THE U.S. INTELLIGENCE COMMUNITY

THE U.S. INTELLIGENCE COMMUNITY

JEFFREY RICHELSON

BALLINGER PUBLISHING COMPANY
Cambridge, Massachusetts
A Subsidiary of Harper & Row, Publishers, Inc.

International Standard Book Number: 0–88730–024–3 (CL)
0–88730–025–1 (PB)

Library of Congress Catalog Card Number: 84–24385

Printed in the United States of America

Library of Congress Cataloging in Publication Data

Richelson, Jeffrey.
 The United States intelligence community.

 Bibliography: p.
 Includes index.
 1. Intelligence service—United States. I. Title.
JK468.I6R53 1985   327.1'2'0973   84–24385
ISBN 0–88730–024–3
ISBN 0–88730–025–1 (pbk.)

274529

To Herbert and Edna Richelson

CONTENTS

List of Figures   xi

List of Tables   xiii

List of Abbreviations   xv

Preface   xxv

Chapter 1
Intelligence   1

Intelligence   2
The Intelligence Cycle   3
The Utility of Intelligence   4
Varieties of Intelligence Information   6

Chapter 2
National Intelligence Organizations   11

National Reconnaissance Office   12
National Security Agency   15
Central Intelligence Agency   20

Chapter 3
Defense Department Intelligence Organizations   35

Defense Intelligence Agency   35
Defense Mapping Agency   42
Armed Forces Medical Intelligence Center   43
Special Operations Division, J–3, JCS   44
Defense Special Plans Office/Monarch Eagle   45

Chapter 4
Military Service Intelligence Organizations   49

Air Force Intelligence Community   49
Naval Intelligence Community   58
Army Intelligence Community   66
Marine Corps Intelligence   72

Chapter 5
Intelligence Components of the Unified
and Specified Commands   75

Strategic Air Command Intelligence   76
Air Force Space Command/NORAD   78
Unified Geographic Commands   79
Selected Subordinate Geographic Commands   84
Fleet Intelligence Centers and Fleet Ocean Surveillance Information
    Centers   87
Unified Command ELINT Centers   90
Reconnaissance Technical Groups   90

Chapter 6
Civilian Intelligence Organizations   95

State Department Intelligence   95
Department of Commerce Intelligence   98
Department of the Treasury Intelligence   100
Department of Energy Intelligence   100
Department of Agriculture Intelligence   101
Drug Enforcement Administration Intelligence   101
Federal Bureau of Investigation   103
Federal Research Division, Library of Congress   104

Chapter 7
Imaging and Signals Intelligence 107

Imaging 107
Signals Intelligence 118

Chapter 8
Ocean Surveillance, Space Surveillance,
and Nuclear Detonation Monitoring 139

Ocean Surveillance 139
Space Surveillance 150
Nuclear Detonation Monitoring 156

Chapter 9
Human and Other Sources 171

Open Source Collection 173
Human Sources 177
Technical Surveillance and Mail Opening 185
Material Exploitation and Recovery Operations 187

Chapter 10
Cooperative Arrangements and Overseas Bases 195

The UKUSA Agreement 195
Ocean Surveillance 199
Radio Broadcast Monitoring 201
Overhead Reconnaissance 202
Human Intelligence Cooperation with Australia 203
The Israeli Connection 205
Cooperation with the PRC 207
Estimates: Cooperation Among the Anglo-Saxon Countries 208
Overseas Bases 210

Chapter 11
Counterintelligence and Covert Action 219

Counterintelligence 220
Covert Action 227

Chapter 12
Analysis and Estimates   241

National Intelligence   241
Central Intelligence Agency   246
Defense Intelligence Agency   248
Bureau of Intelligence and Research   253
Military Service Scientific and Technical Intelligence Centers   254
Unified, Specified, and Theater Commands   255

Chapter 13
Management and Direction   263

Orders, Directives, and Regulations   263
Individuals, Committees, and Offices   275
Programs, Plans, and Requirements Documents   287

Chapter 14
Managing Intelligence Collection   297

Managing Satellite Reconnaissance   297
Managing SIGINT   301
Managing Sensitive Reconnaissance Missions   303
Managing Human Collection   306

Chapter 15
Managing Information Access and Analysis   313

Managing the Access to Information   314
Managing the Analytic Process   327

Chapter 16
Issues   337

Management Issues   338
Policy Issues   342

Index   349

About the Author   359

LIST OF FIGURES

2-1   Organization of the National Security Agency   18
2-2   Organization of the Central Intelligence Agency   22
2-3   Organization of the Directorate of Operations   26
2-4   Organization of the Directorate of Intelligence   27

3-1   Organization of the Defense Intelligence Agency   38

4-1   Organization of the Air Force Intelligence Service   51
4-2   Organization of the Air Force Electronic Security Command   54
4-3   Electronic Security Command Units Worldwide   55
4-4   Organization of the Foreign Technology Division   57
4-5   Organization of the Air Force Technical Applications Center   59
4-6   Organization of Task Force 168   61
4-7   Organization of the Navy Operational Intelligence Center   65
4-8   Organization of the Missile Intelligence Agency   70

5-1   SAC DCSI Organization   77
5-2   Organization of PACOM Intelligence   81
5-3   Organization of the Atlantic Command Intelligence Division   83
5-4   Organization of USAFE Intelligence   86
5-5   Available CASPER Patterns   89
5-6   Organization of the Atlantic Command Electronic Intelligence
       Center   91

6-1   Organization of the INR   97

8-1   Clipper Bow in Operation—Artist's Conception   144

9-1   Navy FMEP Proposal   191

13-1   Intelligence Community Staff   281

LIST OF TABLES

7-1	Resolution Required for Different Levels of Precision	110
8-1	Launch Dates and Orbital Parameters for White Cloud Satellites	142
8-2	Varieties of Aerial Sampling Operations	159
11-1	Table of Contents for Foreign Intelligence and Security Services: Israel	226
12-1	NIE-11 Series, 1960-1962	244
12-2	SNIEs Concerning the 1961 Berlin Crisis	245
12-3	SNIEs 1960-1962 on Southeast Asia	246
12-4	Table of Contents for WIS 29-82	250
12-5	General Intelligence Production Responsibilities	256
13-1	NSCIDs Issued on February 17, 1972	266
13-2	Selected Air Force Regulations Concerning Intelligence	273
13-3	Selected Army Regulations Concerning Intelligence	274
15-1	Sensitive Compartmented Information Nondisclosure Agreement	324

LIST OF ABBREVIATIONS
AND ACRONYMS

AAA	Anti-Aircraft Artillery
AB	Air Base
ABM	antiballistic missile
ACOUSTINT	acoustic intelligence
ACSI	Assistant Chief of Staff, Intelligence
ADC	Aerospace Defense Command
ADIC	Aerospace Defense Intelligence Center
AEDS	Atomic Energy Detection System
AFAR	Azores Fixed Acoustic Range
AFB	Air Force Base
AFIS	Air Force Intelligence Service
AFMIC	Air Force Medical Intelligence Center
AFOSI	Air Force Office of Special Investigations
AFR	Air Force Regulation
AFSA	Armed Forces Security Agency
AFSAC/IRC	Armed Forces Security Agency Council/Intelligence Requirements Committee
AFSSO/SAO	Air Force Special Security Offices and Special Activities Offices
AFTAC	Air Force Technical Applications Center
AGER	Auxiliary General Environmental Research
AGTR	Auxiliary General Technical Research
AIS	Army Intelligence Survey
ALPA	Alaska Long Period Array
ANZMIS	Australia–New Zealand Military Intelligence Service
AR	Advanced Rhyolite
	Army Regulation

AR papers	Assessment and Research papers
ARC	Acoustic Research Center
ARGUS	Advanced Rhyolite satellite
ARIA	Advanced Range Instrumentation Aircraft
ARIS	Advanced Range Instrumentation Ships
ASIS	Australian Secret Intelligence Service
ASTIB	*Army Scientific and Technical Intelligence Bulletin*
ASW	Antisubmarine Warfare
AUTEC	Atlantic Undersea Test and Evaluation Center
B	Byeman
BBC	British Broadcasting Corporation
BfV	Federal Office for Protection of the Constitution (West Germany)
BIOT	British Indian Ocean Territory
BMD	Ballistic Missile Defense
BMEWS	Ballistic Missile Early Warning System
BND	Federal Intelligence Service (W. Germany)
BSTIS	*BiWeekly Scientific and Technical Intelligence Summary*
CANUS	Canadian–U.S.
CASPER	Contact Area Summary Report
CBW	Chemical Biological Warfare
CCD	charged couple devices
CCF	Collection Coordination Facility
CCP	Consolidated Cryptographic Program
CCPC	Critical Collection Problems Committee
CDAA	Circularly Disposed Antenna Array
CERP	Combined Economic Reporting Program
CFI	Committee on Foreign Intelligence
CIA	Central Intelligence Agency
CIG	Central Intelligence Group
CINC	Commander in Chief
CINCPACFLT	Commander in Chief Pacific Fleet
CINCSAC	Commander in Chief of Strategic Air Command
CIOC	Current Intelligence Operations Center
CIPC	Critical Intelligence Problems Committee
CIRL	Current Intelligence Reporting List
COIC	Combat Operations Intelligence Center
COMINT	Communications Intelligence
COMIREX	Committee on Imagery Requirements and Exploitation
COMOR	Committee on Overhead Reconnaissance
COMSEC	Communications Security
COMSOTFE	Commander Support Operations Task Force Europe

CNWDI	Critical Nuclear Weapons Design Information
CRC	Cuban Revolutionary Council
C/S	Country Intelligence study
CSAW	Communications Supplementary Activity Washington
CSE	Communications Security Establishment (Canada)
CSS	Central Security Service
C^{3}I	Command Control Communications and Intelligence
DARCOM	Development and Readiness Command
DCD	Domestic Collection Division
DCI	Director of Central Intelligence
DCIB	Defence Counterintelligence Board
DCID	Director of Central Intelligence Directive
DCS	Deputy Chief of Staff
	Domestic Contact Service
DCSI	Deputy Chief of Staff for Intelligence
DDIA	Director of the Defense Intelligence Agency
DDNI	Deputy Director of Naval Intelligence
DEA	Drug Enforcement Administration
DEFSMAC	Defense Special Missile and Astronautics Center
DEPLOC	Daily Estimated Position Locator
DF	Direction Finding
DIA	Defense Intelligence Agency
DIN	Defense Intelligence Notice
	Digital Network
DIO	Defense Intelligence Officer
DMA	Defense Mapping Agency
DMSP	Defense Meteorological Satellite Program
DNI	Director of Naval Intelligence
DOD	Department of Defense
DRM-4	Department of Defense Reference Mission 4
DRSP	Defense Reconnaissance Support Program
DS&T	Directorate of Science and Technology
DSCS	Defense Satellite Communications System
DSD	Defense Signals Directorate (Australia)
DSP	Defense Support Program
DSPO	Defense Support Project Office
	Defense Special Plans Office
DSSCS	Defense Special Security Communications System
DUSD(P)	Deputy Undersecretary of Defense for Policy
EAL	Economic Alert List
EC	Exploitation Center
ECM	electronic countermeasures

EIC	Economic Intelligence Committee
ELINT	Electronic Intelligence
EMP	electromagnetic pulses
EPDS	Evaluation, Plans, and Designs Staff
EPL	Emitter Programs Listing
ESC	Electronic Security Command
ESI	Extremely Sensitive Information
ESG	Electronic Security Group
EUDAC	European Defense Analysis Center
EW	early warning
FAS	Foreign Agriculture Service
FBI	Federal Bureau of Investigation
FBIS	Foreign Broadcast Information Service
FICEURLANT	Fleet Intelligence Center Europe and Atlantic
FISINT	Foreign Instrumentation Signals Intelligence
FLIR	forward-looking infrared
FM	frequency modulated
FMEP	Foreign Material Exploitation Program
FNLA	National Front for the Liberation of Angola
FOIA	Freedom of Information Act
FOSIC	Fleet Ocean Surveillance Information Center
FRD	Federal Research Division
FSTC	Foreign Science and Technology Center
FTD	Foreign Technology Division
GATT	General Agreement on Tariffs and Trade
GCHQ	Government Communications Headquarters (Britain)
GCSB	Government Communications Security Bureau (New Zealand)
GDIP	General Defense Intelligence Program
GEODSS	Ground Based Electro-Optical Deep Space Surveillance System
GHz	gigahertz
GIUK	Greenland–Iceland–U.K.
GMAIC	Guided Missile and Astronautics Intelligence Committee
GMI	general medical intelligence
GPS	Global Positioning System
GRU	Chief Intelligence Directorate of the General Staff
HUMINT	Human Intelligence
IAC	Intelligence Advisory Committee
I&W	Indications and Warning
ICBM	intercontinental ballistic missile
ICS	Intelligence Community Staff
IDC	Interagency Defector Committee

IG-CI	Interagency Group for Counterintelligence
IG-CM	Interagency Group for Countermeasures
IIM	Interagency Intelligence Memorandum
IMEMO	Institute of World Economy and International Affairs (USSR)
INR	Intelligence and Research (Bureau of, State Dept.)
INSCOM	Intelligence and Security Command (Army)
INTELSAT	International Telecommunications Satellite
IOB	Intelligence Oversight Board
IPAC	Intelligence Center Pacific
IPC	Intelligence Producers Council
IRAC	Intelligence Resources Advisory Committee
IRSIG	International Regulations on SIGINT
ISA	Intelligence Support Activity
ITAC	Intelligence and Threat Analysis Center
ITSS	Integrated Tactical Surveillance System
JAEIC	Joint Atomic Energy Intelligence Committee
JCS	Joint Chiefs of Staff
JRC	Joint Reconnaissance Center
JRS	Joint Reconnaissance Schedule
JSCO	Joint Systems Collection Officer
JSTPS	Joint Strategic Target Planning Staff
KGB	Committee for State Security (Soviet Union)
KIQ	Key Intelligence Questions
KH	Keyhole
Kt	kiloton
LARIAT	Laser Radar Intelligence Acquisition Technology
LASA	Large Aperture Seismic Array
MAD	magnetic anomaly detector
MBFR	Mutual and Balanced Force Reduction
mc	megacycles
MHz	megahertz
MIA	Missile Intelligence Agency
MIIA	Medical Intelligence and Information Agency
MIRV	multiple independently targeted reentry vehicles
mm	millimeter
MOL	Manned Orbiting Laboratory
MOTIF	Main Optical Tracking and Identification Facility
MPA	Main Political Administration of the Soviet Army and Navy
MPLA	People's Movement for the Liberation of Angola
MRR	Movement for the Recovery of the Revolution

NASA	National Aeronautics and Space Administration
NATO	North Atlantic Treaty Organization
NAVALEX	Naval Electronics Systems Command
NAVSPASUR	Naval Space Surveillance
NCSC	National Communications Security Committee
NDS	Nuclear Detection System
NEACP	National Emergency Airborne Command Post
NETCAP	National Exploitation of Tactical Capabilities
NFAC	National Foreign Assessment Center
NFIB	National Foreign Intelligence Board
NFIC	National Foreign Intelligence Council
NFIP	National Foreign Intelligence Program
NFMP	Navy Foreign Material Program
NFOIO	Navy Field Operational Intelligence Office
NIAM	National Intelligence Analytical Memorandum
NIC	Naval Intelligence Command
	National Intelligence Council
NIE	National Intelligence Estimate
NITC	National Intelligence Tasking Center
NIO	National Intelligence Officer
NIPE	National Intelligence Program Evaluation
NIPSSA	Naval Intelligence Processing System Support Activity
NISC	Naval Intelligence Support Center
NISR	National Intelligence Situation Report
NIT	National Intelligence Topic
NITC	National Intelligence Tasking Center
NMIC	National Military Intelligence Center
NOIC	Navy Operational Intelligence Center
NORSAR	Norwegian Seismic Array
NPIC	National Photographic Interpretation Center
NREC	National Reconnaissance Executive Committee
NRL	Naval Research Laboratory
NRO	National Reconnaissance Office
NSA	National Security Agency
NSAM	National Security Action Memorandum
NSC	National Security Council
NSCG	Naval Security Group Command
NSCIC	National Security Council Intelligence Committee
NSCID	National Security Council Intelligence Directive
NSDM	National Security Decision Memorandum
NSG	Naval Security Group
NSP	Navy Space Project
NSRL	National SIGINT Requirements List

NTIS	National Technical Information Service
NUDET	Nuclear Detonation
OACSI	Office of the Assistant Chief of Staff for Intelligence
OAG	Operations Advisory Group
OAS	Organization of American States
OASIS	Operational Applications of Special Intelligence Systems
OID	Operational Intelligence Division
OJCS	Office of the Joint Chiefs of Staff
OL–A	Operating Location–A
ONI	Office of Naval Intelligence
OPA	Office of Political Analysis
OPEC	Organization of Petroleum Exporting Countries
OpFors	Opposing Forces
OPC	Office of Policy Coordination
OPSEC	Operations Security
OSD	Office of the Secretary of Defense
OSI	Office of Strategic Information
OSIS	Ocean Surveillance Information System
OSR	Office of Strategic Research
OSS	Office of Strategic Services
OTS	Oakhanger Tracking Station
PACBAR	Pacific Radar Barrier
PACCS	Post Attack Command and Control System
PACOM	Pacific Command
PARCS	Perimeter Acquisition Radar Characterization System
PBCFIA	President's Board of Consultants on Foreign Intelligence Activities
PD	Presidential Directive
PDB	President's Daily Brief
PFIAB	President's Foreign Intelligence Advisory Board
PIB	PACOM Intelligence Board
PID	Photographic Intelligence Division
PLO	Palestine Liberation Organization
PNE	Peaceful Nuclear Explosion (Treaty)
PNIO	Priority National Intelligence Objectives
POW	Prisoner of War
PPC	Precision Processing Center
PRC	People's Republic of China
	Policy Review Committee
RAF	Royal Air Force
RDSS	Rapidly Deployable Surveillance Systems

REWSON	Reconnaissance, Electronic Warfare, Special Operations, and Naval Intelligence Systems
RORSAT	radar ocean surveillance satellite
RPV	Remotely Piloted Vehicle
R/T	radio/telephone
RTG	Reconnaissance Technical Group
RWO	Ramstein Warning Office
SAC	Strategic Air Command
SALT	Strategic Arms Limitation Talks
SAM	surface-to-air missile
SAMOS	Satellite and Missile Observation System
S&TI	scientific and technical intelligence
SATRAN	Satellite Reconnaissance Advance Notice
SCA	Service Cryptological Authorities
SCARS	System Control and Receiving Station
SCC	Special Coordination Committee
SCF	Satellite Control Facility (U.S.A.F.)
SCI	Sensitive Compartmented Information
SDAC	Seismic Data Analysis Center
SDIN	*Special Defense Intelligence Notice*
SDS	Satellite Data System
SECOM	Security Committee
SHF	Super High Frequency
SI	Special Intelligence
SID	Signals Intelligence Directive
SIG	Senior Interagency Group
SIG-I	Senior Interagency Group–Intelligence
SIGINT	Signals Intelligence
SIGSEC	Signals Security
SIOP	Single Integrated Operational Plan
SIPRI	Stockholm International Peace Research Institute
SIRE	Space Infrared Experiments
SIS	Secret Intelligence Service (Britain)
SLBM	Submarine Launched Ballistic Missile
SNIE	Special National Intelligence Estimate
SOSUS	Sound Surveillance System
SOUTHCOM	Southern Command
SPADATS	Space Tracking and Detection System
SPADOC	Space Defense Operations Center
SPINTCOMM	Special Intelligence Communications
SPOEM	Special Program Office for Exploitation Modernization
SR	Strategic Reconnaissance

SSN	Nuclear Powered Submarine
START	Strategic Arms Reduction Talks
STS	Space Transportation System
SURTASS	Surface Towed Array Surveillance System
TAC	Target Assessment Center
TCP	Tactical Cryptologic Program
TENCAP	Tactical Exploitation of National Capabilities
TDI	Target Data Inventory
TELINT	Telemetry Intelligence
TERCOM	Terrain Contour Matching
TF	Task Force
TIARA	Tactical Intelligence and Related Activities
TIP	Travelers in Panama (file)
TK	Talent-Keyhole
TSD	Technical Services Division
TTIC	Technology Transfer Intelligence Committee
UHF	Ultra High Frequencies
U.N.	United Nations
UNITA	National Union for the Total Independence of Angola
USAFE	United States Air Forces Europe
USCIB	United States Communications Intelligence Board
USCIB/IC	United States Communications Intelligence Board/ Intelligence Committee
USCSB	United States Communications Security Board
VHF	Very High Frequencies
VLF	Very Low Frequencies
WDD	Western Development Division
WIS	*Weekly Intelligence Summary*
WSSIC	Weapons and Space Systems Intelligence Committee
WWR	*Weekly Watch Report*

PREFACE

This book tries to accomplish in one volume what requires several volumes. It attempts to provide a comprehensive and detailed order of battle of the U.S. intelligence community—to describe its organizations, activities, and management structure. The reader who is not already aware of it will soon discover the complexity involved.

Given the purpose of the book, I have not commented in the first fifteen chapters on the acceptability, morality, or wisdom of the activities described. In Chapter 16, I set forth what I consider to be some pertinent issues concerning U.S. intelligence activities. Hopefully, the reader interested in pursuing such questions will turn to the vast available literature pertaining to such issues as covert action, secrecy, and the ethics of intelligence collection operations.

I owe a great debt to the individuals who contributed directly or indirectly to this book, including those who provided me with documents, information, critical analyses, and their perspective on the activities of the U.S. intelligence community. Unfortunately, not all of them can be named. Those who can be are: William Arkin, Scott Armstrong, James Bamford, Desmond Ball, Richard Fieldhouse, Jay Peterzell, and John Prados.

Finally, I am grateful to those at American University and Ballinger Publishing Company who, by providing a variety of support services, eased and speeded the transition from handwritten manuscript to published book.

1 INTELLIGENCE

Informed policymaking and decisionmaking requires adequate information and analysis. Only if policymakers and decisionmakers are sufficiently informed about the state of the world and the likely consequences of policies and actions can they be expected to make intelligent judgments. If their responsibilities have foreign aspects, they will require the acquisition and analysis of foreign intelligence information.

The individuals with the most prominent need for foreign intelligence are those concerned with national security policymaking and decisionmaking. Hence, those involved in foreign and defense policy—the President, the National Security Council (NSC), the State Department, and the Defense Department (DOD)—are the most visible consumers of foreign intelligence.

However, there are many other policymakers who have a need for foreign intelligence, just as there are ways other than political or military action that foreign governments or groups can affect the U.S. national security or public welfare. This has become particularly evident in recent years. Edward Boland, Chairman of the House Permanent Select Committee on Intelligence, has noted that "many believe in fact that energy and related economic problems can threaten us more deeply and affect our national security more rapidly than any change in the military picture short of war."[1] Clearly, the availability of energy resources as well as the stability of the dollar can be influenced by the actions of foreign governments or groups.

As a result, there are many government agencies that engage in intelligence activities. As will be seen in the chapters that follow, these departments and agencies extend well beyond those involved in foreign and defense policy to include units of the Commerce, Energy, and Treasury Departments among

1

others. Before turning to the examination of these agencies and offices, it would be useful to examine the various types of intelligence activities—collection, analysis, counterintelligence, and covert action—as well as the utility and type of intelligence that can be gathered and produced.

INTELLIGENCE

Strictly speaking, intelligence can be defined as "the product resulting from the collection, evaluation, analysis, integration and interpretation of all available information which concerns one or more aspects of foreign nations or of areas of operation which is immediately or potentially significant for planning."[2]

Collection can be defined as the purposeful acquisition of any information that might be desired by analyst, consumer, or operator. Collection activity can take any one of several overlapping forms: open source collection, clandestine collection, human source collection, or technical collection. Open source collection includes the acquisition of material in the public domain: radio and television broadcasts, newspapers, magazines, technical and scholarly journals, books, government reports, and reports by foreign service officers and defense attachés concerning public activities. The extent to which open source collection yields valuable information will vary greatly with the nature of the targeted society and the subject involved. The information might be collected by human sources—individuals who purchase the books and journals or observe public events—or by technical resources—recordings of television and radio programs.

Clandestine collection involves the acquisition of data that are not publicly available. As with open source collection, both human and technical resources may be employed. The traditional human spy may be employed to provide vast quantities of sensitive political and military information. Alternatively, technical systems can be used to photograph military installations or intercept strategic communications.

Great secrecy and sensitivity are more characteristic of human source clandestine collection. Although much technical collection is also clandestine, secrecy is not always as vital as in the case of human collection. Thus, the United States and Soviet Union are well aware of, if not totally informed of, each other's satellite reconnaissance programs. Even in the absence of a SALT or START agreement prohibiting concealment and deception measures with respect to certain activities, some of these activities would be extremely difficult, if not impossible, to conceal from technical collectors. In such cases, the ability to collect effectively the required data does not depend on its being done clandestinely.

Analysis involves the integration of collected information or raw intelligence from all sources into finished intelligence. The finished intelligence product might be a simple statement of facts, an estimate of the capabilities of another nation's military forces, or a projection of the likely course of political events in another nation.

Strictly speaking, intelligence activities involve solely the collection and analysis of information and its transformation into intelligence, but several other activities have come to be considered examples of intelligence activity—specifically, counterintelligence and covert action.

Counterintelligence is the acquisition of information or activity designed to neutralize hostile intelligence services. These activities might involve espionage against hostile services, debriefing of defectors, and analysis of the methods of operation of the hostile services. They might also involve the direct penetration and disruption of those services and their activities.

Covert action is also known as "special activities," "secret political action" (Britain), and "active measures" (Soviet Union). Covert action can be defined as any operation or activity designed to influence foreign governments, persons, or events in support of the sponsoring government's foreign policy objectives while keeping the sponsoring government's *support* of the operation a secret. Thus, while in the case of clandestine collection the emphasis is on keeping the activity secret, the emphasis in covert action is on keeping sponsorship secret.

There are several distinct types of covert action: black propaganda (propaganda that purports to emanate from a source other than the true one); gray propaganda (in which true sponsorship is not acknowledged); paramilitary or political actions designed to overthrow or support a regime; support (aid, arms, training) of individuals and organizations (newspapers, labor unions, political parties); economic operations; and disinformation.[3]

THE INTELLIGENCE CYCLE

It is important to put the collection and analysis activities conducted by various intelligence units into proper perspective—one that relates these activities to the requirements and needs of the decisionmakers and the use made of the finished intelligence product. This is done through the concept of the "intelligence cycle."

The intelligence cycle is the process by which information is acquired, converted into intelligence, and made available to policymakers. Generally, it comprises five steps: planning and direction, collection, processing, production and analysis, and dissemination.[4]

Planning and direction involves the management of the entire intelligence effort, from the identification of the need for data to the final delivery of an intelligence product to a consumer. The process is initiated by requests or requirements for intelligence on certain subjects based on the needs of the customers—the President, Department of State, DOD, or others. In some cases, the requests and requirements become institutionalized. Thus, the President does not need to remind the intelligence community to collect information on Soviet strategic forces.

Collection, as indicated above, involves the gathering of raw data from which finished intelligence will be produced. The collection process involves open sources, clandestine agents, and technical systems. Processing is concerned with the conversion of the vast amount of information coming into the system to a form more suitable for the production of finished intelligence. It involves language translation, decryption, and sorting by subject matters as well as data reduction—interpretation of the information stored on film and tape through the use of photographic and electronic processes.

Production and analysis refers to the conversion of basic information into finished intelligence. It includes the integration, evaluation, and analysis of all available data and the preparation of various intelligence products. The "raw intelligence" that is collected may often be fragmentary and at times contradictory, requiring specialists to give it meaning and significance.

The final step in the cycle is dissemination. This involves the distribution and handling of the finished intelligence to the consumers—the policymakers (and operators) whose needs triggered the process.

Like any model, this outline of the intelligence cycle is a simplification of the real world. As noted above, certain requirements become "standing requirements." Similarly, policymakers will not specify, except in rare cases, specific items of information. Rather, they will indicate a desire for reports on, for example, Chinese strategic forces or the political situation in Egypt, the collection agencies being given the responsibility of determining how to obtain the information necessary to prepare such reports. Finally, the collection agencies will have a certain internal need to acquire information to provide for their continued operation—information related to counterintelligence and security and information that will be useful in potential future operations.

THE UTILITY OF INTELLIGENCE

The utility of intelligence activity, here narrowly construed to mean collection and analysis, depends on the extent to which it aids national decisionmakers. Two questions arise in this regard: In what ways does intelligence aid decisionmakers, and what attributes make intelligence useful? With respect to the first question, four distinct areas exist in which intelligence can be useful to national decisionmakers: policymaking, planning, conflict situations, and warning.

In their policymaking roles, national decisionmakers set the basic outlines of foreign, defense, and international economic policy. Their need for intelligence in order to make sound decisions is summed up in the report of the Rockefeller Commission:

> Intelligence is information gathered for policymakers in government which illuminates the range of choices available to them and enables them to exer-

cise judgment. Good intelligence will not necessarily lead to wise policy choices. But without sound intelligence, national policy decisions and actions cannot effectively respond to actual conditions and reflect the best national interests or adequately protect . . . national security.[5]

In addition to its value in policymaking, intelligence is vital to the specific decisions needed to implement policy and decisions that might be labeled planning decisions. Such decisions involve the building and deployment of new weapons systems, the development of strategic war plans (in the case of the United States, the Single Integrated Operational Plan or SIOP), suspension or resumption of foreign aid, and the employment of trade restrictions. Here intelligence might be able to tell the decisionmaker the likely or expected effects of such actions, including the reactions of those nations toward which a particular decision is directed. Thus, Zbigniew Brzezinski has written that President Carter's decision to embargo grain sales to the Soviet Union was based in part on the Agriculture Department's estimate that no other country could replace the United States as a major seller to the Soviet Union—"a conclusion which within days was shaken by Argentina's announcement that it would partially replace the American grain shipment." In another case, the Carter administration went ahead with a planned sale of planes to Saudi Arabia partially on the basis of intelligence indicating that if the United States backed out of the deal the Saudis would simply buy French planes.[6]

Conflict situations in which intelligence is of value need not be exclusively of a military nature. Any situation where nations have at least partially conflicting interests, such as in arms control negotiations, trade negotiations, or international conferences, would qualify. Intelligence can indicate how far the other negotiator can be pushed and the extent to which a position must be modified for it to be adopted.

Warning is also a prime benefit of intelligence. Warning might concern military or other action to be taken against the decisionmaker's own government or nation or against a country the fate of which concerns the decisionmaker. The warning mission requires, to the greatest extent possible, the monitoring of the adversary nation's armed forces. For the United States, this means monitoring the status of the entire range of Soviet forces—knowing the numbers deployed, their locations, and usual pattern of activity, and notifying the proper authorities in the event of major anomalies. On the basis of advance notice, defenses can be prepared, responses considered and implemented, and preemptive actions (diplomatic or military) taken to forestall or negate action.

The overall utility of intelligence in regard to military matters was concisely summarized by the Eisenhower administration's Technological Capabilities Panel:

If intelligence can uncover a new military threat, we may take steps to meet it. If intelligence can reveal an opponent's specific weakness, we may prepare to exploit it. With good intelligence we can avoid wasting our resources by arming for the wrong danger at the wrong time. Beyond this, in the broadest sense, intelligence underlies our estimate of the enemy and thus helps to guide our political strategy.[7]

The utility of intelligence, in addition to being dependent on its addressing relevant subjects, is also dependent on its having the attributes of quality and timeliness. Unless all relevant information is marshaled when assessing intelligence on a subject, the quality of the finished product might suffer. Covertly obtained intelligence should not be assessed in isolation from overtly obtained intelligence. As Professor H. Trevor-Roper observed:

> Secret intelligence is the continuation of open intelligence by other means. So long as governments conceal a part of their activities, other governments, if they wish to base their policy on full and correct information, must seek to penetrate the veil. This inevitably entails varying methods.
>
> But, however the means may vary, the end must still be the same. It is to complement the results of what for convenience, we may call "public" intelligence: that is, the intelligence derived from the rational study of public or at least available sources. Intelligence, in fact, is indivisible.[8]

In addition to being based on all relevant information, the assessment process must be objective. As former Secretary of State Henry Kissinger told the U.S. Senate in 1973: "Anyone concerned with national policy must have a profound interest in making sure that intelligence guides and does not follow, national policy."[9]

Further, intelligence must reach decisionmakers in good time for them to act decisively. Intelligence as foreknowledge has always had particular relevance in military matters. It can give the military commander or domestic policymaker the great advantage of not being taken unaware—an advantage the value of which was recognized by Sun Tzu 2,500 years ago: "The reason the enlightened prince and the wise general conquer the enemy whenever they move and their achievements surpass those of ordinary men is foreknowledge."[10]

VARIETIES OF INTELLIGENCE INFORMATION

To understand how specific varieties of intelligence can be useful to government officials one need only consider the components of those varieties. To begin, one might identify several general categories of intelligence—political, military, scientific and technical, economic.

Political intelligence will include intelligence about both a nation's foreign policy and its domestic politics. Clearly, the foreign policies of other nations have an impact on the United States. A variety of issues might be involved: support of the United States on a U.N. issue, a nation's relations with the Soviet Union or Cuba, attitudes and policies concerning the Arab-Israeli conflict, the support of revolutionary groups, or leadership perceptions of the United States.

The domestic politics of other nations—whether friendly, neutral, allied, or hostile—is also of significant concern to the United States since the resolution of domestic political conflict can have a direct effect on foreign policy. The outcome of such conflict—whether by coup, election, or civil war—can affect the orientation of that nation in the world, the regional balance of power, the accessibility of critical resources to the United States, or the continued presence of U.S. military bases.

Thus, the outcome of elections in Spain and Greece may affect those countries' continued participation in NATO and the status of major U.S. military bases. Likewise, the resolution of the internal conflict in Iran deprived the United States of several assets: oil, a military ally, and critical intelligence bases from which Soviet missile telemetry could be intercepted. Similarly, the extent of the nationality problem in the Soviet Union can have a significant effect on its Middle Eastern policy as well as its ability to maintain high manpower levels in the armed forces.[11]

Military intelligence is useful and required with respect to a wide variety of situations. The United States, in order to determine its own requirements in strategic weapons, must know the nature of Soviet strategic forces (numbers of delivery vehicles and warheads; their yield, accuracy, and reliability) as well as the characteristics of the Soviet target base (numbers, blast resistance, locations). Much of this information is also vital to the negotiation and monitoring of arms limitation agreements. The same basic requirements exist with respect to conventional forces. The size and capabilities as well as the location and readiness of Warsaw Pact forces must be continually monitored—either as a guide to NATO planning requirements or as a means of warning against possible attack or as a means of monitoring a Mutual and Balanced Force Reduction (MBFR) agreement.

Scientific and technical intelligence includes both civilian- and military-related scientific and technical development. A nation's ability to produce steel or oil may influence both that country's stability and U.S. fortunes. In many cases, technological developments that occur in the civilian sector have military applications. Areas such as computer technology, ball bearing production, mirrors and optical systems, and lasers all have significant military applications. Hence, intelligence concerning a nation's progress in those areas or its ability to absorb foreign-produced technology in those areas is relevant to its potential military standing.

One aspect of scientific and technological intelligence that has been of constant concern for over thirty years is atomic energy intelligence. Whether the announced purpose of a nation's atomic energy activities has been civilian or military, those activities have received high intelligence priority. In addition to the obvious need to determine if a foreign government is developing nuclear weapons independent of U.S. government actions, there has also been a perceived need to acquire secret intelligence in support of decisionmaking concerning applications for nuclear technology exports. Thus, the first Director of Central Intelligence (DCI) noted in 1947 that the United States "cannot rely on information submitted by a licensee" and that it was necessary to the United States to "determine actual use, [to] endeavor to discover secondary diversions."[12]

Economic intelligence is also of great importance. The activities of, for example, OPEC and the Common Market are matters of concern to U.S. national security and economic policy officials. In 1975 the DCI noted that economic intelligence of value to U.S. policymakers includes "topics such as the activities of multi-national corporations, international development programs, regional economic arrangements and the workings of international commodity markets."[13] Specific areas of interest included:

- Rates of production, consumption, pricing of raw materials and energy sources, and international commodity arrangements as a means to share the burden of price fluctuation between producers and consumers of primary commodities.

- Price and nonprice restrictions on international trade.

- The international payments mechanism and the coordination of national fiscal monetary policies.[14]

With regard to any one nation, U.S. officials may have a need for intelligence concerning all aspects of domestic and foreign affairs. In the case of the Soviet Union, intelligence of value would include (but by no means be limited to) intelligence concerning the forthcoming grain harvest, ethnic problems in the armed forces, strategic weapons systems deployed and under development, Soviet oil production, Chernenko's consolidation of power, and Soviet negotiating strategy for START. With regard to the Middle East, U.S. officials would need intelligence concerning the health of the Israeli Prime Minister, the ability of the Likud coalition to remain in power, Israeli plans for future settlements on the West Bank, Arab government support for the PLO, the internal stability of the Saudi and Egyptian regimes, the willingness of various Arab governments to recognize Israel's right to exist, and the military capabilities of all nations in the region.

NOTES TO CHAPTER 1

1. U.S. Congress, House Permanent Select Committee on Intelligence, *Intelligence on the World Energy Future* (Washington, D.C.: U.S. Government Printing Office, 1979), p. 2.

2. *Dictionary of United States Military Terms for Joint Usage* (Washington, D.C.: Departments of the Army, Navy, and Air Force, May 1955), p. 53.

3. Disinformation is the anglicization of the Soviet term *Desinformatsiya* — the propagation of false, incomplete, or misleading information that is

passed, fed, or confirmed to a targeted individual, group, or country. See Paul W. Blackstock, *Agents of Deceit* (Chicago: Quadrangle, 1966).

4. CIA, *Intelligence: The Acme of Skill* (Washington, D.C.: CIA, 1978), p. 6.

5. Commission on CIA Activities within the United States, *Report to the President* (Washington, D.C.: U.S. Government Printing Office, 1975), p. 6.

6. Zbigniew Brzezinski, *Power and Principle: Memories of the National Security Adviser 1977-1981* (New York: Farrar, Straus & Giroux, 1983), pp. 243, 431.

7. James J. Killian, Jr., *Sputnik, Scientists, and Eisenhower: A Memoir of the First Special Assistant to the President for Science and Technology* (Cambridge, Mass.: MIT Press, 1977), p. 80.

8. Hugh Trevor-Roper, *The Philby Affair — Espionage, Treason and Secret Services* (London: Kimber, 1968), p. 66.

9. U.S. Congress, Senate Committee on Foreign Relations, *Nomination of Henry A. Kissinger* (Washington, D.C.: U.S. Government Printing Office, 1973). For evidence that Kissinger did not always follow his own advice, see Seymour Hersh, *The Price of Power: Kissinger in the Nixon White House* (New York: Summit, 1983), pp. 529-560.

10. Samuel Griffith, trans., *Sun Tzu, The Art of War* (London: Oxford Press, 1963), p. 144.

11. See Jeremy Azrael, *Emergent Nationality Problems in the USSR* (Santa Monica, Cal.: RAND Corporation, 1977).

12. Sidney Souers, "Atomic Energy Intelligence," *RG 218 Joint Chiefs of Staff, File 131*, July 1, 1947, Modern Military Branch, National Archives.

13. "Director of Central Intelligence Perspectives for Intelligence 1976-1981," *Covert Action Information Bulletin* 6 (October 1979): 13-24.

14. Ibid.

2 NATIONAL INTELLIGENCE ORGANIZATIONS

The activities of the U.S. intelligence services are similar to the intelligence services of many other nations—collection and analysis, covert action, and counterintelligence. However, the extent of these activities and the methods employed, especially with respect to technical collection, far surpass those of every other nation except the Soviet Union.

The United States collects information via reconnaissance satellites, aircraft, ships, signals intelligence stations, radar, and underseas surveillance as well as via the traditional overt and clandestine human sources. The total cost of these activities is well in excess of $10 billion per year.

Given this wide range of activity and the large number of intelligence consumers, it is not surprising that a plethora of organizations are involved in intelligence activities. The exact number of members of the U.S. intelligence community is somewhat ambiguous or subjective. Some organizations are clearly members—the Central Intelligence Agency, the State Department's Bureau of Intelligence and Research (INR), the National Security Agency (NSA), the National Reconnaissance Office (NRO), and the Defense Intelligence Agency (DIA). In addition, each of the major military services (Army, Navy, Air Force) has its own intelligence community, with several distinct subordinate organizations reporting to an assistant chief of staff for intelligence. Further, there are other agencies and offices that perform intelligence functions either marginally related to the production of national security intelligence or intelligence in support of foreign economic and trade policy formulation.

Three organizations are considered national intelligence organizations: the NRO, the NSA, and the CIA. They perform intelligence functions for the entire

11

government (rather than just a department). Their activities provide intelligence for national-level policymakers and they are responsive to direction by supra-departmental authority.

NATIONAL RECONNAISSANCE OFFICE

The NRO manages satellite reconnaissance programs for the entire U.S. intelligence community. These programs involve the collection of photographic and signals intelligence via satellite. The specific programs involved include the Air Force's Keyhole-8 and Keyhole-9 photographic reconnaissance satellites, the CIA's Keyhole-11 (KH-11) photographic reconnaissance satellites, and Rhyolite signals intelligence satellites as well as the Navy Space Project's White Cloud ocean surveillance satellite.

The NRO has a broad range of functions. It has participated in various policy committees, such as the NSAM 156 committee established by President Kennedy in 1962 to review the political aspects of U.S. policy on satellite reconnaissance.[1] It has also played a significant role in drawing a curtain of secrecy around the reconnaissance program. Thus, in a memorandum to President Kennedy concerning the SAMOS II (Satellite and Missile Observation System, the Air Force's first photographic reconnaissance satellite) launch, Assistant Secretary of Defense for Public Affairs Arthur Sylvester noted that the material to be made available to newsmen concerning the launch and the program "represents a severe reduction from what had previously been issued." Sylvester further stated that "Dr. Charyk [Director of NRO] has reviewed those changes and is satisfied that they meet all his security requirements and those of his SAMOS Project Director, Brigadier General Greer."[2] More recently, the NRO has been heavily involved in developing security regulations concerning the release of information concerning military satellite payloads to be placed in orbit by the Space Transportation System (STS).

The NRO is also responsible for the routine operation of the satellites, including maneuvers such as turning them on and off and facing them toward or away from the sun.[3] More importantly, the NRO implements and helps prepare a joint reconnaissance schedule that details the assignment of reconnaissance systems to targets.[4]

Although the NRO has existed under the "cover" of the Under Secretary of the Air Force and the Office of Space Systems, it is, as its name indicates, a national-level organization. And, in fact, it is directly supervised by one of two National Executive Committees chaired by the Director of Central Intelligence (DCI), the National Reconnaissance Executive Committee.[5]

The NRO came into existence on August 25, 1960 after several months of debate within and among the White House, Department of Defense (DOD), Air Force, and CIA concerning the nature and duties of such an organization. Its creation was a response to various problems plaguing the early missile and satellite programs as well as to the May 1, 1960 shooting down of a U-2 over the Soviet Union.[6] As a result of this latter event, the Office of the Secretary of Defense and the Air Force sought a revised program to exploit as early as possible any reconnaissance data that could be obtained from SAMOS test flights. On June 10 President Eisenhower asked Secretary of Defense Gates, Jr. to reevaluate the program and brief the National Security Council (NSC) on intelligence requirements, the technical feasibility of meeting those requirements, and the DOD's plans.[7]

Gates in turn appointed a panel of three—Dr. Joseph Charyk, Undersecretary of the Air Force; John H. Rubel, Deputy Director of the Defense Directorate of Research and Engineering; and Dr. George B. Kistiakowsky, the President's science adviser. The eventual product of their work was their briefing of August 25 which was followed, according to an official Air Force history, by "a key decision by the NSC and the President which, eliminating previous uncertainties, signaled the start of a highest priority program reminiscent of the wartime Manhattan Project effort"—the creation of the NRO.[8] The NRO superseded an office (the Directorate of Advanced Technology) that coordinated satellite development for the Air Force Chief of Staff.[9]

The national-level character of the organization was a major point of importance to those involved in its formation. Thus, George Kistiakowsky, President Eisenhower's Special Assistant for Science and Technology, noted that it was important "that the organization have a clear line of authority and that on the top level direction be of a national character, including OSD [Office of the Secretary of Defense] and CIA and not the Air Force alone."[10] One reason such a framework was desired was to be certain that the utilization of the photographic "take" not be left solely in the hands of the Air Force.[11]

The existence of an office known as the National Reconnaissance Office was kept secret from the U.S. public and most of the rest of the government for thirteen years, until 1973. An obscure reference to its creation, but not its name, appeared in the September 12, 1960 issue of *Aviation Week*. In that issue it was noted that "development of SAMOS is being moved directly under the Secretary of the Air Force. . . . Brig. Gen. Richard B. Curtin will head SAMOS development in the new office."[12]

The first public revelation of the NRO's existence came in 1973 as the result of an error made in editing a Senate Committee report. The name National Reconnaissance Office was, by error, not deleted from a list of intelligence agencies that the committee recommended should make their budgets public.[13] The slip led to a fairly extensive article in the *Washington Post* a few months later in which the NRO's functions, budget, and cover were discussed.[14] The following year the CIA lost in its attempt to have a similar discussion deleted from Marchetti and Marks's *The CIA and the Cult of Intelligence*.

The NRO is still officially considered a secret or "black" institution, at least by the NRO and the DOD. References to it in the *Department of Defense Annual Report* and Executive Orders are to offices charged with "the collection of specialized foreign intelligence through reconnaissance programs." The closest an executive branch document has come to admitting the existence of the NRO was the report of the Murphy Commission, which referred to "a semi-autonomous office within the Defense Department with the largest budget of any intelligence agency that operates overhead reconnaissance programs for the entire intelligence community."[15] At the same time, the CIA's Publication Review Board cleared for publication two books by former high CIA officials, including former Director William Colby, that referred to the organization.[16]

Headquarters of the NRO is located at 4C-956 in the Pentagon, which is officially the Office of Space Systems and subordinate to the Deputy Undersecretary of the Air Force for Space Systems.[17] Both the Director, Office of Space Systems and the Deputy Under Secretary are high-ranking officials of the NRO.

Traditionally, the Director is the Under Secretary of the Air Force. The NRO's first Director, Joseph Charyk, held the position at the same time that he was Under Secretary of the Air Force, as did Hans Mark in the Carter administration. The only apparent exception to this rule was the appointment of Robert J. Hermann as successor to Mark while he was Assistant Secretary of the Air Force for Research, Development, and Logistics. This break in tradition was apparently due to the lack of knowledge of Antonia Chayes, Mark's successor as Under Secretary, concerning reconnaissance matters.[18] Hermann, on the other hand, had served as chief of W Group in NSA, the unit charged with conducting intercept operations.[19] The break with tradition was only temporary, as the Under Secretary of the Air Force appointed by the Reagan administration, Edward C. Aldridge, became the NRO's most recent Director.

As noted above, the NRO is responsible for managing the entire satellite reconnaissance effort. At the same time, it is known that the CIA's Directorate of Science and Technology is heavily involved in reconnaissance satellite development through its Office of Development and Engineering and its Office of SIGINT (Signals Intelligence) Operations.[20] Specifically, it is these offices that appear to have been responsible for the development of the KH-11 and Rhyolite satellites.[21] Likewise, development of Navy satellites, including the White Cloud ocean surveillance satellite, is the responsibility of the Navy Space Project of the Naval Electronics Systems Command (NAVALEX). Thus, these offices constitute subordinate units of the NRO as well as of their own agencies.

Another unit that is a subordinate unit of the NRO is the Air Force Special Projects Office, located at the Space Division in El Segundo, California. Thus, in discussing the appointment of a new Special Projects Director to head that office, *Aviation Week and Space Technology* noted that

> the special projects group has the responsibility for gathering satellite strategic reconnaissance data for use by national intelligence organizations. It directs the design, development and procurement of photographic and other types of military reconnaissance satellites and their subsystems, operating under an annual budget of $250 to $350 million. The group is resident . . .

at the Air Force's [Space Division] but reports directly to the Secretary of the Air Force.[22]

Location of an NRO component in El Segundo allows direct and frequent contact with the corporations that develop and build reconnaissance satellites—TRW, Hughes, and Lockheed—as well as with the Aerospace Corporation, which serves in an advisory capacity.

The NRO's present budget appears to be in the $3 to $4 billion range.[23] The number of people employed by the NRO is not known, but it is probably small compared to the other national intelligence agencies.

NATIONAL SECURITY AGENCY

After the NRO, the NSA is the most secret (and secretive) member of the U.S. intelligence community. The predecessor of NSA, the Armed Forces Security Agency (AFSA) was established within the DOD on May 20, 1949 by Secretary of Defense Louis Johnson, who made it subordinate to the Joint Chiefs of Staff.[24] AFSA had little power to direct the activities of the service cryptological elements, its functions being defined in terms of what the service elements did not do.[25]

On October 24, 1952, President Harry S. Truman, in a Top Secret eight-page memorandum (now partially declassified) entitled "Communications Intelligence Activities," to the Secretary of State and Secretary of Defense, abolished the AFSA and transferred its personnel to the newly created NSA.[26] The Truman Directive had its origins in a memo sent by Walter Bedell Smith to National Security Council Executive Secretary James B. Lay on December 10, 1951 stating that "control over, and coordination of, the collection and processing of communications intelligence have proved ineffective" and recommending a survey of communications intelligence activities.[27] This proposal was approved on December 13, 1951; the study authorized on December 28, 1951; and the report completed by June 13, 1952.[28] The report, known as the "Brownell Committee Report," surveyed the history of U.S. communications intelligence activities and suggested the need for a much greater degree of coordination and national-level direction.[29] As the change in the security agency's name indicated, the role of the NSA was to extend beyond the armed forces. Thus, the NSA is considered to be "within but not part of DOD."[30]

The charter for the NSA is National Security Council Intelligence Directive (NSCID) 6. In its most recently available form, NSCID 6 of February 17, 1972, "Signals Intelligence," directs the NSA to produce intelligence "in accordance with the objectives, requirements and priorities established by the Director of Central Intelligence and the United States Intelligence Board."[31] The Directive also authorizes the Director of the NSA "to issue direction to any operating elements engaged in SIGINT operations such instructions and assignments as are required. All instructions issued by the Director under the authority provided in this paragraph shall be mandatory, subject only to appeal to the Secretary of Defense."[32]

In regard to the scope of SIGINT activities which comprise Communications Intelligence (COMINT) and Electronics Intelligence (ELINT), the Directive further states that

COMINT activities shall be construed to mean those activities which produce COMINT by interception and processing of foreign communications passed by radio, wire, or other electromagnetic means, with specific exception stated below and by the processing of foreign encrypted communications, however transmitted. Interception comprises range estimation, transmitter operator identification, signal analysis, traffic analysis, cryptanalysis, decryption, study of plain text, the fusion of those processes, and the reporting of the results.

COMINT and COMINT activities are defined herein shall not include (a) any intercept and processing of unencrypted written communications, press and propaganda broadcasts, or (b) censorship.

ELINT activities are defined as the collection (observation and recording) and the processing for subsequent intelligence purposes, of information derived from foreign non-communications, electromagnetic radiations emanating from other than atomic detonation or radioactive sources. ELINT is the technical and intelligence information product of ELINT activities.[33]

Although created in 1952, it was not until 1957 that the NSA's existence was officially acknowledged in the *U.S. Government Organization Manual* as a "separately organized agency within the Department of Defense" that "performs highly specialized technical and coordinating functions relating to national security."[34] Despite the lack of official acknowledgment, the NSA's existence was a matter of public knowledge from at least mid-1953. In that year the Washington newspapers ran several stories concerning the construction of its new headquarters at Fort George G. Meade, Maryland.[35] In late 1954 the NSA was again in the news when an NSA employee was caught taking secret documents home, apparently with the intention of transmitting them to the Soviet Union.[36]

NSCID 6 defines the extent of the NSA's SIGINT mission. The NSA has another mission: Communications Security (COMSEC). In its COMSEC role it creates, reviews, and authorizes the communications procedures and codes of eighteen government agencies, including the State Department, DOD, CIA, and FBI.[37] This role includes development of secure data and voice transmission links on such satellite systems as the Defense Satellite Communications System (DSCS) and the Satellite Data System (SDS).[38] Likewise, FBI agents use a special scrambler phone for sensitive communications that requires a different code each day from the NSA.[39] The NSA's COMSEC responsibilities also include ensuring communications security for strategic weapons systems such as the Minuteman and MX missiles, so as to prevent unauthorized intrusion, interference, or jamming. In addition, the NSA is responsible for developing the codes by which the President must identify himself in order to authorize a nuclear strike.[40] In fulfilling these responsibilities, the NSA produces documents such as the *National COMSEC Plan for Fixed Plant and Strategic Communications* (1977) and the *National COMSEC Plan for Space Systems and Nuclear Weapons Systems* (1972).

The NSA's COMSEC responsibilities also include more mundane activities. One such activity is data-processing security, ensuring that unauthorized individuals or governments are not able to tap into data banks. The data banks to be protected from such intrusion include both government and private data banks, regardless of whether they hold classified data. Thus, the NSA has created a Computer Security Center to cooperate with business organizations in evaluating methods for preventing unauthorized access to computer systems.[41]

Just as the NSA's communications security role extends far beyond the traditional code-making role, so its signals intelligence role extends far beyond the code-breaking role and is directed at gathering foreign military, political, and economic intelligence. This intelligence concerns not only the Soviet Union and other hostile nations but Third World and allied nations.

Signals intercepted may include diplomatic communications, conversations between military personnel and among military-political leaders as well as commercial communications. Thus, in the early 1970s the NSA managed, via a Moscow embassy listening post, to intercept the radio-telephone conversations conducted by Soviet leaders when they were in their limousines.[42] At the same time, the NSA is alleged to intercept personal and commercial international communications transmitted via satellite, transatlantic cables, and microwave telephone links, including INTELSAT/COMSAT and the London–Paris phone links.[43]

In pursuit of military intelligence concerning the Soviet Union and other countries, the NSA monitors the electronic emissions of radars and aircraft, the telemetry of missiles, the signatures of Soviet submarines, and the data transmitted by Soviet spacecraft. Thus, in 1967 the NSA monitored the conversation between Premier Alexei Kosygin and Cosmonaut Vladimir M. Komarov, who had been informed by Soviet ground control that the braking parachutes designed to bring his spacecraft safely to earth were malfunctioning and there was no hope.[44]

Clearly, the NSA provides intelligence relevant to a wide range of government activities. COMINT provides data of use in analyzing possible courses of action of foreign governments and in determining negotiating strategy, whether in regard to military or economic negotiations. Thus, the NSA apparently obtained advance warning of the Arab attack on Israel in 1973 as well as knowledge of the Soviet bargaining position in SALT I.[45] ELINT helps determine the order of battle and capabilities of foreign forces, both conventional and strategic. Intelligence about foreign radar systems is useful in pinpointing their location and developing electronic countermeasures (ECMs). On the basis of intelligence

Figure 2-1.   Organization of the National Security Agency.

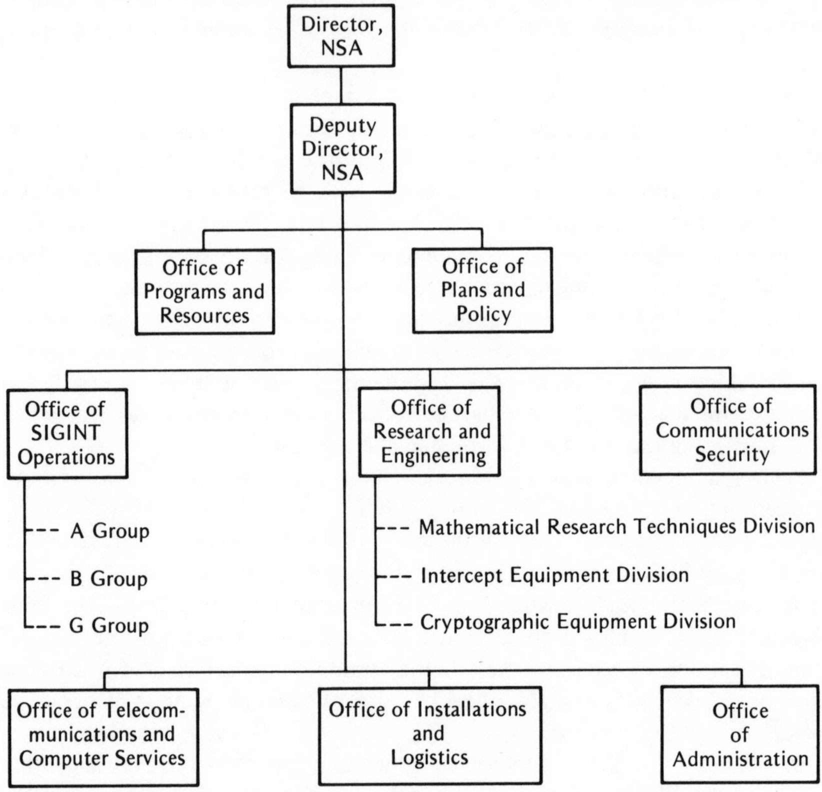

```
                    ┌──────────────┐
                    │  Director,   │
                    │    NSA       │
                    └──────────────┘
                    ┌──────────────┐
                    │   Deputy     │
                    │  Director,   │
                    │    NSA       │
                    └──────────────┘
        ┌────────────────┐      ┌────────────────┐
        │   Office of    │      │   Office of    │
        │  Programs and  │      │   Plans and    │
        │   Resources    │      │    Policy      │
        └────────────────┘      └────────────────┘
  ┌────────────┐   ┌────────────┐   ┌────────────────┐
  │ Office of  │   │ Office of  │   │   Office of     │
  │  SIGINT    │   │ Research and│  │ Communications  │
  │ Operations │   │ Engineering │  │   Security      │
  └────────────┘   └────────────┘   └────────────────┘
```

--- A Group   --- Mathematical Research Techniques Division

--- B Group   --- Intercept Equipment Division

L-- G Group   L-- Cryptographic Equipment Division

| Office of Telecom- munications and Computer Services | Office of Installations and Logistics | Office of Administration |

Source: James Bamford, *The Puzzle Palace: A Report on NSA, America's Most Secret Agency* (Boston: Houghton Mifflin 1982), pp. 56-117.

about foreign radars, NSA prepares Emitter Programs Listings (EPLs) detailing radar frequencies and locations.[46] Identification of Soviet submarines by their signatures is a significant aid to antisubmarine and underseas surveillance activities.

NSA headquarters at Fort Meade houses somewhere between 20,000 and 24,000 employees.[47] As indicated in Figure 2-1, it is divided into several offices/organizations, the three most prominent being the Office of Signals Intelligence Operations, the Office of Communications Security, and the Office of Research and Engineering.[48] The Office of Signals Intelligence Operations has three production units responsible for different geographical areas. A Group is responsible for the Soviet Union and its satellites. Within A Group the A2 Office is responsible for the Soviet Union and A3 for Soviet satellites. Within the A3 Office the A31 Division (or Northern European Communist Division) is responsible for Poland, East Germany, and Czechoslovakia, the A32 Division (South European Communist Division) being responsible for Hungary and Bulgaria (A-321), Yugoslavia and Albania (A-322), and Rumania (A-323). B Group is responsible for China, Korea, Vietnam, and the rest of Communist Asia, and G Group is responsible for all other nations (it used to be known as ALLO), both Third World and allied.

The Office of Communications Security is responsible for COMSEC with respect to the various forms of communications discussed above—diplomatic communications, sensitive secure phone links, satellite voice and data transmissions, and data processing. The Office of Research and Engineering has the responsibility for developing the techniques and equipment necessary for conducting intercept operations, breaking codes, and ensuring secure U.S. codes. The Office's Mathematical Research Techniques Division explores code-breaking possibilities. The Intercept Equipment Divison concentrates on developing the equipment required for the NSA's COMINT and ELINT intercept programs. The Cryptographic Equipment Division seeks to develop secure coding machines.

In addition to the three main offices there are several others of importance. The Office of Telecommunications and Computer Services is responsible for both computer support and the functioning of the NSA's communications network, the Digital Network–Defense Special Security Communications System (DIN/DSSCS). Information transmitted on this system, via the Defense Satellite Communications System (DSCS), includes intercepts from overseas stations. The Office of Installations and Logistics is responsible for overseas housing, disposal of classified waste, construction of facilities at Fort Meade, and procurement of computers. The Office of Administration has a variety of functions including personnel matters, training, employment, and security—the latter being handled by the Office of Security, M5.

Other offices of importance are the Office of Plans and Policy and the Office of Programs and Resources. The Office of Plans and Policy serves as a staff for the Director with the Deputy Director for Plans and Policy serving as a Chief of Staff. The Office of Programs and Resources is charged with the management and allocation of SIGINT/COMSEC resources, most specifically with the preparation of the Consolidated Cryptographic Program (discussed in Chapter 14).

The size of the NSA budget has been variously estimated at $1.2 billion, $3 billion, and $10 billion.[49] The disparities may be a function of one-time equipment purchases and the difference between NSA headquarters budget and the total NSA-controlled SIGINT/COMSEC budget. The latter budget would incorporate the funds spent under the direction of the NSA's "other half," the Central Security Service (CSS). The CSS is responsible, in theory, for supervising and directing the activities of the Service Cryptological Authorities (SCAs)—the Army Intelligence and Security Command, the Air Force Electronic Security

Command, and the Naval Security Group Command. The CSS function of the NSA, with the Director of the NSA serving simultaneously as Chief of the CSS, was established in 1971 in order "to provide a unified, more economical and more effective structure for executing cryptologic and related operations presently conducted under the Military Departments."[50] There is however, at present, no separate CSS Staff.[51]

In addition to performing tactical COMSEC and SIGINT missions, the SCAs provide personnel to man strategic SIGINT collection facilities in the United States and overseas. Assuming that the SCAs employ approximately equal numbers of personnel, the total number of NSA/SCA personnel is in the 50,000 to 60,000 range, and the overall budget for NSA-directed SIGINT and COMSEC activities is in the $5 to $10 billion range.

CENTRAL INTELLIGENCE AGENCY

In the aftermath of World War II, the U.S. central intelligence organization that had been created for the conflict—the Office of Strategic Services (OSS)—was disbanded. Several branches of the organization were distributed among other departments of the government. Thus, the X-2 (counterintelligence) and Secret Intelligence Branches were transferred to the War Department as the Strategic Services Unit, and the Research and Analysis Branch was relocated in the State Department.[52]

Shortly afterward, however, President Truman found himself deluged by intelligence reports from several government agencies and set up the National Intelligence Authority and its operational element, the Central Intelligence Group (CIG), to coordinate and collate the reports.[53] The CIG served as a coordinating mechanism as well as having some responsibility for intelligence collection.[54]

As part of the general consideration of national security needs and organization, the question of intelligence organization was addressed in the National Security Act of 1947. The Act established the CIA as an independent agency within the Executive Office of the President to replace the CIG. According to the Act, the CIA was to have five functions:

1. to advise the National Security Council in matters concerning such intelligence activities of the government departments and agencies as related to national security;
2. to make recommendations to the National Security Council for the coordination of such intelligence activities of the departments and agencies of the government as relate to national security;
3. to correlate and evaluate intelligence relating to the national security, and to provide for the appropriate dissemination of such intelligence within the government using, where appropriate, existing agencies and facilities;

4. to perform for the benefit of the existing intelligence agencies such additional services of common concern as the National Security Council determines can be more effectively accomplished centrally; and

5. to perform other such functions and duties related to intelligence affecting the national security as the National Security Council may from time to time direct.[55]

The CIA was to have no domestic role or powers of arrest.

The provisions of the Act left a great deal of room for interpretation. Thus, the final provision (5) has been cited as authorizing covert action measures. Whatever the intentions of Congress in 1947, the CIA developed in accord with a maximalist interpretation of the Act. Thus, the CIA has become the primary U.S. government agency for intelligence analysis, clandestine human intelligence collection, and covert action. As noted above, it has played a major role in the development of overhead reconnaissance systems, such as the U-2, KH-11, and Rhyolite. Additionally, the Director of the CIA is also Director of Central Intelligence and is responsible for managing the activities of the entire intelligence community.

In addition, under President Reagan's 1981 Executive Order 12333, the CIA is permitted to collect "significant" foreign intelligence secretly within the United States if that effort is not aimed at learning about the domestic activities of U.S. citizens and corporations. The order also gives the CIA authority to conduct, within the United States, "special activities" or covert operations if approved by the President that are not intended to influence U.S. political processes, public opinion, or the media.[56]

Headquarters of the CIA is in Langley, Virginia, although it has many offices and over 3,000 employees scattered around the Washington area.[57] In 1983 it had between 16,500 and 20,000 employees in the Washington area and a budget of $800 million.[58] It is divided into four major components, each headed by a Deputy Director, and six offices directly subordinate to the Director and Deputy Director. The offices are those of the General Counsel, the Inspector General, the Comptroller, Equal Employment Opportunity, Director of Personnel, and Director of Policy and Planning. The major components are the Directorate of Administration, the Directorate of Operations, the Directorate of Science and Technology, and the Directorate of Intelligence. Thus, the general structure of the CIA is that depicted in Figure 2-2.

Within the Directorate of Administration are eight offices which perform a wide range of administrative services: the Office of Communications, the Office of Logistics, the Office of Security, the Office of Training and Education, the Office of Finance, the Office of Data Processing, the Office of Medical Services, and the Office of Personnel.[59] The Office of Communications, with over 2,000 employees in 1973, maintains facilities for secret communications between CIA headquarters and overseas bases and agents.[60] Presumably, this includes control over the CIA Pyramider type agent communications satellites.[61]

Figure 2-2. Organization of the Central Intelligence Agency.

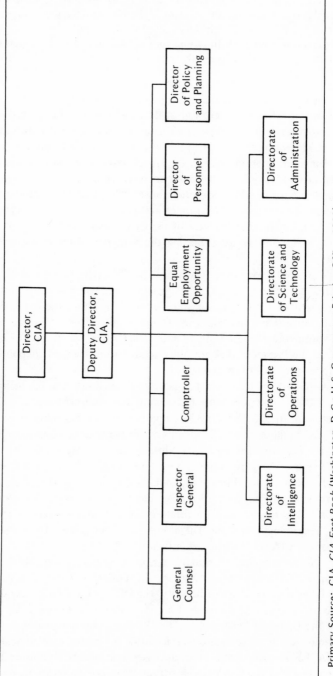

Primary Source: CIA, *CIA Fact Book* (Washington, D.C.: U.S. Government Printing Office, 1980).

The Office of Logistics operates weapons and other warehouses in the United States as well as supplying office equipment.[62]

The Office of Security is responsible for the physical protection of CIA installations, overt and covert, at home and abroad. It also administers polygraph tests to applicants and contractor personnel.[63] The Office of Finance maintains field units in Hong Kong, Beirut, Buenos Aires, and Geneva with easy access to monetary markets. It is also responsible for payroll and maintaining centralized financial records.[64] The Office of Medical Services provides cleared psychiatrists and physicians to treat agency officers.[65] The Office of Personnel is responsible for recruitment and maintenance of personnel files and with the Office of Training and Education operates CIA training facilities, including the main facility, "The Farm," at Camp Peary, Virginia.[66] Along with the Office of Medical Services and the Office of Security, it shares the responsibility for screening applicants. In response to the statement of personnel needs from agency components, it prepares an Advanced Staffing Plan for the ensuing fiscal year, listing the total personnel requirements by category of personnel and occupation job titles.[67] The Office of Training and Education conducts over sixty courses on world affairs, management theories and techniques, foreign languages, and intelligence evaluation and production.[68]

The Directorate of Operations, formerly the Directorate of Plans, is in charge of clandestine collection and covert actions (special activities). It is organized into various headquarters staffs, area divisions, and support divisions. The headquarters staffs are the Foreign Intelligence Staff; the Counterintelligence Staff; Covert Action Staff; Staff D; Central Cover Staff (formerly Cover and Commercial Staff); and the Evaluation, Plans, and Design Staff.

The Counterintelligence Staff (CIS) is responsible for offensive counterintelligence operations—penetration of hostile services, collection and analysis of information concerning such services, and the debriefing of defectors. Through its Operational Approval Branch, the CIS can "cast a vote" concerning proposed recruitments by an area division.[69] Among its analysis functions, the CIS prepares surveys of 50 to 100 pages concerning the structure, history, key personnel, and operations of foreign intelligence services, both hostile and friendly. At the height of its influence, under James Jesus Angleton, it had about 200 employees. After Angleton's dismissal at the end of 1975, the size of the staff was radically reduced and assignment to the staff made a temporary tour of duty. Operational counterintelligence responsibility was assigned to the geographical divisions of the directorate.[70]

The Foreign Intelligence Staff is responsible for checking the authenticity of sources and information; screening clandestine collection requirements; and reviewing the regional divisions projects, budget information, and operational cable traffic.[71] The responsibilities and authorities of the Foreign Intelligence Staff were summarized by a former head of the Staff, Peer de Silva:

> The Foreign Intelligence Staff had a continuing responsibility for monitoring intelligence collection projects and programs carried out abroad. These oper-

ations and collection programs were of course controlled and directed by the area divisions concerned; the FI Staff simply read the progress charts on the various projects (or the lack of progress) and played the role of determining which intelligence collection programs should be continued, changed or terminated. With the exception of a few individual operations of special sensitivity, this FI Staff function was worldwide.[72]

The Covert Action Staff, in cooperation with the area divisions, develops the plans for covert action operations which have included: (1) political advice and counsel; (2) subsidies to an individual; (3) financial support and "technical assistance" to political parties; (4) support to private organizations, including labor unions and business firms; (5) covert propaganda; (6) private training of individuals and exchange of persons; (7) economic operations; (8) paramilitary or political action operations designed to overthrow or support a regime; and (9) attempted assassinations.[73] Thus, during the presidency of Salvador Allende the Covert Action Staff might have devised an article uncomplimentary to Allende in cooperation with the Chilean desk of the Western Hemisphere Division. A CIA front, such as Forum World Features in London, would then be used to write and transmit the article.[74]

Staff D is in charge of bugging, wiretapping, and COMINT activities—some in support of other government agencies. Thus, the U.S. Secret Service regularly tasks the CIA to provide real-time communications intelligence close support to the Secret Service during the foreign travel of the President. The CIA monitors on-the-scene local, foreign military, and internal security support elements responsible for the physical protection of the President.[75] In 1973, at the request of the NSA, the staff monitored telephone conversations between the United States and Latin America for a period of three (or six) months in an effort to identify narcotics traffickers.[76] On another occasion, Staff D apparently gave money to a code clerk working in the Washington embassy of a U.S. ally for supplying information that assisted in breaking the Allies' code.[77] At one time, Staff D also housed the CIA "Executive Action" capability, ZR/RIFLE.[78]

In addition to the operational staffs are two support and evaluation staffs. The Central Cover Staff is the apparent successor to the Operational Services Division, which supplied cover for agents under nondiplomatic cover. The Central Cover Staff may also set up CIA proprietary organizations—business organizations that serve as cover for CIA operations.[79]

The Evaluation, Plans, and Designs Staff (EPDS) does much of the bureaucratic planning and budgeting for the Directorate for Operations. It also serves as a catchall staff for "unwanted" elements of other staffs and offices. Thus, the International Communism Branch of the Counterintelligence Staff was transferred to EPDS as a result of the downgrading of the stature of the CIS.[80]

Actual implementation of staff-planned activities are generally the responsibility of the area divisions, of which there are nine: Soviet Bloc, Western Hemisphere, European, East Asia, Africa, Near East, Special Operations, Foreign Resources, and Domestic Collection.[81] Each of the regional area divisions has staffs for support, covert action, counterintelligence, and foreign intelligence. In addition, each division is broken down into branches and desks representing ever more specific geographic areas. The Special Operations Division handles paramilitary activities such as the Bay of Pigs invasion, CIA secret armies in Laos and Vietnam, and the present efforts directed at the Sandinista government of Nicaragua. The Foreign Resources Division was created in 1963 as the Domestic Operations Division and given the responsibility for "clandestine operational activities of the Clandestine Services conducted within the United States against foreign targets."[82] The present functions of the Division are to locate and recruit foreign nationals residing in the United States who are of special interest to cooperate with the CIA abroad.[83]

The Domestic Collection Division (DCD), known until 1973 as the Domestic Contact Service (and part of the Directorate of Intelligence until then), openly collects intelligence from U.S. residents who have traveled abroad. The intelligence concerns a wide variety of subjects, primarily of an economic and technical nature.[84] One of the DCD's continuing responsibilities is the resettlement of defectors.[85]

An organizational chart of the Directorate of Operations is shown as Figure 2-3. As of 1973 the Directorate had 6,000 employees and a budget of $440 million. About $260 million was spent on covert action, and 4,800 employees were located in the area divisions.[86] Cutbacks by Directors James Schlesinger and Stansfield Turner reduced personnel by about 2,000, but Director William Casey, appointed in 1981, restored many of the slots eliminated by Schlesinger and Turner.[87]

The Directorate of Intelligence, known from 1978 to 1981 as the National Foreign Assessment Center (NFAC), is the primary U.S. government organization for intelligence analysis. As such, it has been the unit primarily responsible for preparing the various National Intelligence Estimates and Special National Intelligence Estimates, the most important of these being the yearly NIE-11-3/8 on Soviet strategic forces. As shown in Figure 2-4, the present structure of the Directorate includes three staffs (Management and Analysis Support, Arms Control Intelligence, and Collection Requirements and Evaluation), five regional offices and five functional offices, and one independent center. Regional offices such as the Office of Soviet Analysis were created by grouping Soviet analysts from all areas of research—political, military, economic, agricultural, and sociological. The functional offices—the Office of Global Issues, the Office of Imagery Analysis, the Office of Scientific and Weapons Research, the Office of Central Reference, the Office of Current Operations—are, with one exception (Global Issues), carryovers from the NFAC organizational framework, which was strictly functional. In 1981 an independent (within the Directorate) center, the Technology Transfer Assessment Center, was established to coordinate the production of technology transfer intelligence.[88]

Figure 2-3.   Organization of the Directorate of Operations.

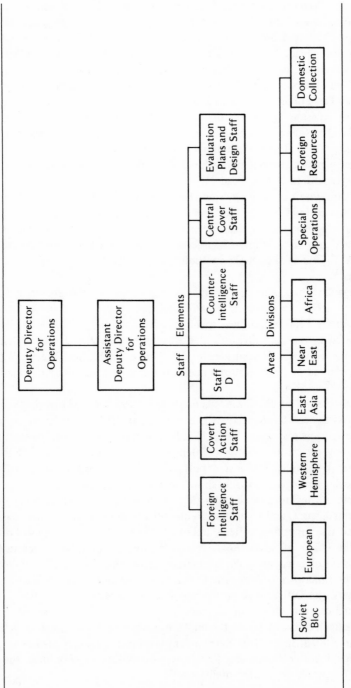

Source: Victor Marchetti and John Marks, *The CIA and the Cult of Intelligence* (New York: Knopf 1974), pp. 58–86; U.S. Congress, House Permanent Select Committee on Intelligence, *Prepublication Review and Secrecy Arrangements* (Washington, D.C.: U.S. Government Printing Office, 1980), p. 10; Interview with author.

Figure 2-4. Organization of the Directorate of Intelligence.

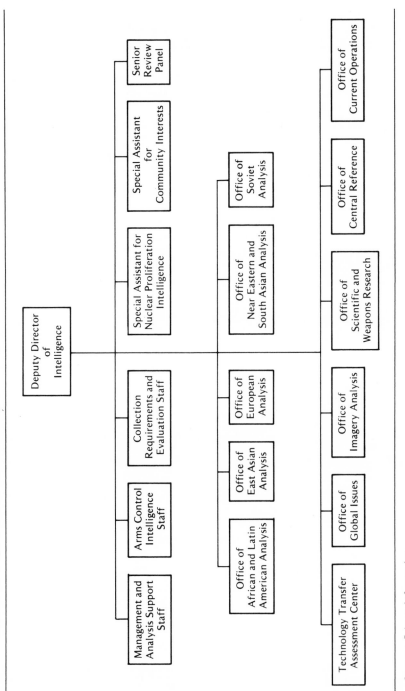

Source: Private information.

A more instructive picture of the Directorate of Intelligence's functions and actual output can be obtained by noting that the Office of Global Issues is concerned with subjects such as narcotics, international terrorism (via the Office's Center for Insurgency, Instability, and Terrorism), and human rights and by considering the functions of the NFAC offices as they stood in April 1979. At that time NFAC consisted of nine offices, an Operations Center, and a Publications and Presentations Group.[89]

The Office of Central Reference provided (and still provides) data in the form of directories of foreign government officials, lists of organizations and of public appearances by foreign officials, and biographies of interest. Among its publications have been "Dmitry Ustinov: USSR Minister of Defense," "The Leadership of the USSR Academy of Science," and "Directory of Officials of the People's Republic of China."

The Office of Imagery Analysis was created in 1961 as the Imagery Analysis Service to give the CIA a photo imagery analysis capability apart from the CIA-run National Photographic Interpretation Center (NPIC), which was to serve the entire intelligence community.[90] The Office of Strategic Research (OSR) was responsible for military intelligence matters. It was primarily concerned, through its Strategic Evaluation Center, with Soviet strategic forces. OSR publications included "Chinese Defense Spending 1965-1979," "A Dollar Cost Comparison of Soviet and U.S. Defense Activities 1968-1978," and "The Egyptian Arms Industry."

The Office of Political Analysis (OPA) was concerned with all aspects of political activity—the outcome of elections, terrorism, the standing of political parties, the political power of factions, and the impact of domestic politics on foreign policy. OPA publications have included "Patterns of International Terrorism," "Profile of Violence: An Analytical Model," and "A Guide to Political Acronyms." The Office of Geographic and Cartographic Research studied demographic, cultural, and social questions. Its publications included "Kampuchea: A Demographic Catastrophe," "The Refugee Resettlement Problem in Thailand," "Relating Climate Change to Its Effects," and "Pakistan: The Ethnic Equation."

The Office of Scientific and Weapons Research was formed by merging the Office of Scientific Intelligence and Office of Weapons Intelligence. Its primary concern is with the analysis of foreign weapon systems—the number, type, quality, and capability. The Office of Economic Research examined a wide variety of economic subjects, particularly those concerning major issues such as the availability of oil and other crucial resources, economic policies, and currency stability. Its publications included "The World Oil Market in the Years Ahead," "Arms Flows to LDC's: U.S.-Soviet Comparisons 1974-1977," "Korea: The Economic Race Between North and South," "USSR: The Long Term Outlook for Grain Imports," "China: In Pursuit of Economic Modernization," and "Soviet Strategy and Tactics in Economic and Commercial Negotiations with the United States."

The Office of Current Operations is in charge of the Operations Center, which maintains watch over incoming data from a variety of collection assets and can inform higher authorities if incoming intelligence indicates a crisis situation is developing.

The Directorate of Science and Technology (DS&T) was created in 1962 as the Directorate for Research and was given its present name in 1963. At that time, various CIA offices dealing with technical intelligence collection were consolidated into one unit.[91] The DS&T has undergone several reorganizations and has gained and lost responsibilities in the twenty years since it was created. Both the Directorate of Intelligence and the Directorate of Operations have at times disputed actual or planned DS&T control of various offices and divisions. Thus, at various times the Directorate has been assigned scientific intelligence analysis functions to the dismay of the Directorate of Intelligence. At one time, the Directorate controlled the Office of Weapons Intelligence (formed by merging the Foreign Missile and Space Analysis Center with certain functions of the Office of Scientific Intelligence).[92]

In 1973 the NPIC was transferred to the DS&T from the Directorate of Intelligence. The NPIC is the successor to a series of CIA photo interpretation units first set up in 1953 as the Photographic Intelligence Division (PID) with thirteen interpreters. In 1958 the PID was merged with a statistical analysis division of the Office of Current Intelligence to form the Photographic Interpretation Center.[93] Under the provision of NSCID 8 of 1961 and its successors, the NPIC is run by the CIA as a "service of common concern" serving the entire intelligence community.[94] It presently has over 1,000 photo interpreters and is located in Building 213 of the Washington Navy Yard at 1st and M Streets.[95]

In addition to the NPIC, the DS&T presently directs the activities of the previously mentioned Office of Development and Engineering and Office of SIGINT Operations as well as the Office of Research and Development, the Office of Technical Service, and the Foreign Broadcast Information Service (FBIS). The Office of Development and Engineering is the successor to a long line of CIA components involved in overhead reconnaissance R&D. The first such CIA component was created in 1954 to develop the U-2 and was named the Development Project Staff. It subsequently became known as the Office of Special Activities, the Office of Special Projects and, in 1973, the Office of Development and Engineering.[96]

The Office of Technical Service was previously the Technical Services Division (TSD) of the Directorate of Operations. It was acquired by the DS&T in 1973—an acquisition that took over ten years. When the DS&T was formed its leadership argued that the TSD should be brought under its control—a suggestion resisted by the leaders of the Operations (then Plans) Directorate, who argued that the division should be close to its consumers, the men in Plans. The TSD was transferred to the DS&T as part of a series of transfers and changes initiated by William Colby.[97]

The Office of Signals Intelligence Operations is involved in all forms of SIGINT R&D, including, as noted above, reconnaissance satellite development. However, CIA SIGINT activities include much nonstrategic collection, such as airborne collection in Central America.

A second service of common concern run by the DS&T is the FBIS, which monitors the public radio and television broadcasts of foreign nations and prepares summaries of those broadcasts of interest for use by intelligence analysts and officials.[98] The FBIS dates back to 1941, when the Federal Communications Commission established the Foreign Broadcast Monitoring Service at the request of the State Department.[99] From that point on, the U.S. government has had an organization to "record, translate, analyze and report to other agencies of the government on broadcasts of foreign origin."[100]

NOTES TO CHAPTER 2

1. Raymond Garthoff, "Banning the Bomb in Outer Space," *International Security* 5 (1980/1981): 25–40.
2. Arthur Sylvester, "Memorandum for the President, White House; SAMOS II Launch," (Washington, D.C.: Office of the Assistant Secretary of Defense for Public Affairs, 1961). *Declassified Documents Reference System 1979-364B.*
3. Philip Taubman, "Secrecy of U.S. Reconnaissance Office is Challenged," *New York Times*, February 29, 1980, p. 10.
4. Victor Marchetti and John Marks, *The CIA and the Cult of Intelligence* (New York: Knopf, 1974), p. 332. The U.S. government obtained a court injunction preventing certain classified portions of the original manuscript from being published. As a result, there have been three different versions of *The CIA and the Cult of Intelligence*: the 1974 version, and the 1980 and 1983 paperback versions. The latter two each contain additional information resulting from the declassification of previously censored portions. Unless otherwise noted, all citations refer to the 1974 edition.
5. William Colby and Peter Forbath, *Honorable Men: My Life in the CIA* (New York: Simon & Schuster, 1978), p. 370; Philip Agee, "How the Director of Central Intelligence Projected U.S. Intelligence Activities 1976–1981," *Covert Action Information Bulletin* 6 (1979): 13–24.
6. George B. Kistiakowsky, *A Scientist in the White House: The Private Diary of President Eisenhower's Special Assistant for Science and Technology* (Cambridge, Mass.: Harvard University Press, 1976), pp. 378–79.
7. Carl Berger, *The Air Force in Space Fiscal Year 1961* (Washington, D.C.: USAF Historical Division Liaison Office, April 1966), p. 34.
8. Ibid.
9. Ibid., p. 42; Larry Booda, "New Capsule to Be Developed for Samos," *Aviation Week*, September 12, 1960, pp. 21–27.
10. Kistiakowsky, *A Scientist in the White House*, p. 382.
11. Ibid.

12. "USAF Strengthens SAMOS Effort," *Aviation Week*, September 12, 1960, p. 31.
13. Special Senate Committee on Secret and Confidential Documents, *Report 93-466* (Washington, D.C.: U.S. Government Printing Office, 1973), p. 16.
14. Laurence Stern, "$1.5 Billion Secret in the Sky," *Washington Post*, December 9, 1973, pp. 1, 9.
15. *Report of the Commission on the Organization of the Government for the Conduct of Foreign Policy* (Washington, D.C.: U.S. Government Printing Office, 1975), p. 95.
16. Colby and Forbath, *Honorable Men*; Theodore Shackley, *The Third Option* (New York: McGraw-Hill, 1981).
17. James Canan, *War in Space* (New York: Harper & Row, 1982), pp. 110–11; *Department of Defense Telephone Directory* (Washington, D.C.: U.S. Government Printing Office, April 1984), p. 0–114.
18. Canan, *War in Space*, pp. 110–11.
19. James Bamford, *The Puzzle Palace: A Report on NSA, America's Most Secret Agency* (Boston: Houghton Mifflin, 1982), p. 78.
20. James Ott, "Espionage Trial Highlights CIA Problems," *Aviation Week and Space Technology*, November 27, 1978, pp. 21–22; Desmond Ball, *A Suitable Piece of Real Estate* (Sydney: Hale and Iremonger, 1980), p. 84.
21. Ibid.
22. "New USAF Special Projects Director," *Aviation Week and Space Technology*, August 11, 1985, p. 51.
23. Taubman, "Secrecy of Reconnaissance Office Challenged."
24. The Brownell Committee, *The Origin and Development of the National Security Agency* (Laguna Hills, Cal.: Aegean Park Press, 1981), p. 30.
25. Ibid., p. 1.
26. U.S. Congress, Senate Select Committee to Study Governmental Operations with Respect to Intelligence Activities, *Foreign and Military Intelligence, Book III* (Washington, D.C.: U.S. Government Printing Office, 1976), p. 736.
27. Walter Bedell Smith, "Proposed Survey of Communications Intelligence Activities," December 10, 1951.
28. The Brownell Committee, *The Origin and Development of the National Security Agency*, p. 181.
29. Ibid., pp. 1–6.
30. U.S. Congress, Senate Select Committee, *Foreign and Military Intelligence, Book III*, p. 736.
31. National Security Council Directive 6, "Signals Intelligence," February 17, 1972. Sanitized version, *Declassified Documents Reference System 1976–168A*.
32. Department of Justice, *Report on CIA Related Electronic Surveillance Activities* (Washington, D.C.: Department of Justice, 1976), p. 78.
33. National Security Council Intelligence Directive 6.
34. *United States Government Organization Manual 1957-1958* (Washington, D.C.: U.S. Government Printing Office, 1957), p. 137.

35. "Washington Firm Will Install Ft. Meade Utilities," *Washington Post*, January 7, 1954, p. 7.

36. "U.S. Security Aide Accused of Taking Secret Documents," *New York Times*, October 10, 1954, pp. 1, 33.

37. U.S. Congress, Senate Select Committee to Study Governmental Operations with Respect to Intelligence Activities, *Foreign and Military Intelligence, Book I* (Washington, D.C.: U.S. Government Printing Office, 1976), p. 354.

38. U.S. Congress, House Committee on Appropriations, *Department of Defense Appropriations for FY 1982, Part 2* (Washington, D.C.: U.S. Government Printing Office, 1981), pp. 824–29.

39. Leslie Maitland, "FBI Says New York is a 'Hub' of Spying in U.S.," *New York Times*, November 14, 1981, p. 12.

40. Patrick E. Tyler and Bob Woodward, "FBI Held War Code of Reagan," *Los Angeles Times*, December 13, 1981, pp. 1, 27.

41. Walter Sullivan, "U.S. Seeks to Link Industry on Computer Defenses," *New York Times*, August 12, 1981, p. A17.

42. Seymour Hersh, "The President and the Plumbers: A Look at Two Security Questions," *New York Times*, December 9, 1973, pp, 1, 76.

43. Duncan Campbell and Linda Malvern, "America's Big Ear on Europe," *New Statesman*, July 18, 1980, pp. 10–14; Bamford, *The Puzzle Palace*, pp. 172–74.

44. Winslow Peck, "U.S. Electronic Espionage: A Memoir," *Ramparts*, August 1972, pp. 36–50.

45. "Eavesdropping on the World's Secrets," *U.S. News and World Report*, June 26, 1978, pp. 45–49.

46. Harry F. Eustace, "Changing Intelligence Priorities," *Electronic Warfare/ Defense Electronics*, November 1978, pp. 30ff.

47. Ibid.; "Shaping Tomorrow's CIA," *Time*, February 6, 1978, pp. 10ff.

48. Except where noted, all material on NSA organization is based on Bamford, ch. 3 and the 1983 Penguin paperback edition p. 518.

49. "Shaping Tomorrow's CIA"; Eustace, "Changing Intelligence Priorities"; Tad Szulc, "The NSA—America's $10 Billion Frankenstein," *Penthouse*, November 1978, pp. 55ff.

50. *National Security Strategy of Realistic Deterrence: Secretary of Defense Melvin Laird's Annual Defense Department Report FY 1973* (Washington, D.C.: U.S. Government Printing Office, 1972), p. 135.

51. Bamford, *The Puzzle Palace* (1982), pp. 155–57.

52. For a history of the OSS, see R. Harris Smith, *OSS: The Secret History of America's First Central Intelligence Agency* (Berkeley: University of California Press, 1972); and Bradley F. Smith, *The Shadow Warriors: O.S.S. and the Origins of the C.I.A.* (New York: Basic Books, 1983).

53. U.S. Congress Senate Select Committee to Study Governmental Operations with Respect to Intelligence Activities, *Supplementary Detailed Reports on Foreign and Military Intelligence, Book IV* (Washington, D.C.: U.S. Government Printing Office, 1976), pp. 4–6.

54. Ibid.

55. U.S. Congress, House Permanent Select Committee on Intelligence, *Compilation of Intelligence Laws* (Washington, D.C.: U.S. Government Printing Office, 1981), p. 7.
56. Judith Miller, "Reagan Widens Intelligence Role, Gives C.I.A. Domestic Spy Power," *New York Times*, December 5, 1981, pp. 1, 11.
57. Paul Hodge, "CIA Plans for Major New Building," *Washington Post*, October 2, 1981, p. B1.
58. Private information.
59. CIA, *CIA Fact Book* (Washington, D.C.: U.S. Government Printing Office, 1980), unpaginated.
60. Marchetti and Marks, *The CIA and the Cult of Intelligence*, p. 74.
61. Jeffrey Lenorovitz, "CIA Satellite Data Task Study Revealed," *Aviation Week and Space Technology*, May 2, 1977, p. 25; Arnaud De Bourchgrave, "Space-Age Spies," *Newsweek*, March 6, 1978, p. 7.
62. Marchetti and Marks, *The CIA and the Cult of Intelligence*, p. 74.
63. Ibid., p. 73.
64. Marchetti and Marks, *The CIA and the Cult of Intelligence*, p. 73; Commission on CIA Activities within the United States, *Report to the President* (Washington, D.C.: U.S. Government Printing Office, 1975), p. 91.
65. Marchetti and Marks, *The CIA and the Cult of Intelligence*, p. 74.
66. Ibid.
67. U.S. Congress House Permanent Select Committee on Intelligence, *Preemployment Security Procedures of the Intelligence Agencies* (Washington, D.C.: U.S. Government Printing Office, 1980), p. 31.
68. Commission on CIA Activities, p. 92.
69. Philip Agee, *Inside the Company: A CIA Diary* (New York: Stonehill, 1975), pp. 56–58.
70. Seymour Hersh, "The Angleton Story," *New York Times Magazine*, June 25, 1978, pp. 13ff; Henry Hurt, *Shadrin: The Spy Who Never Came Back* (New York: Reader's Digest, 1981), p. 147; Samuel T. Francis, "The Intelligence Community," in Charles L. Heatherly, ed., *Mandate for Leadership: Policy Management in a Conservative Administration* (Washington, D.C.: Heritage Foundation, 1980).
71. U.S. Congress, Senate Select Committee, *Supplementary Detailed Reports, Book IV*, p. 46, n. 4.
72. Peer de Silva, *Sub Rosa: The CIA and the Uses of Intelligence* (New York: Times Books, 1978), p. 291.
73. Marchetti and Marks, *The CIA and the Cult of Intelligence*, pp. 387–88.
74. Ibid., p. 4.
75. *Report on CIA Related Electronic Surveillance Activities*, p. 13.
76. Ibid., p. 4.
77. Bamford, *The Puzzle Palace* (1982), pp. 130–33.
78. David Martin, *Wilderness of Mirrors* (New York: Harper & Row, 1980), pp. 121, 127–28; "3 Tales of the CIA," *Ramparts*, April 1967, pp. 17–21.
79. U.S. Congress, House Permanent Select Committee on Intelligence, *Prepublication Review and Secrecy Arrangements* (Washington, D.C.: U.S. Government Printing Office, 1980), p. 10.

80. Author's inverview.
81. Marchetti and Marks, *The CIA and the Cult of Intelligence*, pp. 70–75; David Wise, *The American Police State* (New York: Vintage, 1976), pp. 188–92.
82. Wise, *The American Police State*, p. 188.
83. U.S. Congress, Senate Select Committee, *Foreign and Military Intelligence, Book I*, p. 439.
84. Ibid.; Wise, *The American Police State*, p. 189.
85. Wise, *The American Police State* pp. 70–75.
86. Marchetti and Marks, *The CIA and the Cult of Intelligence*, pp. 70–75.
87. Robert L. Jackson, "CIA Spy Chief Resigns Over Fraud Charges," *Los Angeles Times*, July 15, 1981, pp. 1, 8.
88. Philip Taubman, "Ouster of 3 Russians Linked to Crackdown on Theft of Technology," *New York Times*, April 24, 1983, p. 8.
89. *CIA Fact Book*.
90. Bamford, *The Puzzle Palace* (1982), p. 189.
91. U.S. Congress, Senate Select Committee to Study Governmental Operations, *Supplementary Detailed Staff Reports, Book IV*, pp. 77–78.
92. Ibid., pp. 537–44.
93. John Prados, *The Soviet Estimate: U.S. Intelligence Analysis and Russian Military Strength* (New York: Dial, 1982), p. 156.
94. NSCID 8, "Photographic Interpretation," February 17, 1972, *Declassified Documents Reference System 1976–253G*.
95. George Wilson, "N-Pic Technicians Ferret Out Secrets Behind Closed Windows," *Los Angeles Times*, January 12, 1975, p. 25; Gerald L. Borrowman, "Satellite Photographic Interpretation," *Spaceflight*, October 1982, pp. 161–63.
96. U.S. Congress, House Select Committee on Intelligence, *U.S. Intelligence Agencies and Activities: Intelligence Costs and Fiscal Procedures* (Washington, D.C.: U.S. Government Printing Office, 1976), pp. 537–44.
97. Thomas Powers, *The Man Who Kept the Secrets: Richard Helms and the CIA* (New York: Knopf, 1979), p. 341, n. 38.
98. *CIA Fact Book*.
99. Ray S. Cline, *Secret, Spies and Scholars* (Washington, D.C.: Acropolis, 1976), pp. 11–12.
100. Harold C. Relyea, *The Evolution and Organization of the Federal Intelligence Function: A Brief Overview (1776–1975)* (Washington, D.C.: U.S. Government Printing Office, 1976), p. 236.

3 DEFENSE DEPARTMENT INTELLIGENCE ORGANIZATIONS

In addition to the national intelligence organizations within the Department of Defense (DOD)—the National Reconnaissance Office (NRO) and the National Security Agency (NSA)—there are several agencies that are department-level agencies, their primary function being to satisfy intelligence requirements of the Secretary of Defense and DOD components.

Two of these agencies can trace their origins to the centralization trend that began at the end of the Eisenhower administration and continued through the early 1970s—the Defense Intelligence Agency and the Defense Mapping Agency. Another is more recent: the Armed Forces Medical Intelligence Center. Other organizations examined are the Special Operations Division of the J-3 section of the Joint Chiefs of Staff (JCS) and the possibly defunct Defense Special Plans Office.

DEFENSE INTELLIGENCE AGENCY

Creation of the Defense Intelligence Agency (DIA) was one manifestation of the trend toward centralization that began in the Eisenhower administration and reached its peak in the Kennedy administration. The Eisenhower administration concluded in the late 1950s that a consolidation of the services' general intelligence activities (defined as all non-SIGINT, nonoverhead, nonorganic intelligence activities) was needed.[1] This belief was, according to one analyst, a by-product of the missile gap controversy of the late 1950s.

Faced with the disparate estimates of Soviet missile strength from each of the armed services which translated into what have been called self-serving budget requests for weapons for defense, the United States Intelligence Board [USIB] created a Joint Study Group in 1957 to study the intelligence producing agencies. In 1960 this panel returned various recommendations among which were proposals for the consignment of the defense departments to observer rather than member status on the Intelligence Board and the creation of a coordinating Defense Intelligence Agency which would represent the armed services as a member of the USIB.[2]

The JCS disagreed over form. They were concerned with preserving the responsiveness of the service efforts to the military's tactical intelligence requirements. Thus, they preferred a "Joint Military Intelligence Agency" subordinate to them, within which the independence of the several military components, and hence their sensitivity to the needs of the parent service, would be retained. Kennedy administration Defense Secretary Robert McNamara wanted a much stronger bond—one that would allow for better utilization of service assets to support policymakers and force structure planners as well as to achieve management economies.[3]

The agency that emerged was a compromise between those opposing viewpoints. DIA reports to the Secretary of Defense but does so through the JCS. As a result, the Joint Staff Director for Intelligence (J-2) was abolished, as was the Office of Special Operations, the small intelligence arm of the Secretary of Defense.[4]

The DIA was established by a DOD Directive (DOD 5105.21) on August 1, 1961. The Directive made DIA responsible for:

1. organizing, directing, managing, and controlling Department of Defense intelligence resources assigned to or included within DIA;

2. reviewing and coordinating those Department of Defense intelligence functions retained by or assigned to the military departments. Guiding the conduct and management of such functions as will be developed by the Director, DIA, for review, approval, and promulgation by the Secretary of Defense;

3. supervising the execution of all approved plans, programs, policies and procedures for intelligence functions not assigned to DIA;

4. obtaining the maximum economy and efficiency in the allocation and management of Department of Defense intelligence resources. This includes analysis of those DOD intelligence activities and facilities which can be fully integrated and collocated with non–DOD intelligence organizations;

5. responding directly to priority requests levied upon the Defense Intelligence Agency by the USIB; and

6. satisfying the intelligence requirements of the major components of the Department of Defense.[5]

In 1964–1965 DIA was assigned several additional functions:

1. the photographic intelligence functions previously performed at the Washington level by separate armed services; the new responsibilities of DIA were to establish and operate facilities for military photographic processing, printing, interpretation, analysis and library intelligence services for the entire defense establishment;

2. the consolidation of intelligence dissemination so that the DIA became the agency for communicating both raw and "finished" intelligence, from Defense and non–Defense sources, to the entire defense establishment and to authorized non–DOD and international organizations;

3. the management of all automated, data-handling projects and services of the Department of Defense, including plans for validation of information, assignment of data handling tasks and priorities, and the development of policies and programs guidance for all Defense automated data processing for intelligence purposes. The program is decentralized at the operational level within the Departments of the Army, Navy and Air Force.

4. a program of classified "extraordinary military activities."[6]

Since its creation, DIA has undergone numerous reorganizations (four between 1961 and 1970) and has been subjected to severe criticism by several commentators. The criticism has been directed at the quality of its intelligence output as well as its inability to supervise effectively and constrain the growth of the service intelligence components.[7]

Abolition of the DIA has often been suggested, including by the Pike Committee.[8] Such an outcome is not a likely prospect, and the DIA continues to be the prime intelligence component of the DOD with respect to strategic intelligence matters. Thus, the DIA takes part in the formulation of the National Intelligence Estimates and Special National Intelligence Estimates on such topics as Soviet strategic forces and terrorism. It also serves as the validating authority for much of the work done by service intelligence components such as the Air Force Systems Command's Foreign Technology Division. Additionally, it is responsible for production of the Target Data Inventory (TDI), which is a data bank containing all the facilities that U.S. strategic nuclear planners might want to target. The TDI serves as the data base from which the National Strategic Target List and ultimately the Single Integrated Operational Plan (SIOP) is drawn.[9]

The DIA also engages in R&D Test and Evaluation programs related to intelligence technology. In its Fiscal Year 1982 request, the DIA specified four areas of research: crisis management, scientific and technical intelligence, automated data-processing capabilities, and collection management capabilities. Specifically, it requested funding to develop an automated system to "support timely analysis of Indicator and Warning Intelligence" as well as funding to "develop methodology and data bases to accommodate added intelligence requirements as a direct result of ... U.S. policy regarding nuclear targeting in PD #59." The

Figure 3-1. Organization of the Defense Intelligence Agency.

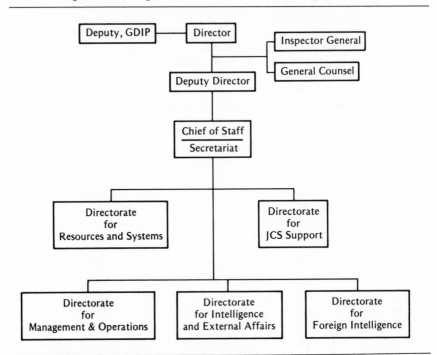

Source: *Department of Defense Telephone Directory* (Washington, D. C.: U.S. Government Printing Office, April 1984), pp. 0-11-0-14.

DIA also requested $0.7 million for development of the Advanced Imagery Requirements and Exploitation System.[10] In its request for the 1983 Fiscal Year, it sought funds for a real-time technical data collection effort designated SUDDEN DAWN as well as for an electro-optical collection program designated STEEL EYE.[11]

Organizationally, the DIA consists of, in addition to various minor offices, the General Defense Intelligence Program (GDIP) Staff, five independent directorates, and an Office of Security, as shown in Figure 3-1.[12] The Director of the GDIP directs the GDIP Staff in preparing, with military service and Central Intelligence Agency collaboration, the budget estimates for the GDIP (discussed in Chapter 13). Further, it tasks organizations under its direction to fulfill GDIP objectives.

The Directorate for Intelligence and External Affairs is divided into five divisions: the Director's Staff Group Division, the Military Operational Support Division, the Legislative and Public Affairs Division, the Foreign Liaison Division, and the International Negotiations Support Division (with Strategic Negotiations and Regional/Special Negotiations Branches). The Directorate is the DIA's link to the National Foreign Intelligence Program, the rest of the intelligence community, and DIA customers outside the intelligence community including negotiating teams (SALT, START, MBFR). It also handles liaison with such defense intelligence organizations as Australia's Joint Intelligence Organization and Britain's Defense Intelligence Staff.

The Directorate for Resources and Systems is divided into five directorates: Defense Intelligence Systems, Technical Services and Support, DIA Systems, Human Resources, and Communications. The Directorate for Defense Intelligence Systems manages and coordinates all DOD information systems programs and the interface of such systems with intelligence community and DOD systems. It also handles the dissemination of research and storage and retrieval functions. This includes the indexing of all aerial imagery and maintenance of automated index files of all DOD and nationally acquired imagery held in the DIA's central DOD depository.

The Directorate of Human Resources is the personnel office, and the Directorate of Communications provides overall management of the worldwide Special Intelligence Communications (SPINTCOMM) portion of the Defense Special Security Communications Systems (DSSCS). The Directorate for Technical Services and Support provides central reference, photo processing, and presentation support.

The Directorate for JCS Support consists of four directorates: the Directorate for OJCS Intelligence Support, the Directorate for Current Intelligence, the Directorate for Indications and Warning (I&W), and the Directorate for NMIC Operations. The Directorate for OJCS Intelligence Support has primary responsibility for all actions (within capabilities) assigned to the DIA by JCS/OJCS and maintains liaison with the NSA/CSS (Central Security Service) to ensure participation in pertinent Joint Staff actions. Additionally, it provides personnel to the National Emergency Airborne Command Post (NEACP). The Directorate for Current Intelligence provides all-source DOD and national-level current indications and warning intelligence as well as preparing Defense Intelligence Notices and Weekly Intelligence Summaries. The Directorate for I&W consists of three divisions: I&W Operations, Development and Implementation, and ELINT (Electronics Intelligence). Whereas the Current Intelligence Directorate focuses on producing indications and warning related to finished intelligence, the I&W Directorate is concerned with the methods of producing the raw I&W data. The Directorate for NMIC Operations is responsible for running the National Military Intelligence Center portion of the National Military Command Center.

The Directorate for Management and Operations is divided into three directorates: the Directorate for Collection Management, the Directorate for Attachés and Training, and the Directorate for Plans and Policy. The Directorate for Collection Management (which consists of five divisions—Current Operations, Requirements and Evaluation, Human Resources, Imagery, and SIGINT and Technical Sensors) manages, levies, and evaluates all intelligence collection and processing requirements of the DOD, including HUMINT (Human Intelligence), Imagery, SIGINT, and technical sensors. It also manages and coordinates DOD imagery processing and exploitation activities. It provides a single DIA focus for coordination and support of national and departmental reconnaissance activities. In this regard, it operates the Collection Coordination Facility (CCF) for interactive tasking of collection systems and maintains liaison with the Joint Reconnaissance Center (JRC) and other reconnaissance authorities.

The Directorate provides for DIA participation in the Defense Special Missile and Astronautics Center (DEFSMAC). DEFSMAC is run jointly with the NSA and is located at Fort Meade, Maryland. Created in September 1966, the function of DEFSMAC is to provide warning of missile and space launches with the objective of allowing U.S. intelligence assets to be targets on those launches.[13] DEFSMAC may also serve as the site for receipt of KH-11 photography.[14]

The Directorate for Attachés and Training runs DIA training and education programs (e.g., the Defense Intelligence School) as well as the Defense Attaché System. Defense attachés are accredited diplomats, as well as military officers, stationed at U.S. embassies throughout the world. Their functions include interaction with the military of friendly host countries and the overt collection of defense intelligence in whatever country they are stationed.

In some cases, attachés have been involved in clandestine collection activities. Several instances of congressional testimony by DIA officials hint at such activities—in one case, the Deputy Director of the DIA explicitly stated that the DIA conducted covert operations.[15] One of the items allegedly lost in the raid on the U.S. embassy in Iran was a SECRET-RODCA computer print-out that listed the true identities of all DIA sources and agents in the country as well as records of Operation Gray Pan—a joint CIA-DIA plan to steal a Russian-made anti-aircraft gun and armored personnel carrier that the Soviets had sold to the Iranian army in 1978.[16] Also, a U.S. attaché assassinated in France in early 1982 was targeted "for a specific reason," according to one U.S. diplomat, and had a long history of intelligence assignments.[17] Whatever the situation in the past, President Reagan's approval of National Security Decision Directive-138 of April 2, 1984 authorized the DIA to employ intelligence agents to collect information concerning terrorism.[18]

The Directorate for Plans and Policy consists primarily of the Plans and Policy Division with offices for national intelligence and tactical intelligence programs.

The Directorate for Foreign Intelligence is the branch of the DIA responsible for production of finished intelligence. Under the Vice Director of Foreign Intelligence are the Defense Intelligence Officers (DIOs) as well as the Directorates for Estimates, Scientific and Technical Intelligence, and Research. DIOs communicate with National Intelligence Officers in substantive matters of prime interest to the DOD. There are DIOs for East Asia and the Pacific, Latin America, the Middle East and South Asia, European and Soviet Political/Military Affairs, General Purpose Forces and Mutual and Balanced Force Reductions (MBFR), Africa, Strategic Programs, and Defense Intelligence Commentary. The Directorate for Estimates produces all intelligence estimates for the use of the Office of the Secretary of Defense, the Office of the JCS, and the DOD contribution to National Intelligence Estimates. It produces long-range threat forecasts and provides intelligence support for the DOD acquisition process. It initiates estimates of future trends in foreign force structures, weapons systems, overall military capabilities, strategy, and defense policy to alert national and DOD planners and decisionmakers to developments that might affect U.S. national security.

The Directorate for Scientific and Technical Intelligence, with four divisions—Nuclear Energy, Weapons and Systems, Strategic Defense, Command and Control, and Space and Research and Technologies—reviews and validates requirements and establishes production priorities for scientific and technical intelligence. It develops, manages, and technically directs DOD wide production and produces or tasks the scientific and technical intelligence, integrating it to provide selected assessments of combined military threat systems capabilities. It also maintains liaison with other elements of the DIA, other DOD agencies, the CIA, and other government elements to coordinate scientific and technical intelligence activities.

The Directorate of Research produces all-source finished military intelligence on orders of battle, military doctrine, strategy and tactics, C^3, equipment and logistics, biographies, and economics and material production and assistance programs. Its biographies focus on military and civilian defense leadership in allied, neutral, and hostile countries. The Directorate also produces substantive intelligence, estimates and special studies, and I&W intelligence. Among the six Directorate of Research divisions is the Operational and Target Intelligence Support Division, the Strategic Targeting Branch and Target Support Branch of which formulate target intelligence policies and plans. Finally, it exploits multisensor imagery and produces imagery-derived intelligence, participating in the National Photographic Interpretation Center (NPIC) and the development of exploitation equipment.

The Office of Security is divided into a Counterintelligence Division, a Counterterrorist Threat Branch, a Security Division, and a Compartmented Security Policy Division. The Compartmented Security Policy Division is responsible for establishing policy with regard to the three major categories of codeword clearances relating to intelligence systems and their products—Special Intelligence (SI), Talent–Keyhole (TK), and Byeman (B). The office provides counterintelligence and counterterrorist staff support to the Office of the Secretary of Defense and JCS, produces counterintelligence and terrorist threat studies, and coordinates the counterintelligence production of the military departments.

As of 1978, DIA had 4,300 to 5,500 employees (including 1,000 attachés) and a budget in the $200 to $250 million range.[19]

DEFENSE MAPPING AGENCY

The Defense Mapping Agency (DMA) was created in 1972 to consolidate the mapping, charting, and geodesy functions of the various military services. The primary mission of the DMA is to support the military services by providing mapping, charting, and geodesy products and services that are critical to successful military operations. Specifically, the DMA is required to produce strategic and tactical maps, charts, geodetic information, data bases, and specialized products to support current and advanced weapons and navigation systems.[20]

In some instances, this involves the processing of data acquired by technical intelligence sensors. It is the processing of such data that allows the targeting of cruise missiles via Terrain Contour Matching (TERCOM). Such processing is also necessary for precise specification of target location in the SIOP and accurate targeting of U.S. warheads on those targets. This is particularly important since "on all geographic maps published in the U.S.S.R. not one Soviet city or town is shown in its current position with relation to its lines of latitude and longitude."[21]

The DMA has two principal production facilities providing mapping, charting, and geodesy products. The DMA Aerospace Center in St. Louis, Missouri provides aeronautical charts, air target materials, digital data, point positioning data bases, flight information publications, space mission charts, and a wide spectrum of technical data relevant to the earth and its aerospace environment essential to navigation and missilery. This data is partially based on the data acquired by military geodetic satellites and is intended to allow compensation for force fields that might throw missiles off their intended path. Thus, it is crucial to the attainment of missile accuracy for U.S. missiles such as MX and Trident.[22]

The DMA Hydrographic/Topographic Center at Brookmont, Maryland produces hydrographic charts and related material for surface and subsurface navigation, topographic maps for land forces, and Digital Terrain Evaluation Data for the cruise missiles as well as some products for air operations.[23] Thus, the Hydrographic/Topographic Center produces the Precise Bathyspheric Naval Zone Charts (required by submarines to obtain location fixes without surfacing) based on information gathered by DESKTOP reconnaissance missions (discussed in Chapter 8).

In 1982 DMA established a new component, the Special Program Office for Exploitation Modernization (SPOEM), with a mission "to develop the capability to produce DMA products by digital/softcopy techniques from advanced acquisition systems and enhance production capabilities to utilize hard copy source material from a new collection system."[24] In plainer language, SPOEM will give the DMA the capability to receive and utilize the digital readout from KH-11 and KH-12 photographic reconnaissance satellites as well as to improve the capability to make use of such data when they have been transformed into a photograph.

ARMED FORCES MEDICAL INTELLIGENCE CENTER

A very recent example of intelligence centralization at the DOD level was the creation in 1982 of the Armed Forces Medical Intelligence Center (AFMIC).[25] The AFMIC replaces the Army's Medical Intelligence and Information Agency (MIIA), which previously provided medical intelligence for the entire defense community.

Medical intelligence is particularly vital in planning for combat operations, particularly combat operations in areas that are significantly different from the United States—different in terms of the environment and prevalence of disease. This aspect of medical intelligence is best illustrated by the following account of Special Forces (Green Beret) medical intelligence collection in Indochina.

> In order to improve our medical intelligence, the Green Beret doctors developed a plan for using Special Forces as medical intelligence collectors. At Fort Bragg, each Special Forces team member bound for Indochina was given a complete physical prior to boarding the airplane that would take his entire detachment to its overseas destination. Samples of blood serum, carefully identified, taken for each man were to be analyzed and compared with serum that would be drawn when he returned with his detachment at the end of a six month tour of duty. An exhaustive questionnaire administered to returnees by Green Beret doctors was aimed at determining details concerning sanitation, food, insects, climate, rainfall, indigenous customs, living conditions, visible evidence of disease, and scores of other bits of environmental intelligence. This information was then computerized. Little by little a medical map of Indochina began to form. The geographic areas where diseases were prevalent, the times of the year, the times of day or night, the temperatures and relative humidity which marked danger periods were translated into graphs and curves which would be literally a matter of life and death for the Americans who were to come later to S.E. Asia.[26]

In addition to developing and maintaining such medical intelligence data bases, the AFMIC is responsible for assessing foreign biomedical R&D and its impact on the physiological and psychological effectiveness of military forces as well as the exploitation of foreign medical material obtained under the DOD Foreign Materiel Exploitation Program (FMEP).[27] The AFMIC is also responsible for maintaining coordination and liaison with members of the intelligence community concerning medical intelligence matters.

The AFMIC is a joint agency of the military departments under the authority, direction, and control of the Secretary of Defense. AFMIC's formation was possibly a result of unhappiness with the medical intelligence efforts of the MIIA. Discussions of Defense Audit Service personnel with the Director of the General Defense Intelligence Program Staff in 1981 indicated intelligence community concern about a lack of adequate medical intelligence in the Southwest Asian and Third World countries, "where casualties from unusual diseases and environmental conditions could occur."[28] Management of the center is the responsibility of the Secretary of the Army via the Army Assistant Chief of Staff for Intelligence and the Army Surgeon General. The link between the military services, the DOD, and the Secretary of the Army is provided by an Interdepartmental Advisory Panel. The panel consists of representatives from the Assistant Secretary of Defense (Health Affairs), the Surgeons General of the Army and Air Force, and representatives of the Office of Naval Intelligence and Defense Intelligence Agency. The panel, in addition to developing an initial concept of operations for the AFMIC, will continue to provide recommendations to the Secretary of the Army and the Center on DOD and military service medical intelligence requirements.

SPECIAL OPERATIONS DIVISION, J-3, JCS*

The Special Operations Division of the J-3 (Operations) section of the JCS Joint Staff is concerned with developing and evaluating plans and programs for unconventional warfare activities, psychological operations, special plans, contingency operations, and counterterrorist plans. The division consists of five branches: the Unconventional Warfare Operations, the Psychological Operations Branch, the Support Activities Branch, the Special Plans Branch, and the Contingency Operations Branch.[29]

Unconventional Warfare encompasses special operations, guerrilla action, evasion and escape, and subversion. The Unconventional Warfare Operations Branch prepares unconventional warfare annexes for the various military (unified and specified) commands as well as for the Joint Strategic Planning System and monitors R&D programs relating to special operations and unconventional warfare. The Branch also serves as a point of contact with the CIA on matters concerning special operations, with regard to both the plans and the intelligence support required for planning. In the event of a war in Europe, this contact would be especially close inasmuch as the CIA would assign a liaison group to the Commander Support Operations Task Force Europe (COMSOTFE) and the commander would be able to call on CIA assets for use in unconventional warfare activities. In addition, the Branch is charged with representing the Director of J-3 with regard to evasion and escape matters and taking "appropriate"

---

*With the exception of its Special Plans Branch, the Special Operations Division has been transferred from J-3 to the newly created Joint Special Operations Agency (JSOA).

action on such matters and operations directed at recovering U.S. prisoners of war.[30]

The Psychological Operations Branch is responsible for the development of policies, procedures, and doctrine for the conduct of psychological operations—apparently including white, grey, and black propaganda. The Branch monitors the psychological operations and programs of the various unified and specified commands as well as maintaining liaison with U.S. government agencies that engage in such operations—namely, the CIA and the United States Information Agency. It also serves as the Joint Staff's point of contact for intelligence requirements to support psychological operations.[31]

The Special Plans Branch provides "guidance and instructions to appropriate agencies on the conduct of special planning (perception management) activities" and "serves as the JCS member and secretariat of the inter-departmental special plans group and its designated working group."[32] Perception management may well be a euphemism for strategic deception.

DEFENSE SPECIAL PLANS OFFICE/MONARCH EAGLE

During the early years of the Reagan administration, one or more attempts were made to create new intelligence units within the DOD. Thus, the Defense Special Plans Office (DSPO) was established by DOD Directives C-5155.1 and TS-5155.1 of April 24, 1982. However, in a memo of February 2, 1983 Deputy Under Secretary of Defense (Policy) Richard Stillwell requested all holders of those directives to destroy them, as they "were charter documents establishing a DOD activity whose establishment subsequently was not authorized by Congress."[33] The exact functions of the Office have never been revealed. A DOD spokesman would say only that it was concerned with special planning with regard to intelligence matters. One possibility is that the DSPO was created to coordinate and engage in strategic deception (perception management)—supervising the JCS Special Plans Branch, the DIA Special Plans Branch, the Army Special Operations Office, the Naval Special Warfare Group, and the Air Force Special Plans Office.

Another possibility is that the DSPO was the official name for project Monarch Eagle—the attempt by Stillwell to create a DOD human clandestine collection organization to provide tactical intelligence for the military services.[34] That project was also vetoed by Congress on the grounds that it would overlap with CIA human intelligence collection efforts and make control of sensitive operations more difficult.[35] The proposal stemmed partially from military service/DOD dissatisfaction with CIA collection priorities. In light of the events in Grenada and Lebanon in 1983, and subsequent complaints concerning the lack of tactical intelligence available to the military in those situations, requests for such a unit might be revived.

NOTES TO CHAPTER 3

1. U.S. Congress, Senate Select Committee to Study Governmental Operations with Respect to Intelligence Activities, *Foreign and Military Intelligence, Book I* (Washington, D.C.: U.S. Government Printing Office, 1976), p. 325.
2. U.S. Congress, Senate Select Committee, *Supplementary Reports on Intelligence Activities* (Washington, D.C.: U.S. Government Printing Office, 1976), p. 266.
3. U.S. Congress, Senate Select Committee, *Foreign and Military Intelligence Book I*, p. 325.
4. Ibid.
5. U.S. Congress, Senate Select Committee, *Supplementary Reports on Intelligence Activities*, p. 266.
6. Harry Howe Ransom, *The Intelligence Establishment* (Cambridge, Mass.: Harvard University Press, 1970).
7. "Defense Intelligence Organization Criticized," *Aviation Week and Space Technology*, August 3, 1970, p. 17; Patrick McGarvey, *The CIA: The Myth and the Madness* (Baltimore: Penguin, 1972), p. 80.
8. The Pike Committee, *CIA: The Pike Report* (Nottingham, England: Spokesman, 1977), p. 261.
9. Desmond Ball, *Deja Vu: The Return to Counterforce in the Nixon Administration* (Santa Monica, Cal.: California Seminar on Arms Control and Foreign Policy, 1974), pp. 10–11.
10. U.S. Congress, House Committee on Armed Services, *Hearings on Military Posture and HR 2970, Part 4* (Washington, D.C.: U.S. Government Printing Office, 1981), pp. 1143–45.
11. U.S. Congress, House Committee on Armed Services, *Hearings on Military Posture and HR 2970, Part 5* (Washington, D.C.: U.S. Government Printing Office, 1982), p. 1189.
12. The material below, except where noted, is from Defense Intelligence Agency, *DIA Organization, Mission and Key Personnel* (Washington, D.C.: U.S. Government Printing Office, 1980); *Department of Defense Telephone Directory*, April 1984, pp. 0–11–0–14.
13. James Bamford, *The Puzzle Palace: A Report on NSA, America's Most Secret Agency* (Boston: Houghton Mifflin, 1982), pp. 190–91.
14. "The Military Race in Space," *Defense Monitor* 9, no. 9 (1980).
15. U.S. Congress, Senate Committee on Appropriations, *Department of Defense Appropriations FY 1969, Part 4* (Washington, D.C.: U.S. Government Printing Office, 1968), p. 2091.
16. "What the U.S. Lost in Iran," *Newsweek*, December 28, 1981, pp. 33–34.
17. "An American in Paris," *Newsweek*, February 1, 1982, p. 50.
18. Robert C. Toth, "U.S. Acts to Curb Terrorism Abroad," *Los Angeles Times*, April 15, 1984, pp. 1, 28.
19. "Shaping Tomorrow's CIA," *Time*, February 6, 1978, pp. 10ff.

20. In U.S. Congress, House Committee on Armed Services, "Written statement of Maj. Gen. Richard M. Wells," *Hearings on Military Posture and HR 5968, Part 5* (Washington, D.C.: U.S. Government Printing Office, 1982), pp. 1231-34.

21. Leonid Vladimirov, *The Russian Space Bluff* (New York: Dial, 1973), p. 49.

22. U.S. Congress, Senate Committee on Appropriations, "Prepared Statement of Brig. Gen. Donald O. Aldridge," *Department of Defense Appropriations for FY 1982, Part 5* (Washington, D.C.: U.S. Government Printing Office, 1981), p. 262.

23. Ibid.

24. Department of Defense, *Department of Defense Justification of Estimates for Fiscal Year 1984, Submitted to Congress January 1983* (Springfield, Virg.: NTIS, 1983), p. 5.

25. Except where noted, the material in this section is based on DOD Directive 6420.1, "Armed Forces Medical Intelligence Center," December 9, 1982.

26. Charles S. Simpson, III., *Inside the Green Berets: The First Thirty Years* (Novato, Cal.: Presidio, 1983), pp. xiii-xiv.

27. Defense Audit Service, *Semiannual Audit Plan First Half, Fiscal Year 1982* (Washington, D.C.: DAS, 1981), p. 32.

28. Ibid.

29. Joint Chiefs of Staff, *Organization and Functions of the Joint Chiefs of Staff, JCS PUB 4* (Washington, D.C.: JCS, September 2, 1980, with subsequent changes), p. III-3-47.

30. Ibid.

31. Ibid.

32. Ibid.

33. Richard G. Stillwell, "Memorandum for the Director, Washington Headquarters Services: Cancellation of DOD Directives TS-5155.2 and C-5155.1," February 2, 1983.

34. Raymond Bonner, "Secret Pentagon Intelligence Unit is Disclosed," *New York Times*, May 11, 1983, p. A13.

35. Robert C. Toth, "U.S. Spying: Partnership Re-Emerges," *Los Angeles Times*, November 14, 1983, pp. 1, 12.

4 MILITARY SERVICE INTELLIGENCE ORGANIZATIONS

Unlike Britain, which abolished its service intelligence components with the creation of the Defense Intelligence Staff, or Australia, which restricts its service intelligence organizations to the production of low-level tactical intelligence, the United States has maintained elaborate service intelligence organizations. Indeed, each of the three major services has an intelligence community of its own. Further, these communities have grown in budget, personnel, and importance over the last several years.

Part of the explanation of the continued major role of U.S. service intelligence organizations may be found in bureaucratic politics, but it is more significantly a function of U.S. military requirements. A military force with large service components, each with wide-ranging functional and geographical responsibilities, may be better served in terms of intelligence support by organizations that are not too detached from the service components. Additionally, some strategic intelligence and collection functions may be best performed by service organizations. Thus, given an obvious Air Force requirement to be informed on foreign aerospace technology or an obvious Navy requirement to be informed on foreign submarine technology, assignment of such intelligence production tasks to the Air Force and Navy might allow the most efficient production of such intelligence which will inform both service and national policymakers.

AIR FORCE INTELLIGENCE COMMUNITY

Five organizations constitute the Air Force intelligence community: the Office of the Assistant Chief of Staff, Intelligence; the Air Force Intelligence Service (AFIS); the Air Force Electronic Security Command; the Foreign Technology

Division (FTD) of the Air Force Systems Command; and the Air Force Technical Applications Center.

The Office of the Assistant Chief of Staff, Intelligence (OACSI) is the premier organization of the Air Force intelligence community and is divided into two directorates.[1] The Directorate of Estimates consists of four divisions: the General Threat Division; the Regional Estimates Division; the Strategic Studies Division; and the Weapons, Space, and Technology Division. The Directorate of Intelligence Plans and Systems is divided into the Plans Division, Systems Division—divided into HUMINT (Human Intelligence), Imagery, Technical, and SIGINT (Signals Intelligence) Branches—an Electronic Combat Group, and a Resource Management Group.[2]

The OACSI is primarily a management organization, directing the work of the entire Air Force intelligence community with respect to collection and analysis, with the Assistant Chief of Staff, Intelligence representing the Air Force in dealings with the rest of the U.S. intelligence community. This framework was dictated by a 1971 directive by the Secretary of the Air Force mandating reassignment of Air Staff operating and support functions to other organizations.[3] In response to this mandate, the AFIS was created on June 27, 1972. As indicated by Figure 4-1, AFIS is divided into eight directorates and a Special Activities Center.

The Directorate of Operational Intelligence and Directorate of Targets provide the Air Force with all-source intelligence affecting Air Force policies, reserves, force deployment and employment, indications and warning (I&W), intelligence analysis of current operations, and special intelligence research. The directorates provide experts on targeting, weapons, photo research, geodesy, and cartography. The Directorate of Targets also serves as the Department of the Air Force contact with the Defense Mapping Agency and provides intelligence support of electronic warfare activities.[4]

The Directorate of Security and Communications Management oversees worldwide Air Force Special Security Offices and Special Activities Offices (AF SSO/SAO) and ensures compliance with security policies that cover "special intelligence" and intelligence communications. Thus, the AF SSO/SAO oversees the handling of "codeword" material, whether obtained via photographic or signals intelligence platforms. The Directorate of Intelligence Data Management plans, coordinates, and exercises managerial control of worldwide Air Force systems for the handling of intelligence data. The Directorate of Attaché Affairs supports the Defense Attaché System and monitors all matters concerning Air Force participation in that program.[5]

The Directorate of Intelligence Reserve Forces manages the AFIS Intelligence Reserve program. Responsibilities include recruitment, administration, readiness training, and operational utilization of more than 1,200 assigned and attached mobilization augmentees in support of peacetime and contingency mission requirements. The Directorate of Soviet Affairs conducts the Air Force's Soviet Awareness Program, consisting of the "Soviet Military Thought and Studies in

Figure 4–1. Organization of the Air Force Intelligence Service.

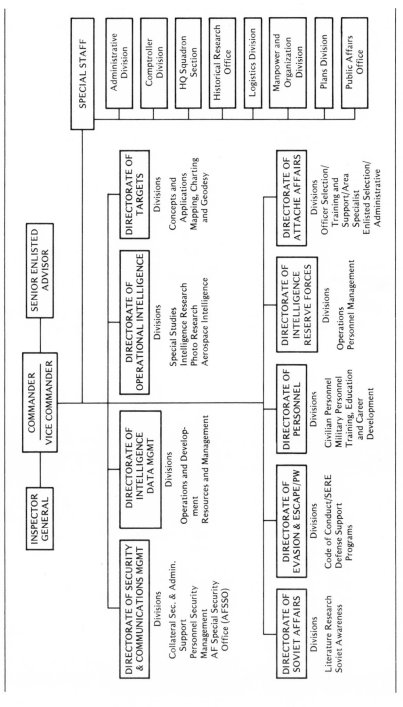

Source: Air Force Intelligence Service.

Communist Affairs" books series, *Soviet Press Selected Translation* periodical, internal publications, Soviet Military Power Week, the Soviet Awareness Team, and the Soviet Military Literature Research facility.[6]

The Directorate of Evasion and Escape/Prisoner of War Matters provides centralized management and cohesive direction to all aspects of intelligence support of evasion and escape/prisoner of war matters and is the action office for Department of Defense (DOD) code-of-conduct training. Escape and evasion intelligence support involves ensuring that intelligence is collected and analyzed concerning the terrain and climate in which U.S. airmen may find themselves when shot down, the location of roads and other paths by which airmen can get back to allied lines, regulations and customs that must be observed to avoid attracting police attention, the escape routes that can be established using friendly indigenous personnel, and optimal survival strategies. The information collected may come from satellite photography, open source collection, and human sources—satellite photography to give a broad view of the terrain, open source collection on regulations and customs, and human sources concerning likely U.S. sympathizers.

Finally, the Air Force Special Activities Center at Fort Belvoir, Virginia provides centralized management of all Air Force activities involved in the collection of information from human sources.[7] These activities include clandestine collection as well as the debriefing of defectors. The Center was previously known as the 7612th Air Intelligence Group and prior to that the 1127th Field Activities Group. The 1127th was described as "an oddball unit, a composite of special intelligence groups who 'conducted worldwide operations to collect intelligence from human sources.' The men of 1127th were con artists. Their job was to get people to talk—Russian defectors, North Vietnamese soldiers taken prisoner."[8]

In addition to two detachments in the United States—Detachment 21 at Fort Belvoir and Detachment 22 at Wright Patterson Air Force Base (AFB), Ohio (FTD headquarters)—there are two overseas Special Activities Areas. The Pacific Special Activities Area is headquartered at Hickam AFB, Hawaii with detachments at Yokota Air Base (AB), Japan (Detachment 31) and Yongsan, Korea (Detachment 32). The European Special Activities Area is headquartered at Lindsey Air Station, Germany and has three German detachments (11 at Munich, 12 at Nierrod, and 13 at Bitburg AB) under its command.[9] As of 1981, the AFIS employed 447 military personnel and 144 civilians.[10]

The Electronic Security Command (ESC) was created in 1947 as the Air Force Security Service and is headquartered at San Antonio, Texas. The ESC performs cryptographic, cryptanalytic, and electronic warfare functions for the Air Force as well as operating under NSA (National Security Agency)/CSS (Central Security Service) direction for purposes of strategic intelligence collection. In the latter capacity it provides personnel for overseas and domestic strategic intelligence collection sites and airborne collection programs. The ESC employs 10,080 military personnel and 877 civilians.[11]

As indicated in Figure 4-2, ESC's main activities are managed by several Deputy Chiefs of Staff. The Deputy Chief of Staff/Intelligence supervises the activities of the Directorates of C^3I Intelligence, Threat Analysis, Security Management, Information Coordination, and Current Intelligence. The Director of C^3I Intelligence examines hostile nations' C^3 systems based on a variety of intelligence sources to facilitate the development of countermeasures. The Directorate of Threat Analysis examines the threat from SIGINT and electronic warfare.[12]

The Deputy Chief of Staff/Operations supervises the activities of the Offensive Operations Directorate, Defense Operations Directorate, Operation and Readiness Management Directorate, Airborne and Remote Reconnaissance Operations Directorate, Operations Training Directorate, and Special Operations Activity.[13]

In addition to its headquarters organization, the ESC maintains a large number of SIGINT collection facilities in the United States and abroad—particularly in Europe and Asia. As indicated in Figure 4-3, there are ESC facilities located at bases in Germany, Greece, Italy, the United Kingdom, Korea, Japan, and the Philippines as well as in the United States.[14]

The ESC is one of the most important Air Force intelligence organizations. Another is the Foreign Technology Division (FTD) of the Air Force Systems Command. FTD is located at Wright Patterson AFB in Dayton, Ohio. It was first established in 1917 as the Foreign Data Section of the Airplane Engineering Department, which was soon transferred from Washington, D.C. to Dayton, Ohio. It was subsequently renamed the Technical Data Section (1927), Technical Data Laboratory (1942), T-2 (Intelligence) of the Air Technical Service Command (1945), the Air Technical Intelligence Center (1951), and the FTD.[15]

The FTD played a major role in Projects Overcast and Paper Clip. With the defeat of the Third Reich ensured, planning began for the identification and control of scientists and technicians who might materially contribute to the revival of German war potential. Furthermore, it was thought that their scientific and technical counsel could benefit the United States in its war with Japan. German scientists were identified, recruited, and in many cases brought to the United States.[16]

In 1947 all nonintelligence functions were removed from FTD's mission statement. Today, the FTD is one of the largest and most important U.S. intelligence units. Its major areas of technical intelligence activity include the prevention of technological surprise, advancement of U.S. technology by use of foreign technology, identification of weaknesses in foreign weapon systems, and use of certain design traits of foreign weapon systems as indicators of strategic intent.[17]

Thus, the FTD

acquires, evaluates, analyzes and disseminates information on foreign aerospace technology in concert with other divisions, laboratories and centers. Information collected from a wide variety of sources is processed on unique electronic data handling and laboratory processing equipment and analyzed by scientific and technical specialists. In quest of human intelligence relevant

Figure 4-2. Organization of the Air Force Electronic Security Command.

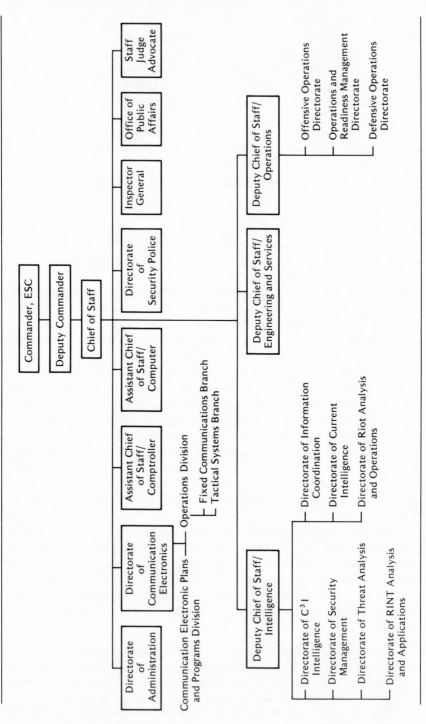

Source: Air Force Electronic Security Command.

Figure 4-3. Electronic Security Command Units Worldwide.

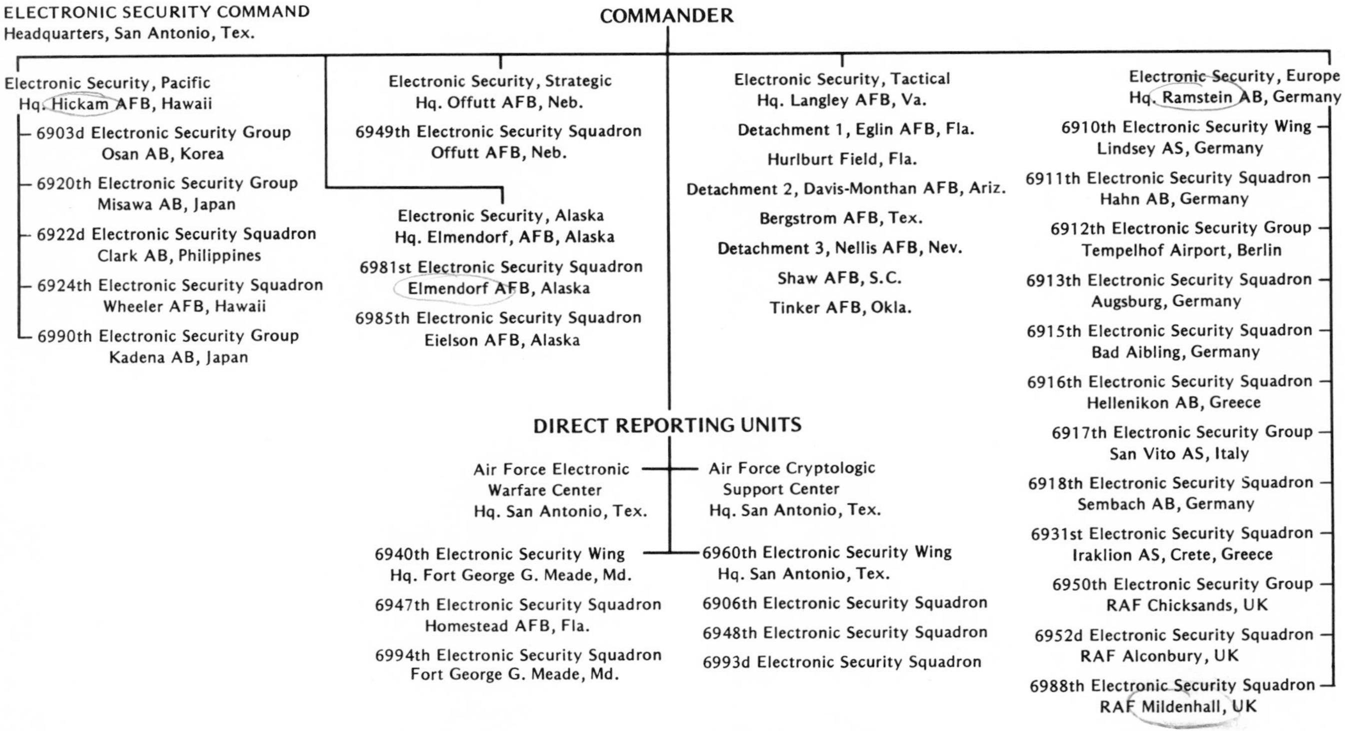

COMMANDER

ELECTRONIC SECURITY COMMAND
Headquarters, San Antonio, Tex.

Electronic Security, Pacific
Hq. Hickam AFB, Hawaii
- 6903d Electronic Security Group, Osan AB, Korea
- 6920th Electronic Security Group, Misawa AB, Japan
- 6922d Electronic Security Squadron, Clark AB, Philippines
- 6924th Electronic Security Squadron, Wheeler AFB, Hawaii
- 6990th Electronic Security Group, Kadena AB, Japan

Electronic Security, Strategic
Hq. Offutt AFB, Neb.
- 6949th Electronic Security Squadron, Offutt AFB, Neb.

Electronic Security, Alaska
Hq. Elmendorf, AFB, Alaska
- 6981st Electronic Security Squadron, Elmendorf AFB, Alaska
- 6985th Electronic Security Squadron, Eielson AFB, Alaska

Electronic Security, Tactical
Hq. Langley AFB, Va.
- Detachment 1, Eglin AFB, Fla. — Hurlburt Field, Fla.
- Detachment 2, Davis-Monthan AFB, Ariz. — Bergstrom AFB, Tex.
- Detachment 3, Nellis AFB, Nev. — Shaw AFB, S.C. — Tinker AFB, Okla.

Electronic Security, Europe
Hq. Ramstein AB, Germany
- 6910th Electronic Security Wing, Lindsey AS, Germany
- 6911th Electronic Security Squadron, Hahn AB, Germany
- 6912th Electronic Security Group, Tempelhof Airport, Berlin
- 6913th Electronic Security Squadron, Augsburg, Germany
- 6915th Electronic Security Squadron, Bad Aibling, Germany
- 6916th Electronic Security Squadron, Hellenikon AB, Greece
- 6917th Electronic Security Group, San Vito AS, Italy
- 6918th Electronic Security Squadron, Sembach AB, Germany
- 6931st Electronic Security Squadron, Iraklion AS, Crete, Greece
- 6950th Electronic Security Group, RAF Chicksands, UK
- 6952d Electronic Security Squadron, RAF Alconbury, UK
- 6988th Electronic Security Squadron, RAF Mildenhall, UK

DIRECT REPORTING UNITS

Air Force Electronic Warfare Center
Hq. San Antonio, Tex.

Air Force Cryptologic Support Center
Hq. San Antonio, Tex.
- 6906th Electronic Security Squadron
- 6948th Electronic Security Squadron
- 6993d Electronic Security Squadron

6940th Electronic Security Wing
Hq. Fort George G. Meade, Md.
- 6947th Electronic Security Squadron, Homestead AFB, Fla.
- 6994th Electronic Security Squadron, Fort George G. Meade, Md.

6960th Electronic Security Wing
Hq. San Antonio, Tex.

Source: *Air Force Magazine* May 1982, p. 95.

to its mission FTD participates in and coordinates humint activity. Thus, in addition to Air Force officers who are assigned as attachés Foreign Technology Activity Officers may be assigned to defense attaché offices to monitor and if possible, acquire sensitive foreign military technologies.[18]

The FTD has primary responsibility for interpreting communications intercepted from Soviet rocket boosters to their ground controls. It conducted the telemetry analysis on 1968 Soviet "triplet" tests and developed the thesis that the Mod-4 might possess some primitive MIRV (multiple independently targeted reentry vehicles) characteristics.[19]

Additionally, in a carry-over from Projects Overcast and Paper Clip, the FTD maintains a detailed list, known as HAVE CHECK, on East Bloc scientists engaged in military aerospace activities. Lists can be used to chart the actions and likely innovations in aerospace development.

As indicated by Figure 4-4, FTD is organized into six main directorates: Administration and Support, Data Services, Plans and Operations, Systems, Sensor Data, and Technology and Threat. Thus, the Directorate of Administration and Support and the Directorate of Data Services provide basic support services to the production and collection management directorates of the FTD. The Directorate of Plans and Operations is responsible for seeing that FTD requirements for raw data are formulated and met, developing production schedules and managing resources for fulfillment of tasks. The Directorate of Sensor Data is responsible for the initial exploitation of data obtained from the variety of technical sensors available to the U.S. intelligence community. The Directorate of Systems and the Directorate of Technology and Threat produce assessments based on this and human source data with regard to the wide variety of foreign aerospace related systems—ballistic missiles, defensive systems, space systems, C^3, and future systems.

The Air Force Technical Application Center (AFTAC), with 1,380 personnel in 1983 and headquartered at Patrick AFB, Florida, operates the U.S. Atomic Energy Detection System (AEDS). AEDS is a worldwide system with operations in more than thirty-five countries.[20] The system uses scientific means to obtain and evaluate technical data on the nuclear energy activities of foreign powers—including determination of whether foreign nations are complying with treaties such as the Limited Test-Ban Treaty, Non-Proliferation Treaty, Threshold Test Ban Treaty of 1974 (which limits the yield of underground tests to 150 Kt), and the Peaceful Nuclear Explosion Treaty of 1976. AFTAC also conducts R&D programs designed to increase the understanding of the technical problem associated with the detection and identification of nuclear events in the atmosphere.[21]

In pursuit of fulfilling its mission, AFTAC has an extensive network of U.S. and foreign (manned and unmanned) ground sites, some of which may be covert, having been implanted on foreign territory without the "host" government's knowledge. AFTAC squadrons are located at McClellan AFB, California; Wheeler AFB, Hawaii; and Lindsey Air Station, Germany. The squadrons at Wheeler and

Figure 4-4. Organization of the Foreign Technology Division.

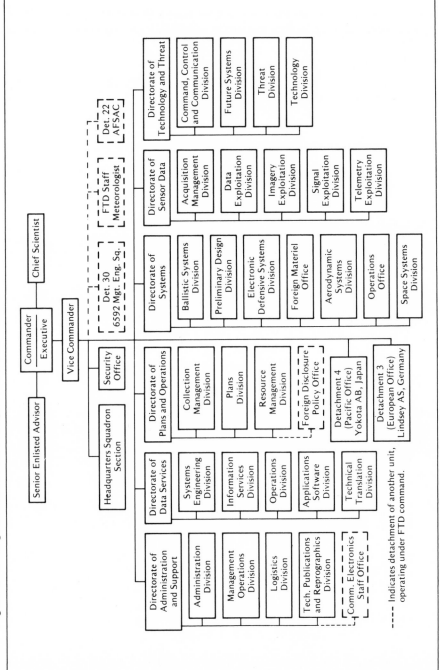

Source: Air Force Foreign Technology Division.

Lindsey provide administrative, logistic, and other support to subordinate activities in their areas. In addition to the three squadrons are nineteen detachments, six operating sites, and fifty equipment locations.[22] An organization chart for AFTAC is shown as Figure 4-5.

In addition to ground sites, AFTAC acquires data via airborne, underwater, and space operations. Present aerospace collection assets include the Vela and Defense Support Program satellites.

NAVAL INTELLIGENCE COMMUNITY

At the top of the naval intelligence community is the Assistant Chief of Naval Operations for Intelligence, who is simultaneously the Director of the Office of Naval Intelligence (ONI). The ONI is primarily a supervisory organization that directs the activities of the various naval intelligence production and collection agencies.

Directly subordinate to the Director of Naval Intelligence (DNI) are the divisions that make up the ONI organization: the Security of Military Information; Plans, Policy, and Estimates; Special Projects; and Plans, Programs, and System Architecture.[23] The Security of Military Information Division is responsible for security review, security education, and classification management. Plans, Policy, and Estimates consists of three branches: Plans, Policy, and Estimates. The Policy Branch establishes priorities for the naval intelligence community. The Estimates Branch is subdivided into both regional and functional units. Thus, there are units for Political Military Affairs, Europe/International Terrorism, Americas/Antarctic, East Asia/Pacific, Middle East/Africa/S. Asia, Air and Electronic Warfare, Surface Warfare, USSR, Submarine Warfare, and Foreign Publications Analysis as well as Assistants for Naval Systems and National Estimates.[24]

The Special Projects Division is probably involved in various technical collection efforts, including those that are space based as well as those that are sea or undersea based. The nature of these projects will be discussed in more detail in subsequent chapters. The Plans, Programs, and System Architecture Division supervises design and construction of various technical naval intelligence systems.

Subordinate to the DNI are two Deputy DNIs (DDNIs), each of whom heads an intelligence organization. These organizations are the Naval Intelligence Command (NIC) and the Naval Security Group Command (NSGC).

The NIC is headquartered at 4600 Silver Hill Road, Suitland, Maryland.[25] The functions of the Command include the direction and coordination of intelligence collection, production, and dissemination to satisfy Navy and national requirements. Specifically, the functions include:

1. directing and coordinating intelligence collection, production, dissemination and other activities necessary to satisfy Department of the Navy and DIA tasking;

Figure 4-5. Organization of the Air Force Technical Applications Center.

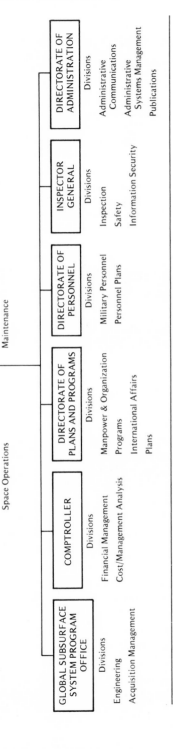

a. External Agency.
Source: Air Force Technical Applications Center.

2. supporting overt fleet intelligence collection planning implementation and evaluation and providing time-sensitive collection guidance, specialized equipment, and qualified personnel;

3. managing overt collection of information from human and other open sources directly accessible to Navy collectors;

4. ensuring that Navy information requirements are introduced into the intelligence community collection requirements mechanism and monitoring their fulfillment;

5. managing intelligence production within the NIC to satisfy Navy, R&D, Department of Defense, and national requirements;

6. managing the dissemination of intelligence products to ensure adequacy and timeliness in meeting national and Department of Defense requirements;

7. promoting effective naval intelligence cooperation and exchange programs with foreign navies and approving intelligence releases to foreign government nationals and intelligence organizations;

8. managing budget and financial requirements; and

9. developing plans for and monitoring the R&D and procurement of intelligence systems and equipment in order to satisfy intelligence requirements.[26]

At the top of the NIC organizational structure is the Commander, who is simultaneously a DDNI. Assistants to the Commander include an Assistant for Navy Attaché Affairs, a Special Assistant for R&D, and a Special Assistant for Processing Systems. The remainder of the NIC headquarters organization fall directly under five Assistant Commanders.[27] The Assistant Commander for Manpower, Training, and Reserve Programs supervises the activities of the Manpower Personnel and Training and Reserve Programs Divisions. The Assistant Commander for Financial Management/Comptroller is responsible for NIC budgetary matters.

The supervision of collection operations is the responsibility of the Assistant Commander for Operations/Commander, Task Force (TF) 168. As Figure 4-6 indicates, TF 168 consists of three divisions and a Collection Advisory Center which determine requirements, manage, and conduct collection operations.

The TF 168 Collection Support Division is responsible for providing personnel, equipment, and analysis in support of collection activities. The International Programs Division is responsible for conducting and monitoring liaison and exchange programs with foreign naval intelligence authorities. The Collection Operations Division (1) collects information from individuals ("designated by higher authority") who, because of their travel or contacts with foreign nationals, may have information of intelligence value to the Navy; (2) collects biographic data on foreign naval officers who attend Navy/Marine Corps school in the United States; and (3) collects information from émigrés and defectors that is of interest to the Navy. The Collection Guidance and Requirements Branch of the Operations Division manages collection guidance, requirements, and reporting in support of the fleet, naval shore establishment, and the intelligence community.[28]

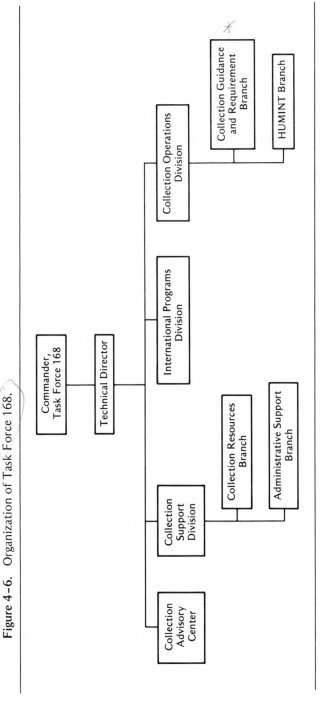

Figure 4-6. Organization of Task Force 168.

Source: *Department of Defense Telephone Directory* (Washington, D.C.: U.S. Government Printing Office, April 1984), pp. 0-96 – 0-97.

The Assistant Commander for Security supervises the SCI (Sensitive Compartmented Information) Programs Administrative Division and SCI Program Management Division. These divisions deal with the distribution of SCI—codeword information obtained via either signals intercepts or photo reconnaissance. The Assistant Commander for Data Management and Production supervises the Data Management Division and Production Management Division.[29]

Also, under the supervision of the Commander of the NIC are three field commands: the Naval Intelligence Processing System Support Activity, the Naval Intelligence Support Center, and the Navy Operational Intelligence Center.

The Naval Intelligence Processing System Support Activity (NIPSSA) is responsible for planning, sponsoring, developing, and managing automated naval intelligence information processing and communications systems. NIPSSA functions include advising the Chief of Naval Operations and Commander of the NIC on matters related to the Naval Intelligence Processing System, Ocean Surveillance Information System (OSIS), all intelligence information systems, intelligence communications systems, and fleet tactical intelligence processing systems as well as managing NIC participation in the operational aspects of the OSIS network.[30]

The Naval Intelligence Support Center (NISC), formerly the Naval Scientific and Technical Intelligence Center, is the scientific and technical intelligence organization for the Navy. Its mission is to process, analyze, produce, and disseminate scientific and technical intelligence on foreign naval systems in order to support national and Navy strategic plans, R&D, and objectives and programs. It also performs such other functions and tasks as are directed by higher authority.[31] Its functions are to:

1. provide scientific and technical intelligence support to the Chief of Naval Operations, Chief of Naval Material, DNI, C, NIC, Director, DIA, Navy Establishment operating forces and other authorized U.S. agencies;
2. process, correlate, and provide detailed analysis of all source intelligence information concerning foreign naval systems and merchant marines; conduct research to analyze foreign basic research and development for naval applications;
3. produce naval intelligence technical assessments and participate in production of naval intelligence assessments and other intelligence forecasts and estimates at the international, national, joint, and service levels;
4. provide naval intelligence threat support to the U.S. naval weapons systems planning, development and acquisition process by: producing threat/ capabilities publications; developing threat assessments and threat support plans in support of specific programs and project managers and other participants in the naval weapons system planning, development, and acquisition process;
5. determine the technical characteristics and warfare capabilities of foreign naval surface, subsurface, and air systems—to include weapons systems; command, control, and communications system; ocean surveillance and

electronics systems; and assess the submarine, antisurface, and antiair warfare capabilities of foreign navies;

6. provide intelligence on foreign applications of undersea technology; assist higher authority in development of intelligence collection sensors; analyze and disseminate undersea technical intelligence; provide administrative support to and cognizance over the technical competence of civilian analysts assigned to Forward Area Support Teams under the CTF-168 organization;

7. provide technical support and liaison to national imagery intelligence collection systems for Navy intelligence requirements; ... develop Navy collection and exploitation imagery requirements in support of national intelligence plans and programs and provide support and exploit material collection by Special Navy and national programs; and

8. act as Executive Agent for the Navy Foreign Material Exploitation Program (FMEP) including finding, exploiting, and disseminating derived intelligence.[32]

The NISC is organized into three offices (Operations, Resources, and Naval Warfare Capabilities) and six departments: Undersea Warfare, Technology, Naval Systems, Naval Weapons, Electromagnetic Systems, Information Services, and Imagery Analysis.[33]

The Navy Operational Intelligence Center (NOIC), until recently known as the Navy Field Operational Intelligence Office (NFOIO), has functions related to ocean and underseas surveillance. A subordinate command of NIC, NOIC is also subject to the area coordination authority of the Commandant, Naval District, Washington, D.C.[34]

In 1971 the Navy Field Operational Intelligence Office was officially assigned the responsibility of providing accurate and timely warning of foreign naval activities "which might ultimately result in a threat to the security of the United States and of its allies."[35]

The functions of NOIC are:

1. to provide current operational intelligence and ocean surveillance information on a continuous watch basis;

2. to provide current locating information on and operational histories of selected foreign merchant and fishing fleets;

3. to provide control data base and intelligence interface for the Navy Ocean Surveillance Information Systems (OSIS);

4. to publish all-source intelligence articles and studies on the organization, tactics, doctrine, and operational patterns of selected foreign naval/naval air forces and merchant/fishing fleets;

5. to provide timely analytical support and feedback to special collection resources;

6. to provide direct support to Commander, NIC on matters relating to foreign antisubmarine warfare threats to the U.S. Navy strategic deterrent force;

7. to provide specialized operational intelligence for the U.S. Navy underseas warfare operations.[36]

The NOIC is organized into six departments and one detachment, as shown in Figure 4-7. The department responsible for the ocean surveillance portion of NOIC's mission is the Current Operations Department, formerly known as the Naval Ocean Surveillance Information Center. In 1978 the Department was officially designated a member of the DOD Indications and Warning Network. In conjunction with a worldwide network of intelligence correlation centers, the Current Operations Department maintains an accounting of the location of foreign military aircraft, surface ships, and submarines as well as foreign merchant and fishing fleets operating in all oceans of the world. It also prepares operational intelligence reports and ocean surveillance information for the Joint Chiefs of Staff (JCS), the Department of the Navy, the Defense Intelligence Agency, and other government organizations.[37]

As with the NIC, the Naval Security Group Command (NSGC), with headquarters in Washington, D.C. at 3801 Nebraska Avenue, N.W., is headed by a Deputy Director of Naval Intelligence. The NSGC began its existence as OP-20-G-G Section (Communications Security) of the 20th division (Office of Naval Communications) of the Office of the Chief of Naval Operations.[38] During World War II it was known by the cover name Communications Supplementary Activity Washington (CSAW).[39]

The NSGC is responsible for naval signals intelligence and communications security. As such, it plays a crucial role in the ocean surveillance activities, providing personnel for Classic Wizard (ocean surveillance satellite) earth terminals as well as for ship-based Classic Outboard and ground-based Classic Bullseye HF-DF systems. In conducting these activities, the NSGC maintains a large number of operating groups in the United States and abroad. Such groups are located in Winter Harbor, Maine; Scotland; Japan; Australia; and Diego Garcia in the Indian Ocean.

Under the Commander of NSGC is a Deputy Commander, several assistants, and five Assistant Commanders. The Assistant Commanders' areas of responsibility are: Telecommunications and Automatic Data Systems, Logistics and Material, Special Operations, Electronic Warfare and Signals Security, and Technical Development.[40]

A naval intelligence R&D organization is the Naval Electronic Systems Command (NAVALEX), which encompasses several important intelligence-related functions. Three branches of NAVALEX with important intelligence functions are the Navy Space Project, the REWSON Project, and the Undersea Surveillance Project.

As discussed earlier, the Navy Space Project (NSP) is closely tied to the National Reconnaissance Office. Thus, the NSP was the project office for the now defunct Clipper Bow radar satellite and is the project office for the White Cloud/ Classic Wizard ocean surveillance satellite. REWSON is an acronym for Recon-

Figure 4-7. Organization of the Navy Operational Intelligence Center.

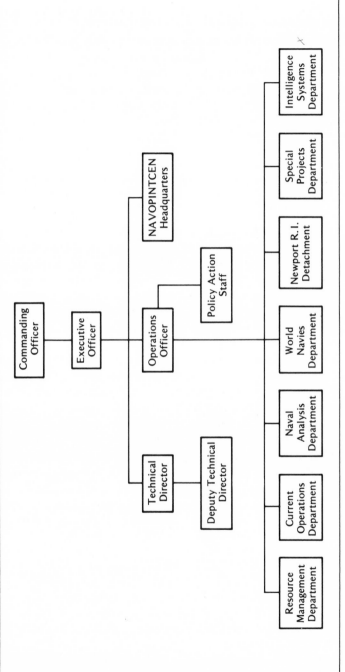

Source: Navy Operational Intelligence Center.

naissance, Electronic Warfare, Special Operations, and Naval Intelligence Systems. With a budget of about $1 billion per year, REWSON is in charge of developing a variety of naval intelligence systems including those concerned with Cover and Deception Programs, Submarine Reconnaissance and Special Operations, Intelligence Systems, and Shore Cryptologic Systems.[41]

The Underseas Surveillance Project is concerned with a variety of hydrophone sensor systems—specifically, the Rapidly Deployable Surveillance Systems (RDSS), the Surface Towed Array Surveillance System (SURTASS), and the Sound Surveillance System (SOSUS), which are discussed in Chapter 7.[42]

ARMY INTELLIGENCE COMMUNITY

At the apex of the Army intelligence community is the Office of the Assistant Chief of Staff for Intelligence which directs the entire army intelligence community. The major operational agency is the Army Intelligence and Security Command (INSCOM) which is charged with general analysis, human intelligence, and SIGINT/COMSEC (Communications Security) functions. Other members of the community are the Missile Intelligence Agency, Foreign Science and Technology Center, and the Intelligence Support Activity. Additionally, the U.S. Army Special Forces (Green Berets) have performed intelligence collection and special operations functions on numerous occasions.

The Office of the Assistant Chief of Staff for Intelligence (OACSI) consists of a Plans, Program, and Budget Office; Intelligence Automation Management Office; and four directorates—Foreign Liaison, Foreign Intelligence, Counterintelligence, and Intelligence Systems.[43]

The Foreign Liaison Directorate conducts liaison with other Army/Military intelligence organizations such as Australia's Military Intelligence Directorate. It coordinates the activities of the Foreign Liaison Office of the U.S. Army Intelligence Operations Detachment as well as developing and coordinating the Foreign Intelligence Assistance Program.[44]

The Foreign Intelligence Directorate is concerned with current intelligence, long-term assessments, establishment of requirements, and technical intelligence. The Counterintelligence Directorate has a wide variety of matters under its purview. These include Freedom of Information Act, Security Review, Personnel, Information Security, SCI Policy, Counterintelligence, OPSEC (Operations Security), and SIGSEC (Signals Security), Foreign Counterintelligence, and Special Operations. It formulates policy for the Army's cryptologic effort, including Communications Intelligence Security Standards.[45] The Intelligence Systems Directorate focuses on major sources of intelligence—SIGINT, Imagery, HUMINT—and their operation.

The United States Army Intelligence Operations Detachment is a field-operating agency under the supervision and control of the Assistant Chief of Staff, Intelligence (ACSI). Each element of the Detachment is authorized to communicate directly with the Office of the Secretary of Defense, Office of the JCS, and the headquarters of the Department of the Army.

The Detachment's Office of Foreign Liaison administers foreign military attaché tours, Department of the Army VIP tours, and foreign counterpart visits. It also processes identification and applications for foreign attachés. The Intelligence Command and Control Office monitors and inspects all Army-wide intelligence activities to ensure compliance with Executive Orders and DOD and Army Directives. The Detachment's OACSI Watch Office monitors global situations to provide I&W support to the Army Operations Center and provides I&W briefings to members of the Army Staff. The Current Intelligence Division provides a daily written current intelligence "Black Book" for distribution to the Army Secretariat or Army Staff.[46]

INSCOM, headquartered at Fort Meade, was created by the merger of the Army Intelligence Command and the Army Security Agency in 1976.[47] The former was created to perform counterintelligence duties within the United States; the latter was successor to the variously named Army signals intelligence/communications security organizations of World War II. INSCOM is thus responsible both to the Army's OACSI and to the Chief of the Central Security Service. INSCOM personnel man SIGINT collection facilities at several overseas bases, including several in Turkey. Further, INSCOM conducts clandestine human intelligence collection and counterintelligence operations as well as performing various analysis activities.

The organizational structure of INSCOM is based on a number of Deputy Chiefs of Staff (DCS) responsible for different areas of activity. Thus, in addition to the Chief of Staff there are DCSs for Personnel; Telecommunications; Operations; Intelligence and Threat Analysis; Counterintelligence; Force Modernization; Resource Management; Information Resource Management; and Plans, Programs, and Modernization.[48]

The DCS for Intelligence and Threat Analysis is Commander of the Intelligence and Threat Analysis Center (ITAC), designated as the Army's only national-level general intelligence and threat analysis production center. Two-thirds of ITAC's production concentrates on the Soviet Union and Warsaw Pact developments which pose a threat to the Army's mission accomplishment now and in the future. This includes the threat posed by hostile multidiscipline intelligence collection efforts and terrorist activities directed against the Army. ITAC also provides, primarily to the scientific and technical intelligence community, detailed and comprehensive imagery exploitation which is often the only way to determine physical characteristics of threat systems, table of organization, and equipment and facilities.[49]

The remaining one-third of the production effort focuses on geographically oriented country studies of those areas where Army contingency missions might exist. This includes the Caribbean, Central America, Africa, Middle East/Persian Gulf, and the Far East. A recent ITAC initiative, the Army Intelligence Survey (AIS), will produce a six-volume study on each of the thirty-one countries from these areas. The AIS will provide the operational commander with basic planning data in sufficient detail for use as a foundation in contingency planning.[50] Finally, it should be noted that, according to INSCOM, it was an ITAC study, *Combat Elements of the North Korean Army*, that was responsible for President Carter's decision to halt the withdrawal of U.S. troops from Korea.[51]

The DCS for Operations directs INSCOM intelligence collection activities. Subordinate to the DCS for Operations are Assistant Directors for HUMINT, OPSEC, Imagery Intelligence, Plans/Training, Intelligence Support, and SIGINT/EW (Electronic Warfare). The Assistant Directors for HUMINT and SIGINT/EW direct the activities of U.S.- and foreign-based INSCOM units involved in collection activities.

Subordinate to the Assistant DCS Operations (HUMINT) are the four divisions and one office that manage the HUMINT collection program. The Collection Management Division (with its Requirements and Reports, Concepts and Targets, and Biographics Branches) prepares the INSCOM HUMINT Collection Plan; maintains the HUMINT target system; and oversees the preparation of Mission Target Analysis for HUMINT collection units and provides guidance on collection emphasis, changing priorities, and new collection objectives.[52]

The Field Activities Division (through its Controlled Collection, Overt Collection, and Source Management Branches) directs both clandestine and overt HUMINT collection activities, including the Emigré Exploitation Program. Other divisions are the TAREX (Target Exploitation) Management and Policy and Programs Divisions.[53] The Special Actions Office "conducts specialized intelligence collection operations in response to INSCOM departmental and national intelligence needs."[54]

The Assistant DCS, Operations (Imagery Intelligence) exercises staff responsibility for national imagery collection and exploitation operations in support of intelligence requirements as well as representing the Army and/or INSCOM on boards involving Army imagery activities including the National Foreign Intelligence Board's Committee on Imagery Requirements and Exploitation.[55]

The DCS, Resource Management supervises and represents INSCOM in regard to resource programs such as the Consolidated Cryptologic Program, Defense Foreign Counterintelligence Program, and General Defense Intelligence Program. The DCS, Force Modernization oversees improvements in technical collection and data-processing capabilities and research development for new systems.[56]

As noted above, a significant aspect of INSCOM's activities occur abroad. Foreign-based units include the 66th Military Intelligence Group in Augsburg, which conducts clandestine HUMINT operations, as well as the INSCOM units at U.S. Army Field Stations in Augsburg, Okinawa, and Sinop, which conduct SIGINT collection activities.[57]

A recently created MI Group located in the United States is the 513th Military Intelligence Group. Activated on September 30, 1982 with 375 personnel, its function is to provide intelligence support to the Army component of the Central Command and the U.S. Army, Europe in times of war.[58]

Unlike the Air Force and Navy, the Army has two separate agencies that are responsible for producing scientific and technical intelligence: the Missile Intelligence Agency (MIA) and the Foreign Science and Technology Center (FSTC).

Located in Huntsville, Alabama, the MIA is responsible for production of intelligence concerning all foreign missile systems relevant to the Army's missions. Such missiles include tactical ground-to-ground, air-to-ground, and ship-to-surface missiles as well as strategic missiles—due to the Army's responsibility for the U.S. ballistic missile defense program.

As indicated in Figure 4-8, the MIA consists of a Material Simulation Office, a Program Management and Support Office, and five divisions: Technical Data Management, System Simulation and Scientific Applications, Land Combat Missile Systems, Tactical Air Defense Missile Systems and, Strategic Ballistic Missile Defense (BMD) and Strategic Air Defense Missile Systems.[59] The Electromagnetic Data Analysis Branch of the Technical Data Management Division has among its functions the maintenance of an all-source (except imagery) data base and the conduct of a continuing survey of intelligence requirements from all sources to support MIA product elements. The Division's Imagery Data Analysis Branch maintains a photographic intelligence data base and considers requirements for augmenting the data base.[60]

The Land Combat Missile Systems Division produces intelligence on short-range ballistic missiles and antitank guided missile weapon systems. The Strategic BMD and Strategic Air Defense Missile Systems Division focuses on strategic ballistic missiles, strategic air defense, and C^3 as well as R&D organizations and personalities.[61]

The FSTC, established in 1962, is located in Charlottesville, Virginia and is directly subordinate to the Army Material Readiness and Development Command. The center

1. develops and maintains a S&T data base;
2. produces S&T intelligence in support of Army R&D programs;
3. seeks to discover S&T threats to the security of U.S. Army ground forces;
4. forecasts foreign military trends and developments;
5. identifies foreign improvements that might be incorporated into U.S. weapons and equipment systems;
6. seeks to identify deficiencies in foreign systems at which U.S. countermeasures can be directed;
7. manages the U.S. Army program for the acquisition and exploitation of foreign material; and
8. provides support to the Army S&T intelligence collection effort.[62]

In addition to numerous support offices, the FSTC consists of an Intelligence Production Directorate, Technical Services Directorate, and Army Foreign Material Program Office. The Intelligence Production Directorate produces current intelligence in several different forms and assesses the capabilities and vulnerabilities of electronic systems employed in ground force operation, of foreign com-

Figure 4-8. Organization of the Missile Intelligence Agency.

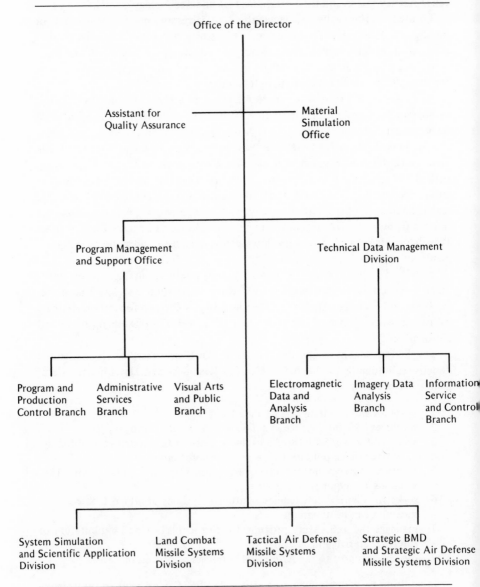

Source: Army Missile Command Regulation 10-2, Chapter 29, "Missile Intelligence Agency" (Huntsville, Ala.: Army Missile Command 1983).

bat arms that constitute ground force firepower, and of air and ground systems that enhance or degrade combat mobility.[63]

The Technical Services Directorate manages the collection of intelligence in support of the FSTC's mission. It operates a foreign scientific and technical information center that seeks to exploit foreign-language literature as well as providing data-processing capabilities. The Foreign Material Program Office is responsible for the acquisition and exploitation of foreign ground material, excluding medical and cryptological material.[64]

A unit only recently revealed to exist is the Intelligence Support Activity (ISA).[65] Despite its innocuous name, the Activity is a clandestine collection and covert operations unit. Its creation appears to stem from the seizure of U.S. hostages by Iranian militants and the subsequent rescue mission. According to one account, "CIA people were preoccupied with keeping their cover and could not provide equipment or information for the [rescue] operation. They had enough to do covering their skins. The military decided that they needed their own outfit to collect intelligence on areas where they are asked to fight."[66]

Since its creation, the ISA has been involved in providing intelligence and equipment in support of Lt. Col. James Bo Gritz's search for American POWs thought by some still to be held in Laos. In Europe the ISA played an unspecified role in the January 1982 rescue of Brig. Gen James Dozier. It has been alleged to have gathered intelligence in support of anti-Sandinista rebels in Nicaragua as well as conducting unspecified operations in El Salvador. It has also been said to have provided military equipment to foreign forces and deployed servicemen using false identities to collect intelligence. In one nation with which the United States has no diplomatic relations, arms and bulletproof vests were provided to cooperative persons for information about military deployments. Some of these operations might have taken place in Africa and Southeast Asia, where the ISA is said to have operated.

Virtually nothing is known about the ISA's structure, headquarters location, officials, budget, or size. Some of its operations have been run out of Fort Bragg, North Carolina, apparently as an extension of Special Forces Activity.

The U.S. Army Special Forces (Green Berets) have performed numerous intelligence and special operations missions. Established in 1952 and headquartered at Fort Bragg, the Special Forces's primary mission is insurgency, particularly in making contact with dissidents behind enemy lines and training them in guerrilla operations, sabotage, and terror.[67]

In the late 1950s the CIA began turning to the Special Forces to provide manpower for covert operations around the world. The relationship flourished in Southeast Asia in the 1960s and 1970s as hundreds of Special Forces troops served in operations supervised by the Central Intelligence Agency. In 1965 the Green Berets and a naval special warfare unit were ordered to develop plans for the assassination of Dominican Republic Colonel Francisco Caamano Deno, who was leading guerrilla forces in an attempt to overthrow the government. The mission was canceled at the last moment.[68]

In late 1967 in Latin America the Green Berets took part in the capture and execution of Che Guevera. Ten to twelve Green Berets from the 8th Army Special Forces Group in Panama were sent to Bolivia in late 1967 as part of a CIA-sponsored plan to train Bolivian forces in counterinsurgency. During training, Guevera's presence in the nearby hills was reported. A dispatched party located and captured him.[69]

In Southeast Asia during the Vietnam War, Special Forces were sent on missions into North Vietnam, Laos, and Cambodia to collect strategic intelligence.[70] They also conducted assassinations as part of Operation Phoenix and to eliminate suspected North Vietnamese/Viet Cong agents. Three Green Berets also trained mercenaries in Thailand for operations in Laos as part of a CIA program.[71] In 1980 a number of Green Berets based in West Germany entered Teheran posing as businessmen to collect intelligence for the rescue mission.[72]

At their peak there were 13,000 Special Forces—a number that had declined to 3,600 by 1980. Present plans are to boost the number of Special Forces personnel to 5,000.[73]

MARINE CORPS INTELLIGENCE

Not being a major service, the Marine Corps intelligence community consists simply of the Office of the Director of Intelligence. Subordinate to the Director are five branches: Counterintelligence, Intelligence Plans and Estimates, Intelligence Management, Signals Intelligence and Electronic Warfare, and National Intelligence Affairs.[74]

NOTES TO CHAPTER 4

1. *Department of Defense Telephone Directory* (Washington, D.C.: U.S. Government Printing Office, April 1984), p. 0–115.
2. Ibid.
3. "Air Force Intelligence Service," *Air Force Magazine*, May 1982, p. 126. For the official statement of AFIS functions, see Air Force Regulation 23–45, "Organization and Mission-Field—Air Force Intelligence Service," June 10, 1974.
4. Ibid.
5. Ibid.
6. Ibid.
7. Ibid.
8. Benjamin F. Schemmer, *The Raid* (New York: Harper & Row, 1975), pp. 26–27.
9. *Air Force Address Directory (AFR 10-4)* (Washington, D.C. Department of the Air Force, 1983), pp. 45, 56, 175.

10. "USAF Personnel By Commands, SOA's and DRU's," *Air Force Magazine*, May 1981, p. 160.
11. Ibid.
12. *USAF Command Organization Chart Book* (Washington, D.C. Department of the Air Force, 1981), pp. 7–7A.
13. Ibid.
14. "Electronic Security Command: A Major Command," *Air Force Magazine*, May 1982, pp. 94–95.
15. *FTD 1917–1967* (Dayton, Ohio: FTD, 1967), pp. 8, 10, 12, 22, 26.
16. Ibid., pp. 16–18.
17. Col. Robert B. Kalisch, "Air Force Technical Intelligence," *Air University Review* 12 (July–August 1971): 2–11.
18. "Special AFSC Organizations," *Air Force Magazine*, May 1982, p. 200; AFSC Regulation 23–2, "Organization and Mission– Field, Foreign Technology Division," May 10, 1979.
19. John Prados, *The Soviet Estimate: U.S. Intelligence and Russian Military Strength* (New York: Dial, 1982), p. 201.
20. "Air Force Technical Applications Center," *Air Force Magazine*, May 1983, pp. 134–37.
21. Ibid.
22. Ibid.
23. *Department of Defense Telephone Directory*, April 1984, pp. 0–60, 0–61.
24. Ibid.
25. Ibid., p. 0–96.
26. Charles David Taylor, *An Alternative Method of Information Handling Within the Naval Intelligence Community* (Monterey, Cal.: Naval Postgraduate School, 1980), pp. 148–49.
27. *Department of Defense Telephone Directory*, April 1984, p. 0–96.
28. Ibid.; NAVINTCOM Instruction 5450.8A, "Naval Intelligence Command Organization," September 30, 1981.
29. *Department of Defense Telephone Directory*, April 1983, pp. 0–92–0–93.
30. Taylor, *An Alternative Method of Information Handling*, pp. 160–61.
31. Ibid., pp. 152–55.
32. Ibid.
33. *Department of Defense Telephone Directory*, April 1984, p. 0–97.
34. Taylor, *An Alternative Method of Information Handling*, pp. 152–55.
35. Navy Operational Intelligence Center, "Naval Intelligence and Ocean Surveillance" (Washington, D.C.: NOIC, 1984).
36. Taylor, *An Alternative Method of Information Handling*, pp. 152–55.
37. NOIC, "Naval Intelligence and Ocean Surveillance."
38. David Kahn, *The Codebreakers* (New York: Macmillan, 1967), pp. 11–12.
39. The Brownell Committee, *The Origin and Development of the National Security Agency* (Laguna Hills, Cal.: Aegean Park Press, 1982), p. 90.
40. *Department of Defense Telephone Directory*, April 1984, p. 0–97.
41. "Rewson Contracts to Exceed $1 billion in '83," *Defense Electronics*, July 1981, pp. 69–76.
42. *Department of Defense Telephone Directory*, April 1984, p. 0–97.
43. AR (Army Regulation) 10–5, November 1978, pp. 2–29, 2–31.

44. Ibid.
45. Ibid.
46. AR (Army Regulation) 10–61, "Organization and Functions, United States Army Intelligence Operations Detachment," March 1, 1983.
47. Jules Spry, "Army Intelligence Unit Moving Headquarters to Meade," *Baltimore Sun*, December 3, 1980, p. E2.
48. INSCOM Regulation 10–2, April 1, 1982; *Department of Defense Telephone Directory*, April 1984, pp. 0–41, 0–42.
49. Capt. John Arbeeny, "ITAC: The Unique Organization," *INSCOM Journal*, February 1982, pp. 3–4.
50. Ibid.
51. Ibid.
52. INSCOM Regulation 10–2.
53. Ibid.
54. Ibid.
55. Ibid.
56. Ibid.
57. Ibid.; Author's inverview.
58. "513 MI Group, INSCOM's Newest Element," *INSCOM Journal*, September 1982, p. 9; "Washington Report," *Journal of Electronic Defense*, September 1982, pp. 14–15.
59. Army Missile Command Regulation 10–2, Chapter 29, "Missile Intelligence Agency." (Huntsville, Ala.: Army Missile Command, 1983).
60. Ibid.
61. Ibid.
62. *U.S. Army Foreign Science and Technology Center* (Charlottesville, Virg.: FSTC, n.d.).
63. Ibid.
64. Ibid.
65. The account of the ISA that follows is based on: Jay Peterzell, "Can Congress Really Check the CIA?" and "What is the Army's ISA Up To?" *Washington Post*, April 24, 1983, pp. C1, C4; Raymond Bonner, "Secret Pentagon Intelligence Unit is Disclosed," *New York Times*, May 11, 1983, p. A13; Robert C. Toth, "White House to Put Limits on Army's Secret Spy Unit," *Los Angeles Times*, May 15, 1983, pp. 1, 10.
66. Toth, "White House to Put Limits on Army's Secret Spy Unit."
67. Richard Halloran, "Military is Quietly Rebuilding Its Special Operations Forces," *New York Times*, July 19, 1982, pp. 1, 9.
68. Philip Taubman, "The Secret World of a Green Beret," *New York Times Magazine*, July 4, 1982, pp. 18ff.
69. Ibid.
70. See Charles Simpson, III, *Inside the Green Berets* (Novato, Cal.: Presidio, 1983), pp. 88–182; Seymour Hersh, *The Price of Power: Kissinger in the Nixon White House* (New York: Summit, 1983), pp. 177–78.
71. Taubman, "The Secret World of a Green Beret."
72. Ibid.
73. "Green Grow the Green Berets," *Newsweek*, October 10, 1983, p. 46.
74. *Department of Defense Telephone Directory*, April 1984, p. 0–68.

5 INTELLIGENCE COMPONENTS OF THE UNIFIED AND SPECIFIED COMMANDS

In addition to the large number of intelligence units subordinate to the Department of Defense (DOD) and the military services, there are a significant number of intelligence units subordinate to the unified and specified commands of the armed forces. These commands are either regional—that is, responsible for a given portion of the world—or functional. Functional commands, such as the Strategic Air Command (SAC), are responsible for carrying out a specific set of missions worldwide. In the case of SAC, the primary mission is the ability to deliver several thousand nuclear warheads, via missile and bomber, to their designated targets in the Soviet Union.

Whether such commands are regional or functional, they have significant intelligence requirements. Many of their requirements will be satisfied by the DOD or military service intelligence units. In some cases, the intelligence units of the commands will serve as little more than conduits by which material is passed from the Central Intelligence Agency, Defense Intelligence Agency (DIA), or other such organizations to the commands and as a channel through which the command can make its intelligence requirements known to the appropriate collectors and analysts.

In other cases, the command intelligence organizations may provide additional intelligence support, especially analysis, geared to command operations. Additionally, the intelligence components of the regional commands may be assigned management responsibilities for the on-scene aspects of national reconnaissance and other sensitive collection operations.

STRATEGIC AIR COMMAND INTELLIGENCE

The Commander in Chief, SAC (CINCSAC) is in fact, Commander of three organizations. Collocated with SAC at Offutt AFB, Nebraska are the Joint Strategic Connectivity Staff and the Joint Strategic Target Planning Staff (JSTPS). The former is responsible for developing and implementing programs that are designed to ensure that in the event of nuclear war an adequate C^3 system will continue to operate through the trans- and post-attack periods. The JSTPS is responsible for developing the National Strategic Target List and, from that list, in response to guidance from the President, Secretary of Defense, and Joint Chiefs of Staff (JCS), the Single Integrated Operational Plan (SIOP).

SAC itself is responsible for the operation and maintenance of two-thirds of the triad of forces that would be used to execute the SIOP in the event of war: land-based ICBMs (intercontinental ballistic missiles) and bombers. It is also responsible for the operation of strategic reconnaissance aircraft—the U-2, SR-71, and RC-135.

The Deputy Chief of Staff, Intelligence (DCSI) is responsible for providing SAC with the intelligence required to accomplish its mission and the JSTPS with the intelligence support directed by the JCS. The DCSI has, as illustrated in Figure 5-1, three directorates and a Special Security Office subordinate to him.[1]

The Directorate of Plans is responsible for all planning, programming, and budget activities required to fulfill SAC's intelligence mission. It formulates and evaluates intelligence policy, concepts, and objectives. As part of its responsibility, it promulgates the *SAC Intelligence Plan* which outlines objectives in regard to intelligence acquisition and production.

Subordinate to the Directorate are three divisions: Systems, Plans and Policy, and Unit Support. The Systems Division formulates policy and develops plans for the development and integration of intelligence collection, processing, data handling, and dissemination systems used by SAC for intelligence purposes. Along with the DCS, Data Systems, the division oversees the design and operation of the SAC Intelligence Data Handling System.

The Plans and Policy Division develops and seeks to ensure the implementation of SAC intelligence policies, concepts, objectives, and plans. In pursuit of this goal, it directs and coordinates the development of intelligence annexes and other intelligence involvement in SAC military capabilities planning. It also represents SAC with regard to the General Defense Intelligence Program. The Unit Support Division coordinates staff support to intelligence elements at SAC units.[2]

The Directorate of Assessments, with its Offensive, Defensive, and Politico-Economic Divisions, is responsible for assessing military, scientific, political, economic, and demographic information on selected foreign countries. The Directorate is responsible for the acquisition and production of intelligence on

Figure 5-1.   Strategic Air Command Deputy Chief of Staff/
Intelligence Organization.

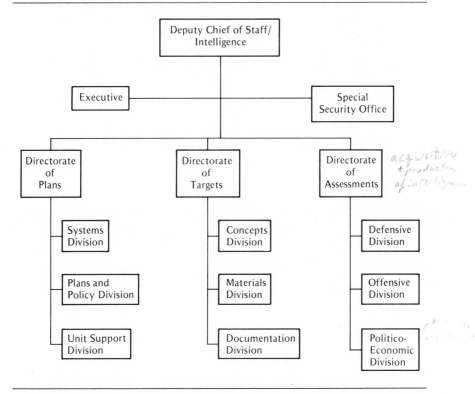

Source: SAC Regulation 23-6, "Organization and Functions—Headquarters Strategic
Air Command," July 1, 1981.

the capabilities, strength, vulnerabilities, and operational activities of both offensive and defensive forces; development of intelligence on foreign strategic doctrines; employment concepts; and tactics. It also assesses scientific and technological factors with an impact on foreign military capabilities, planning, and force structure.[3]

The Politico-Economic Division is responsible for the acquisition and production of all-source intelligence on military-related aspects of the capabilities, strengths, vulnerabilities, and activities of nations in which SAC forces might be employed. It coordinates production of studies on political and economic strategies, doctrines, and ideologies as they relate to the structuring and employment of military forces. It also analyzes the political, sociological, military, economic, and demographic infrastructures supporting the defense policies of foreign nations, alliances, and political organizations. Finally, it prepares and coordinates the preparation of assessments on foreign politico-military and military-economic capabilities and activities.[4]

The Directorate of Targets develops and implements targeting concepts and target weaponry policy based on national and command guidance. It is responsible for the development and maintenance of target intelligence data bases and for SAC inputs to national target files as well as tasking subordinate SAC units for targeting and mapping, charting, and geodesy.[5]

The Directorate's Concepts Division develops and validates concepts, requirements, and plans associated with targeting methodologies, procedures, and policies for non–SIOP and conventional targeting of SAC forces. In collaboration with the Strategic Targeting Intelligence Center, it provides for the acquisition and application of targeting intelligence for SAC military planning activities. The Materials Division directs and manages the aircraft and missile target material program. The Documentation Division manages the documentation of the targeting aspects of operations plans and orders related to the SAC Post Attack Command and Control System (PACCS) and other command and control assets. It also identifies and coordinates support for PACCS intelligence requirements.[6]

In addition, the DCS, via SAC's Strategic Reconnaissance Center, manages the U-2, SR-71, and RC-135 strategic reconnaissance aircraft. The main loci of these activities are the 55th Strategic Reconnaissance Wing at Offutt AFB and the 9th Strategic Reconnaissance Wing at Beale AFB, California. The latter is responsible for the 1st and 99th Strategic Reconnaissance Squadrons at Beale; Detachment 1 at Kadena Air Base, Japan; and Detachment 4 at RAF Mildenhall, England.[7]

AIR FORCE SPACE COMMAND/NORAD

The Air Force Space Command was created on September 1, 1982 to bring under one managerial roof the responsibility for the Air Force's space-related research, development, and acquisition and operational activities. The head of the Space Command is simultaneously Commander in Chief, U.S. Aerospace Defense Command (ADC). The deputy head of the Space Command is the head of the Space Division—the Air Force space research, development, and acquisition organization—located at El Segundo, California.[8]

The primary intelligence functions managed by the Space Command relate to space surveillance; nuclear detection monitoring and weather reconnaissance functions also fall under its purview. The 1st Space Wing of the command is responsible for the operation of two satellite systems—the Defense Support Program, and the Defense Meteorological Satellite Program (DMSP) satellites—as well as a network of twenty-four radar and optical sensor sites for space surveillance.[9]

The Defense Support Program satellites have a primary mission of early warning detection of the launch of Soviet or Chinese ICBMs and SLBMs. The DMSP satellites provide military useful weather information, including the existence of cloud cover. Since present U.S. imaging satellites cannot penetrate cloud covers, knowledge of the existence of clouds allows the avoidance of wasted film. The National Reconnaissance Office (NRO) can simply turn off the satellite cameras until a feasible target emerges.

The ground-based sensors network operated by the 1st Space Wing allows the Space Defense Operations Center (SPADOC), Space Objects Indentification Center, and Space Intelligence Indications Center of the ADC to develop a complete catalog of all U.S. and foreign space objects/satellites. Information included in the catalog involves launch dates, orbit, mission, and the times when the satellites pass over U.S. territory.[10] Such information plays a crucial role in the production of the Satellite Reconnaissance Advance Notice (SATRAN) warnings to U.S. intelligence and military activities that are intended to be kept secret from Soviet reconnaissance satellites.[11] On the basis of the SATRANs, such activities can be suspended when satellites pass overhead.

North American Aerospace Defense Command (NORAD) intelligence is the responsibility of the DCSI. Subordinate to the DCSI is the Directorate of Operational Intelligence, Intelligence Plans, and Programs and Intelligence Systems.[12]

The Intelligence Operations Division of the Directorate of Operational Intelligence is responsible for producing assessments of the military threat to North America and the *Eurasian Space Order of Battle.* In addition, it prepares intelligence estimates and command inputs to national and joint U.S.-Canadian (CANUS) Intelligence Estimates. The Directorate's Strategic Warning Division operates the ADCOM (Aerospace Defense Command) Indications and Warning (I&W) Center, assesses and verifies hostile aerospace events, receives and disseminates warning information, initiates collection requirements, performs initial target signature analyses for space object identification, and executes Satellite Tracking Network reporting.[13]

The Directorate of Intelligence Plans and Programs prepares the NORAD/ ADCOM Intelligence Plan as well as managing Sensitive Compartmented Information (SCI) activities. The Directorate of Intelligence Systems is responsible for computer operations as well as reviewing national intelligence collection capabilities and evaluating and exploiting operational sensors for intelligence value.[14]

In December 1979 the Aerospace Defense Center was established in Colorado Springs to support NORAD and the ADC. Subordinate to the Center is the Aerospace Defense Intelligence Center (ADIC). ADIC provides intelligence support in regard to aerospace defense developments and threats.[15]

UNIFIED GEOGRAPHIC COMMANDS

In recent years the U.S. military has unified the theater activities of the military services by creation of command structures that direct the activities of all four services, the most recent creation being the Central Command for Southwest Asia. In addition to the Central Command, there are five other geographic commands—Pacific Command (PACOM), Atlantic Command (LANTCOM), European Command (EUCOM), Southern Command (SOUTHCOM), and Readiness Command (REDCOM)—all of which maintain intelligence components for the acquisition and dissemination of intelligence and participation in national intelligence activities.

The responsibility of PACOM extends from 100 degrees east to 95 degrees west in the north and 17 degrees east to 92 degrees west in the south. This area covers the Indian Ocean, parts of Africa, India, Australia, Japan, China, parts of the Soviet Union, Alaska, Mexico, and portions of Canada and the United States.

PACOM's Directorate for Intelligence is divided into four divisions: Intelligence Information Systems, Management, Collection Management, and Special Security. The Collection Management Division consists of Imagery, Signals, and Human Intelligence (HUMINT) Branches. These branches manage and oversee theater and national SIGINT (Signals Intelligence) programs and validate and evaluate human intelligence programs. The division also serves as the Pacific arm of the Joint Reconnaissance Center (JRC).[16]

Intelligence production for PACOM is the responsibility of the Intelligence Center Pacific (IPAC). The Center is responsible for providing a constant Indications and Warning Watch for PACOM. It also maintains an all-source data base from which order of battle, estimates, and studies can be provided as well as producing some national orders of battle as delegated by the DIA.[17]

Subordinate to the IPAC and its Commander are a Technical Director, Command Safety and Security Office, Command Resources Office, and three directorates: Intelligence, Production, and Data Systems.

The Directorate of Intelligence produces conventional military intelligence, including portions of the national automated order of battle and produces air, defensive, missile, ground, and AAA (Antiaircraft Artillery) orders of battle. Beyond this conventional military intelligence, the Directorate also produces "all-source intelligence pertaining to the military, internal security, political, economic, sociological and scientific and technological situations in all PACOM countries."[18] The Directorate of Production manages the IPAC intelligence production schedule. It also is responsible for imagery interpretation and ELINT analysis. In the latter capacity it provides all-source operational ELINT, performs technical ELINT analysis in support of Navy ELINT collection programs, and produces ELINT orders of battle.[19]

In addition to the intelligence management and production divisions, there is an extensive management structure to direct PACOM intelligence activities. The PACOM Intelligence Board (PIB) reviews and coordinates intelligence activities as well as making recommendations concerning the establishment of intelligence requirements and procedures as well as validation of the products. In addition to the PIB, there are numerous Management Action Groups to deal

Figure 5-2. Organization of PACOM Intelligence.

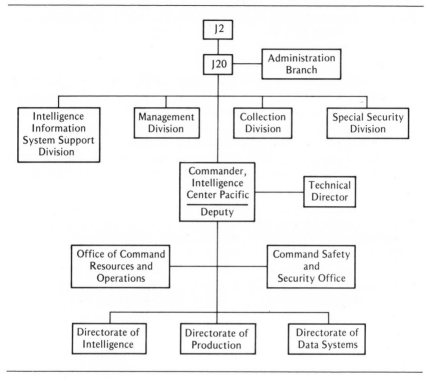

Source: U.S. Pacific Command.

with specific aspects of intelligence collection and production. Included are the Aerial Reconnaissance Review Committee, SIGINT Requirements Committee, HUMINT Board, and the Counterintelligence Advisory Committee.[20] The structure of PACOM intelligence is shown in Figure 5-2.

The Central Command was formed on January 1, 1983 as a successor to the Rapid Deployment Force, with responsibility for the general Southwest Asia region. Included in this area are the countries of the Middle East and Persian Gulf (e.g., Iran, Iraq, Jordan, Saudi Arabia, and Kuwait), Northeast Africa (e.g., Egypt, Somalia, and Sudan), and Southwest Asia (e.g., Pakistan and Afghanistan).[21]

The Intelligence Directorate (J2) of the Central Command consists of four divisions—Intelligence Operations, Resource Management, Collection Management, Targets—and a Special Security Office. The Intelligence Analysis Branch of the Intelligence Operations Division provides finished intelligence on the nations within the Command's area of responsibility.[22]

The U.S. Southern Command is responsible for Central and South America. The J2 (Intelligence Directorate) is divided into four divisions—Collection Management, Indications and Analysis, Plans and Security, and the Contingency Production Support Division—and directs intelligence production as well as managing the U.S. SOUTHCOM Automatic Ground Order of Battle System for Panama.[23]

The Collection Management Division is responsible for determining and delegating intelligence requirements throughout the Command. It also serves as liaison with national agencies and the JRC.[24] The Division also provides collection planning guidance and develops and reviews plans and programs in support of local, national, and DOD intelligence collection activities.[25]

The Indications and Analysis Division produces a variety of SOUTHCOM intelligence products—Special Intelligence Briefs, Annual Intelligence Briefs, and the Country Intelligence Study (CIS), Panama. It maintains the Travelers in Panama (TIP) File as well as operating the Indication and Warning Center. The Plans and Security Division manages Command walk-in and defector programs and publishes the *SOUTHCOM Intelligence Plan.*[26]

The organization of the Intelligence Division, Atlantic Command/Fleet reflects the extent of the Command's responsibilities and activities. Managed by the Assistant Chief of Staff for Intelligence (J2) and his Deputy, the Division has eight subordinate branches, as indicated in Figure 5-3. In addition, the Deputy Chief manages, supervises, and directs the Current Intelligence Operations Center (CIOC). Attached to the CIOC is the Fleet Ocean Surveillance Information Center (FOSIC) and Atlantic Command Forward Area Support Teams.[27]

Of the eight Intelligence Division branches, three are of particular interest: Target Intelligence, FOSIC Detachment and Ocean Surveillance, and Collection Management. The Target Intelligence Branch is responsible for handling nuclear and conventional targeting materials and coordinating with CINCLANT (Commander in Chief, Atlantic) representatives to the JSTPS concerning matters of targeting and reconnaissance planning. The FOSIC Detachment and Ocean Surveillance Branch supervises the fusion, analysis, and dissemination of intelligence on Soviet Bloc surface, subsurface, and air activity in the Atlantic. It also maintains liaison with the Collection Management Branch (to inform it of gaps in operational intelligence) as well as with fleet units and intelligence organizations (to provide for the exchange of time sensitive operational intelligence).[28]

The Collection Management Branch supervises the planning, management, and administration of Atlantic Command/Fleet intelligence collection programs and maintains liaison with other intelligence organizations. The Branch is staffed by several Collections Officers. The Submarine Collections Officer maintains liaison with the Atlantic Command and Fleet and other agencies—the CIA and the Naval Intelligence Command (NIC)—to coordinate special submarine intelligence collection operations. The Special Collection and Requirements Officer

Figure 5-3. Organization of the Atlantic Command Intelligence Division.

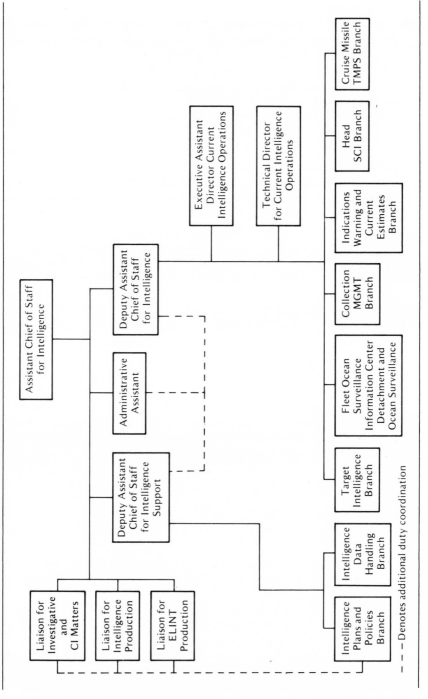

– – – Denotes additional duty coordination

Source: U.S. Atlantic Command.

manages the maintenance and submission of LANTCOM Operational ELINT Requirements as well as supervising the Human Intelligence Tasking System Programs. The Joint Systems Collection Officer (JSCO) is the primary point of contact for liaison with "sensitive national intelligence collection programs." The JSCO also manages intelligence tasking for scheduled peripheral reconnaissance missions and submission of Atlantic Command inputs to the National SIGINT Requirements List.[29]

The J-2 Directorate (Intelligence) of the European Command consists of four Divisions (Intelligence Applications, Intelligence Collection, Intelligence Plans, and Intelligence Targets), an Intelligence Operations Center, and a Special Security and Special Activities Office. The Intelligence Applications Division produces intelligence studies on the Soviet Bloc, the Middle East, and Western Europe; the Intelligence Operations Center produces current intelligence and is responsible for indications and warning. The Intelligence Targets Division is responsible for target development and mapping, charting, and geodesy.[30]

The U.S. Readiness Command is responsible for maintaining general ready reserve forces of the Army and Air Force to reinforce other unified commands and to construct contingency planning for areas not under the responsibility of any unified command. It is also responsible for planning for the land defense of the United States and Canada.[31]

The Directorate of Intelligence, J2, of REDCOM is divided into two offices (Security Programs and Special Security Management) and two divisions (Operational Intelligence and Plans, Training, and Support). The Current Indications Branch of the Operational Intelligence Division (OID) prepares current intelligence briefings to the Commander in Chief, REDCOM and his staff. It also provides current intelligence to support contingency planning, including disaster relief and emergency evacuation operations, in areas not assigned to another unified command. The Analysis Branch of the OID produces orders of battle, intelligence annexes, and prepackaged intelligence data bases for contingency operations.[32]

SELECTED SUBORDINATE
GEOGRAPHICAL COMMANDS

Subordinate to each unified command are the distinct military services commands. Thus, subordinate to the European Command are United States Naval Forces Europe and United States Air Force Europe (USAFE) as well as the United States Army Europe. Likewise, subordinate to the Pacific Command is the Pacific Fleet. In turn, subordinate to the Pacific Fleet are U.S. Naval Forces Japan. Many of these subordinate commands in themselves have significant intelligence responsibilities—either at the theater or, in some cases, at the national level. It would be impossible to examine closely the dozens of such subordinate commands' intelligence activities, but some of them merit special attention.

The organizational structure of USAFE intelligence apparatus is shown in Figure 5-4. Subordinate to the DCSI are seven directorates: Intelligence Plans and Programs, Intelligence Systems, Intelligence Research, Intelligence Applications, Intelligence Operations, Intelligence Requirements, and Intelligence Collection. The Applications, Operations, and Requirements and Reconnaissance Directorates constitute the 7450 Tactical Intelligence Squadron.

The Directorate of Intelligence Plans and Programs is responsible for USAFE intelligence resource actions including planning, programming, budgeting, and manpower allocations. The Operations Division of the Intelligence Systems Directorate manages programs designed to enhance USAFE Intelligence capabilities—including the Operational Applications of Special Intelligence System (OASIS) program for the Tactical Fusion Center and programs to enhance the capabilities of the Combat Operations Intelligence Center (COIC), which is discussed below.[33]

The Directorate of Intelligence Research is responsible for the processing and analysis of "intelligence collected by human and technical sources." This responsibility includes management of the 497th Reconnaissance Technical Group, a photo interpretation unit discussed in detail in a subsequent section.[34]

The Directorate of Intelligence Applications is primarily concerned with targeting matters.[35] Based on signals intelligence and overhead photography from both local and national systems, the Directorate keeps updated folders on potential targets (for both nuclear and conventional systems) and identifies gaps in intelligence information. Located at Ramstein Air Force Base (AFB), the Directorate is collocated with COIC. The COIC operates in a multistory underground concrete bunker across the street from the headquarters building of USAFE. The primary function of the COIC is to provide photographic interpretation support to the Directorate's targeting operations.[36]

The Directorate of Intelligence Operations is the current intelligence/indications and warning unit of USAFE intelligence. In addition to current intelligence and threat analysis branches, the Directorate operates the Tactical Fusion Center at Boerfink, an underground complex for all-source intelligence analysis designed to provide near real-time warning.[37] Boerfink might have a capability for real-time access to the imagery of the KH-11 photographic reconnaissance satellite.[38] At Directorate headquarters is the Ramstein Warning Office (RWO) which provides an extension from Boerfink to the USAFE Commander in Chief and his staff. Finally, the Directorate is also responsible for the I&W activities conducted at Operating Location-A (OL-A), the Fleet Ocean Surveillance Information Facility at Rota, Spain.[39]

The Directorate of Intelligence Requirements and Reconnaissance has three branches: Collection Management, Reconnaissance, and SIGINT.[40] Among its functions, the Directorate is responsible for managing the Creek Misty, Creek Flush overflights of the Berlin Corridor.[41]

The Director of Intelligence Collection is simultaneously the Commander of the 7113 Special Activities Squadron.[42] As noted in Chapter 4, the Squadron is

Figure 5–4.   Organization of USAFE Intelligence.

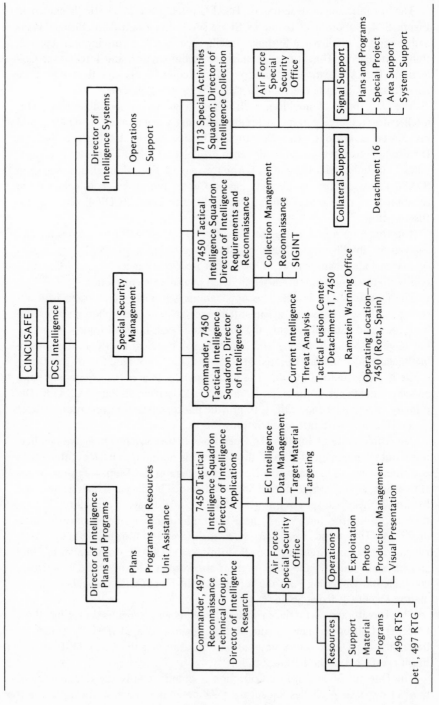

Source: Attachment 2, USAFER 200–2, 1983.

responsible for human intelligence collection activities. This involves handling of detectors and collecting intelligence for escape and evasion plans for U.S. fliers in the event of war as well as for support of targeting and combat forces.

The Commander in Chief, Pacific Fleet (CINCPACFLT) is responsible, via his Intelligence Directorate, for managing national intelligence collection activities in the area of ocean surveillance. Thus, CINCPACFLT Instruction S-3271.1A concerns the "Narrowband Assignment and Reporting Instruction for the Pacific High Frequency Direction Finding Net" and instructs stations in the net to report one fix every thirty minutes for priority ONE targets, to report one fix every two hours for priority TWO targets, and to report one fix every day for priority THREE targets.[43]

A related instruction is CINCPACFLT Instruction C 3431.1C, "Rainform Formatted Message Reporting System," which defines a series of message types for reporting encounters on the high seas with shipping vessels. Included are OSIS (Ocean Surveillance Information System) WHITE for periodic reporting of movements or locations of all merchant and friendly naval shipping (excluding that of special interest) and OSIS RED for reporting the arrival, departure, or routine movement of Communist flag merchant and fishing ships.[44] The OSIS is discussed more fully in Chapter 8.

In the case of U.S. Naval Forces Japan, the N2, Intelligence Division performs functions both in support of both local forces and national collection and liaison programs. N2 is headed by the Assistant Chief of Staff, Intelligence. Subordinate to him are the Force Investigative and Counterintelligence Adviser, Special Security Office, Special Intelligence Communications Section, Intelligence Liaison and Production Section, Special Fleet Support Section, and the Scientific Adviser.[45]

The Special Fleet Support Section provides local coordination and adminis- tration of U.S. Navy Intelligence collection programs in support of national intelligence collection requirements. These programs undoubtedly include the Sound Surveillance System (SOSUS) arrays off the coast of Japan and land, sea, and air-ocean surveillance of Soviet and Chinese naval activities in the vicin- ity of Japan. The Intelligence Liaison and Production Section coordinates the CINCPACFLT and Commander of U.S. Naval Forces Japan intelligence ex- changes with the Chief of Intelligence Division of the Japanese Maritime Staff Office and Intelligence Officer, Commander in Chief of the Japanese Self- Defense Forces fleet.[46]

FLEET INTELLIGENCE CENTERS AND FLEET OCEAN SURVEILLANCE INFORMATION CENTERS

An important means of providing intelligence support to the naval commands are the Fleet Intelligence Centers and the FOSICs. Prior to 1974 there were three Fleet Intelligence Centers: one at Norfolk, Virginia (Atlantic Fleet); one at Jacksonville, Florida (Naval Forces Europe); and one at Pearl Harbor, Hawaii (Pacific Fleet). Effective July 1, 1974, the Europe and Atlantic Centers became the Fleet Intelligence Center Europe and Atlantic (FICEURLANT) headquartered at Norfolk, Virginia.[47] In addition to the two main Fleet Intelligence Centers, the Pacific Fleet Intelligence Center has a satellite activity at Cubi Point in the Philippines.[48]

The mission of the Fleet Intelligence Centers is "to develop an intelligence processing and production capability which is immediately available to U.S. naval forces in the ... ocean areas assigned to their commands for defense responsibility."[49] The mission requires intelligence related to the areas (particularly coasts, ports, and oceans) where naval forces will operate, the targets to be attacked, and their susceptibility to destruction by particular types of attack.

Thus, subordinate to the Commanding Office of FICEURLANT are the Administrative Readiness and Logistics, Intelligence Production, and Production Services Departments. The Intelligence Production Department consists of four divisions: Amphibious Intelligence, Target Intelligence Material, Area Analysis, and Exploitation.[50] The Amphibious Intelligence Division is responsible for acquiring and maintaining information on coastal areas where troops and ships could be landed. The Target Intelligence Material Branch is concerned with both nuclear strike planning and unconventional warfare, and the Area Analysis Division focuses on weapons systems, naval affairs, order of battle information, and geopolitical military affairs.

In addition to the centers there are six FOSICs located at Rota, Spain; Norfolk, Virginia; London; Hawaii; San Francisco; and Kamiseya, Japan.[51] FOSICs receive data from underwater sensors, satellites, ships, land stations, and ocean surveillance aircraft, and they process the data to obtain a picture of naval movements in their area of responsibility. Of particular interest is any indication of buildups in Soviet or other hostile naval activity. The data are then transmitted both to the Navy Operational Intelligence Center (NOIC) and the area Commander in Chief.

Among the products provided by the FOSIC located at Pearl Harbor are two types of reports concerning foreign shipping activities relevant to naval operations. The Contact Area Summary Position Report (CASPER) provides information on shipping passing through an area of operations, in vicinity of a ship or aircraft, or that can provide medical assistance. CASPERs come in four varieties. One variety gives such information in a circular area with up to a 9,999-nautical-mile radius while a second consists of a series of circular patterns with radii as requested. A third variety of CASPER is a polygon with a minimum of three and a maximum of twenty-three points defined by the latitude and longitude; and the fourth is a rectangular corridor defined by two end points and a corridor width in nautical miles. Figure 5-5 illustrates these differing patterns. The Daily Estimated Position Locator (DEPLOC) provides detailed underway and in-port

Figure 5-5. Available CASPER Patterns.

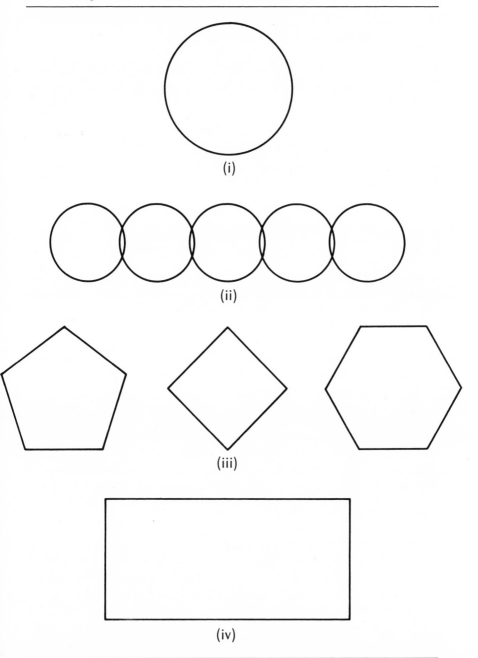

(i)

(ii)

(iii)

(iv)

shipping information on specified geographic areas over an extended period of time.[52]

UNIFIED COMMAND ELINT CENTERS

In ___ ___ intelligence directorates of the European, Atlantic, and Pacific ___ of the Commands maintains centers for the analysis of electronic ___ The centers are responsible for the integration of variously obtained ELINT and its subsequent analysis. The European center is known as the European Defense Analysis Center (EUDAC). The Pacific Command ELINT Center is located at Hospital Point, Honolulu, and the Atlantic Command ELINT Center is located at Norfolk, Virginia.[53] The organization of the Atlantic Command ELINT Center is shown in Figure 5-6.

RECONNAISSANCE TECHNICAL GROUPS

An important aspect of intelligence support to U.S. military forces is the provision of overhead reconnaissance photographs to theater commands. Such commands are interested in the day-to-day location and movements of opposing forces—especially forces that are within striking distance.

Provision of overhead photography to European and Pacific Commands that has been collected by national systems is the focus of the Tactical Exploitation of National Capabilities (TENCAP) program. The Commands maintain photo interpretation units for the immediate analysis of overhead photography provided by airborne collection systems.

The main imagery analysis unit for U.S. forces in the European theater is the 497th Reconnaissance Technical Group (RTG) at the Schierstein Compound outside Weisbaden, Germany and under the command of USAFE. The Group was first activated in 1951 to provide photo processing and photo interpretation services for theater operations.[54] It presently consists of seventy to seventy-five enlisted men and officers from the Air Force, Army, and Marine Corps who are divided into country group. A subordinate Reconnaissance Technical Squadron is located at RAF Alconbury, U.K.[55]

In the Pacific theater, the 548th RTG is supervised by the Assistant Deputy Chief of Staff for Intelligence of Pacific Air Force Headquarters (at Hickam AFB, Hawaii), although the 548th is under the direct authority of USAF headquarters. Located at Hickam AFB, Hawaii and with subordinate Reconnaissance Technical Squadrons at Yokota AB, Japan and possibly at Yongsan AB, Korea, the mission of the 548th is to provide photo interpretation services for PACOM, Pacific Air Forces, and national agencies.[56] The Yokota squadron serves as a primary site for interpretation of SR-71 photos provided by flights from Kadena AB, Japan.[57]

Figure 5–6. Organization of Atlantic Command Electronic Intelligence Center.

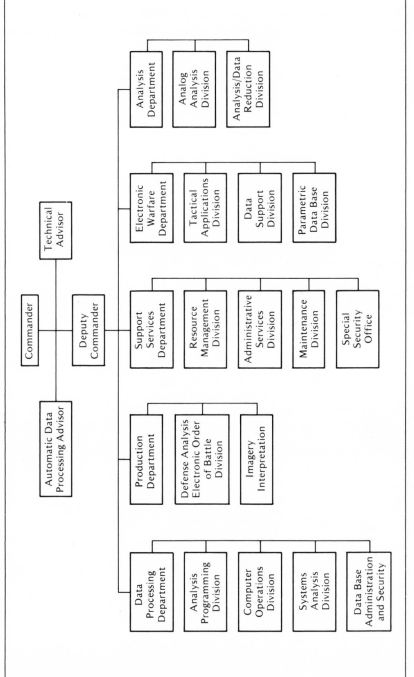

Source: Atlantic Command Electronic Intelligence Center.

The 548th RTG consists of four operational centers and four support elements. The support elements are the Logistics Division, Data Management Division, Production and Programs Management Division, and Document Library Division. The operational centers are the Exploitation Center (EC), the Precision Processing Center (PPC), the Target Assessment Center (TAC), and the Research and Analysis Center.[58] Thus, the raw film is first turned over to the PPC for developing and transformation to photographs, then interpreted at the EC, and then turned over to the Target Assessment and Research and Analysis Centers.

NOTES TO CHAPTER 5

1. SAC Regulation 23-6, "Organization and Functions—Headquarters Strategic Air Command," July 1, 1981.
2. Ibid.
3. Ibid.
4. Ibid.
5. Ibid.
6. Ibid.
7. Brian Bennett, Tony Powell, and John Adams, *The USAF Today* (London: West London Aviation Group Publication, 1981), p. 52.
8. "Space Command," *Air Force Magazine*, May 1983, pp. 96-97.
9. Ibid.
10. Ibid.
11. HQ North American Aerospace Defense Command, HQ Space Command, "Command Regulation 0-2," July 1, 1983.
12. N/A/A Pamphlet 20-4, *Organization and Mission, Headquarters NORAD/ ADCOM/ADC*, June 15, 1982.
13. Ibid.
14. Ibid.
15. "Aerospace Defense Center," *Air Force Magazine*, May 1982, p. 142.
16. Information provided by Pacific Command.
17. Ibid.
18. Ibid.
19. Ibid.
20. Ibid.
21. U.S. Congress, House Committee on Armed Services, *Hearings on HR 1816* (Washington, D.C.: U.S. Government Printing Office, 1983), p. 955.
22. Organization Chart, "Headquarters United States Central Command, MacDill Air Force Base, Fla.," July 1, 1983.
23. Headquarters, U.S. Southern Command Regulation 10-1. "Organization and Functions Manual," October 1, 1982.
24. Ibid.
25. Ibid.
26. Ibid.
27. Organization Chart of Intelligence Division, Atlantic Command/Fleet.

28. Ibid.

29. Ibid.

30. *Headquarters European Command Patch Barracks Telephone Directory*, April 30, 1975.

31. "REDCOM Public Affairs Fact Sheet," October 1981.

32. "U.S. Readiness Command, Directorate of Intelligence, J2," October 1, 1983 (from REDCOM Organization and Functions Manual).

33. "Attachment 2, USAFE R 200-2," 1983.

34. Ibid.

35. Ibid.

36. Private Information.

37. "Attachment 2, USAFE R 200-2."

38. Private information.

39. "Attachment 2, USAFE R 200-2."

40. Ibid.

41. See Peter Pringle and William Arkin, *SIOP* (New York: Norton, 1983).

42. "Attachment 2, USAFE R 200-2."

43. CINCPACFLT Instruction S 3271.1A, "Narrowband Assignment and Reporting Instructions for the Pacific High Frequency Direction Finding Net."

44. CINCPACFLT Instruction C 3431.1C, "RAINFORM Formatted Message Reporting System," May 18, 1981.

45. Commander U.S. Naval Forces Japan, Staff Instruction 5450.1G, May 13, 1983.

46. Ibid., pp. V-5, V-7.

47. "Fleet Intelligence Center Europe and Atlantic," information provided by FICEURLANT.

48. U.S. Congress, Senate Committee on Appropriations, *Department of Defense Appropriations FY 1972, Part 3* (Washington, D.C.: U.S. Government Printing Office, 1971), p. 487.

49. CINCPACFLT Instruction 5450.1L, "Missions and Functions of Fleet Intelligence, Pacific, Pearl Harbor, Hawaii."

50. "Fleet Intelligence Center Europe and Atlantic (FICEURLANT) Organization Chart," July 1, 1983.

51. U.S. Congress, Senate Committee on Appropriations, *Department of Defense Appropriations FY 1972, Part 3*, p. 487; U.S. Congress, Senate Committee on Appropriations, *Department of Defense Appropriations FY 1973, Part 3* (Washington, D.C.: U.S. Government Printing Office, 1972), p. 475; Paul Bracken, *The Command and Control of Nuclear Forces* (New Haven, Conn.: Yale University Press, 1983), p. 38.

52. CINCPACFLT Instruction 3130.6f, "Pacific Area Ocean Surveillance Report Services," November 8, 1982.

53. U.S. Congress, Senate Committee on Appropriations, *Department of Defense Appropriations FY 1973, Part 3*, p. 507; Richard Halloran, "Air Force Seeking Joint Space Unit," *New York Times*, June 19, 1983, p. 17.

54. *497th Reconnaissance Technical Group* (Weisbaden: 497th RTG, 1976).

55. "Attachment 2, USAFE R 200-2."

56.   Department of the Air Force, Hq. Pacific Air Force, Hickam AFB, Hawaii, PACAF Regulation 23–17, "548th Reconnaissance Technical Group," September 29, 1980.

57.   Benjamin Schemmer, *The Raid* (New York: Harper & Row, 1975), p. 254.

58.   Department of the Air Force, "548th Reconnaissance Technical Group."

6 CIVILIAN INTELLIGENCE ORGANIZATIONS

The bulk of U.S. intelligence resources—whether in terms of personnel or dollars—lies in the hands of the national and military intelligence organizations. At the same time, several civilian executive departments have offices that collect and analyze intelligence with respect to either foreign political and military affairs, economic affairs, or narcotics. In some cases, the intelligence units are very small and their main purpose is to serve as liaison with the larger intelligence units, making them aware of their department's intelligence requirements and transmitting intelligence from the larger units to the appropriate department offices. Thus, in addition to the State and Energy Departments, the Commerce, Treasury, and Justice Departments all maintain units with foreign intelligence responsibilities.

STATE DEPARTMENT INTELLIGENCE

With dissolution of the Office of Strategic Services (OSS), its research and analysis functions were transferred to the State Department. Those functions were carried out by the Interim Research and Intelligence Service. Since then there have been two name changes and many more reorganizations. It has been designated the Bureau of Intelligence and Research (INR) since 1957.[1]

The Bureau engages in no collection activity beyond reporting through normal diplomatic channels and open source collection. However, it performs a variety of functions on operational matters in the liaison area between the Department of State and the community to ensure that the actions of other intel-

95

ligence agencies, such as the Central Intelligence Agency, are in accord with U.S. foreign policy.[2]

In terms of its production functions, the INR faces in two directions. One direction is outward, where it is involved in interagency intelligence production efforts—National Intelligence Estimates (NIEs) and Special National Intelligence Estimates (SNIEs). The second direction is inward—toward the State Department internal organization. In this role it prepares a variety of intelligence products. The *Morning Summary* is prepared in collaboration with the Department's Executive Secretariat. It is designed to inform the Secretary of State and his principal deputies of current events and current intelligence. It prepares a variety of regional and functional summaries as well as single-subject reports under three different titles.[3]

The Director of the INR holds rank equivalent to an Assistant Secretary and is assisted by four Deputy Assistant Secretaries who directly supervise the INR's sixteen offices.[4] The Deputy Assistant Secretary for Intelligence and Research is the second-ranking individual in the Bureau. He or she supervises the Office of the Executive Director and Office of Intelligence Support. The Office of the Executive Director handles personnel, budget and finance, and general administrative support for the Bureau. The Office of Intelligence Support is the State Department's center for the receipt of intelligence information, in whatever form, and for its processing and dissemination under security safeguards.[5]

The Deputy Assistant Secretary for Current Analysis supervises six geographic offices and the Offices of Politico–Military Analysis. The geographic offices are the Offices of Analysis for Africa, Inter-American Affairs, East Asia and the Pacific, the Soviet Union and Eastern Europe, Western Europe, and the Near East and South Asia. The primary function of the Current Analysis Offices is to produce analyses of developments and issues that are, or will be, of concern to the policymaker. They are responsible for preparing the regional and other special summaries and for preparing INR contributions to communitywide estimates and assessments. Current Analysis personnel also conduct longer range studies and assessments under the direction and guidance of the Deputy Assistant Secretary for Assessments and Research.[6]

The Deputy Assistant Secretary for Assessments and Research has the primary responsibility for the Bureau's long-range analytical studies. He is responsible for the Office of Long Range Assessments and Research, the Office of Economic Analysis, the Office of the Geographer, the Office of Global Issues, and the Reports Coordination and Review Staff. The Office of Long Range Assessments and Research prepares its own long-range assessments on selected topics, contributes on occasion to assessments on selected topics, contributes on occasion to assessments prepared elsewhere in the Bureau, and commissions contractors and consultants for those projects that cannot be done in the INR. The Office of Economic Analysis produces reports for policymakers on current and

Figure 6-1. Organization of the Bureau of Intelligence Research.

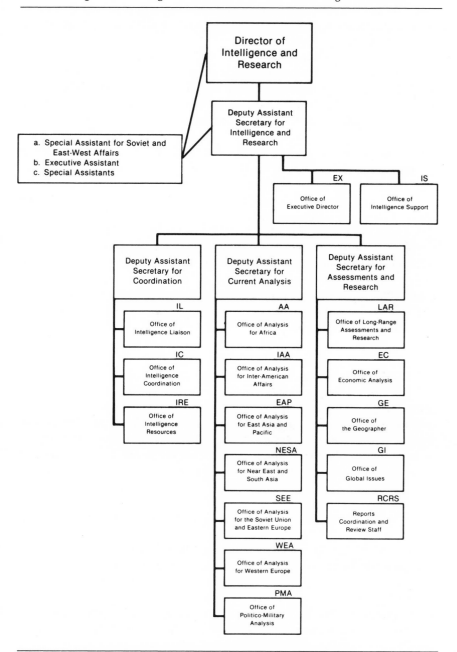

Source: *INR* (Washington, D.C.: Department of State, 1983).

longer range issues involving international economic concerns such as foreign economic policies, business cycles, trade, financial affairs, food, population, energy, and economic relations between the industrialized countries and the developing nations.[7]

The Office of the Geographer prepares studies of policy issues associated with physical, cultural, economic, and political geography, emphasizing the law of the sea, U.S. maritime issues, and international boundaries and jurisdictional problems. The Global Issues Staff produces finished intelligence on selected transnational, regional, and global topics including science and technology, narcotics, human rights and refugees, oceans, and the environment. The Reports Coordination and Review Staff is responsible for the final production of the INR's formal reports. It is responsible for editorial review, format, printing, and distribution.[8]

The Deputy Assistant Secretary for Intelligence Coordination supervises the Office of Intelligence Liaison, the Office of Intelligence Coordination, and the Office of Intelligence Resources. The Office of Intelligence Liaison works with intelligence agencies on human collection efforts and coordinates proposals for special political (covert) activities. Its basic responsibility in connection with those programs is to ensure "thorough consideration of their support of and implications for U.S. foreign policy."[9] The Office also handles defector cases and requests for biographic data and other intelligence agency documents and conducts briefings on intelligence matters for Department officers going to and returning from overseas posts. It also handles liaison with designated foreign intelligence representatives.

The Office of Intelligence Resources provides staff support, representation, and coordination for the Department's interests in the National Foreign Intelligence Program and budget. It works with other intelligence community agencies; concerned areas of the Department; and overseas missions in planning, tasking, deploying, and evaluating technical collection activities. It also advises Department officers on the use of intelligence produced by major technical systems.[10] An organization chart for INR is shown as Figure 6-1.

DEPARTMENT OF COMMERCE INTELLIGENCE

Department of Commerce participation in intelligence activities has been heightened in recent years by many factors—most recently, the concern over technology transfer operations. Such operations require intelligence concerning (1) those who wish to acquire such technology, (2) those who may attempt or are attempting to provide it, and (3) its accessibility, particularly with respect to dual use of civilian technology. Additionally, the Export Administration Act requires that restrictions be placed on technology transfers only if there is no sufficient foreign availability.

Neither the concern over technology transfer nor an intelligence role for the Department of Commerce in that area are new. For a brief period during the 1950s, U.S. efforts to regulate the flow of information and goods to the Soviet Union and other potential adversary nations involved the Department of Commerce in an intelligence role. At the urging of the National Security Council (NSC), the Office of Strategic Information (OSI) was established within the Department of Commerce in 1954.[11]

The OSI was never authorized by legislation but created by presidential directive on November 1, 1954 in response to the NSC recommendation—a recommendation that resulted from concern about Soviet efforts to obtain U.S. industrial and military information. The OSI tried to create "prepublication awareness" concerning the "danger" resulting from the availability of certain unclassified scientific and technical information. Particular concern focused on aerial photography, resulting in creation of an OSI Task Force on Aerial Photography. The OSI recommended a specific educational program through the government and industry "to alert producers and users of the strategic intelligence value of aerial photographs."[12] The OSI clashed with the Department of Defense (DOD) and Congress. The DOD considered the OSI's security role redundant; Congress was concerned about the OSI's negative impact on scientific projects. As a result, the OSI ceased operation in June 1957.[13]

At present, the Department of Commerce has three units with intelligence functions, including the Office of Intelligence Liaison and the Intelligence Division of the Office of Export Enforcement (OEE). The Office of Intelligence Liaison serves as a liaison office between the Department of Commerce and the intelligence community—particularly with respect to technology transfer intelligence issues. The Office is the recipient of all information transmitted from the intelligence community to the Department of Commerce.[14] It then distributes the information to the appropriate Department of Commerce unit.

The Office also provides day-to-day intelligence support to key Department of Commerce officials having international policy or program responsibilities. This support includes preparation of a daily departmental foreign intelligence summary covering major international developments. Support also includes intelligence information for key department officials traveling abroad.[15]

Additionally, the Office is responsible for reviewing and assessing Department of Commerce intelligence requirements. Basing its directives on the results of these assessments, it tasks the intelligence community to provide the necessary data.[16]

The OEE was formerly the Compliance Division of the Office of Export Administration. In either form, its function has been to ensure that the proper approvals have been obtained for the export of sensitive technology and to prevent unauthorized shipments of such technology. The Intelligence Division of the OEE is responsible for detecting indications of prospective violations for the Office to act on in conjunction with the Customs Service.

Creation of the OEE stemmed from perceived inadequacies in the operation of the Compliance Division. It was found to be understaffed, poorly equipped, and inadequately trained. Its incompetence led to the 1980 investigation of grain embargo violations being conducted by an interagency working group consisting of representatives from the CIA, State Department, Navy, Department of Agriculture, and other agencies.[17]

The Foreign Availability Assessments Division (FAAD) of the Office of Export Administration was formed in 1984. FAAD develops and maintains a data base to allow assessment of the foreign availability of high technology products to the Soviet Bloc and the People's Republic of China.[18] Such assessments would influence U.S. decisions concerning the export of U.S. high technology. The Division will have about 10 employees divided into Data Collection, Information Analysis, and Capabilities Assessments branches.[19]

DEPARTMENT OF THE TREASURY INTELLIGENCE

The Treasury's Office of Intelligence Support overtly collects foreign economic, financial, and monetary data, participating with the Department of State in the collection of such data. It also produces and disseminates foreign intelligence relating to U.S. economic policy as required by the Secretary of the Treasury.[20] Additionally, it develops intelligence requirements and informs the remainder of the intelligence community of them as well as generally representing the Department in intelligence community deliberations.

The Office is subordinate to the Executive Secretary of the Department of the Treasury and consists of nine individuals: a Special Assistant to the Secretary (National Security), three National Intelligence Advisers, two Technical Librarians, a Secretary, and two Intelligence Support Assistants. The National Intelligence Advisers are responsible for (1) Latin America, Asia, Terrorism, and Narcotics; (2) the Middle East, Energy, and International Monetary Affairs; and (3) Europe, Africa, Trade, and Investment. In addition, a National Security Agency (NSA) representative is assigned to the Office.[21]

DEPARTMENT OF ENERGY INTELLIGENCE

The Department of Energy participates with the Department of State in the overt collection of information with respect to foreign energy matters, produces and disseminates foreign intelligence necessary for Energy Department operations, participates in formulating intelligence collection and analysis requirements where the expert capability of the department can contribute, and provides technical analytical and research capability to other agencies of the intelligence community.[22] Most importantly, Energy Department analysts are heavily involved in the analysis of civilian and military Soviet nuclear energy activities, including weapons-testing capabilities and effects.

These intelligence functions are performed by the Defense Intelligence Division of the Office of International Security Affairs, which is headed by an Assistant Secretary. The Division is subdivided into four branches: the Technology Intelligence, Weapons Intelligence, Intelligence Support and Policy, and Intelligence Secretariat.[23]

The Department also manages, via Lawrence Livermore Laboratory, a Proliferation Intelligence Program, which seeks to provide:

1. national capability assessments of potential proliferant countries;
2. analyses of state-of-the-art fuel cycle technologies, such as enrichment and reprocessing that proliferants could use to acquire fissile material;
3. assessments of worldwide availability of nuclear weapons technology that could enable a proliferant to build the physics package of a weapon;
4. assessments of worldwide availability of related but non-nuclear weapon technology such as safety, arming, firing, and fusing systems;
5. assessments of the activities and behavior of nuclear supplier states and international organizations involved in nuclear commerce, safeguards, and physical security.[24]

DEPARTMENT OF AGRICULTURE INTELLIGENCE

The Department of Agriculture's intelligence consumers are in general more likely to be U.S. farmers than the national security officials. However, in certain circumstances—such as proposed grain sales to the Soviet Union—the Department's Foreign Agriculture Service (FAS) might contribute to the production of intelligence relevant to foreign policy decisionmaking.

The FAS maintains a worldwide agricultural intelligence and reporting system. This system consists of approximately 100 professional agriculturists posted at approximately seventy U.S. embassies as agricultural attachés. Attaché reporting includes information and data on foreign government policies, analysis of supply and demand conditions, commercial trade relationships, and market opportunities. In Washington, part of the FAS staff analyzes the activities of international trade conducted under the General Agreement on Tarrifs and Trade (GATT).[25]

DRUG ENFORCEMENT ADMINISTRATION INTELLIGENCE

The Drug Enforcement Administration (DEA) operates in the United States and abroad. Its external functions include the collection, analysis, and dissemination of foreign intelligence concerning narcotics operations—growing, processing, distribution, and any other facets of the process.

DEA intelligence operations are the responsibility of the Assistant Administrator for Intelligence, who heads the Office of Intelligence of the DEA Operations Division. The Office is subdivided into three sections: the Operational Intelligence Section, the Strategic Intelligence Section, and the El Paso Intelligence Center.[26]

The Office's Special Field Intelligence Program provides funding "to exploit high-specialized or unique collection opportunities against a wide variety of intelligence problems in foreign areas."[27] The target of such activities is the collection of data on the entire narcotics raw material production process, smuggling routes and methods, trafficking, and terrorist or financial matters relating to narcotics activities.[28]

According to the DEA's 1984 congressional budget submission, its major activities and accomplishments include:

- development of sources of information knowledgeable of illicit cultivation, production, and transportation activities;

- undercover penetration of trafficking organizations in support of host country operations;

- surveillance assistance and development of evidence against major traffickers of drugs destined for the United States;

- intelligence support to governments in Mexico and Central America in eradicating marijuana and poppyfields.[29]

Additionally, the DEA reports that intelligence probes in West Germany have identified a sizable number of Turkish and Pakistani traffickers transporting Southwest Asian, heroin into Western Europe. Likewise, intelligence probes in Pakistan, Turkey, and Mexico are reported to have pinpointed illicit laboratory locations, identified the operators, and assessed the potential output of a number of sophisticated morphine, heroin, and opium production operations.[30]

In the course of its activities, the DEA interacts with several major intelligence agencies. Detection of drug trafficking operations can involve human agents—both DEA and CIA—as well as a variety of technical sensors—for example, infrared photo reconnaissance and ocean surveillance satellites. Hence, the DEA has contacts with agencies such as the CIA, the NSA, the Navy Space Project (NSP), and the National Reconnaissance Office (NRO). Thus, the Administrator of DEA stated in 1981 congressional testimony that he

> met with Deputy Director of CIA, Admiral Inman for quite some time at their headquarters and discussed our narcotics priorities. He'll be well familiar with this problem. I've worked with him in the past, both at NSA and on other matters, and we are expecting increased attention from that agency, and we need it desperately. Because without intelligence, the enforcement effort is immediately limited.[31]

Thus, the CIA has provided the DEA with international narcotics intelligence derived from both human sources and electronic surveillance operations overseas.[32]

FEDERAL BUREAU OF INVESTIGATION

The responsibilities of the FBI are predominately in the criminal law enforcement and domestic counterintelligence areas, the latter responsibilities being performed by the Bureau's Intelligence Division. The Intelligence Division also does have some present-day responsibility with regard to collection of foreign intelligence in the United States.

Over the years the FBI has tried to expand its role in the foreign intelligence area. In 1939 President Roosevelt gave responsibility for the collection of intelligence in the Western Hemisphere to the FBI, which created a Special Intelligence Service (SIS) for this function. The SIS had approximately 360 agents, mostly in Mexico, Argentina, and Brazil.[33] Although it was stripped of this function after the war, the Bureau maintained representatives as Legal Attachés in ten embassies as of 1970. The Attachés' official function was to be a liaison with national police forces on matters of common concern and to deal with Americans who found themselves in trouble with the law. In 1970 the Bureau expanded from ten to twenty the number of embassies with FBI representation and instructed agents to collect foreign intelligence, particularly interesting intelligence being slugged with the designation HILEV (High Level) by overseas agents. Some such material was distributed to high officials—for example, Henry Kissinger—outside normal intelligence channels.[34] In the aftermath of Director J. Edgar Hoover's death and FBI revelations, this program was terminated, and FBI representation abroad was reduced to fifteen embassies.

At least one recent instance of an FBI attempt to engage in foreign clandestine collection has come to light. During the investigation of the murder of former Chilean Defense Minister Orlando Letelier, the FBI operated an undercover informer in Chile, codenamed "Gopher." Gopher told the FBI that the right-wing Partia y Libertad had contracted with Chilean narcotics traffickers to murder Letelier. Gopher turned out to be a former DEA informant who had been terminated and blacklisted years earlier for double dealing, misrepresentation, and moral turpitude.[35]

Despite its failure to acquire a significant *overseas* role in the collection and production of foreign intelligence, the FBI is involved in domestic activities designed to generate foreign intelligence. Thus, Executive Order 12333 allows the FBI to:

Conduct within the United States, when requested by the officials of the intelligence community designated by the President, activities undertaken to collect foreign intelligence or support foreign intelligence collection requirements of other agencies within the intelligence community.[36]

In the past such activities have included wiretapping and break-ins. According to Marchetti and Marks, the FBI has operated wiretaps against numerous foreign embassies in Washington. FBI agents regularly monitored the phones in the offices of all Communist governments represented in Washington. Additionally, the phones in the offices of non-Communist governments are tapped, especially when those nations are engaged in negotiations with the United States or when significant developments are taking place in the countries.[37] This has included the phones of an allied Trade Mission in San Francisco.[38] In addition, the FBI has conducted break-ins at foreign embassies to obtain cryptanalytical and other foreign intelligence.[39]

FEDERAL RESEARCH DIVISION, LIBRARY OF CONGRESS

The Federal Research Division (FRD) of the Library of Congress analyzes open source information concerning foreign military activities. Although part of the Library of Congress, it is also under the jurisdiction of the Defense Intelligence Agency (DIA). As a military intelligence unit, it participates along with the DIA and the military services in the General Intelligence Career Development Program.[40]

NOTES TO CHAPTER 6

1. U.S. Congress, Senate Select Committee to Study Governmental Operations, *Supplementary Reports on Intelligence Activities* (Washington, D.C.: U.S. Government Printing Office, 1976), pp. 271–76.
2. U.S. Congress, House Committee on Foreign Affairs, *The Role of Intelligence in the Foreign Policy Process* (Washington, D.C.: U.S. Government Printing Office, 1980), p. 57.
3. *INR* (Washington, D.C.: Department of State, 1983).
4. Ibid., p. 7.
5. Ibid., pp. 15–16.
6. Ibid., pp. 11–12.
7. Ibid., pp. 12–13.
8. Ibid., p. 13.
9. Ibid., p. 14.
10. Ibid.
11. National Academy of Sciences, *Scientific Communication and National Security* (Washington, D.C.: National Academy Press, 1982), p. 99.
12. U.S. Congress, House Committee on Government Operations, *Availability of Information from Federal Departments and Agencies, Part 6* (Washington, D.C.: U.S. Government Printing Office, 1956), pp. 1671–72.
13. National Academy of Sciences, *Scientific Communication and National Security*, p. 99.

14. U.S. Congress, Senate Committee on Governmental Affairs, *Transfer of United States High Technology to the Soviet Union and Soviet Bloc Nations* (Washington, D.C.: U.S. Government Printing Office, 1982), p. 42.
15. Department of Commerce, "Department Organization Order Series 10–6, Appendix A. June 10, 1981."
16. Ibid.
17. U.S. Congress, Senate Committee on Governmental Affairs, p. 42.
18. Telephone conversation between author and Deputy Director, FAAD. September 12, 1984.
19. Ibid.
20. Ronald Reagan, "United States Intelligence Activities," Executive Order 12333 *Federal Register* 46, no. 235 (December 5, 1981): 59941–54; "Foreign Intelligence—It's More than the CIA," *U.S. News and World Report*, May 1, 1981, pp. 35–37.
21. Organization Chart, Department of the Treasury, Office of Intelligence Support, 1983.
22. Reagan, "Executive Order 12333."
23. *Federal Executive Directory* (Washington, D.C.: Carroll, November–December, 1982), p. 65.
24. U.S. Congress, House Committee on Armed Services, *Department of Energy: National Security and Military Applications of Nuclear Energy Authorization Act of 1984* (Washington, D.C.: U.S. Government Printing Office, 1983), p. 394.
25. Department of Agriculture, *FAS USA: The Farmers' Export Arm* (Washington, D.C.: Department of Agriculture, 1980).
26. U.S. Congress, House Committee on Appropriations, *Department of Commerce, Justice and State, the Judiciary and Related Appropriations for 1984, Part 6 – Department of Justice* (Washington, D.C.: U.S. Government Printing Office, 1983), p. 3.
27. Ibid.
28. Ibid., p. 21.
29. Ibid., p. 22.
30. Ibid.
31. U.S. Congress, Senate Committee on the Judiciary, *Oversight of the Drug Enforcement Administration* (Washington, D.C.: U.S. Government Printing Office, 1981), p. 9.
32. Department of Justice, *Report on Inquiry Into CIA-Related Electronic Surveillance Activities* (Washington, D.C.: Department of Justice, 1976), p. 20.
33. Sanford J. Ungar, *The FBI* (Boston: Little, Brown, 1976), p. 240.
34. Ibid., p. 242.
35. Taylor Branch and Eugene M. Proper, *Labyrinth* (New York: Viking, 1982), pp. 231, 350, 358.
36. Reagan, "Executive Order 12333," Section 1.14, provision c.
37. Victor Marchetti and John Marks, *The CIA and the Cult of Intelligence* (New York: Knopf, 1974), p. 204.
38. "Mole Tunnels Under a Soviet Consulate," *Newsweek*, August 15, 1983, p. 21.

39. Douglas Watson, "Huston Says NSA Urged Break-Ins," *Washington Post*, March 3, 1975, pp. 1, 6.
40. Defense Intelligence Agency, *Defense Intelligence Agency Review and Analysis of the General Intelligence Career Development Program (ICDP) Annual Status Report for FY 1980 and FY 1981.* (Washington, D.C.: DIA, 1982), p. III–12.

7 IMAGING AND SIGNALS INTELLIGENCE

Technical intelligence collection activities can be traced back to the latter part of the nineteenth and early years of the twentieth century. The development of radio led to its use for military and diplomatic communications, which led in turn to the interception and deciphering of those communications. The invention of the airplane was followed in World War I by the development of photographic reconnaissance techniques.

Technical intelligence collection techniques were developed further in World War II. Indeed, the interception of German military communications played a crucial role in the outcome of the war. Further, development of techniques such as radar demonstrated the feasibility of producing information about foreign military weapons systems by electronic means.

However, it was not until the postwar period that technical intelligence attained its preeminence. The ability to develop a detailed, if not complete, picture of the Soviet order of battle by means of such things as satellite and radar had far-reaching implications. The intelligence produced by imaging and signals intelligence systems is of such quality that significant information concerning Soviet strategic capabilities can be obtained. Consequently, participation in arms limitation agreements and avoidance of unnecessary weapons programs becomes far more feasible (if not inevitable) than would be the case otherwise.

IMAGING

The sensors deployed on photographic reconnaissance satellites may include more than photographic equipment. Hence, the term "photographic reconnaissance satellite" could be misleading. Photography is only one means, albeit the most significant, of obtaining imagery. Imagery includes pictures obtained by photography as well as picturelike representations using other sensor systems.

The basic difference between alternative means of obtaining imagery is that they rely on different portions of the electromagnetic spectrum to produce images. Photographic equipment is sensitive to electromagnetic radiation with a wavelength between 0.0004 mm and 0.00075 mm—the visible light portion of the spectrum.[1]

Photographic equipment can be of either the film-based or television types. A conventional camera records on film the varying light levels reflected from a scene and all of the separate objects in that scene. On the other hand, an electro-optical camera works by converting the varying light levels into electrical signals. A numerical value is assigned to each of the signals—called picture elements or pixels. The process transforms a picture (analog) image to a digital image which can then be transmitted electrically to distant points. The signal can then be reconstructed from the digital to the analog format. The analog signal can then be displayed on a video screen or made into a photograph.[2]

Imagery can also be obtained by infrared photography, which uses radiation in a portion of the near-infrared segment of the electromagnetic spectrum to produce imagery. Unlike the portion used by photographic equipment, infrared photography is not visible to the human eye. At the same time, infrared photography, like visible light photography, depends on the reflective properties of objects rather than their emission of radiation.[3]

Color infrared film is also known as "false color" film because the objects are recorded in different colors than they appear in nature. Thus, healthy vegetation appears in exotic magenta-red tones, and cut vegetation does not reflect infrared radiation at all.[4] Such film can be used as a means of detecting camouflaged field installations, weapons, or vehicles.

Other sensors are employed to obtain imagery from the mid and far infrared portion of the electromagnetic spectrum. Thus, thermal infrared scanners work at long wavelengths and produce imagery via the radiation (heat) emitted by objects. Such devices can detect buried structures, such as missile silos, or underground construction by measuring temperature differences between targets and the earth's surface.[5] Since infrared photography and thermal infrared scanners do not depend on visible light to develop imagery, these techniques can be employed during darkness.[6] However, as with visible light photography, infrared imagery is dependent on the sky being relatively free of cloud cover. Further, the resolution of infrared photography is substantially poorer than that of visible light photography.

A means of producing imagery in the presence of cloud cover is imaging radar (*ra*dio *d*etection *a*nd *r*anging). Radar imagery is produced by bouncing radio waves off an area or object. The data concerning the time required for the pulses to return is used to produce an image. Since radio waves are not attenuated by the water vapor in the atmosphere, they are able to penetrate cloud cover.[7]

In addition to the basic sensors that can be used to produce imagery, there are several means of enhancing the effectiveness of the sensor-produced data. Multispectral scanners use separate lenses to shoot several pictures simultaneously, each in a different region of the visible light and photographic infrared bands. Special coloring and combination of the multiple images reveals camouflaged military facilities that regular photos would conceal.[8]

Image enhancement pulls out more submerged detail. Computers disassemble a picture into millions of electronic Morse Code pulses and then use mathematical formulas to manipulate the color contrast and intensity of each spot. Each image can be reassembled in various ways to highlight special features and objects that were hidden in the original image.[9]

A third technique is optical subtraction. Electronic optical subtraction of earlier pictures from later ones makes unchanged buildings or landscapes in a scene disappear while new objects, such as missile silos under construction, stand out.[10]

The ultimate utility of any imaging satellite is a function of several factors — the most prominent being resolution. Resolution can be defined as the minimum size that an object must be in order to be measurable and identifiable by photo analysts.[11] The smaller the resolution, the greater the detail that can be extracted from a photo. It should be noted that resolution is a product of several factors — the optical or imaging system, atmospheric conditions, and orbital parameters, for example.[12]

The degree of resolution required depends on the specificity of the intelligence desired. Five different interpretation tasks have been differentiated. Detection involves the location of a class of units, objects, or activity of military interest. General identification involves the determination of general target type. Precise identification involves discrimination within target type of known types. Description involves specification of the size-dimension, configuration-layout, components-construction, and number of units. Technical Intelligence involves determination of the specific characteristics and performance capabilities of weapons and equipment.[13] Table 7-1 gives estimates of resolution capability required for the interpretation tasks.

Factors other than resolution that are considered significant in evaluating the utility of an imaging satellite include coverage speed, readout speed, analysis speed, reliability, and enhancement capability. Coverage speed is the area that can be surveyed in a given time, readout speed is the speed with which the information is processed into a form that is meaningful to photo interpreters, and reliability is the fraction of time the system produces useful data. Enhancement capability refers to whether the initial images can be enhanced to draw out more useful data.[14]

Table 7-1. Resolution Required for Different Levels of Precision.

Target	Detection	General Identification	Precise Identification	Description	Technical Intelligence
Bridge	20 ft.	15 ft.	5 ft.	3 ft.	1 ft.
Communications radar/radio	10 ft./10 ft.	3 ft./5 ft.	1 ft./1 ft.	6 in./6 in.	1.5 in./6 in.
Supply dump	5 ft.	2 ft.	1 ft.	1 in.	1 in.
Troop units (bivouac, road)	20 ft.	7 ft.	4 ft.	1 ft.	3 in.
Airfield facilities	20 ft.	15 ft.	10 ft.	1 ft.	6 in.
Rockets and artillery	3 ft.	2 ft.	6 in.	2 in.	.4 in.
Aircraft	15 ft.	5 ft.	3 ft.	6 in.	1 in.
Command and control hq.	10 ft.	5 ft.	3 ft.	6 in.	1 in.
Missile sites (SSM/SAM)	10 ft.	5 ft.	2 ft.	1 ft.	3 in.
Surface ships	25 ft.	15 ft.	2 ft.	1 ft.	3 in.
Nuclear weapons components	8 ft.	5 ft.	1 ft.	2 in.	.4 in.
Vehicles	5 ft.	2 ft.	1 ft.	2 in.	1 in.
Land minefields	30 ft.	20 ft.	3 ft.	1 in.	—
Ports and harbors	100 ft.	50 ft.	20 ft.	10 ft.	1 ft.
Coasts and landing beaches	100 ft.	15 ft.	10 ft.	5 ft.	3 in.
Railroad yards and shops	100 ft.	50 ft.	20 ft.	5 ft.	2 ft.
Roads	30 ft.	20 ft.	6 ft.	2 ft.	6 in.
Urban area	200 ft.	100 ft.	10 ft.	10 ft.	1 ft.
Terrain	—	300 ft.	15 ft.	5 ft.	6 in.
Surfaced submarines	100 ft.	20 ft.	5 ft.	3 ft.	1 in.

Source: Adapted from U.S. Congress, Senate Committee on Commerce, Science, and Transportation, *NASA Authorization for Fiscal Year 1978, Part 3* (Washington, D.C.: U.S. Government Printing Office, 1977), pp. 1642–43; and Bhupendra Jasani, ed., *Outer Space – A New Dimension in the Arms Race* Cambridge, Mass.: Oelgeschlager, Gunn & Hain, 1982), p. 47.

Imaging sensors can be carried aboard three types of vehicles: spacecraft, aircraft, Remotely Piloted Vehicles or drones. It was not until October 1, 1978 in a speech at Cape Canaveral, Florida, that a U.S. President acknowledged that the United States had been using space satellites to conduct photographic reconnaissance.[15] U.S. development and employment of satellites for photographic reconnaissance had not been officially acknowledged for seventeen years—since the very beginning of the program's operation—although the program was well known and often written about.

It was on March 16, 1955 that the Air Force issued "General Operational Requirement No. 80," a formal requirements document calling for the development of a photographic reconnaissance satellite.[16] Martin, RCA, and Lockheed participated in the competition that followed, Lockheed being the winner. Thus, on October 29, 1956 the Air Force awarded Lockheed a contract for the development of Weapons System 117L, the Advance Reconnaissance System or Pied Piper.[17]

The Pied Piper project was revealed in an article in *Aviation Week and Space Technology* on October 14, 1957.[18] This revelation created concern over the secrecy of the reconnaissance satellite program. Combined with the belief that the Pied Piper technology could not produce a near-term satellite (to match the Soviet Sputnik), this concern led to consideration of alternative courses of action. One alternative was to accept the Army's proposal for development of a reconnaissance satellite. An Army briefing on November 10, 1957 made the case for 500-pound Army photo intelligence satellite that would orbit at 300 miles.[19]

A more attractive proposal was made by the Central Intelligence Agency, which had experience in the development of a secret photo intelligence system (the U–2) and could provide funding directly from the Director of Central Intelligence's (DCI's) Contingency Fund. Thus, in February 1958, President Eisenhower approved project CORONA, with the expectation that it would result in an operational photographic reconnaissance satellite employing a recoverable capsule system by the spring of 1959.[20]

While the CIA pursued the objective of a recoverable film satellite, the Air Force considered other options in the belief that a recoverable system was not a near-term possibility. The options considered by the Air Force were a conventional camera system and a television camera system. The television option had been rejected in August 1957, after a study by RCA had shown that resolution would be extremely poor.[21] Instead, the decision was made to develop a film-scanning technique in which a conventional camera is used to photograph the target. The film was to be developed on board and scanned by a fine light beam, the resulting signal being transmitted to a receiving station on the ground, where it would be used to build up a picture.[22] While the scanning process would somewhat degrade picture quality, it was expected to be far superior to television.[23]

The ultimate result of those R&D projects was the Air Force's Satellite and Missile Observation System (SAMOS) and the CIA's Keyhole-4 (KH-4)/CORONA Satellite. SAMOS 1, launched on October 11, 1960, did not achieve orbit, but SAMOS 2, launched on January 31, 1961, did. Its orbit was inclined 97.4 degrees to take it over the Soviet Union and China, with a perigee of 296 miles and an apogee of 348 miles.[24] It has been estimated by some that SAMOS's/radio-transmitted pictures had a resolution of twenty feet from 300 miles; later SAMOS resolution was in the five-to-ten-foot range.[25]

According to some accounts, SAMOS produced a significant and immediate payoff. Philip Klass suggests that SAMOS-2 transmitted over 1,000 photos before its transmitter was turned off and these photos led to a sharp reduction—from 120 to 60—of Soviet ICBM strength. Freedman, on the other hand, suggests that the SAMOS photos were of extremely poor quality and that the program was, in general, a failure—a view confirmed by former CIA officials involved with the program.[26]

The purpose of the SAMOS satellite was to provide the United States with an area surveillance photographic reconnaissance satellite—a satellite the cameras of which could cover large areas in a short period of time. On the other hand, the CORONA program, which was conducted under cover of the Discoverer experimental satellite program, was designed to provide a close-look, higher resolution capability. This capability was attained on March 7, 1962, when a KH-4 was placed in an orbit with a 157-mile perigee and 423-mile apogee at an inclination of 90.98 degrees.[27]

As of 1983, the United States was operating its fourth generation of area surveillance satellite and third generation close-look satellite. The fourth generation area surveillance satellite was introduced in 1971 and has been nicknamed "Big Bird" but is officially the Keyhole-9 (KH-9).

The KH-9 was developed initially as a back-up to the Air Force's Manned Orbiting Laboratory (MOL), a program to test man's usefulness in space. A contract was awarded to Lockheed's Missile and Space Division to develop the system which was given the code number 612.[28] By 1967 the design was set well enough to permit the Air Force to contract for a launch vehicle: the Titan IIID. In 1968 its code number was changed to 467. With cancellation of the MOL in 1969, 467 became a primary rather than back-up system.[29]

The first launch of a KH-9 took place on June 15, 1971 and had a lifetime of fifty-two days. The spacecraft is reported to weigh approximately 30,000 pounds and to be fifty feet long and ten feet in diameter.[30] It has been reported to carry infrared and multispectral scanners in addition to a conventional photographic camera.[31] It carries four returnable film capsules which are recovered either during descent or afterward by frogmen.[32]

Big Bird satellites are launched into a north-south polar orbit with an apogee of approximately 155 miles and a perigee of about 100 miles. Its inclination is approximately 96.4 degrees, taking it over the Soviet Union and China.[33] The north-south polar orbit is also a sun-synchronous orbit; hence, each daylight pass over an area is made at an identical sun-angle, avoiding differences in pictures of the same area that result from different sun-angles. Each area is overflown twice a day—once in daylight and once in darkness.[34] The ground track repeats every 3.5 days—that is, Big Bird passes over the same territory every 3.5 days.[35]

Initial reports concerning Big Bird suggested that it was to be a SIGINT (Signals Intelligence) satellite.[36] Subsequent reports suggested that it was equipped with both close-look and area surveillance cameras as well as infrared and multispectral scanners.[37] Most recent reports, however, describe it as purely an area surveillance satellite.[38]

The lifetime of the KH-9 has increased dramatically since its initial use. As noted above, the lifetime of the first satellite was 52 days. Lifetimes of the next four launches were 40 days, 68 days, 90 days, and 71 days, respectively. By 1974-75 lifetimes were in the area of 150 days. By 1977 a lifetime of 180 days was attainable, and the Big Bird launched on June 18, 1980 had a lifetime of 261 days. The most recent Big Bird, the eighteenth, was launched on June 20, 1983 and had lifetime of over 300 days.[39]

Big Bird satellites have overflown areas of interest at times of particular concern: May 16 to 24, 1974, during which time the Indian nuclear test occurred; July 14 to 28, 1974, during which a crisis over Cyprus occurred; and July 1977, when South Africa was possibly planning a nuclear test.

The third generation close-look (high resolution) satellites, known as the Keyhole-8 (KH-8), have been launched by a Titan 3B–Agena D rocket. Dimensions of the spacecraft have been given as 24 feet long with a diameter of 4.5 feet and a weight of 6,600 pounds.[40] This satellite has had a significantly shorter lifetime than the KH-9—approximately eighty days. This represents a significant increase from the 1966 close-look satellites initially launched by the Titan 3B–Agena D. Its orbit has included a 77-mile perigee and 215-mile apogee, with a 96.4 degree inclination. Thus, it has flown along the same path as the Big Bird satellites but closer to the ground, film being returned in at least two reentry vehicles which are recovered in midair by Lockheed C-130s stationed at Hickam Air Force Base (AFB), Hawaii. The resolution of the photographic images has been estimated at six inches.[41]

The three most recent KH-8 launches are interesting in different respects. The launch of February 28, 1981 (1981-19A) corresponded to a buildup of Soviet forces near the Polish border that was reaching its peak.[42] The launch of January 21, 1982 (1982-6A) has been *assumed* to be close-look satellite, as it was launched on Titan 3B–Agena D and entered into an 88-by-332-mile orbit with a 97.32 degree inclination—characteristics indicative of a close-look satellite. The satellite's mission has been reported to include producing pictures of a suspected Libyan troop buildup and TU-22 Blinder bombers amassed along Libya's borders with Chad and the Sudan.[43] However, after its initial orbits the satellite subsequently moved in sharp leaps to an orbit of 350 by 415 miles, far higher than that for a photo reconnaissance satellite and more typical of an electronic ferret. Specifically, twenty-four hours after launch, a major two-burn manuever was performed, raising its orbit from 109 by 339 miles to 346 by 403 miles. Subsequently, on January 29 the satellite's perigee was raised to 364 miles, and over the next thirty-nine days it adjusted its orbit until it was in a 389-by-409-mile orbit.

Following a small manuever on March 21, it emitted three objects into orbits similar to that of the main satellite. Another object was emitted on May 3. After 122 days in orbit and seventeen manuevers, the satellite was deorbited on May 23, 1982. In that the satellite maintained a sun-synchronous orbit, it has been speculated that the mission involved a test of cameras for the KH-11 follow-on system.[44] The most recent KH-8 launch occurred on April 15, 1983, the spacecraft being launched into an 84-by-192-mile orbit with an inclination of 96.53 degrees.[45]

Both the Big Bird and KH-8 systems was slated to be phased out by the end of 1984. The decision to terminate them is due largely to the successful development and operation of the Keyhole-11 (KH-11) spacecraft, first introduced in December 1976.

The KH-11 was developed by TRW under the code number 1010.[46] Unlike the KH-8 or KH-9 satellites, the KH-11 transmits its pictures in real time, probably either to a facility at Fort Belvoir, Virginia or to the Defense Special Missile and Astronautics Center at Fort Meade.[47] Instead of using film, the KH-11 converts its pictures into digital radio pulses and transmits immediately to a Satellite Data System spacecraft, which relays them to a Washington-area ground station.[48] Although the KH-11 has high resolution, it is not as good as that of the close-look satellite. Lower resolution results from a combination of factors— its higher orbit as well as the transmission of pictures rather than use of a film-based system.

As with the Big Bird, the KH-11 is launched by a Titan 3D booster.[49] As with the other imaging spacecraft, the KH-11 flies in a north-south sun-synchronous polar orbit that covers each area twice a day with an inclination of 97 degrees.[50] It is sixty-four feet long and weighs 30,000 pounds.[51]

Although the KH-11 has inferior resolution to the close-look satellite, it has an important advantage over both film-based systems with regard to lifetimes. The lifetime of the first KH-11, launched on December 19, 1976, was 770 days—three times greater than that of the longest Big Bird. The second KH-11, launched on June 14, 1978, had a lifetime of 760 days. The third KH-11, launched on February 7, 1980, had a lifetime of 555 days—the shortest of any KH-11. The shortened lifetime may have been a product of its being maneuvered to cover aspects of the Iran-Iraq war in 1980, during which time it malfunctioned.[52]

The two most recent KH-11 launches occurred on September 3, 1981 and November 17, 1982. The 1981 launch placed the fourth KH-11 into a 153-by-

329-mile orbit inclined 96.99 degrees. The 1982 launch placed the fifth KH-11 in a 169-by-311-mile orbit inclined 97 degrees.[53]

Several accomplishments of the KH-11 have been noted in the press. According to one report, a KH-11 revealed that the Soviet Union was constructing a new super submarine and a new miniaircraft carrier and disproved reports of a new Soviet CBW center by showing it actually to be a reserve arms storage facility. A KH-11 also apparently discovered an SS-20 ballistic missile in its canister alongside an encapsulated SS-16 ICBM. It has been suggested that the Soviets were seeking to have Soviet reconnaissance satellites compare the two so that steps could be taken to increase the similarity and hence increase the chances for successful disguise.[54] Finally, the KH-11 was also used during the 1980 Iranian crisis to try to determine exactly where in the U.S. Embassy in Teheran U.S. personnel were being held.[55]

With two systems on the verge of elimination, there appear to be at least two imaging systems under development. One is a 32,000-pound follow-on to the KH-11 which will have resolution equal to the KH-8 satellite.[56] The first space shuttle launched from Vandenberg AFB in 1986 will carry a Department of Defense (DOD) Reference Mission 4 (DRM-4) satellite, which is the code term for the improved KH-11.[57] Once these new spacecraft are operational in 1986, plans call for launch of an individual satellite into about a 150-nautical-mile polar orbit. The same shuttle mission then would retrieve another spacecraft that had been in orbit for some time and return it to earth for refurbishment.[58]

In addition, there are plans for at least one imaging radar satellite.[59] Such a satellite has been considered in the past; in 1964 the Air Force planned to develop a recoverable payload satellite equipped with high-resolution radar for ground mapping.[60] The presently planned system is to be directed at Soviet and Warsaw Pact targets—targets often obscured by cloud cover.[61] Intelligence gathered will be relayed through the Tracking Data and Relay System Satellite to a ground station in White Sands, New Mexico.[62]

Satellites are the most productive of U.S. photo reconnaissance/imaging collection systems—in terms of being able to overfly any location without hindrance and, in the case of the KH-11, being able to provide information almost instantaneously. However, satellites possess certain limitations. They cannot, even if already in orbit, be dispatched to cover events on short notice. Further, such systems are extraordinarily expensive and priorities must be set; inevitably, some areas are neglected. Aircraft reconnaissance systems can supplement satellite coverage as well as provide a quick reaction capability.

The United States relies on two aircraft for strategic photo reconnaissance collection activities: the SR-71 and the U-2. The SR-71 (SR for Strategic Reconnaissance) was known as OX CART when it was managed by the National Reconnaissance Office (NRO). At least thirty of the SR-71s, nicknamed Blackbird's for their black epoxy heat-resistant paint job, are thought to have been built.[63] At present, there are nine SR-71s operational.[64]

Built by Lockheed, the SR-71, originally known as the A-12, first became operational on January 7, 1966 with the delivery of plane 64-17956 to the 4200th Strategic Reconnaissance Wing at Beale AFB, California.[65] It is capable of attaining Mach 3 speed (over 2,000 miles per hour) and a height of 85,000 feet. It has a wingspan of 55 feet, 7 inches; a length of 107 feet, 5 inches; and a height of 18 feet, 6 inches.[66] The plane is armed with a variety of electronic warfare material, including a radar detector, and possibly Electronic Counter-measures (ECMs) which allows it to wipe itself off opposition radar screens.[67]

Flying at 85,000 feet the SR-71 can film 60,000 square miles in one hour.[68] It is equipped with three high-power cameras that can map the United States in three passes as well as three-dimensional filming equipment that can cover 150 square miles so precisely as to locate a mailbox on a country road.[69] It is also reportedly equipped with a synthetic aperture radar for high-altitude night imaging.[70] In addition to the SR-71s stationed at Beale AFB, permanent SR-71 detachments (consisting of two to three planes) are stationed at Kadena AFB, Okinawa and RAF Mildenhall, England.[71] The SR-71s at Mildenhall or additional SR-71s might be used for target mapping in support of the Pershing II missile.[72]

An SR-71 photographed the entire first Chinese nuclear test.[73] Until 1971 it was used constantly to conduct surveillance operations over the People's Republic of China (PRC). These operations were suspended as part of the agreement to open up relations with the PRC. Other prominent Southeast Asian targets have included North Korea, Vietnam, and Laos. The SR-71 was used to gather photographic intelligence concerning the Sontay POW camp in preparation for the raid that was designed to rescue the POWs.[74]

Outside of Asia, the SR-71 has been used for reconnaissance over Cuba and the Middle East. During the 1973 Arab-Israeli war, an SR-71 was sent to overfly the Negev desert on the basis of information that Israel was preparing to arm its Jericho missiles with nuclear warheads.[75]

The SR-71 is the second strategic reconnaissance aircraft built by Lockheed. Prior to the 1966 deployment of the SR-71, the primary U.S. strategic reconnaissance aircraft was the U-2, codenamed IDEALIST. More than fifty-five U-2s in various versions are believed to have been built.[76] In 1984 there were eight U-2s in the U.S. arsenal, and Lockheed is under contract to build at least two more over the next two years.[77]

Development of the U-2 by the CIA and Lockheed Aircraft began in 1954 at the urging of the Eisenhower Surprise Attack Panel. It became operational in 1956 and began overflying the Soviet Union that year. The U-2 brought back significant intelligence on airfields, aircraft, missile testing and training, nuclear weapons storage, submarine production, atomic production, and aircraft deployment.[78] The center of U-2 operations against the Soviet Union, was Adana, Turkey, where U-2 operations were conducted by the 10-10 Detachment under the cover of the Second Weather Observational Squadron (Provisional).

It was the flight of May 1, 1960 that began in Peshawar, Pakistan and was to conclude 3,788 miles later in Bodo, Norway that brought the U-2 to world attention.[79] The plane was shot down but its pilot, Francis Gary Powers, survived to stand trial.[80] Powers's plane contained a camera with a rotating 944.6-mm lens which peered out through seven holes in the belly of the plane. It would take 4,000 paired pictures of a 125-mile-wide, 2,174-mile-long strip of the Soviet Union.

The U-2R (the main present version) has a wingspan of 103 feet, a height of 16 feet, and a length of 63 feet. It has a range of 3,000 miles and a maximum speed of 528 knots at an altitude of 40,000 feet. Its operational ceiling is more than 70,000 feet.[81] U-2Rs are capable of slant photography—looking in the target area at an angle. Thus, one can be flying along the borders of a region and still get pictures inside those borders.[82]

U-2s have been flown from bases in Cyprus, Turkey, Pakistan, Japan, Formosa, Okinawa, the Philippines, Alaska, West Germany, and England.[83] The flights provided photographic intelligence coverage of not only the Soviet Union but the PRC, North Korea, and the Middle East. With the advent of satellite reconnaissance capabilities as well as the SR-71, reliance on U-2 coverage was reduced. However, U-2s still provide coverage in some areas. The U-2s photographic capabilities have been used to document the buildup of military forces in Nicaragua and have been making regular flights taking pictures of military construction and arms depots. These flights have operated (most probably) from bases in Texas and Patrick AFB, Florida.[84] U-2s are also used for overhead reconnaissance directed against other targets in the Caribbean and Central America—for example, Cuba and Grenada. At present, U-2s fly from bases in the United States, Europe (RAF Akrotiri in Cyprus, RAF Mildenhall in England), and Asia (Osan in Korea and Kadena on Okinawa).[85]

In some cases, neither satellites nor aircraft provide satisfactory means of conducting overhead reconnaissance. As noted above, satellites are somewhat inflexible in that missions must be planned in advance and once in orbit there is a limited capability to reorient their targets, particularly within the space of several hours. Although aircraft can compensate for these deficiencies, they too have their limitations. Overflights using SR-71s and U-2s are politically sensitive operations and create the possibility of an international incident if they go down—whether due to hostile action or malfunction.

An alternative to both satellite and aircraft reconnaissance is the use of Remotely Piloted Vehicles (RPVs) or drones. RPVs can be launched from carrier aircraft and directed toward targets of interest. With no crew, RPVs or drones can be used for extremely low altitude photography when required, and they are expendable. Such craft were used extensively during the Vietnam War as well as to overfly the Chinese mainland. One drone, the D-21, was used in combination with the SR-71.[86] At present, the United States does not appear to have any strategic reconnaissance RPVs or drones in operation or development.

SIGNALS INTELLIGENCE

Signals intelligence (SIGINT) is a term that encompasses a wide variety of technical intelligence. The most general division between types of signals intelligence distinguishes between Communications Intelligence (COMINT) and Electronic Intelligence (ELINT).

COMINT is technical and intelligence information derived from the interception of encrypted or unencrypted communications.[87] These communications include diplomatic, commercial, political, and military communications conducted by a variety of means—telephone, radio-telephone, radio satellite, landline, or undersea cable.

The use of microwave relay stations for transmission of telephone, telex, and other means of communication has made interception very feasible. As one observer has written with regard to microwave relay stations,

> With modern communications, "target" messages travel not simply over individually tappable wires like those that connect the ordinary telephone, but as part of entire message streams, which can contain up to 970 individual message circuits, and have voice, telegram, telex and high speed data bunched together.[88]

Satellite transmissions can be intercepted from various ground locations. Ground stations that send messages to satellites have antennas that can direct the signals to the satellite with great accuracy; satellite antennas, on the other hand, are smaller and the signals they send back to earth are less narrowly focused—perhaps covering several thousand square miles.[89]

Landline and undersea cables are less susceptible to interception. Tapping cable requires physical access to the cable and operation and maintenance of the tapping equipment at the point of access. This might be an unattainable requirement with respect to hardened and protected internal landlines—the type of landline that carries much high-priority secret command and control communications. Undersea cables are more vulnerable since the messages transmitted by them undersea are then transmitted by microwave relay once the cable reaches land.[90]

ELINT—technical and intelligence information derived from foreign noncommunications electromagnetic radiations emanating from other than atomic detonations or radioactive sources—also encompasses a wide variety of technical intelligence.[91] One prominent example of ELINT is RADINT—the intelligence derived from monitoring the electronic emanations of the radars of foreign nations, particularly those of the Soviet Union and the PRC. The intelligence derived allows for the mapping of locations and hence targeting of early warning (EW) stations, air defense systems, antiballistic missile (ABM) systems, airfields, air bases, satellite tracking and control stations, and ships at sea. Recording their frequencies, signal strengths, pulse lengths, pulse rates, and other specifications allows for the ability to jam the transmitters in the event of war. Knowing the location of air defense systems would give the United States and allied bomber fleets a better chance of evading those systems en route to their targets. Monitoring Soviet radar systems has an arms control verification aspect, since the 1972 treaty between the United States and Soviet Union on the limitation of ABM systems restricts the use of radars in an ABM mode.

ELINT also includes the intelligence derived from nonimaging radar systems. Such systems do not have adequate resolution to produce images but can detect the presence of objects. They can determine the distance between the radar and the object, altitude, and size as well as speed and directional data.[92]

Another subcategory of ELINT is Telemetry Intelligence (TELINT). Telemetry is the set of signals by which a missile, stage of a missile, or missile warhead sends back to earth data about its performance during a test flight. The data relate to features such as structural stress, rocket motor thrust, fuel consumption, guidance system performance, and the physical conditions of the ambient environment. Intercepted telemetry can provide intelligence on such questions as the number of warheads carried by a given missile, the range of the missile, its payload and throw-weight, and hence the probable size of its warheads and accuracy with which the warheads are guided at the point of release from the missile's post-boost vehicles.[93]

TELINT is also a subcategory of Foreign Instrumentation Signals Intelligence (FISINT). Foreign Instrumentation Signals are electromagnetic emissions associated with the testing and operational deployment of aerospace, surface, and subsurface systems that may have military or civilian application. FISINT includes, but is not limited to, signals from telemetry, beaconing, electronic interrogators, tracking/fusing/aiming/command systems, and video data links.[94]

Two further subcategories of SIGINT/ELINT were listed in the proposed National Security Agency (NSA) charter of 1980: information derived from the collection and processing of (1) nonimaging infrared and (2) coherent light signals. The former involves sensors that can detect the absence or presence and movement of an object or event via temperature. The latter term is another expression for laser and hence refers to the interception of laser communications, such as future communications between Soviet satellites and submarines using blue green laser communications techniques.[95]

Collection of signals intelligence is achieved by a multitude of means—satellite, aircraft, ships, submarine, and ground facilities. There are basically two types of SIGINT satellites: high-orbiting satellites with apogees over 20,000 miles and low-orbiting satellites with apogees under 1,000 miles. The first U.S. SIGINT satellite was launched in March 1962 and weighed one ton. In 1963 it was replaced by a 3,300-pound vehicle that operated at an altitude of approximately 300 miles. In 1968 a 4,400-pound version succeeded it in approximately the same orbit.[96] For the seven years following its inception, the SIGINT satellite program exclusively involved low-orbiting satellites. But with the improvement of interception technology, SIGINT satellites operating at high altitudes became a possibility. Today it is the high-orbiting satellites that form the basis of the U.S. SIGINT satellite program.

The United States is presently operating in high-altitude orbits at least three SIGINT satellites—Rhyolite, Chalet, and a third the codename of which is unknown. Rhyolite, developed by the CIA and built by TRW, was described in a TRW briefing as being a "multipurpose covert electronic surveillance system."[97]

Rhyolite is capable of being targeted against telemetry, radars, and communications. Rhyolite's communications intercept capability against Soviet and Chinese telephonic and radio communications extends across the VHF, UHF, and microwave frequency bands.[98] With respect to microwave frequencies, Robert Lindsey has written that the Rhyolite satellites "could monitor Communist microwave radio and long-distance telephone traffic over much of the European land mass, eavesdropping on a Soviet Commissar in Moscow talking to his mistress in Yalta or on a general talking to his lieutenants across the great continent."[99]

Additionally, the Rhyolite radio-telephonic (R/T) traffic intercepts may include early morning stock exchange and other business calls. Interception of commercial communications might include those transmitted by INTELSAT satellites.[100] These satellites, first launched in 1965, have a capacity for the simultaneous transmission of 11,000 two-way telephone conversations. In the VHF–UHF range, Rhyolite satellites regularly monitor the walkie-talkie traffic between aircraft and air traffic controllers.[101]

The highest priority of the Rhyolite program has always been telemetry interception. The telemetry from Soviet missile tests is generally transmitted on about fifty channels. It is frequency modulated (FM) and ranges in frequency from 150 MHz in the VHF band to perhaps 3 GHz in the S-band, thus substantially falling in the microwave range.[102]

In the initial stages of the program, Rhyolite had significant success in the area, for it was not until 1975, when informed of Rhyolite's capability by Christopher Boyce and Andrew Daulton Lee, that (according to several sources) the Soviet Union abandoned the conventional wisdom that signals at VHF and higher frequencies could not be intercepted by satellites at geostationary altitudes. However, no attempt was made to encrypt the telemetry data until mid-1977, or six months after the arrest of Boyce and Lee.[103] Presumably, the Soviets feared the encryption might give away Soviet acquisition of material on Rhyolite.

At the same time, it should be noted that former CIA Director Stansfield Turner, in response to being asked whether the information passed by Boyce and Lee led to Soviet encryption, replied "probably not."[104] The encryption has reached the point where, according to one U.S. official, the Soviets are encrypting "essentially all the telemetry" on two new weapons systems (an ICBM and an SLBM), making it "almost impossible to determine anything of significance."[105] Perhaps this represents the last stage in a series of actions begun in 1977 to encrypt telemetry—an action possibly based on a decision to keep as secret as possible the characteristics of the next generation of strategic weapons.

According to a 1979 account there were, as of May 1979, four Rhyolite launches: March 6, 1973; May 23, 1977; December 11, 1977; and April 7, 1978.[106] According to this account, two of the satellites are stationed near the Horn of Africa, primarily to intercept telemetry signals transmitted by liquid-fueled ICBMs launched from Tyuratam in a northeasterly direction toward the Kamchatka Peninsula; two stationed further east are intended to monitor telemetry from the SS-16 and SS-20 missiles launched from Plesetsk in north Russia.[107]

It appears that the March 6, 1973 launch was actually the second launch. Christopher Boyce was told at a briefing in late 1974 that the first Rhyolite satellite had been in operation "for almost four years."[108] An Australian computer operator who began work at Pine Gap, the Australian control station for Rhyolite, in November 1970 has stated that the first Rhyolite satellite had become operational just at the time of his arrival.[109] Additionally, a former U.S. intelligence official has stated that Rhyolite ground facilities were installed in Britain in 1970.[110] Based on launch vehicle and orbital parameters, the most likely satellite is the one designated 1970-46A, launched on June 18, 1970.

All known Rhyolite launches have employed an Atlas-Agena D booster to propel the spacecraft into orbit and have taken place from the Eastern Test Range at Cape Canaveral. Little is known about the physical characteristics of the Rhyolite spacecraft. One source lists it at 1,540 pounds, five feet seven inches in length, four feet seven inches in diameter, and cylindrical.[111] The main antenna is a concave dish more than seventy feet in diameter, backed and supported by a framework to which are also attached a number of other appendages, including large panels of solar cells and several lesser antennas.[112]

The Rhyolite project was described by former CIA official Victor Marchetti in the following terms:

This was a very interesting project, a very much advanced project in terms of technology and a very desirable project because getting information of the type that we wanted and needed on Soviet ICBM testing, anti-ballistic missile programs, anti-satellite programs and the like, much of this activity of course takes place in the Eastern Siberia and Central Asia, getting information on the Chinese ICBM program.[113]

Rhyolite is not the only high-orbiting U.S. SIGINT satellite. In June 1979 the existence of a satellite codenamed Chalet, apparently in geosynchronous orbit, which was being reconfigured to give it a capacity to intercept Soviet missile telemetry, was revealed.[114] Chalet launches, from the Eastern Test Range and employing Titan 3C boosters, apparently occurred on June 10, 1978; October 1, 1979; and October 31, 1981.[115]

The third SIGINT satellite is apparently operated under the cover of the Satellite Data System (SDS) program. The known functions of SDS include transmitting KH-11 photography and acting as a communications link (1) for the Strategic Air Command (SAC) bombers flying over the poles and (2) between the Air Force Satellite Test Center in Sunnyvale and the other components of the Air Force Satellite Control Facility.[116] In its highly elliptical orbit of 200-by-24,000 miles, SDS "hovers" over the northern Soviet Union/Arctic for long periods of time. At those times it is ideally suited to receive and transmit photos from the KH-11 as it flies over Russia or to communicate with bombers flying over the Arctic.[117]

No picture of the SDS satellite has ever appeared in published congressional hearings—unlike other "white" (unclassified) satellites. More significantly, in 1979, when five U.S. spacecraft had been launched into the distinctive SDS orbit since 1975, the Air Force Director of C[3] stated that as of 1979 the fourth and fifth satellites were in the process of being *manufactured.*[118] The satellites were not *delivered* until 1980.[119]

In addition to presently operational systems, one or more new systems appear to be in the later stages of development. In the wake of the loss of Iranian ground stations, a revised version of ARGUS was approved.[120] Argus or AR (for Advanced Rhyolite) was intended to be a follow-on to the Rhyolite satellite, with an antenna twice the diameter of Rhyolite's. This revised version may well have already been orbited, possibly early in 1984.

In addition to having high-orbiting SIGINT satellites, the United States also has low-orbiting Ferret satellites. The purpose of these satellites has been to map Soviet, Chinese, and other radars. The radars include Soviet air defense, surface-to-air missiles (SAMs), and early warning radars that operate in the 1-to-50-Hz frequencies. The satellite operates in orbits that, with rare exceptions, are always distinctively higher than those for photo reconnaissance satellites but lower than all other U.S. military satellites.

The Ferret program was initiated in 1962, long before the introduction of high-orbiting SIGINT satellites, with a launch on May 15. The satellite was placed into an orbit with an 82.33 degree inclination, a perigee of 190 miles, and an apogee of 396 miles. This program continued until 1972 with launch of between one and three satellites per year.[121]

In the midst of the original Ferret program, another type of ferret satellite was developed. These satellites were launched "piggyback" with another, larger satellite which was ejected in its own orbit. The first such launch occurred on August 29, 1963. The most recent version of these ferrets have been launched on board KH-9 photo reconnaissance satellites, including the May 11, 1982 launch.

With a 96-degree inclination and orbit of 375 miles, these octagonal satellites weighing 132 pounds continued to map Soviet and Chinese radars.[122]

Since the end of World War II, the United States had relied on aircraft for a significant portion of its SIGINT collection program. In the late 1940s Special Electronic Airborne Operations were flown by Air Force bombers and transports as well as by Navy patrol planes. These operations had the objective of "ferreting out" Soviet radar capabilities for the purpose of developing electronic countermeasures and locating Soviet air defenses.[123]

The procedure and rationale were described in 1960 by two ex-NSA employees, who defected to the Soviet Union, as follows:

In advance of a reconnaissance flight of a United States military plane along the Chinese or Soviet Far Eastern borders, a top-secret message would be sent to Kamiseya and other communications intelligence stations, informing them as to the flight time and course of the plane.

At the designated flight time, monitors at these stations would tune in on the frequencies used by radar reporting stations of the target country, i.e., the Soviet Union or Communist China. At the same time, radio direction finders would tune in on these frequencies to seek out the locations of the radar reporting stations.

Information gathered in this manner would then be forwarded to the National Security Agency. There, analysts study the communications and code systems used by the radar stations. N.S.A. is then able to estimate the degree of alertness, accuracy and efficiency of the radar defenses of the target nation, and it is also able to collect information about the organization of command within the target nation's internal defense system.

After going to work for the National Security Agency, we learned about another type of aerial intelligence mission which involves incursion into the airspace of the target nation. These missions, known as ELINT missions ("electronic intelligence" missions), consist of flights in the immediate proximity of radar installations of the Soviet Union and other countries to obtain data about the physical nature of radiations from radar transmitters. This information is used in an attempt to find ways to render the radar defense system ineffective, for instance through the use of radar jamming devices operating from bases close to the Soviet borders.[124]

Occasionally, such flights ended in disaster. On September 2, 1958 an EC-130 on assignment to the NSA crashed in Soviet Armenia, killing six of the crew of seventeen according to Soviet statements. The fate of the remaining eleven members has never been revealed.[125] According to the secret testimony of Allen Dulles in 1960, released in 1982, a CIA plane with a crew of eight or nine went down in the Caucasus in the late 1950s.[126]

With the development of ferret satellites and changes in the world situation, such provocative missions were curtailed. However, the United States still relies on aircraft for a variety of SIGINT missions. Both the SR-71 and the U-2 aircraft have SIGINT as well as photographic capabilities. The SR-71 signals intelligence capability includes equipment for monitoring radio and radar transmissions.[127] Some of the new SR-71As stationed at Mildenhall have been seen configured for ELINT or COMINT surveillance and have flown missions at regular intervals. Many of these missions spanned in excess of ten hours and involved peripheral flight work along the borders of the Soviet Union and other Warsaw Pact nations.[128] The purpose of these peripheral intelligence missions is to pinpoint locations and characteristics of potentially hostile signal emitters for the same reasons described above.[129]

The U-2 SIGINT capability has been recently upgraded by the addition of the SENIOR RUBY ELINT system.[130] Some of the U-2s that fly from RAF Mildenhall and Akrotiri airfield in Cyprus conduct signals intelligence missions on the periphery of the Soviet Union and Eastern Europe and in the Mediterranean area.[131]

In addition to the U-2 and SR-71 planes used in SIGINT collection, the EC-135, EC-121, and RC-135 have all been used. The EC-121, which has been phased out, was for many years a significant SIGINT collection system.

The plane, which carried a crew of thirty and six tons of electronic equipment, is a derivative of the C-121 super constellation transport and is distinguished by the massive radomes above and below the fuselage. The EC-121 had a crusing speed of 300 mph, produced by its four-piston engines. With a range of 6,500 miles and an ability to stay aloft for twenty hours, it could monitor communications longer and more intensively than a speedier jet.[132]

Because many of the signals to be monitored travel in straight lines rather than bending with the earth's curvature, an airborne collecter sees a much more distant horizon and keeps signals within range for a longer period of time. One EC-121 radar could sweep a 40,000-square-mile area. From the 1950s to the 1970s EC-121s flew the Atlantic and Pacific regularly as radar picket aircraft. The EC-121 first pinpointed a radar site and then, by analyzing the signal picked up, determined just what the particular radar was used for: detecting incoming vehicles, guiding SAMs, controlling nuclear weapons. Its antennas, tuned to a wide range of radio frequencies used in military communications, could overhear conversations between major command posts 200 miles away and thus plot troop movements and combat readiness.[133]

The EC-135 is a modified KC-135 Stratotanker. It is equipped as a flying command post for SAC's airborne alert role. Seven EC-135Ns, also known as Advanced Range Instrumentation Aircraft (ARIA), are equipped as airborne radio and telemetry stations for the Apollo program and have also been used to monitor U.S. and Soviet missile tests and space activities. Eventually, the ARIA fleet will consist of six EC-18B and two EC-135E aircraft.[134]

The most important strategic intelligence collection aircraft devoted solely to SIGINT collection is the RC-135, and it has assumed much of the work of the retired EC-121s. The RC-135, of which there are several versions, is a modified

Boeing 707 which can stay aloft for eighteen hours. It is packed with a variety of equipment for COMINT and ELINT gathering.[135] Some of the RC-135s named RIVET JOINT are equipped with COMBAT SENT—"a classified scientific and technical ELINT system."[136]

Presently, there are eighteen RC-135s in the U.S. inventory.[137] U.S.-based RC-135s include those at Offutt AFB, Nebraska; Eielson AFB, Alaska; and Shemya Island, Alaska.[138] European-based RC-135s include those at RAF Mildenhall, U.K. and Hellenikon, Greece; Asian-based RC-135s are stationed at Kadena AB, Okinawa.[139]

RC-135s based in Alaska are used to monitor Soviet air exercises, missile tests, and the alert status of Soviet defenses. Thus, several RC-135s routinely patrol off the Soviet coast near Kamchatka and the Sakhalin Islands—flying in an elliptical pattern on an average of twenty days or nights a month.[140]

Under normal circumstances, the primary mission of the RC-135 is to document the electronic order of battle of Soviet radar stations, antiaircraft missile bases, and overall Soviet air defense procedures.[141] When a test of a new missile is believed imminent, the recording of telemetry from such a test becomes the primary goal. On the night of August 21, 1983, when the RC-135 from Eielson AFB flew a parallel course to the doomed KAL 007 flight, its objective was interception of telemetry from an anticipated test of an SS-X-24.[142]

An extremely important set of SIGINT collectors are the radars and antennas placed throughout the world—including on the periphery of the Soviet Union and PRC and on the paths of their ballistic missile test trajectories. Among the radars, the most important is the COBRA DANE radar on Shemya Island in the Aleutians, situated 480 nautical miles from Kamchatka Peninsula and the surrounding ocean area—the primary impact point for practically all Soviet missile tests.[143] COBRA DANE is a phased array radar (i.e., it electronically scans the field of view rather than moving an antenna dish across the field of view). The phased array portion is ninety-five feet in diameter and contains 15,360 active radiating elements.[144]

COBRA DANE was designed to track Soviet reentry vehicles during ICBM tests and to track foreign satellites. Specifically, the primary purpose and value of COBRA DANE is

> to acquire precise radar metric and signature data on developing Soviet ballistic missile weapon systems for weapon system characteristics determination. The Soviet developmental test to Kamchatka and the Pacific Ocean provide the U.S. the primary source for collection of this data early in the Soviet developmental program.[145]

From Shemya, COBRA DANE can obtain data on missile trajectories, separation velocities, payload maneuvers, and signature data on reentry vehicles from missiles fired from both the Russian land mass and the Soviet's primary SLBM launch site.[146]

COBRA DANE can detect an object the size of a basketball at a range of 2,000 miles and simultaneously track more than 100 objects. Processed data on objects being tracked are transmitted in real time to the continental United States via the Defense Satellite Communications System and distributed to the NORAD Space Defense Center and the Foreign Technology Division. In the event of a missile attack, the radar would function as an early warning sensor. In this mode, COBRA DANE can detect and track up to 300 objects simultaneously as well as providing predicted impact points for up to 200 objects.[147]

To supplement COBRA DANE, the United States recently deployed another phased array radar, COBRA JUDY, on the U.S.N.S. Observation Island. With its operational base at Pearl Harbor, COBRA JUDY operates in the Pacific Ocean to complement COBRA DANE. The COBRA JUDY system, designated AN/SPQ-11, was designed to monitor the final near-earth trajectories of Soviet reentry test vehicles. That portion of their flight is not visible to COBRA DANE because of line-of-sight constraints imposed by the curvature of the earth.[148]

COBRA TALON is a radar that was first deployed in Thailand in 1972–1973. In 1981 it was relocated at San Miguel in the Philippines in a space surveillance role.[149]

Possibly also part of the COBRA series are the FPS-17 detection and FPS-79 tracking radars located at an Intelligence and Security Command (INSCOM) base near Diyarbakir, Turkey. FPS-79 is part of the Air Force's 466L Electromagnetic Intelligence System and was developed as project BLUE NINE.[150] These radars are targeted against missiles launched from Kapustin Yar and Tyuratam.[151] As discussed below, the FPS-79 has an important space surveillance role.

A second system used for a variety of SIGINT missions is the AN/FLR-9 system, also known as Wullenweber or Circularly Disposed Antenna Array (CDAA). They are designed to locate and intercept signals from the low to high bands. Low-band traffic includes submarine traffic; radio-telephone traffic falls in the high band.[152]

The outermost circle of an AN/FLR-9 is the size of about three football fields—875 feet—and has the shortest antenna of the four rings that constitute the array. This ring consists of 120 equally spaced antenna elements—one for each 3 degrees of azimuth. The second ring consists of a high-band reflector screen which consists of vertical wires suspended from pole-supported horizontal braces. The screen is designed to shield the high-band antenna from signals emanating from any direction other than the one being monitored. The third ring, the elements of which are taller than those of the second, is the low-band receiving array. It is made up of forty equally spaced "folded monoples" similar to the first ring. The fourth and innermost ring is the giant low-band reflector screen, which "looks like an enormous circle of ten-story high telephone poles, with thin copper wires stretched vertically between them and suspended from above."[153]

Each antenna element is connected to a separate buried coaxial cable that terminates inside the operations building located at the center of the array. A goniometer is used to determine which receiving element was the first to have picked up a signal.[154] Inasmuch as the first receiving element to be struck is the one closest to the transmitting station, this will give a vague indication of the location of the transmitting station. Specific locations can be obtained from a number of CDAAs over a wide area.

The United States maintains CDAAs at bases in the Philippines, England (Menwith Hill and Chicksands), Korea, Germany, and Italy (San Vito dei Normanni).[155]

A highly directional antenna system—one that is used against specific targets—is the Rhombic array.[156] Each element or antenna of that array consists of a wire several feet off the ground and attached to four posts spaced in the shape of a diamond, each side being approximately ten feet long. At one end the wire is connected to a coaxial cable that runs underground to a centrally located operations building. The entire array consists of between thirty and forty structures over several hundred acres.

A Rhombic array is located at the Vint Hills Farm, Virginia, an INSCOM station as well as a home of the Army Signal Warfare Laboratory. Among Vint Hills monitoring tasks is the interception of British diplomatic traffic.[157]

The United States also maintains, either at its own bases overseas or in cooperation with several foreign governments, VHF–UHF–SHF receivers capable of intercepting telemetry from Soviet launch sites. Telemetry from missiles launched from Kapustin Yar and Tyuratam are intercepted by the VHF–UHF–SHF receivers at the Karamursel facility. Such receivers may also be present at Iraklion Station, Greece for the same purpose.[158]

At one time, the United States placed great reliance on signals intelligence gathered by ship-based sensors. The United States began by using combat ships in this role. Destroyers and destroyer escorts often carried mobile vans packed with antennas as well as special detachments to operate the equipment.[159] Use of destroyers and destroyer escorts, however, degraded fighting capabilities as combat ships were assigned intelligence missions. Further, some Navy officials felt the stationing of a destroyer off a foreign shore, especially that of a hostile nation, to be provocative.[160] As an alternative to the use of destroyers and other combat ships, the Auxiliary General Technical Research (AGTR) ship was introduced.

AGTRs, which were equipped with a variety of SIGINT equipment, were converted Victory- and Liberty-class vessels of World War II vintage. The first AGTR—the U.S.S. Oxford (AGTR-1)—was commissioned on July 8, 1961. Subsequently, the Georgetown (AGTR-2), Jamestown (AGTR-3), Belmont (AGTR-4), Liberty (AGTR-5), Valdez (AGTR-6), and Muller (AGTR-7) were commissioned for the same purpose.[161]

In 1965 a second set of ships, to be designated Auxiliary General Environmental Research (AGER), were authorized and converted. The ships were built and equipped under the joint command of the Naval Security Group Command, REWSON (Reconnaissance, Electric Warfare, Special Operations, and Naval Intelligence Systems—then subordinate to the Naval Ship Systems Command), and the NSA.[162] They operated under an integrated naval surveillance and intelligence ship program established by the Chief of Naval Operations in August 1965 after coordination with the NSA.[163]

The initial vessel approved for this type of activity of the AGER type was the U.S.S. Banner, subsequently followed by the U.S.S. Pueblo and the U.S.S. Palm Beach. The ships were old World War II converted diesel-driven light-cargo ships approximately 170 feet in length with a maximum speed of thirteen knots and a crusiing speed of ten knots. Each had an estimated range of 4,000 nautical miles.[164]

AGER collection capability was more restricted than AGTR capability, being concerned with SIGINT and hydrographic information. Elimination of AGER and AGTR collection ships resulted from the events of 1967 and 1969. The AGTR U.S.S. Liberty was sunk by Israeli war planes in the midst of the 1967 war. It was alleged by the Israeli government that the ship was mistaken for an Egyptian vessel; others have alleged the attack was deliberate and intended to prevent the United States from learning of Israeli military gains that would lead the United States to pressure Israel into a "premature" cease-fire.[165]

In 1969 the U.S.S. Pueblo was captured by the North Koreans and its crew held hostage. Up to the time of its capture, the Pueblo was involved with the Banner in a threefold mission from January to July 1968 to:

1. determine the nature and extent of naval activity of North Korean ports;
2. sample electronic environment off the east coast of North Korea; and
3. intercept the communications of and conduct surveillance of Soviet naval units.[166]

Shortly after the Pueblo was seized, the U.S.S. Sergeant Joseph P. Muller almost drifted into Cuban waters. When the Muller lost power and started drifting toward Cuban waters, she was given the additional protection of a combat air patrol. After several failures, she was finally towed to safety by the escorting destroyer.[167] Subsequently, the AGERs and AGTRs were decommissioned as intelligence collection vessels.

Since then, the United States has employed two Advanced Range Instrumentation Ships (ARIS) for the collection of foreign intelligence, the use of these ships for intelligence purposes being given the codename COBRA JEAN.[168] The primary missions of the ships are to provide tracking data on U.S. missile and space launches, and they are normally deployed off the Eastern and Western Test Ranges (Cape Canaveral and Vandenberg AFB). They have also been deployed on secondary missions for forty-five-day periods off the Kamchatka Peninsula to collect data on Soviet ballistic missile tests. The ship that is operated off Cape Canaveral is the Redstone. With dimensions of 595 by 75 by 25 feet, it is operated by a crew of 165 and carries approximately 450 tons of electronic equipment.[169]

More recently, the United States has employed Spruance-class destroyers and frigates to collect intelligence concerning Nicaragua and El Salvador. The 7,800-ton destroyer Deyo, as well as her sister ship Caron, were stationed in the Gulf of Fonzeca.[170] The ships can monitor suspect shipping, intercept communications and encrypted messages, and probe the shore surveillance and defense capabilities of other nations. With regard to the latter use, they can induce a nation to switch on shore-to-sea, ship-to-ship, and air-to-sea radar.[171]

In addition to being in the Gulf of Fonzeca, the Caron has been present in the Baltic, the Northern Sea, and off the Libyan coast. During the birth of Solidarity in Poland in August 1980, the Caron cruised fourteen miles off the coast of Gdansk, and in the summer of 1981 she was among the ships that constituted the task force that was on an exercise off the Libyan Coast in the Gulf of Sidra.[172] During a North Atlantic cruise, she came as close to the Soviet naval base at Murmansk as the Chesapeake Bay Bridge is to the U.S. Naval Base at Norfolk, Virginia.[173]

Two Navy frigates stationed in the Pacific have also been used against targets in Nicaragua, El Salvador, and Honduras. One—the 3,900-ton Blakely—is a Knox-class frigate commissioned in 1970; the other—the 3,400-ton Julius A. Furei—is a Brooke-class guided-missile frigate. The missions involved homing and recording voice and signals communications, locating transmitting stations, logging ships' movements, and studying their waterlines to help determine if they are riding low in the water when entering post and high when exiting—indicating the unloading of cargo.[174]

In addition to employing surface vessels, the United States has used submarines for the collection of signals intelligence. In 1975 it was revealed that the United States had been conducting, via submarine, intelligence collection activities near Soviet coastlines for over fifteen years.[175] The program apparently began in the last years of the Eisenhower administration.[176] The ships employed were Sturgeon 637-class submarines with electronic gear and a special NSA unit aboard. The project was codenamed, at various times, Holystone, Pinnacle, and Bollard.[177]

Holystone missions collected a variety of valuable intelligence by several means. The submarines were able to plug into Soviet land communications cables that were strewn across the ocean bottom and thus were able to intercept high-level military messages and other communications considered too important to be sent by radio or less secure means. They also took photos of the underside of an E-class Soviet submarine, apparently in Vladivostok harbor. In addition, they observed missile launches of Soviet SLBMs inland and obtained voice autographs of Soviet submarines.[178]

The Holystone operations produced several near confrontations. In late 1969 a Holystone submarine collided with a Soviet ship fifteen to thirty-five miles from the entrance to the White Sea, in the Barents Sea of northern Russia. The Commander of the submarine Gato, which had been as close as one mile off the Soviet coast, was ordered to file a series of falsified reports stating that the submarine had broken off her patrol two days before the date of collision because of propeller shaft malfunction.[179] Earlier that year, a Holystone submarine was beached for about two hours on the Soviet coast.[180] In another incident, a Holystone vessel surfaced underneath a Soviet ship in the midst of a Soviet fleet naval exercise.[181]

In addition to whatever Holystone missions are still being performed, there are two U.S. nuclear submarines codenamed Watchdog and Tomcat on station on the floor of the Sea of Okhotsk to follow their Soviet counterparts and monitor military communications.[182]

NOTES TO CHAPTER 7

1. Bhupendra Jasani, *Outer Space — Battlefield of the Future?* (New York: Crane, Russak, 1978), p. 12.

2. Farouk El-Baz, "EO Imaging Will Replace Film in Reconnaissance," *Defense Systems Review*, October 1983, pp. 48–52.

3. Richard D. Hudson, Jr. and Jacqueline W. Hudson, "The Military Applications of Remote Sensing by Infrared," *Proceedings of the IEEE* 63, no. 1 (1975): 104–28.

4. "An Introduction to Remote Sensing," *Spaceworld* M–5–149 (May 1979), pp. 5–14.

5. Hudson and Hudson, "The Military Applications of Remote Sensing by Infrared;" Bruce G. Blair and Garry D. Brewer, "Verifying SALT Agreements," in William C. Potter, ed., *Verification and SALT: The Challenge of Strategic Deception* (Boulder, Colo.: Westview, 1980), pp. 7–48.

6. There are also nonimaging infrared sensors such as infrared radiometers that detect the absence or presence of an object or event via temperature. The basis of U.S. early warning (Defense Support Program) satellites is infrared detection of missile launches.

7. Homer Jensen, L. C. Graham, Leonard J. Porcello, and Emmet N. Leith, "Side-looking Airborne Radar," *Scientific American* 237 (October 1977): 84–95.

8. Paul Bennett, *Strategic Surveillance* (Cambridge, Mass.: Union of Concerned Scientists, 1979).

9. Ibid.

10. John F. Ebersole and James C. Wyant, "Real-time Optical Subtraction of Photographic Imagery for Difference Detection," *Applied Optics* 15 no. 4 (1976): 871–76.

11. Jasani, *Outer Space*, p. 21.

12. See James Fusca, "Space Surveillance," *Space/Aeronautics*, June 1964, pp. 92-103.

13. U.S. Congress, Senate Committee on Commerce, Science and Transportation, *NASA Authorization for Fiscal Year 1978, Part 3* (Washington, D.C.: U.S. Government Printing Office, 1977), pp. 1642-43.

14. Ibid.; National Photographic Interpretation Center, *Problems of Photographic Imagery Analysis*, in *Declassified Documents Reference System* 1981-13B (Washington, D.C.: CIA, 1968).

15. Don Irwin, "Satellites Spy on Soviets, Carter Says," *Los Angeles Times*, October 2, 1978, pp. 1, 8.

16. Herbert F. York and G. Allen Greb, "Strategic Reconnaissance," *Bulletin of the Atomic Scientists* 33 (April 1977): 33-41.

17. Anthony Kenden, "U.S. Reconnaissance Satellite Programs," *Spaceflight* 20, no. 7 (1978): 243ff.

18. "USAF Pushes Pied Piper Space Vehicle," *Aviation Week*, October 14, 1957, p. 26.

19. "Briefing on Army Satellite Program," November 10, 1957, *Declassified Documents Reference System* 1977-101B.

20. John Prados, *The Soviet Estimate: U.S. Intelligence Analysis and Russian Military Strength* (New York: Dial, 1982).

21. Kenden, "U.S. Reconnaissance Satellite Programs."

22. Ibid.

23. Ibid.

24. Ibid.

25. Philip Klass, *Secret Sentries in Space* (New York: Random House, 1971), pp. 104-106.

26. Ibid., p. 105; Lawrence Freedman, *U.S. Intelligence and the Soviet Strategic Threat* (London: Macmillan, 1972), p. 72; Interviews with author.

27. Kenden, "U.S. Satellite Reconnaissance Programs."

28. Curtis L. Peebles, "The Guardians," *Spaceflight*, November 1978, pp. 381ff.

29. Ibid.

30. "Big Bird: America's Spy in Space," *Flight International*, January 27, 1977.

31. Klass, *Secret Sentries in Space*, pp. 170-72.

32. "Space Reconnaissance Dwindles," *Aviation Week and Space Technology*, October 6, 1980, pp. 18-20.

33. Ibid.

34. Peebles, "The Guardians."

35. Jasani, *Outer Space*.

36. "Perspective," *Space/Aeronautics*, February 1970, pp. 22-24.

37. For example, Philip Klass, *Secret Sentries in Space*, pp. 170-72.

38. "Space Reconnaissance Dwindles."

39. See Jeffrey Richelson, "The Keyhole Satellite Program," *Journal of Strategic Studies* 7, no. 2 (1984): 121-153.

40. Ibid.

41. "Space Reconnaissance Dwindles."

42. Mark Hewlish, "Satellites Show Their Warlike Face," *New Scientist*, October 1, 1981, pp. 36–40.

43. James B. Schultz, "Inside the Blue Cube," *Defense Electronics*, April 1983, pp. 52–59.

44. Anthony Kenden, "A New U.S. Military Space Mission," *Journal of the British Interplanetary Society* 35 (October 1982): 441–44.

45. Richelson, "The Keyhole Satellite Program."

46. Klass, *Secret Sentries in Space*, p. 172.

47. "The Military Race in Space," *Defense Monitor* 9, no. 9 (1980): 2.

48. John Pike, "Reagan Prepares for War in Outer Space," *Counter Spy* 7, no. 1 (September–November 1982): 17–22.

49. "Space Reconnaissance Dwindles."; John Noble Wilford, "Spy Satellite Reportedly Aided in Shuttle Flight," *New York Times*, October 20, 1981, p. C4.

50. "Space Reconnaissance Dwindles."

51. Wilford, "Spy Satellite Reportedly Aided in Shuttle Flight."

52. "CBS Evening News with Walter Cronkite," October 3, 1980.

53. D. C. King-Hele et al., *The RAE Table of Earth Satellites 1957–1980* (New York: Facts on File, 1981); *The RAE Table of Earth Satellites 1981–1982* (Farnborough, England: Royal Aircraft Establishment, January 1983), pp. 661, 715; "Industry Observer," *Aviation Week and Space Technology*, December 6, 1982, p. 17.

54. "Missile Disguise," *Aviation Week and Space Technology*, September 29, 1980, p. 17.

55. "Inside the Rescue Mission," *Newsweek*, July 12, 1982, pp. 19ff.

56. "New Payload Could Boost Shuttle Cost," *Aviation Week and Space Technology*, August 14, 1978, pp. 16–17.

57. Pike, "Reagan Prepares for War in Outer Space."

58. Gerald L. Borrowman, "Recent Trends in Orbital Reconnaissance," *Spaceflight* 24 (January 1982): 10ff; Pike, "Reagan Prepares for War in Outer Space," "New Payload Could Boost Shuttle Cost."

59. "Space Reconnaissance Dwindles."; "Navy Will Develop All-Weather Ocean Monitor Satellite," *Aviation Week and Space Technology*, October 6, 1980, pp. 18–20.

60. "Industry Observer," *Aviation Week and Space Technology*, December 14, 1962, p. 12.

61. "Space Reconnaissance Dwindles."

62. "Washington Round-Up," *Aviation Week and Space Technology*, June 4, 1979, p. 11; Robert C. Toth, "Anaheim Firm May Have Sought Spy Satellite Data," *Los Angeles Times*, October 10, 1982, pp. 1, 32.

63. "Reconnaissance and Special Duty Aircraft," *Air Force Magazine*, May 1978, p. 118.

64. Joint Chiefs of Staff, *JCS Posture Statement 1982* (Washington, D.C.: U.S. Government Printing Office, 1981).

65. Jay Miller, *The Lockheed A-12/Y-12/SR-71 Story* (Austin, Texas: Aerofax, 1983), p. 2.

66. "Reconnaissance and Special Duty Aircraft."

67. "Shaping Tomorrow's CIA," *Time*, February 6, 1978, pp. 10ff; "Radar Detector Abroad SR-71 Alerted to Missile Attack," *New York Times*, August 29, 1981, p. 3.

68. "Shaping Tomorrow's CIA."

69. Ibid.

70. Leslie Gelb, "Korean Jet: Points Still to be Settled," *New York Times*, September 26, 1983, p. A6.

71. Brian Bennett, Tony Powell, and John Adams, *The USAF Today* (London: West Aviation Group Publication, 1981), p. 52.

72. Walter Pincus, "Pershings Packed to Go," *Washington Post*.

73. Col. Asa Bates, "National Technical Means of Verification," *Royal United Services Institute Journal*, 123, 2 (June 1978): 64–73.

74. Benjamin Schemmer, *The Raid* (New York: Harper & Row, 1975), p. 169.

75. Colonel William V. Kennedy, *Intelligence Warfare* (New York: Crescent, 1983), p. 124.

76. "U-2 Facts and Figures," *Air Force Magazine*, January 1976, p. 55.

77. Joint Chiefs of Staff, *JCS Posture Statement 1982*; "Lockheed Back into U-2 Spy Plane Business," *Defense Week*, February 22, 1983, p. 16.

78. David Wise and Thomas B. Ross, *The U-2 Affair* (New York: Random House, 1962), p. 56.

79. Ibid., p. 11.

80. Ibid.

81. Ibid.

82. Bates, "National Technical Means of Verification."

83. Wise and Ross, *The U-2 Affair*, p. 58.

84. Howard Silber, "SAC U-2's Provided Nicaraguan Pictures," *Omaha World Herald*, March 10, 1982, p. 2; Detachment 5 of 9th Strategic Reconnaissance Wing is located at Patrick AFB, Fla.

85. Bennett, Powell, and Adams, *The USAF Today*.

86. Duncan Campbell, *The Unsinkable Aircraft Carrier* (London: Michael Joseph, 1984), p. 135.

87. U.S. Congress, House Permanent Select Committee on Intelligence, *Annual Report* (Washington, D.C.: U.S. Government Printing Office, 1978), p. 31.

88. Deborah Shapely, "Who's Listening?: How NSA Turns on America's Overseas Phone Calls and Messages," *Washington Post*, October 9, 1977, pp. C1, C4.

89. Ibid.

90. Ibid.; James Bamford, *The Puzzle Palace: A Report on NSA, America's Most Secret Agency* (Boston: Houghton Mifflin, 1982), pp. 173–74.

91. U.S. Congress, House Permanent Select Committee, *Annual Report*, p. 36.

92. Prados, *The Soviet Estimate*, p. 35. See also, Richard G. Wiley, *Electronic Intelligence: The Analysis of Radar Signals* (Dedham, Mass.: Artech House, 1982).

93. Prados, *The Soviet Estimate*, p. 203; Farooq Hussain, *The Future of Arms Control: Part IV, The Impact of Weapons Test Restrictions* (London: International Institute for Strategic Studies, 1980); Robert Kaiser, "Verification of SALT II: Art and Science," *Washington Post*, June 15, 1979, p. 1.

94. U.S. Congress, House Permanent Select Committee, *Annual Report*, pp. 28, 38.

95. U.S. Congress, House Permanent Select Committee on Intelligence, *HR 6588, The National Intelligence Act of 1980* (Washington, D.C.: U.S. Government Printing Office, 1980), p. 521.

96. Thomas Karas, *The New High Ground: Strategies and Weapons of Space Age War* (New York: Simon & Schuster, 1983), p. 109.

97. Robert Lindsey, *The Falcon and the Snowman* (New York: Simon & Schuster, 1979), p. 54.

98. Frequency is a term used to describe either the number of times an alternating current goes through its complete cycle per second or the vibration rate of sound waves in the air. 1 cycle per second is referred to as a hertz (Hz). 1,000 Hz is a kilohertz; 1,000,000,000 Hz is a gigahertz (GHz). Frequencies may range from 0.001 Hz to 8×10^{21} Hz. The terms used in this study and the corresponding frequency limits are given in the table below.

Terms Used	Frequency Limits
Very Low Frequencies (VLF)	3 to 30 KHz
Low Frequencies (LF)	30 to 300 KHz
High Frequencies (HF)	3 to 30 MHz
Very High Frequencies (VHF)	30 to 300 MHz
Ultra High Frequencies (UHF)	300 MHz to 3 GHz (GC)
Super High Frequencies (SHF)	3 to 30 GHz
Extremely High Frequencies (EHF)	30 to 300 GHz

Microwave frequencies overlap the UHF, SHF, and EHF bands, running from 1 to 50 GHz. See Robert L. Shrader, *Electronic Communications* (New York: McGraw-Hill, 1980), pp. 64–65, 627.

99. Lindsey, *The Falcon and the Snowman*, p. 157.

100. Desmond Ball, *Secret Satellites Over Australia*, forthcoming.

101. Ibid.

102. Ibid.

103. Lindsey, *The Falcon and the Snowman*, pp. 345–46; Robert Lindsey, "Soviet Spies Got Data on Satellites Intended for Monitoring Arms Pact," *New York Times*, April 29, 1979, p. 1; Clarence Robinson, "Soviet Push Telemetry Bypass," *Aviation Week and Space Technology*, April 16, 1979, p. 14.

104. U.S. Congress, House Committee on Foreign Affairs, *The Role of Intelligence in the Foreign Policy Process* (Washington, D.C.: U.S. Government Printing Office, 1980), p. 232.

105. Richard Halloran, "U.S. Aides Uneasy on Soviet Coding," *New York Times*, January 4, 1982, p. 3; "Are the Soviets Cheating?," *Newsweek*, January 10, 1983, p. 31.

106. Philip J. Klass, "U.S. Monitoring Capability Impaired," *Aviation Week and Space Technology*, May 14, 1979, p. 18.

107.   Ibid.
108.   Lindsey, *The Falcon and the Snowman*, p. 111.
109.   Ball, *Secret Satellites Over Australia*.
110.   Duncan Campbell, "Target Britain," *New Statesman*, October 31, 1980, pp. 6–9.
111.   King-Hele et al., *The RAE Table of Earth Satellites 1957–1980*, p. 324.
112.   Ball, *Secret Satellites Over Australia*.
113.   Victor Marchetti interview in the film *Allies*.
114.   Richard Burt, "U.S. Plans New Way to Check Soviet Missile Tests," *New York Times*, June 29, 1979, p. A3.
115.   Anthony Kenden, "U.S. Military Activities in Space, 1983," *Journal of the British Interplanetary Society*, forthcoming.
116.   "Washington Round-up," *Aviation Week and Space Technology*, January 2, 1984, p. 13.
117.   Pike, "Reagan Prepares for War in Outer Space."
118.   U.S. Congress, House Committee on Appropriations, *Department of Defense Appropriations for 1980, Part 6* (Washington, D.C.: U.S. Government Printing Office, 1979), p. 160.
119.   Department of Defense, *DOD C^3 I Program Management Structure and Major Programs* (Washington, D.C.: DOD, December 10, 1980).
120.   "Washington Round-up," *Aviation Week and Space Technology*, June 4, 1979, p. 11.
121.   Kenden, "U.S. Reconnaissance Satellite Programs."
122.   Ibid.
123.   David Alan Rosenberg, "The Origins of Overkill: Nuclear Weapons and American Strategy, 1945–1960," *International Security* 7, no. 4 (Spring 1983): 3–71.
124.   Wayne G. Baker and Rodney E. Coffman, *The Anatomy of Two Traitors: The Defection of Bernon F. Mitchell and William H. Martin* (Laguna Hills, Cal.: Aegean Park, 1981), p. 71.
125.   Bamford, *The Puzzle Palace*, pp. 178–84.
126.   U.S. Congress, Senate Foreign Relations Committee, *Executive Sessions of the Senate Foreign Relations Committee (Historical Series), XII (1960)* (Washington, D.C.: U.S. Government Printing Office, 1982), pp. 295–96.
127.   Ted Greenwood, "Reconnaissance, Surveillance and Arms Control," *Adelphi Papers* #88, 1972.
128.   Jay Miller, *Lockheed U–2* (Austin, Tex.: Aerofax, 1983), p. 51.
129.   Duncan Campbell, "Spy in the Sky," *New Statesman*, September 9, 1983, pp. 8–9.
130.   Harry F. Eustace, "Changing Intelligence Priorities," *Electronic Warfare/Defense Electronics*, November 1978, p. 85ff.
131.   Duncan Campbell, "How We Spy on Argentina," *New Statesman*, April 30, 1982, p. 5; Dennis MacShane, "Spy Stations in Cyprus," *New Statesman*, June 30, 1978, p. 870; Miller, *Lockheed U–2*, p. 51.
132.   "Reconnaissance and Special Duty Aircraft," *Air Force*, May 1979, p. 121.

133.   Ibid.
134.   "Reconnaissance and Special Duty Aircraft"; Charles W. Corddry and Albert Schistedt, Jr., "Planes' Covert Role is to Monitor Soviet Space Flights and Missile Tests," *Baltimore Sun*, May 7, 1981, p. 1; Department of the Air Force, *Supporting Data for Fiscal Year 1984, Budget Estimates Submitted to Congress Descriptive Summaries, Research, Development, Test and Evaluation* (Washington, D.C.: Department of the Air Force, 1983), pp. 862–63.
135.   T. Edward Eshelon and Tom Bernard, "A Personal View: Former RC-135 Crewmen Question U.S. Version of Jet Liner Incident," *Baltimore News American*, September 15, 1983, p. 8.
136.   *Code Name Handbook 1981* (Greenwich, Conn.: Defense Marketing Service, 1981), p. 81.
137.   U.S. Congress, House Committee on Appropriations, *Department of Defense Appropriations for 1984, Part 8* (Washington, D.C.: U.S. Government Printing Office, 1983), p. 384.
138.   Bennett, Powell, and Adams, *The USAF Today*, pp. 42–53.
139.   Ibid.
140.   Philip Taubman, "U.S. Says Intelligence Plane Was on a Routine Mission," *New York Times*, September 5, 1983, p. 4.
141.   Campbell, "Spy in the Sky."
142.   Michael Getler, "Soviets Held Test of New Missile Three Days After Jet Downed," *Washington Post*, September 16, 1983, p. A28.
143.   For a history of COBRA DANE, see E. Michael Del Papa, *Meeting the Challenge: ESD and the COBRA DANE Construction Effort on Shemya Island* (Bedford, Mass.: Electronic Systems Division, 1979).
144.   Philip J. Klass, "USAF Tracking Radar Details Disclosed," *Aviation Week and Space Technology*, October 25, 1976, pp. 41ff.
145.   Del Papa, *Meeting the Challenge.*
146.   Ibid., p. 3.
147.   Klass, "USAF Tracking Radar."
148.   Kenneth J. Stein, "Cobra Judy Phased Array Radar Tested," *Aviation Week and Space Technology*, August 10, 1981, pp. 70–73.
149.   U.S. Congress, Senate Committee on Appropriations, *Department of Defense Appropriations FY 1973, Part 4* (Washington, D.C.: U.S. Government Printing Office, 1972), pp. 358, 361; *Code Name Handbook 1981*, p. 74; U.S. Congress, House Committee on Appropriations, *Department of Defense Appropriations for 1981, Part 2* (Washington, D.C.: U.S. Government Printing Office, 1980), p. 240.
150.   *Code Name Handbook 1981*, p. 58.
151.   Stockholm International Peace Research Institute, *World Armaments and Disarmaments, SIPRI Yearbook 1980* (London: Taylor & Francis, 1980).
152.   The description of the AN/FLR-9 is from *Cryptologic Collection Equipments* (Pensacola, Fla.: Naval Education and Training Command, 1977) and Bamford, *The Puzzle Palace*, p. 162.
153.   Ibid.

154. J. Hockley, "A Goniometer for Use with High Frequency Circularly Diposed Aerial Arrays," *Radio and Electronic Engineer* 43 (August 1973): 475-85.

155. See Jeffrey T. Richelson and Desmond Ball, *The Ties that Bind: The UKUSA Intelligence Network* (London: Allen & Unwin, 1985).

156. Bamford, *The Puzzle Palace*, p. 163.

157. Duncan Campbell, "Thatcher Bugged by Closest Ally," *New Statesman*, July 25, 1980, p. 4.

158. SIPRI, *World Armaments*. See note 98 for an explanation of VHF, UHF, and SHF.

159. Trevor Armbrister, *A Matter of Accountability* (New York: Coward McCann, 1970), p. 87.

160. Ibid.

161. U.S. Congress, House Committee on Armed Services, *Inquiry into the U.S.S. Pueblo and EC-121 Plane Incidents* (Washington, D.C.: U.S. Government Printing Office, 1969), p. 1632.

162. Armbrister, *A Matter of Accountability*, p. 87.

163. U.S. Congress, House Committee on Armed Services, *Inquiry into the U.S.S. Pueblo*, p. 1634.

164. Ibid., p. 1632.

165. James Ennes, *Assault on the Liberty* (New York: Random House, 1980).

166. U.S. Congress, House Committee on Armed Services, *Inquiry into the U.S.S. Pueblo*, p. 1639.

167. Paul Backus, "ESM and SIGINT Problems at the Interface," *Journal of Electronic Defense*, July–August 1981, pp. 23ff.

168. Department of the Air Force, *Administrative Practices: Nicknames and Exercise Terms*, AF Pamphlet 11-6 (Washington, D.C.: Department of the Air Force, 1982), p. 5.

169. U.S. Congress, Senate Committee on Appropriations, *Department of Defense Appropriations FY 1973, Part 4*, p. 363; *Jane's Fighting Ships 1983-1984* (London: Jane's Publishing, 1983), p. 714.

170. Richard Halloran, "U.S. Says Navy Surveillance Ship is Stationed Off Central America," *New York Times*, February 25, 1982, p. 1, 6.

171. Private information.

172. Ibid.

173. Ibid.

174. George C. Wilson, "U.S. Detects Slowdown in Shipments of Weapons to El Salvador," *Washington Post*, April 29, 1983, p. A13.

175. Seymour M. Hersh, "Submarines of US Stage Spy Missions Inside Soviet Waters," *New York Times*, May 25, 1975, pp. 1, 42.

176. George Kistiakowsky, *A Scientist at the White House: The Private Diary of President Eisenhower's Special Assistant for Science and Technology* (Cambridge, Mass.: Harvard University Press, 1976), p. 153.

177. Hersh, "Submarines of US Stage Spy Missions"; Hersh, "A False Navy Report Alleged in Sub Crash," *New York Times*, July 6, 1975, pp. 1, 26.

178. Ibid.

179.   Hersh, "A False Navy Report Alleged."
180.   Ibid.
181.   Ibid.
182.   Geoffrey Murray, "Under Soviet Eyes, U.S. and Japan Hold Sea Exercises," *Christian Science Monitor*, September 22, 1983, p. 6.

8 OCEAN SURVEILLANCE, SPACE SURVEILLANCE, AND NUCLEAR DETONATION MONITORING

Although the most prominent aspects of U.S. technical intelligence collection are the photographic reconnaissance and signals intelligence efforts directed against land-based targets and missiles, the United States devotes a considerable effort to the collection of intelligence by technical means against ocean- and space-based targets. The intelligence produced is valuable in monitoring Soviet compliance with a variety of treaties and developing an order of battle concerning the Soviet naval and space efforts. Likewise, the monitoring of nuclear detonations by technical means provides intelligence related to both treaty compliance and weapons development.

OCEAN SURVEILLANCE

In the last decade there has been a significant expansion of Soviet naval capabilities. Most recently, launches of the Alfa, Viktor III, and Typhoon have further enhanced Soviet capabilities. The Typhoon SSBN with the multiple warhead SS-N-20 will significantly upgrade Soviet sea-based strategic nuclear capabilities.

Even before such improvements, however, watching the Soviet fleet was already a major activity of U.S. intelligence—particularly of the technical intelligence community. In addition to their military combat uses, Soviet ships (whether military or "civilian") have for many years been employed to collect intelligence as well as to ship arms. Though less sophisticated than the present Typhoon, the Soviets' SSBN fleet has been a significant force—over sixty boats—for several years. Hence, tracking the Soviet Navy has been a major intelligence requirement, the goal being to know the location of every Soviet naval vessel at any point in time. Additionally, the naval activities of numerous other nations, both hostile and friendly, are of interest to the U.S. intelligence community and policymakers. Further, any naval activity in sensitive political, military, or economic areas—for example, the Suez Canal, Sea of Japan, and Hawaiian Islands—is an intelligence target.

As with signals intelligence, ocean surveillance data are collected by a wide variety of collection systems: satellite, aircraft, ground station, and surface ships. Since underseas activities are also a major target of intelligence collection, underseas collection systems are also employed. All the systems constitute the Ocean Surveillance Information System, the data they produce being transmitted to regional Fleet Ocean Surveillance Information Centers and to the Current Operations Department of the Navy Operational Intelligence Center.

Until 1976 the United States Navy did not have a dedicated overhead reconnaissance system for ocean surveillance. Ocean surveillance data were obtained from U.S. photo-reconnaissance satellites, with the Air Force and Navy cooperating on reconnaissance matters.[1] Thus, it was suggested at the time that the April 18, 1975 launch of a high-resolution Keyhole-8 satellite was intended to acquire data on the massive Soviet naval exercise then taking place.[2]

Initial studies for a dedicated ocean surveillance satellite system began in 1968.[3] In 1970 the Chief of Naval Operations ordered a study of overall ocean surveillance requirements, which resulted in a five-volume Ocean Surveillance Requirements Study by the Naval Research Laboratory (NRL).[4] Such studies were initiated by the Navy in response to the significant buildup that was occurring in Soviet naval forces and capabilities. Designated Program 749, the ocean surveillance satellite study focused on the development of high-resolution, phased array radars that would allow all-weather ocean surveillance monitoring as well as detection of low-trajectory sea-launched missiles.[5] Also explored was the possibility of equipping the satellites with an infrared scanner, operating in the eight- to fourteen-micron band.[6] Experimental phased array radars were developed by Hughes Aircraft and Westinghouse Electric.[7]

Despite the emphasis of these initial studies, the ocean surveillance satellite system, Classic Wizard, lacked any radar capability. Rather, White Cloud, the satellite portion of the Classic Wizard System is a passive interceptor.[8] It is apparently equipped with a passive infrared scanner and millimeter wave radiometers as well as radio-frequency antennas capable of monitoring radio communications and radar emissions from Soviet submarines and ships.[9] Passive interferometry techniques are used to determine the location of Soviet vessels: The craft computes a ship's position from data provided by several antennas that measure the direction from which a vessel's radar or radio signals arrive.[10]

The satellite system consists of a mother ship and three subsatellites. The basic techniques involved in using multiple spacecraft to eavesdrop and direction find on Soviet surface vessels and submarines were first demonstrated using three NRL spacecraft launched on December 14, 1971. The launch vehicle was a McDonnell–Douglas Thorad. A Lockheed Agena was used as the satellite dispenser to place the spacecraft in appropriate orbits.[11]

The present satellites are launched from the Western Test Range – Vandenberg Air Force Base (AFB)—into a near circular 63-degree inclined orbit at an altitude of approximately 700 miles, employing a General Dynamics Atlas F booster. The three spacecraft are dispersed from the main vehicle into three parallel orbits with latitude separation as well as time/distance separation along their orbital paths. At the 700-mile altitude, the spacecraft can receive signals from surface vessels more than 2,000 miles away, providing overlapping coverage on successive passes.[12] There is a displacement of approximately 1,866 miles between passes.[13]

In addition to the 1971 test mentioned above, there was apparently a test of the subsatellite on June 8, 1975, the subsatellite being ejected from a Keyhole-9 satellite.[14] Subsequently, as indicated in Table 8–1, there have been five operational clusters placed into orbit: on April 30, 1976; on December 8, 1977; on March 3, 1980; on February 9, 1983; and on June 9, 1983.[15]

The subsatellites are relatively small, measuring approximately three by eight by one feet. The largest surface area on one side is covered by solar cells; four spherical objects that are deployed on the end of metal booms are believed to be sensors.[16]

Each satellite transmits its collected intelligence at a slightly different frequency—1,430.2 mc, 1,432.2 mc, and 1,434.2 mc—using approximately 1 mc of bandwidth. Narrow-band telemetry transmissions are made at frequencies of 1,427.23 mc, 1,427.43 mc, and 1,427.63 mc. Transmissions at these frequencies have been allocated for spaceborne position-fixing functions by the International Telecommunications Union.[17]

Naval ocean surveillance satellite transmissions have generated protests from radio astronomers because of their proximity to the 1,400- to 1,427-mc hydrogen-line band allocated for radio astronomy. Astronomers at Canada's Dominion Radio Astrophysical Observatory in Penticton, British Columbia raised the issue in a letter to *Science Magazine* published March 11, 1977.[18]

Several months later, the Canadian scientists identified the signal as coming from the White Cloud/Classic Wizard satellite, based on their 107.5-minute period and 63.5-degree inclination. The scientists stated that "the wide-bandwidth and rapid modulation indicate that the satellites are transmitting large amounts of information or radar pulses."[19]

The ground segment of the Classic Wizard system consists of five ground stations at the Naval Security Group facilities at Diego Garcia; Guam; Adak, Alaska; Winter Harbor, Maine; and Edzell, Scotland.[20] Several tracking domes have been built at Edzell to control and receive information from the satellites.[21]

Table 8-1. Launch Dates and Orbital Parameters for White Cloud Satellites.

Designation	Date	Launch Vehicle/ Launch Site	Inclination	Perigee (ml)	Apogee (ml)
1971–110A	Dec. 14, 1971	Thorad-Agena D/ WTR	70.02	983	999
1971–110C	Dec. 14, 1971		70.01	983	999
1971–110D	Dec. 14, 1971		70.01	982	997
1971–110E	Dec. 14, 1971		70.01	981	997
NOSS–1 1976–38A	Apr. 30, 1976	Atlas/WTR	63.46	683	705
SSU–1 1976–38C	Apr. 30, 1976		63.44	683	706
SSU–2 1976–38D	Apr. 30, 1976		63.43	683	706
SSU–3 1976–38J	Apr. 30, 1976		63.45	677	712
NOSS–2 1977–112A	Dec. 8, 1977	Atlas F/WTR	63.43	659	730
SSU–4 1977–112D	Dec. 8, 1977		63.44	659	730
SSU–5 1977–112E	Dec. 8, 1977		63.44	659	730
SSU–6 1977–112F	Dec. 8, 1977		63.44	659	730
NOSS–3 1980–19A	Mar. 3, 1980	Atlas/WTR	63.03	647	719
SSU–7 1980–19C	Mar. 3, 1980		63.49	655	729
SSU–8 1980–19E	Mar. 3, 1980		63.49	655	729
SSU–9 1980–19G	Mar. 3, 1980		63.49	655	729
NOSS–4 1983–008A	Feb. 9, 1983	Atlas/WTR	63.43	665	741
SSD 1980–08B	Feb. 9, 1983		63.39	655	741
SSA 1983–08E	Feb. 9, 1983		63.44	658	730
SSB 1983–08F	Feb. 9, 1983		63.44	658	730
SSC	Feb. 9, 1983		63.44	658	730
NOSS–5 1983–066A	June 10, 1983	Atlas/WTR	63.34	655	730
GB1 1983–56C	June 10, 1983		63.43	657	733
GB2 1983–56D	June 10, 1983		63.44	657	733
GB3 1983–56G	June 10, 1983		63.45	657	733

Source: Various volumes of *The RAFs Table of Earth Satellites.*

Given the increased frequency of ocean surveillance satellite launches in recent years, funds have been requested for antenna upgrades at all Classic Wizard sites.

The two principal pieces of processing equipment at the Classic Wizard sites are designated AN/FYK-IIA and AN/FSQ-III. The AN/FYK-IIA processing system was designed by the NRL and the Naval Electronics System Command and produced by TRW. It is described as a "data processing set for telemetric data" and was first fielded in 1975. The AN/FSQ-III was designed and produced by NRL and is described as a "digital data set" for the generation, transmission, and reception of "special telemetry signals." It was first fielded in 1981.[22]

Production and management of the Classic Wizard system involves several organizations. The satellite system was developed and initially produced by the NRL. After the initial two operational clusters were built, the production role was turned over to the Martin–Marietta Corporation.[23] Technical assistance is provided by the NRL.[24] E-Systems of Dallas, Texas provides the electronic intelligence receivers and antennas for the satellites.[25] The program office for Classic Wizard is located in the Navy Space Project Office of the Naval Electronic Systems Command, and actual operation of the Classic Wizard ground terminals is the responsibility of the Naval Security Group Command.[26]

Related to Classic Wizard is Sea Nymph, an integrated satellite and shipboard electronic signal collection system that allows identification of the nature and sources of unknown radar and communications signals collected by destroyers by correlating data with information obtained by the White Cloud satellites.[27]

Although the Classic Wizard system did not incorporate the use of radar into its sensor package, such a capability (as indicated above) has long been desired by Navy planners. It has even been alleged that the Navy launched a successful radar ocean surveillance satellite in the early 1960s on an experimental basis.[28] The Soviet Union has long employed nuclear-powered radar ocean surveillance satellites (RORSATs). COSMOS 954, which malfunctioned and spread radioactive debris over Canada on January 24, 1978, was one of those RORSATs.[29]

The Navy did intend to develop and launch a radar ocean surveillance satellite with the unclassified codename Clipper Bow. Clipper Bow was intended, through the use of radar, to provide Navy commanders at sea with an all-weather/day-night active global coverage for surveillance and targeting of hostile ships in the area around a task force.[30]

Unlike the Classic Wizard system, Clipper Bow was intended to be effective even in the absence of enemy signals emissions. It would have been capable of pinpointing the location of surface ships via radar and, by correlating these data with signals emissions, establishing at a minimum the class of the vessel.[31] Possibly, more detailed information would also be determinable.[32]

Clipper Bow, depicted in Figure 8-1, was intended, according to David E. Mann, Assistant Secretary of the Navy for Research, Engineering, and Systems in 1979, to be "a tactical support satellite, no more and no less. It is not intended

Figure 8-1. Clipper Bow in Operation—Artist's Conception.

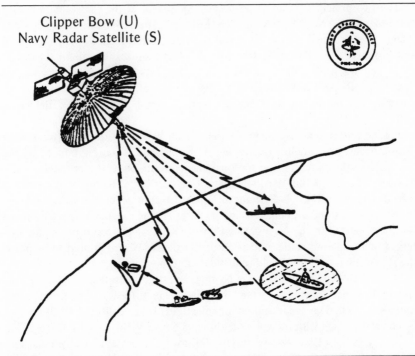

Clipper Bow (U)
Navy Radar Satellite (S)

Source: U.S. Congress, House Committee on Armed Services, *Hearings on Military Posture and HR 5068 Book 1, Part 3* (Washington, D.C.: U.S. Government Printing Office 1977) p. 751.

to provide, except as a completely adjunct capability national intelligence or surveillance that is primarily useful on a national scene."[33] Further, Mann stated:

> What it [Clipper Bow] is intended to do is to provide the tactical force commander with information that is necessary for his own protection, for his deployment, and movement of his own resources and assets, to provide him with, so to speak, eyes over the horizon, to warn him of the presence of other approaching or attacking battle groups, to provide him the targeting information he would need to fire or vector his assets at enemy targets well beyond horizon range.[34]

The information provided was to be continuous but not of high-resolution variety. The intended resolution was to be sufficient to locate and provide course or track information on ships and shipping, for targeting purposes, and to provide the task force Commander with a view of the area into which he is moving.[35]

The Clipper Bow development program as of 1977 envisaged a first launch in 1983.[36] However, considerable delays began to plague the program, primarily due to considerable congressional resistance to funding the satellite. Preliminary studies were conducted by the Aerospace Corporation and industry teams fielded by Lockheed/Westinghouse, Martin Marietta/Hughes Aircraft and McDonnel Douglas/General Electric.[37] In 1979 it was decided not to request full-scale development funds for Fiscal Year 1980. Rather, residual Fiscal Year 1979 funds were used to finance low-level studies while the program was reassessed.[38] In 1980 the Clipper Bow program was canceled.[39]

Much of the controversy over funding of Clipper Bow has been due to the apparent plans, discussed above, by the CIA for construction of a radar satellite with a late 1980s initial operating capability. In addition, Air Force studies of spaceborne radar have been directed toward its possible use to detail and track aircraft and cruise missiles, possibly from geosynchronous orbit. Such a satellite would be of the nonimaging variety.[40]

Despite the formal cancellation of Clipper Bow, a spaceborne radar capability for ocean surveillance is still a possibility—as part of the Navy's Integrated Tactical Surveillance System (ITSS). The ITSS Study, which calls for a worldwide ship and aircraft detection capability, has been used by Navy planners to justify the investigation of the use of spaceborne assets to satisfy the requirements.[41]

Thus, in describing the ITSS effort, Navy spokesmen stated that they wanted "to develop an architecture that is going to give us worldwide coverage, day and night, and which will support our forces no matter where our commitments may be or where we are asked to respond."[42] They then go on to indicate that the sensor systems involved include both terrestrial and spaceborne systems.[43] Indeed, recent reports indicate the ITSS will be part of an Air Force-Navy-Department of Defense space-based radar program involving both national and tactical intelligence collection.[44]

As was the case with photographic and signals reconnaissance activities directed at land-based targets, the United States employs several aircraft in an ocean surveillance role. Included are the EP-3E, EA-3B, P-3, and modified U-2s.

The EP-3E Orion and EA-3B Skywarrior are operated by the Fleet Air Reconnaissance Squadrons and detachments in Rota, Spain; Agana, Guam; and Atsugi, Japan. Both planes are employed to monitor signals emanating from Soviet vessels in the Atlantic and Pacific regions. In the case of the EP-3E, which is a modified P-3, some of its targets may also be land based. The EA-3B is often employed on aircraft carriers for periods ranging from days to months in order to extend the range of coverage.[45]

The P-3 Orion is a four-engined aircraft capable of flying 1,560 miles, patrolling for four hours, and returning to base.[46] P-3s, operated in two versions—the P-3B and P-3C—are engaged in surveillance on both surface and submersible vessels, although in wartime antisubmarine warfare functions would take precedence.[47] The P-3C is equipped with a general purpose digital computer that coordinates the returns from sensor systems and presents them in visual form by means of cathode ray display tubes. Sensor systems include active or passive sonobouys, magnetic anomaly detector (MAD), forward-looking infrared (FLIR) sensors, and radar.[48]

U.S. Orions are based at sixteen major bases throughout the world, including Clark AFB in the Philippines, Misawa and Kadena (Okinawa) in Japan, Alaska, Iceland, Hawaii, Guam, Spain, Italy, Ascension Island, and Diego Garcia. For occasional surveillance in remote areas, the Navy has initiated a program to provide an in-flight refueling capability for the P-3Cs.[49]

Two U-2s also serve in an ocean surveillance role. These are U-2 variants with a long-loiter capability and specially equipped with a Westinghouse high-resolution radar, infrared scanner, and ELINT and COMINT receivers designed for ocean surveillance purposes.[50]

In addition to the aerospace systems used for ocean surveillance, the United States also relies on ship- and land-based HF/DF systems. These systems form part of the overall Classic network. Thus HF/DF equipment codenamed Classic Outboard can be found on a large number of Navy destroyers. Land-based HF/DF systems are codenamed Classic Bullseye.[51] Most of the stations in the worldwide Bullseye network use the FLR-15 antenna array for signals interception purposes.[52] Others use Circularly Disposed Antenna Arrays (CDAAs).

The Bullseye network is managed by the Naval Security Group Command and includes stations in Diego Garcia; Rota, Spain; Edzell, Scotland; Keflavik, Iceland; Japan; Guam; and Brawdy, Wales. European stations such as those in Edzell, Brawdy, and Keflavik monitor passage of ships from the Soviet port of Murmansk through the GIUK (Greenland-Iceland-U.K.) Gap; the Diego Garcia station performs similar duties for the Indian Ocean area. Monitoring of the western and southwestern Pacific is the responsibility of the Japanese and Guam stations in cooperation with Australian and British stations in Australia and Hong Kong.[53]

As important as is intelligence concerning surface naval activities, intelligence concerning underseas activities—particularly those of submarines—is even more important. The Soviet Union has placed the preponderance of strategic nuclear weapons capability on land, but it also maintains sixty-two submarines armed with SLBMs and has begun to deploy the modern Typhoon SSBN armed with multiwarhead SS-N-20 missiles. Hence, locating and tracking these submarines is of the greatest importance.

Additionally, Soviet attack submarines represent a threat to the U.S. SSBN fleet. In the midst of a transition from Poseidon to Trident submarines, the U.S. SSBN fleet represents only half of the number of Soviet SSBNs—although they have substantial advantages in the most important aspects. Since these submarines play a more significant role in U.S. nuclear strategy than Soviet SSBNs play in Soviet strategy, it is imperative to detect and track any possible threats to U.S. SSBNs.

Much of the data gathered fall under the heading of Acoustic Intelligence (ACOUSTINT)—intelligence information derived from the analysis of acoustic waves radiated either intentionally or unintentionally by the target into the surrounding medium. This includes the underwater acoustic waves from ships and submarines that can be used to develop the "signature" of those vehicles, much in the same manner as voice autographs can be developed of individual people.

The most important submarine detection and tracking system is a global network of large fixed sea-bottom arrays of hydrophones that passively listen for sounds generated by submarines. These arrays are collectively known as the SOSUS (Sound Surveillance System) although only about two-thirds of the arrays are part of the SOSUS network proper, the other one-third being allied systems. The SOSUS system was described by one U.S. Admiral in 1979 as "the backbone or ASW [Antisubmarine Warfare] detection capability."[54]

SOSUS was described by the Stockholm International Peace Research Institute (SIPRI) in 1979 as follows:

> Each SOSUS installation consists of an array of hundreds of hydrophones laid out on the sea floor, or moored at depths most conducive to sound propagation, and connected by submarine cables for transmission of telemetry. In such an array a sound wave arriving from a distant submarine will be successively detected by different hydrophones according to their geometric relationship to the direction from which the wave arrives. This direction can be determined by noting the order in which the wave is detected at the different hydrophones. In practice the sensitivity of the array is enhanced many times by adding the signals from several individual hydrophones after introducing appropriate time delays between them. The result is a listening "beam" that can be "steered" in various directions towards various sectors of the ocean by varying the pattern of time delays. The distance from the array to the sound source can be calculated by measuring the divergence of the sound rays within the array or by triangulating from adjacent arrays.[55]

Development work on SOSUS began in 1950, at which time the hydrophone arrays were codenamed Caesar. Installation of the first SOSUS/Caesar array was completed on the continental shelf off the east coast of the United States in 1954;[56] subsequent Caesar arrays were installed elsewhere off the east coast; at Brawdy in Wales,[57] and perhaps other locations as well. The Caesar arrays have been progressively updated and the technology is now in its fifth generation of development. Caesar uses AN/FQQ-6 and AN/FQQ-9V sonars and AN/VQA-5 spectrum analyzers.[58]

The Caesar arrays proved extremely effective during the Cuban missile crisis of October 1962, and it was decided to expand further and upgrade this network and to construct variants codenamed Colossus along the Pacific coast of the

United States. Colossus uses a more advanced form of sonar than Caesar, designated AN/FQQ-10 (V).[59] In 1966 the existence of a joint U.S.-Canadian sophisticated detection system, codenamed Nutmeg but similar to Caesar, was reported; it is presumably located at Argentia, Newfoundland.[60] One of the largest underwater hydrophone arrays, codenamed Sea Spider, is located off the north coast of Hawaii; it was reportedly this array that monitored and localized the breakup of the Soviet submarine that sank north of Hawaii in March 1968 and was subsequently the subject of the Central Intelligence Agency/Glomar Explorer recovery effort.[61] In October 1963 the United States signed a lease agreement with the United Kingdom for the use of a complex of deep underwater facilities, collectively known as the Atlantic Undersea Test and Evaluation Center (AUTEC), in the Bahamas, with the major shore facility on Andros Island; the acoustic range became operational in 1968 and was certified in 1969.[62] In September 1968 construction of a large fixed underwater system known as the Azores Fixed Acoustic Range (AFAR) began off the island of Santa Maria, the southernmost of the Azores group. Commissioned by NATO on May 19, 1972, the AFAR system is intended to track Soviet submarines approaching the Straits of Gibraltar or on passage to round the Cape of Good Hope.[63] Other related projects are codenamed Barrier and Bronco.[64]

It was stated in 1974 that there were twenty-two SOSUS installations located along the east and west coasts of the United States and at various choke points around the world;[65] the locations of an additional fourteen similar installations have also been identified. These thirty-six arrays are distributed around the world as follows: eight on the east and west coasts of the continental United States (including the AUTEC facility on Andros Island), two in the United Kingdom (one at Brawdy in Wales and the other at Scatsa in the Shetland Islands), two in Turkey, two in Japan, and one each in Alaska, Hawaii ("Sea Spider"), Puerto Rico, Bermuda, Barbados, Canada (Argentia, Newfoundland), Norway, Iceland (Keflavik), Santa Maria Island in the Azores (AFAR), Ascension Island, Italy, Denmark, Gibraltar, the Ryukus, Galeta Island in the Panama Canal Zone, the Philippines, Guam, Diego Garcia, and in the northeastern part of the Indian Ocean.[66] The Japanese arrays may have detected the sinking of a Soviet nuclear-powered submarine that sank in the northern Pacific in the summer of 1983.[67]

Data from these arrays are initially transmitted to the associated shore facilities and then retransmitted via FLTSATCOM (Fleet Satellite Communications) and DSCS (Defense Satellite Communications System) satellites to "a central shore station" at the Acoustic Research Center (ARC) at Moffett Field, California, where it is integrated with data from other sources and processed by the Illiac 4 computer complex to provide a real-time submarine monitoring capability.[68] According to one report, the detection capabilities of SOSUS are sufficient to localize a submarine to within a radius of fifty miles at ranges of several thousand miles,[69] but other reports suggest that radii of ten miles are now possible.[70] In one test of an array deployed off the coast of Oregon, a submarine was detected off the coast of Japan, some 6,000 miles away, but ranges up to about half this are more typical.[71] According to testimony submitted to Congress in May 1980, "SOSUS has demonstrated a substantial capability to detect submarines patrolling or transitting through SOSUS areas of coverage. . . . Since the first U.S.S.R. deployment of SSBNs, a large fraction of the SSBN deployed force has been subject to SOSUS detection and tracking."[72] Other reports have been even more categoric, to the effect that SOSUS has been able to detect all Soviet submarine movements.[73]

The extraordinary capabilities of SOSUS notwithstanding, the U.S. Navy has established requirements for other complimentary systems. SOSUS performance is contingent upon sound propagation conditions, which are quite variable, and in some circumstances the performance of fixed arrays is inferior to that of other systems. Moreover, the SOSUS network—the sensors, the cables, and the shore stations—is rather vulnerable.[74] The two most important complementary systems currently under development are a Rapidly Deployable Surveillance System (RDSS) and the Surface Towed Array Sensor System (SURTASS). Together with SOSUS, they form the Integrated Undersea Surveillance System.[75]

RDSS is designed to operate in areas where fixed or manned systems cannot operate safely or reliably. The system consists of large sonobuoys that can be remotely deployed by aircraft and ships (from frigates on up) or launched through submarine torpedo tubes and that moor themselves automatically to the ocean bottom. RDSS would be particularly useful in monitoring "such high interest areas as the Dardanelles, Baltic approaches, Straits of Gibralter, and the Greenland–Iceland–United Kingdom (GIUK) gap."[76]

SURTASS is designed to provide a mobile back-up to the SOSUS network. It will be used in areas where SOSUS is unavailable or inoperative, or it can be used to enhance coverage within SOSUS regions. SURTASS is slated for operation in late 1984.[77] The program involves the acquisition of twelve 217-foot ships, designated T–AGOS, designed to tow a very long aperture hydrophone array (some 1,220 meters long) by a 2,000-meter cable. The T–AGOS ships are designed to operate for up to ninety days on station. Transit speeds are eleven knots and towing speeds must be three knots or less, allowing a mission radius of about 3,000 nautical miles. Data from the hydrophone array will be preprocessed on board ship and then sent via FLTSTACOM and DSCS satellites to the Central Shore Station at Moffett Field.[78]

Several other special Navy programs have been identified relating to underseas surveillance. DESKTOP is designed to collect information concerning undersea plateaus in areas from which U.S. submarines might launch missiles at Soviet targets—areas such as the Norwegian Sea and Mediterranean. By using a secure sonar signal to correlate the contour of the ocean bottom to Precise Bathymetric Navigational Zone Charts maintained in the submarine's computer system, the submarine can determine its precise location without surfacing.[79] By determining precise locations and coordinates, the accuracy of U.S. SLBMs can be enhanced, which in turn allows for their more effective use against hardened targets such as missile silos and command and control bunkers—targets that can be destroyed only by highly accurate missiles.

A second program, PILOT FISH, apparently involves placing transmitters on the ocean bottom to pick up sonar data from approaching submarines and transmitting them to ASW craft. A third program, PRAIRIE SCHOONER, has been described as an "advanced submarine surveillance program" that involves optical systems, direction finding, and laser signal detection.[80]

SPACE SURVEILLANCE

Initially, U.S. concern for tracking and detection of space objects resulted from the requirements of the U.S. space program—the ability to monitor and control U.S. satellites. In preparation for the 1957–1958 International Geophysical Year, two global tracking networks were set up. The Navy established a number of low-cost Minitrack antennas that could locate a transmitting satellite by interferometric measurements of satellite transmissions. The Smithsonian Astrophysical Observatory set up a network of twelve Baker-Nunn cameras around the world to photograph the satellite.[81]

However, with the launch of Sputnik I in 1957, the United States came to place a high priority on developing a dedicated system for the tracking of Soviet satellite systems. Neither the Minitrack nor the Baker-Nunn network was able adequately to track the Sputnik. The Minitrack antennas were tuned to the wrong frequency, and the Baker-Nunn cameras had such a narrow field of view that they had to be pointed quite accurately before they could detect a satellite.

Since that time, the military's use of space has become a major aspect of Soviet and U.S. military strategy. In addition to their reconnaissance and surveillance functions discussed above, satellites play important roles in military communications, navigation, and weather reporting. Consequently, the significance of the space surveillance mission has grown sharply. The detection, tracking, and investigation of Soviet satellites, from their launch through their orbital lifetime and eventual reentry, provides the United States with several significant items of intelligence.

Space surveillance helps provide the United States with intelligence on the characteristics and capabilities of Soviet space systems and their contribution to overall Soviet military capabilities. Such data aid the United States in developing countermeasures to Soviet systems, provide a data base for U.S. Anti-Satellite (ASAT) targeting, and allow the United States to assess the threat represented by Soviet ASAT systems. The detection and tracking of Soviet satellites allows the United States to avoid coverage of certain sensitive U.S. military activities—

for example, the tests of Stealth aircraft—via the Satellite Reconnaissance Advance Notice (SATRAN) system.[82] U.S. military forces conducting sensitive activities are notified whenever Soviet reconnaissance satellites are due to pass overhead and instructed to cease and camouflage such activities during the relevant period. Hence, during preparations for the attempted rescue of the U.S. hostages held by Iranian militants in 1980, the U.S. forces involved were instructed to dismantle the mock embassy used in the practice raids so as to prevent the Soviets from detecting the preparations.[83]

The means of detecting, tracking, and investigating foreign—especially Soviet—satellites are primarily ground based, although the feasibility of space-based surveillance has been demonstrated in several instances. During Shuttle Mission 7, the shuttle was photographed by a West German Shuttle Pallet Satellite released from the shuttle itself. During the initial shuttle flight—that of the Columbia—the Keyhole-11 (KH-11) was apparently maneuvered into position to examine the tiles damaged during the launch phase. The quality and content of those images convinced NASA that the damaged tiles would not interfere with reentry, allowing completion of the orbital phase of the shuttle's mission.[84] Thus, the KH-11 would appear to have the capability to photograph Soviet satellites in low earth orbit.

Additionally, R&D is underway to give the United States a dedicated space-to-space reconnaissance capability. The Air Force is developing one such system, and the Defense Advanced Research Projects Agency (DARPA) has conducted Space Infrared Experiments (SIRE) as part of its Space Infrared Surveillance Program to develop an infrared system to detect hostile satellites. The system has been successfully tested on the ground.[85] Development of a space-based space surveillance system in the far term has been described by the Air Force Deputy Chief of Staff for Research, Development, and Acquisition as the "primary thrust of the Space Surveillance Technology Program." The system is intended to provide full earth orbit coverage, reduce overseas basing of sensors, and provide near-real-time "operationally responsive coverage of objects and events in space."[86]

Thus, the Air Force requested $22.6 million for Fiscal Year 1984 for research, development, test, and evaluation of a Space Based Surveillance System with a deployment goal of the early 1990s. The system would consist of four satellites in low-altitude equatorial orbit. The long-wave infrared (eight to fourteen micron) mosaic staring sensor on each satellite would view the volume of space from approximately sixty nautical miles to geosynchronous altitude.[87]

At present though, U.S. space surveillance activities are predominately ground based. The overall military system is known as the Space Tracking and Detection System (SPADATS); the Air Force portion of this system is the SPACETRACK system. SPADATS consists of three types of sensors: dedicated, collateral, and contributing. Dedicated sensors are Strategic Air Command (SAC) and Navy sensors the primary mission of which is space surveillance. Collateral sensors are SAC sensors with a secondary space surveillance role. Contributing sensors are non-SAC sensors with a secondary space surveillance mission.[88]

Until recently, the main dedicated sensor system was a series of Baker-Nunn optical cameras located at Edwards AFB, California; Mt. John, New Zealand; Pulmosan, Korea; St. Margarets, New Brunswick (Canada); and San Vito, Italy.[89] These cameras, which are ten feet tall and weigh three tons, can photograph at night a lighted object the size of a basketball over 20,000 miles in space.[90]

Despite its impressive photographic capability, the Baker-Nunn system also suffers from several limitations. It operates only in clear weather and during those hours when satellites are still illuminated by the sun. It is slow in terms of both data acquisition rate and response time—that is, it takes several minutes to get a fix on one satellite and takes an hour or more to process the film and measure image positions. Finally, it is useful for tracking but not detection: The approximate position of a satellite must be known beforehand so the Baker-Nunn can be pointed toward the satellite.[91]

The Baker-Nunn system is in the process of being replaced by the Ground Based Electro-Optical Deep Space Surveillance System (GEODSS). As with the Baker-Nunn system, the GEODSS will have five locations: White Sands, New Mexico; Maui, Hawaii; Taego, South Korea; Diego Garcia; and the southern coast of Portugal. Construction has been completed at White Sands, Maui, Taego, and Diego Garcia.[92]

GEODSS provides the capability to track objects optically from above 3,000 nautical miles out to 22,000 miles.[93] It is also able to search up to 17,400 square degrees per hour.[94] Further, GEODSS installations will be close enough together to provide overlapping coverage as a means of overcoming poor weather at any one site.[95]

As with the Baker-Nunn system, GEODSS depends on the collection of light reflected by the objects under investigation and is operational only at night during clear weather. Additionally, sensitivity and resolution is downgraded by adverse atmospheric conditions.[96] At the same time, GEODSS is able to provide real-time data—with a computer-managed instantaneous video display of surveillance data. Further, the computer automatically filters stars from the night sky backdrop and then uses its memory of known space objects to determine the existence of new or unknown space objects, alerting the user when such objects are found.[97]

GEODSS consists of three telescopes at each site which work together under computer control. Two forty-inch telescopes, designed primarily for high-altitude object observation, are capable of examining up to 2,400 square degrees of the night sky each hour. A fifteen-inch telescope is employed mainly for low-altitude observations, searching up to 15,000 square degrees per hour. Each telescope has a sensitive Ebiscon tube which will register the image of an object for real-time processing as well as a radiometer for optical signature characterization and identification.[98]

According to one account,

> In a typical operational scenario the small telescope will be conducting a low-altitude, high speed search, one of the large telescopes will be tracking an object at high altitude and the other large telescope will be tracking an object – at either high or low altitudes and collecting radiometric data.[99]

To locate an object, the system computes an object's position from information on its orbit and points the telescope to the required position. The operator may then pick out the spacecraft by locating a stationary object in a moving star field. The operator may also fix the telescope on the moving star background and collect camera frames that show a satellite streak building up. Most recently, a GEODSS site photographed a FLTSATCOM satellite at geosynchronous altitude.[100]

The present sensor capability of GEODSS is scheduled to be improved by the replacement of the Ebiscon by charged couple devices (CCDs). The CCDs will allow for higher quality images of space objects.[101]

A second set of dedicated SPADATS sensors are those that constitute the Naval Space Surveillance (NAVSPASUR) system. The NAVSPASUR system detects and tracks satellites that pass through an electronic fence that consists of a fan-shaped radar beam with a 6,000-mile range extending in an east–west direction from San Diego, California to Fort Stewart, Georgia. The beam cannot be steered. Detection results when the satellite passing through the beam deflects some of the beam's energy back to earth, where it is detected by several arrays of dipole antennas – "a form of cheap, unsophisticated antenna not unlike a television receiving aerial."[102]

The central transmitter for the beam is located at Lake Kicapoo, Texas with two smaller transmitting stations at Gila River, Arizona and Lake Jordan, Atlanta. The six receiver stations – at San Diego, California; Elephant Butte, New Mexico; Red River, Arkansas; Silver Lake, Mississippi; Hawkinsville, Georgia; and Fort Stewart, Georgia – are all located, as are the transmitting stations, across the southern part of the United States along a great circle inclined at about 33 degrees to the Equator.[103] The data obtained are then transmitted to the NAVSPASUR Headquarters and Computation Center at Dahlgren, Virginia.[104]

A third set of dedicated sensors are located at Cloudcroft, New Mexico and Haleakala, Hawaii (Kaena Point) for the electro-optical observation of spacecraft. At Haleakala is an AN/FPS-2 "optical radar." The AN/FPS-2 employ electronic detectors, as opposed to photographic film, which record the light collected by a telescope to produce an "optical signature" of any particular satellite. Spectral analysis allows scientists to determine the surface nature of the satellite, and characteristics such as tumbling rate and spacecraft shape can be deduced from the time-varying intensity of the reflected light.[105]

At both Cloudcraft and Haleakala are instruments known as LARIAT—Laser Radar Intelligence Acquisition Technology. LARIAT is equipped with a laser that can be used for two purposes. It allows satellites to be observed at times when they are not illuminated by sunlight, and it can be used to determine whether any particular satellite has an optical (i.e., camera-based) surveillance capability by "observing" the reflection from any camera lenses that might be aboard the targeted satellite.[106]

A planned addition to the set of dedicated sensors is the Pacific Radar Barrier (PACBAR). The barrier will consist of three radars—located on Guam; at San Miguel, Philippines; and on Kwajalein—which together will provide the capability to determine the orbit of a satellite within its first revolution. The Guam radar may be a newly constructed radar known as SEEK SAIL.[107] The Philippines radar is a AN/GPS-10 search radar with a sixty-foot dish that had been installed in Thailand in the early 1970s and codenamed COBRA TALON.[108] Subsequently, it was withdrawn and moved to storage at Clark AFB, Philippines.[109] The Kwajalein radar (ALTAIR-4) employed will be an upgrade of the system already installed there.[110]

The collateral SPACETRACK sensors are systems employed in either an early warning or strategic verification role. Early warning systems that serve as SPACETRACK collateral sensors are the Ballistic Missile Early Warning System (BMEWS) as well as the FSS-7, Pave Paws, PARCS, and FPS-85 radars. The main function of the BMEWS is tracking missiles and determining the quantity of missiles launched and their targets. The system consists of three sites—Clear, Alaska; Thule, Greenland; and Fylingdales, Moor (Great Britain)—each with a pair of radars. The Thule and Fylingdales sites each are equipped with AN/FPS-49 tracking and AN/FPS-50 detection radars while the Clear site is equipped with an AN/FPS-92 tracking radar in addition to its AN/FPS-50.[111] The AN/FPS-50 antennas direct a fan of radio energy for detection purposes; the steerable AN/FPS-49 consist of dish antennas within radomes to track targets acquired by the "50."[112] Together the radars provide a 3,000-mile detection and tracking range.[113]

Early warning of SLBM launches has been provided by the FSS-7's radars at six locations—Mt. Helo, Washington; Mill Valley, California; Mt. Laguna, California; MacDill AFB, Florida; Fort Fisher, North Carolina; and Charlestown, Maine—on the east and west coasts that constituted the SLBM Detection and Warning System.[114] The system is being replaced by four PAVE PAWS (AN/FPS-115) phased array radars at Otis AFB, Massachusetts; Beale AFB, California; Robins AFB, Georgia; and Goodfellow AFB, Texas.[115] The Otis AFB and Beale AFB radars are already operational. The Robins AFB and Goodfellow AFB radars will become operational in the 1986-1987 period. Each radar has two arrays, providing a total of 240 degrees of coverage.[116] The primary mission of the system will be SLBM detection, but the Robins site will also support NORAD tracking of space objects.[117] The Perimeter Acquisition Radar Characterization System (PARCS) is located in Concrete, North Dakota. It has a 2,500-mile range and is employed in both an early warning and space tracking role.

At Eglin AFB, Florida a Long Range Phased Array Radar, the AN/FPS-85, was constructed in 1967. The radar, thirteen stories high and as long as a city block, has its principal axis aligned due south across the Gulf of Mexico and is capable of receiving and transmitting over an arc extending 60 degrees on either side. Most satellites must pass through its beam, which has a range of 2,500 miles, twice a day.[118]

As with COBRA DANE, the AN/FPS-85 "consists of several thousand individual transmitters the power outputs of which are added together by controlling their phases to form a single beam which can be electronically swept across the sky in millionths of a second."[119] The radar can search for unknown objects across 120 degrees of azimuth, from horizon to zenith, while simultaneously tracking several already acquired targets. In a typical twenty-four-hour period, it makes 10,000 observations.[120]

When first established, the radar was the main U.S.-based active sensor of the Spacetrack system, 30 percent of its operating time being devoted to search and surveillance, 50 percent to tracking specific satellite targets requested by NORAD, and 20 percent to SLBM early warning role. Today, one-third of its operating time is devoted to space surveillance. Its remaining time is occupied by SLBM detection and other tasks.[121]

Strategic verification radars also used in a space surveillance role are the COBRA DANE (AN/FPS-108) and AN/FPS-79 (Pirinclik/Diyarbakir, Turkey) radars, which have been discussed above.[122] With its coverage extending northward over an arc from Khamchatka to the Bering Straits, COBRA DANE can be used for tracking satellites in polar and near-polar orbits in addition to its role in observing Soviet missile test reentry vehicles.[123]

Contributing sensors provide inputs to the SPADATS data base on the basis of contracts or agreements negotiated by SAC with their governmental or nongovernmental operators. Included among the contributing sensors are the Millstone Hill and Haysack deep space tracking radars of MIT's Lincoln Laboratory.[124] The Haystack radar can resolve down to one foot objects in low-earth orbit and has been described in congressional hearings as providing "images of orbiting satellites that we can get from no other location. [It is a] long range, high altitude capable radar which provides extremely good intelligence data and now has a real-time operational reporting capability."[125]

Additional contributing sensors include the Antigua and Ascension Island sensors of the Eastern Space and Missile Center at Patrick AFB, Florida. These sensors are simply tracking antennas down range from the center that are leased by NORAD.[126] The Maui Optical Tracking and Identification Facility (MOTIF) also provides space surveillance data.[127]

NUCLEAR DETONATION MONITORING

As noted in Chapter 1, a subject of considerable U.S. intelligence interest is the nuclear energy programs of foreign nations. Of greatest priority are the nuclear weapons aspects of these programs, particularly when actual nuclear detonations are involved.

Detection of such detonations is important in several respects. It allows the United States to verify, or attempt to verify, several international agreements and treaties concerning such activity. The United States is a signatory to the 1963 Partial Test Ban Treaty which banned atmospheric testing and testing in space, the 1974 Threshold Test Ban Treaty barring underground nuclear testing of devices of greater than 150 kilotons, and the Peaceful Nuclear Explosion (PNE) Treaty of 1976.[128] Should a Comprehensive Test Ban Treaty be signed, even greater demands would be placed on detecting nuclear explosions.

The same collection systems that can be employed for treaty verification purposes obviously can also be employed to monitor the nuclear detonation activities of nonsignatories such as France, China, South Africa, and Israel. Whether a country is a treaty signatory or not, the United States is concerned with the sophistication and likely future development of nuclear weapons. Nuclear monitoring can provide, at least, some clues in this regard. Additionally, nuclear detonation monitoring can provide data on the characteristics of the detonated devices that can be employed to develop countermeasures. Thus, it has been noted in congressional testimony that

> another aspect [of the U.S. worldwide nuclear test detection system] is devoted to the general area of nuclear weapon diagnostics. As a general rule, the assessment of the sophistication of a foreign weapons development program and the estimation of the probable intent of the developing nation in the application of nuclear weapons require some knowledge of the internal details of the device.
>
> Such questions as yield, nuclear materials employed and the construction characteristics that determine size, weight and output of the device are all-important to determine the type of delivery system that might be required and the vulnerability of U.S. systems to the output of such devices. In other words, in order to determine the response of the U.S. to a foreign nuclear weapons development program, more information than the mere existence of a nuclear explosion is required.[129]

Thus, the Atomic Energy Commission was able to announce a few days after China's first nuclear explosion on October 16, 1964 that the bomb used uranium 235 rather than plutonium based on examination of the radioactive cloud.[130]

Recently, an additional factor has appeared. Revisions in U.S. nuclear strategy, as expressed in President Carter's Presidential Directive (PD)/NSC–59, "Nuclear Weapons Employment Policy," and President Reagan's National Security Decision Directive (NSDD)-13, require the United States to possess the capability to fight a prolonged nuclear war—one that could last up to six months. Such a strategy requires the U.S. leadership to determine the precise location of nuclear detonations and assess the damage that results.[131]

The United States began a systematic R&D program in 1960 under the code-name VELA.[132] The program had three components: VELA UNIFORM, VELA SIERRA, and VELA HOTEL. VELA UNIFORM was concerned with the detection of underground nuclear explosions, VELA SIERRA with the detection of nuclear detonations in the atmosphere and space from the ground, and VELA HOTEL with space-based detection of nuclear detonations in space.[133]

The VELA HOTEL satellite, developed by TRW, has become an important part of the overall U.S. nuclear detonation monitoring capability. The first pair of VELA satellites was launched on October 17, 1963, the sixth and last pair on April 8, 1970.[134] Although originally designed to last for only six months, the last pair are still operational in the summer of 1984.

Each of the initial series of VELA satellites was a twenty-six-sided structure. All but two of the twenty-six sides were covered with solar cells to provide the main source of electrical power for the satellite. Additionally, two nickel-cadmium batteries were built in for maintaining power during eclipses and for maintaining a constant voltage to the detectors.[135] Weighing about 300 pounds each, the VELAs were placed on opposite sides of the earth at altitudes of between 60,000 and 70,000 miles—making them the highest orbiting military satellites.[136]

The VELAs could store instructions from the ground and carry a variety of detectors that would be sensitive to the x-rays, gamma rays, and neutrons created by a nuclear explosion. In April 1967 the fourth pair of VELAs, with improved capabilities, was launched. This and following pairs weighed between 506 and 770 pounds and carried an enhanced command and control capability; more sensitive versions of the x-ray, gamma ray, and neutron sensors; optical and electromagnetic pulse sensors; background radiation counters; and an "improved logic circuitry better to discriminate between natural events and man-made bursts of radiation."[137] The optical light sensors, known as Bhangmeters, were designed to detect atmospheric nuclear explosions by means of the detonations' very brief but intense burst of light. Each satellite possesses two Bhangmeters, each with a different sensitivity.[138]

The strategy for determining whether the data acquired by a VELA satellite indicate the occurrence of a nuclear detonation involves requiring "high-order coincidences" among the various detectors.[139] That the detectors can yield ambiguous results is illustrated by the still-disputed event of September 22, 1979. On that day a VELA detected a flash of light possibly indicating a nuclear explosion in the area of Prince Edward Island, South Africa or Antartica. Because of the lack of corroborating evidence and because one of the Bhangmeters recorded more light than the other, considerable debate resulted. A presidential panel concluded that it was most likely an "anomalous" signal resulting from the impact of a small meteoriod on the satellite or sunlight reflected off debris.[140] On the other hand, both the Defense Intelligence Agency and Naval Research Laboratory concluded a nuclear explosion did occur.[141]

As the remaining functional VELAs come to the end of their useful life, U.S. space-based nuclear detection monitoring will be the secondary function of at least two satellite systems. Since the Defense Support Program (DSP) satellites' initial launch in 1971, their secondary function has been the detection of nuclear explosions in space or the atmosphere.

The principal mission of DSP satellites is to provide early warning of Soviet or Chinese ballistic missile attack. Hence, they also provide notification of missile tests. The means of detection is a twelve-foot-long Schmidt infrared telescope thirty-nine inches in diameter. The telescope has a two-dimensional array of lead sulfide detectors at its focus to sense energy emitted by ballistic missile exhausts during the powered stages of their flights.[142] One satellite is maintained on station over the Indian Ocean (70 degrees E) to provide first warning of a Soviet or Chinese ICBM launch, and two are maintained on station over the Western Hemisphere (over Brazil, 70 degrees W and the eastern central Pacific, 135 degrees W) to monitor SLBM launchings off the east and west coasts of the United States.[143] Modifications in DSP sensors are planned to improve atmospheric burst location and advanced radiation detection capabilities. The latter improvement would increase the detection range for nuclear detonations in space.[144]

DSP satellites are launched into a geosynchronous orbit aboard a Titan 3C booster from the Eastern Test Range at Cape Canaveral. At 22,300 miles the orbit of the satellite matches the rotation of the earth. Hence, the satellites "hover" over the same spot continuously.

The prime means for providing trans- and postattack nuclear detonation monitoring will be the Nuclear Detonation (NUDET) Detection System (NDS) carried on board the NAVSTAR Global Positioning System (GPS). The primary function of the GPS is to provide accurate locational data for targeting and navigation purposes; the NDS will represent a major secondary function. The GPS satellite constellation will consist of eighteen satellites in near-circular 17,610-mile orbits with an inclination of 55 degrees. The eighteen satellites will be deployed in three or more planes, each plane containing no more than six equally spaced satellites. The arrangement will guarantee that at least four to six satellites are in view at all times from any point on or near the earth.

The entire GPS constellation is intended to be operational 1988. Seven Block 1 "developmental" satellites have been launched since 1978. Beginning with the launch of GPS–8 in 1983, the NDS will be carried on all subsequent GPS satellites.[145] The two NDS packages will include x-ray and optical sensors, Bhangmeters, EMP sensors, and a data-processing capability that, according to congressional testimony, allow the detection of nuclear weapons detonations "anywhere in the world at any time and get its location down to less than a [mile]."[146] Data will be reported on a real-time basis either directly to ground stations or first to airborne terminals or other GPS satellites for subsequent downlink transmissions.[147]

Besides nuclear detection packages on the VELA, DSP, and GPS satellites, there also appear to be NUDET packages on at least one other satellite system, the NUDET capability of which is considered classified. This might be the previously discussed Satellite Data System (SDS) satellites or the Defense Meteorological Satellite Program (DMSP) spacecraft. The latter are acknowledged to have "classified sensors" in addition to their weather sensors.[148]

In addition to space-based detection systems, aerial sampling is employed to detect the atomic particles emitted by a nuclear explosion. Aircraft employed in aerial sampling operations include the U-2, P-3, C-135, and B-52.[149] Aerial sampling operations are conducted over the United States, Southern Hemisphere, and other areas under a variety of codenames, as indicated in Table 8-2. One version of the C-130 employed, the HC-130, is outfitted with a seawater sampler for sorties flown against possible foreign underwater nuclear tests.[150]

Detection of underground nuclear explosions depends on distinguishing between the seismic waves generated by a nuclear explosion and those created by an earthquake. In most cases, determining the location of seismic events eliminates the large majority of earthquakes from consideration as possible nuclear detonations. Otherwise, analysts may be able to distinguish earthquakes from detonations by the differing nature of the signals produced by each phenomenon—detonations being a point source, earthquakes the result of two bodies of rock slipping past each other. At distances of less than 625 miles from an event, explosions greater than a few kilotons can easily be distinguished from earthquakes. At greater distances, such distinctions become far more difficult.[151]

Table 8-2.   Varieties of Aerial Sampling Operations.

Code Name	Type of Operation
VOLANT CHUCK	Southern Hemisphere Reconnaissance for HQ, USAF
VOLANT CURRY	Special Weather Reconnaissance
VOLANT DOME	Domestic Reconnaissance for HQ USAF
VOLANT FISH	Water Sampler
VOLANT SPECK	Special Reconnaissance for HQ USAF
VOLANT TRACK	Special Sampling Requirement
COMBAT CATCH	Special USAF Reconnaissance
CONSTANT GLOBE	Worldwide Sampling Operations
CONSTANT DOME	Domestic Reconnaissance for HQ USAF
CONSTANT FISH	Special Operations for HQ USAF[a]
PONY EXPRESS	Special Reconnaissance for JCS

a. Special Operations are sorties flown against foreign nuclear atmospheric and underground tests.

Source: Air Force Technical Applications Center Regulation CENR55-3, "Aerial Sampling Operations," October 22, 1982.

Moreover, the actual recording of a seismic signal is disturbed by both instrumental and natural background noise, the latter setting a threshold of detectability.[152]

These limitations place a premium on locating monitoring stations or equipment in suitable locations and developing techniques to enhance the signal-to-noise ratio obtained at any location. The simplest form of earth-based monitoring equipment is the seismometer, which is basically composed of a magnet fixed to the ground and a spring-suspended mass with an electric coil.[153] According to SIPRI, "When seismic waves move the ground and the magnet attached to it, they leave the mass with the coil relatively unaffected. The relative motion of the magnet and coil generates a current in the coil which is proportional to their relative velocity."[154]

One means of enhancing the signal-to-noise ratio is the use of several seismometers in an array. Arrays increase the data set available for analysis in several ways including providing different arrival times of the seismic waves at the different seismometers. Three major (non–AFTAC) arrays are located in Montana, Alaska, and Norway. The largest and most modern of these is the Large Arperture Seismic Array (LASA) in Montana. It consists of thirteen subarrays, each made up of twenty-five short-period instruments and a three-component set of long-period seismometers. The Alaska Long Period Army (ALPA) originally consisted of nineteen long-period seismometers. It has been refitted with newly developed long-period borehole seismometers and now consists of seven three-component seismometers with an aperture of twenty-five miles. The Norwegian Seismic Array (NORSAR) consists of seven subarrays, each with forty-nine short- and seven long-period seismometers, extending over a distance of thirty-two miles.[155]

The seismic arrays and seismometers operated by the Air Force Technical Applications Center (AFTAC) are distributed throughout the world. Among AFTAC's nineteen detachments are those located in Torrejon, Spain; Crete, Greece; Lakenheath, U.K.; Okinawa, Japan; Alice Springs, Australia; Clark AFB, Philippines; and Misawa, Japan.[156] There are also unmanned locations consisting of unattended sensors.

The installation at Alice Springs, codenamed Oak Tree, is operated by Detachment 421 of AFTAC. An underground seismic array located about 1.5 miles northeast of the detachment consists of nineteen seismometers arranged in a circular pattern over 7.25 miles. Thirteen of the seismometers are buried approximately 200 feet in the ground and designed to pick up the long-period waves that pass through the surface layer of the earth. The remaining six seismometers are buried 1.1 miles deep and tuned to detect the short-period waves that pass through the mantle and core of the earth.[157]

The seismometers are linked by cables to a central recording station where the signals are processed to provide an indication of the direction and speed at which they are traveling and the amplitude of the ground motion. The processing involves the amplification of signals, filtering out of the background noise, and addition to the data of a timing standard.[158] Under favorable conditions, the station can monitor seismic events on a worldwide basis, determining the severity of the disturbances, their time of occurrence, and their approximate distance and direction. Combining the data from several other stations, a station can make an accurate estimate of location, magnitude, and cause.[159]

In addition to present systems for the collection of nuclear intelligence and treaty monitoring, experimental work on both ground- and sea-based systems is continuing. The Department of Energy, for example, has established a Regional Seismic Test Network (RSTN) for learning how an "in-country" system might be used for monitoring compliance with a comprehensive nuclear test ban treaty.[160]

The Network consists of five transmitting stations in the United States and Canada spaced about 1,250 miles apart—at Yellowknife, N.W. Territory; Red Lake, Ontario; Black Hills, South Dakota; Adirondacks, New York; CPO Tennessee; and the Nevada Test Site—and three receiving stations. The latter stations are located at Washington, D.C., the Lawrence Livermore National Laboratory in California, and the main System Control and Receiving Station (SCARS) at Sandia National Laboratory in Albuquerque, New Mexico.[161]

The instrumentation at each transmitting station consists of two three-component borehole seismometers, a broadband Geotech KS-3600, and a KS Geotech S-75D as a back-up to the 3600. The seismometers are sealed in a tamper proof package six meters long that is emplaced in a borehole nineteen centimeters in diameter at a depth of 100 meters to reduce the effect of atmospheric noise.[162]

The RSTN is designed to provide digital seismic data at regional (less than 2,000 kilometers) and teleseismic (greater than 2,000 kilometers) over a broad frequency range from 0.02 to 10 Hz. The data is transmitted to a satellite through a special unattended electronics package located on the surface near the borehole and then to the ground stations. The electronics package and a transmitting antenna are housed in a fiberglass dome five meters in diameter.[163]

The goals of the RSTN experiment include providing engineering experience in the siting and operation of sophisticated seismic equipment under severe climactic conditions as well as evaluating the performance of a regional network in a geological environment similar to that of the Soviet Union.[164] Additionally, the network experiment is intended to help determine the number of seismic stations and the data-processing capabilities required to distinguish earthquakes and explosions of low magnitudes.[165]

With respect to undersea monitoring of nuclear explosions, present R&D efforts that form the Fiscal Year 1983–Fiscal Year 1984 Nuclear Monitoring Programs include the testing of an ocean bottom seismic sensor system involving the deployment of seismometers in boreholes beneath the sea floor in international waters. The concept was tested in an experiment in the mid-Atlantic in which a seismometer was successfully installed and recovered from a borehole 2,000 feet below the sea floor in 15,000 feet of water using the drill ship GLOMAR CHALLENGER. Installation of a prototype station was attempted in September 1982, but unfavorable geological conditions prevented the CHALLENGER from completing the drilling of the borehole.[166]

NOTES TO CHAPTER 8

1. "U.S. Launches Recon Satellite Soviet Fleet Maneuvers May Be Target," *Aerospace Daily*, April 22, 1975, pp. 290–91.
2. Ibid.
3. Anthony Kenden, "U.S. Reconnaissance Satellite Programs," *Spaceflight*, July 20, 1973, p. 257.
4. Janko Jackson, "A Methodology for Ocean Surveillance Analysis," *Naval War College Review* 27, no. 2 (September/October 1974): 71–89.
5. "Navy Plans Ocean Surveillance Satellite," *Aviation Week and Space Technology*, August 30, 1971, p. 13; "Industry Observer," *Aviation Week and Space Technology*, February 28, 1972, p. 9.
6. "Navy Plans Ocean Surveillance Satellite."
7. "Industry Observer," February 28, 1972.
8. The entire system consists of the satellite/spacecraft (White Cloud) plus ground terminals for data receipt from the satellite as well as data-processing equipment.
9. "Navy Ocean Surveillance Satellite Depicted," *Aviation Week and Space Technology*, May 24, 1976, p. 22.
10. "Expanded Ocean Surveillance Effort Set," *Aviation Week and Space Technology*, June 10, 1978, pp. 22–23; Mark Hewlish, "Satellites Show Their Warlike Face," *New Scientist*, October 1, 1981, pp. 36–40.
11. Ibid.
12. Ibid.
13. Ibid.
14. Ibid.
15. D. G. King–Hele, J. A. Pilkington, H. Hiller, and D. M. C. Walker, *The RAE Table of Earth Satellites 1957-1980* (New York: Facts on File, 1981); *The RAE Table of Earth Satellites 1983* (Farnborough, England: Royal Aircraft Establishment, 1984).
16. "Expanded Ocean Surveillance Effort Set."
17. Ibid.
18. Ibid.
19. Ibid.
20. Defense Marketing Survey, *Code Name Handbook* (Greenwich, Conn.: DMS, 1980), p. 78; U.S. Congress, House Committee on Appropriations, *Military Construction Appropriations for 1981* (Washington, D.C.: U.S. Government Printing Office, 1980), pp. 1474–77, 1504–09, and 1516–19; U.S. Congress, House Committee on Appropriations, *Military Con-*

struction Appropriations for 1982 (Washington, D.C.: U.S. Government Printing Office, 1981), pp. 1231–36 and 1301–06; U.S. Congress, House Committee on Appropriations, *Military Construction Appropriations for 1983, Part I* (Washington, D.C.: U.S. Government Printing Office, 1982), p. 842; U.S. Congress, Senate Armed Services Committee, *Military Construction Authorization Fiscal Year 1980* (Washington, D.C.: U.S. Government Printing Office, 1979); U.S. Congress, House Armed Services Committee, *Military Construction Authorization Fiscal Year 1980* (Washington, D.C.: U.S. Government Printing Office, 1979), p. 474.

21. Duncan Campbell, "How We Spy on Argentina," *New Statesman*, April 30, 1982, p. 5.

22. *Joint Electronic Type Designation System* (Fort Monmouth, N.J.: Army Communications Command, 1981).

23. "Expanded Ocean Surveillance Effort Set."

24. "Industry Observer," *Aviation Week and Space Technology*, June 20, 1977, p. 11.

25. "Expanded Ocean Surveillance Efforts Set."

26. Naval Military Personnel Command, *Catalog of Navy Training Courses* (Washington, D.C.: Department of the Navy, 1980).

27. "Industry Observer," *Aviation Week and Space Technology*, December 16, 1974, p. 9.

28. "Navy Space Expansion Requires Dedicated Satellites," *Defense Electronics*, July 1981, pp. 79–84.

29. "Industry Observer," *Aviation Week and Space Technology*, July 7, 1980, p. 13.

30. U.S. Congress, House Committee on Armed Services, *Hearings on Military Posture and HR5068 Book 1, Part 3* (Washington, D.C.: U.S. Government Printing Office, 1977), p. 751.

31. *The Military Reconnaissance and Surveillance Market* (New York: Frost & Sullivan, 1979), pp. 21–22.

32. U.S. Congress, Senate Committee on Armed Services, *Department of Defense Authorization for Fiscal Year 1979, Part 8* (Washington, D.C.: U.S. Government Printing Office, 1978), p. 6268.

33. Ibid.

34. Ibid.

35. Ibid., p. 6269.

36. U.S. Congress, House Committee on Armed Services, *Hearings on Military Posture and HR5068 Book 1, Part 3*, p. 751.

37. "Industry Observer," *Aviation Week and Space Technology*, July 26, 1976, p. 11; "Filter Center," *Aviation Week and Space Technology*, June 20, 1977, p. 65.

38. U.S. Congress, Senate Committee on Commerce, Science, and Transportation, *NASA Authorization for Fiscal Year 1980* (Washington, D.C.: U.S. Government Printing Office), p. 1721; "Industry Observer," *Aviation Week and Space Technology*, April 2, 1979, p. 9 and April 16, 1979, p. 11.

39. National Aeronautics and Space Administration, *Satellite Situation Report* 24, no. 2 (April 30, 1984): 46.

40. "Navy Will Develop All-Weather Ocean Monitor Satellite," *Aviation Week and Space Technology*, August 28, 1978, p. 50; "Space Reonnaissance Dwindles."

41. "Future of Space Communications Dedicated on EHF Use," *Defense Electronics*, July 1981, p. 80.

42. U.S. Congress, House Committee on Armed Services, *Hearings on Military Posture and HR 5968, Part 5* (Washington, D.C.: U.S. Government Printing Office, 1981), p. 575.

43. Ibid., pp. 580–81.

44. U.S. Congress, Senate Committee on Armed Services, *Department of Defense Authorization for Appropriations for FY 1983, Part 6* (Washington, D.C.: U.S. Government Printing Office, 1982), p. 3825; Clarence A. Robinson, Jr., "Defense Decisions Hike Strategy Funds," *Aviation Week and Space Technology*, August 23, 1982, p. 19.

45. L. T. Peacock, *U.S. Naval Aviation Today* (Uxbridge, England: Cheney Press, 1977), p. 25.

46. Defense Marketing Service, "Lockheed P–3 Orion," *DMS Market Intelligence Report* (Greenwich, Conn.: DMS, 1982), pp. 1–7.

47. Peacock, *U.S. Naval Aviation Today*, p. 25.

48. Ibid.

49. Owen Wilkes, "Strategic Anti-Submarine Warfare and Its Implications for a Counterforce First Strike," *SIPRI Yearbook 1979* (London: Taylor & Francis Ltd., 1979), p. 430.

50. Defense Marketing Service "Program 749," *DMS Market Intelligence Report* (Greenwich, Conn.: DMS, 1977), pp. 1, 2.

51. U.S. Congress, Senate Committee on Commerce, Science and Transportation, *NASA Authorization for Fiscal Year 1980*, p. 1723.

52. Defense Marketing Service, "FLR–15," *DMS Market Intelligence Report* (Greenwich, Conn.: DMS, 1977).

53. Jeffrey Richelson and Desmond Ball, *The Ties that Bind: The UKUSA Intelligence Network* (London: Allen & Unwin, 1985).

54. "Testimony of Admiral Metzel," in Senate Armed Services Committee, *Department of Defense Authorization for Appropriations for Fiscal Year 1980, Part 6* (Washington, D.C.: U.S. Government Printing Office, 1979), p. 2925.

55. Wilkes, "Strategic Anti-Submarine Warfare."

56. *Fiscal Year 1981 Arms Control Impact Statements* (Washington, D.C.: U.S. Government Printing Office, 1980), p. 239; Norman Friedman, "SOSUS and US ASW Tactics," *U.S. Naval Institute Proceedings*, March 1980, pp. 120–22.

57. U.S. Congress, House Appropriations Committee, *Department of Defense Appropriations for Fiscal Year 1977, Part 5* (Washington, D.C.: U.S. Government Printing Office, 1976), p. 1255; Drew Middleton, "Expert Predicts A Big U.S. Gain in Sub Warfare," *New York Times*, July 18, 1979, p. A5; Chapman Pincher, "U.S. to Set Up Sub Spy Station," *Daily Express*, January 6, 1973.

58. Harvey B. Silverstein, "Caesar, SOSUS and Submarines: Economic and Institutional Implications of ASW Technologies," *Ocean '78* (Proceedings of the Fourth Annual Combined Conference Sponsored by the Marine Technology Society and the Institute of Electrical and Electronics Engineers, Washington, D.C., September 6–8, 1978), p. 407.

59. Ibid.; Defense Marketing Service, "Sonar-Sub-Surface-Caesar," *DMS Market Intelligence Report* (Greenwich, Conn.: DMS, 1980), p. 1.

60. Bernard Kovit, "New Anti-Sub Aircraft," *Space/Aeronautics* 45 (February 1966): 58–71.

61. Silverstein, "Caeser, SOSUS and Submarines"; Clyde W. Burleson, *The Jennifer Project* (Englewood Cliffs, N.J.: Prentice Hall, 1977).

62. Defense Marketing Service, "Sonar Technology–AUTEC," *DMS Market Intelligence Report* (Greenwich, Conn.: DMS, 1981).

63. Howard B. Dratch, "High Stakes in Azores," *The Nation*, November 8, 1975, pp. 455–56; "NATO Fixed Sonar Range Commissioned," *Armed Forces Journal*, August 1972, p. 29; "Atlantic Islands: NATO Seeks Wider Facilities," *International Herald Tribune*, June 1981, p. 25; Richard Tismar, "Portugal Bargains for U.S. Military Aid with Strategic Mid-Atlantic Base," *Christian Science Monitor*, March 24, 1981, p. 9.

64. Defense Marketing Service, "Sonar-Sub-Surface-Caesar," p. 1.

65. U.S. Congress, Senate Appropriations Committee, *Department of Defense Appropriations, Fiscal Year 1975, Part 3* (Washington, D.C.: U.S. Government Printing Office, 1974): 444.

66. Joel S. Wit, "Advances in Anti-Submarine Warfare," *Scientific American* 224 (February 1981): 36–37.

67. George C. Wilson, "Soviet Nuclear Sub Reported Sunk," *Washington Post*, August 11, 1983, p. A9.

68. U.S. Congress Senate Armed Services Committee, *Department of Defense Authorization for Appropriations for Fiscal Year 1980, Part 6*, pp. 2947–49; Wilkes, "Strategic Anti-Submarine Warfare," p. 431; U.S. Congress, House Committee on International Relations, *Evaluation of Fiscal Year 1979 Arms Control Impact Statements*, p. 112.

69. Kosta Tsipis, "Antisubmarine Warfare: Fact & Fiction," *New Scientist*, January 16, 1975, p. 147.

70. Defense Marketing Service, "ASW," *DMS Market Intelligence Report* (Greenwich, Conn.: DMS, 1980).

71. Larry L. Booda, "Antisubmarine Warfare Reacts to Strategic Indicators," *Sea Technology*, November 1981, p. 12.

72. U.S. Congress, House Committee on Foreign Affairs and Senate Committee on Foreign Relations, *Fiscal Year 1981 Arms Control Impact Statement* (Washington, D.C.: U.S. Government Printing Office, 1980), pp. 347–48.

73. "British Say Soviet Lags in Sub Detection," *Baltimore Sun*, December 31, 1980, p. 4.

74. U.S. Congress, Senate Armed Service Committee, *Department of Defense Authorization for Appropriation for Fiscal Year 1980, Part 6*, p. 2984;

U.S. Congress, Senate Armed Services Committee, *Department of Defense Authorization for Appropriations for Fiscal Year 1979, Part 8* (Washington, D.C.: U.S. Government Printing Office, 1978), p. 6350.

75. U.S. Congress, Senate Committee on Armed Services, *Department of Defense Authorization for FY 1983, Part 6*, p. 3825.

76. U.S. Congress, House Committee on International Relations, *Evaluation of Fiscal Year 1979 Arms Control Impact Statements*, p. 111.

77. Ibid.; James Schultz, "Anti-Sub Warfare Escalates," *Defense Electronics*, June 1983, pp. 76–89.

78. U.S. Congress, Senate Armed Services Committee, *Department of Defense Authorization for Appropriations for Fiscal Year 1980, Part 6*, pp. 2947–49; Larry L. Booda, "SURTASS, RDSS Augment Ocean Surveillance," *Sea Technology*, November 1981, pp. 19–29; Norman Polmar, "SURTASS and T–AGOS," *U.S. Naval Institute Proceedings*, March 1980, pp. 120–24; U.S. Congress, House Committee on Foreign Affairs and Senate Committee on Foreign Relations, *Fiscal Year 1981 Arms Control Impact Statement*, p. 342.

79. Jack Anderson, "U.S. Missile Subs Are Vulnerable to Surveillance," *Washington Post*, December 9, 1983, p. E7, citing a classified General Accounting Office report, "The Need for Improving Mapping, Charting and Geodesy Support of the Strategic Ballistic Missile Submarine Force."

80. Defense Marketing Service, *Code Name Handbook 1981* (Greenwich, Conn.: DMS, 1981), pp. 291, 296.

81. Owen Wilkes and Nils Peter Gleditsch, "Optical Satellite Tracking: A Case Study of University Participation in Space Warfare," *Journal of Peace Research* 15, no. 3 (1978): 205–25.

82. NORAD/SPACECOM, *Numerical Index of Standard Publications*, Command Regulation 0–2, July 1, 1983, p. 14.

83. Philip Taubman, "How We Know That They Know That . . . ," *New York Times*, September 11, 1983, p. 2E.

84. Anthony Kenden, "Was Columbia Photographed by a KH–11?" *Journal of the British Interplanetary Society* 36 (1983): 73–77.

85. "Washington Round-Up," *Aviation Week and Space Technology*, April 18, 1983, p. 17; Jack Cushman, "Space Eyes Stretch the Limits of IR Budget and Technologies," *Defense Week* 4, no. 4 (January 1983): 1, 18–19.

86. U.S. Congress, House Committee on Appropriations, *Department of Defense Appropriations for 1984, Part 4* (Washington, D.C.: U.S. Government Printing Office, 1983), pp. 618–19.

87. U.S. Congress, House Committee on Appropriations, *Department of Defense Appropriations for 1984, Part 8*, pp. 506–8.

88. U.S. Air Force, "SAC Fact Sheet," August 1981, p. 81–001.415.

89. Ibid.

90. Richard Halloran, "Nuclear Missiles: Warning System and the Question of When to Fire," *New York Times*, May 29, 1983, pp. 1, 38.

91. Wilkes and Gleditsch, "Optical Satellite Tracking."

92. Craig Covault, "USAF Awaits Space Defense Guidance," *Aviation Week and Space Technology*, February 22, 1982, p. 65; David Russell, "NORAD

Adds Radar Optics to Increase Space Defense," *Defense Electronics*, July 1982, pp. 82–86.

93. U.S. Congress, Senate Committee on Armed Services, *Department of Defense Authorization for Appropriations for Fiscal Year 1980, Part 6*, p. 3022.

94. "U.S. Upgrading Ground-Based Sensors," *Aviation Week and Space Technology*, June 16, 1980, pp. 239–42.

95. Russell, "NORAD Adds Radar Optics to Increase Space Defense."

96. "U.S. Upgrading Ground-Based Sensors."

97. Russell, "NORAD Adds Radar Optics to Increase Space Defense."

98. "U.S. Upgrading Ground-Based Sensors."

99. Ibid.

100. "GEODSS Photographs Orbiting Satellite," *Aviation Week and Space Technology*, December 5, 1983, pp. 146–47.

101. "Focus," *Defense Electronics*, November 1983, p. 30; Department of the Air Force, *Justification of Estimates for Fiscal Year 1984 Submitted to Congress January 1983* (Springfield, Virg.: National Technical Information Service, 1983), pp. 137–38.

102. "Spacetrack," *Jane's Weapon's Systems 1982–1983* (London: Jane's Publishing, 1982), p. 233–34; Russell, "NORAD Adds Radar,"; "The Arms Race in Space," *SIPRI Yearbook 1978 World Disarmament and Armaments* (New York: Crane, Russell, 1978), pp. 114–24.

103. "Spacetrack," *Jane's Weapon's Systems 1982–1983*.

104. Ibid.

105. "The Arms Race in Space," *SIPRI Yearbook 1978*, pp. 114–24.

106. Ibid.

107. "Spacetrack," *Jane's Weapon's Systems 1982–1983*.

108. U.S. Congress Senate Committee on Armed Services, *Department of Defense Authorization for Appropriations for Fiscal Year 1980, Part 6*, p. 3021; Covault, "USAF Awaits . . . "; U.S. Congress, House Committee on Appropriations, *Department of Defense Appropriations for 1981, Part 8* (Washington, D.C.: U.S. Government Printing Office, 1980), p. 240.

109. Ibid.

110. Covault, "USAF Awaits . . . "

111. "BMEWS," *Jane's Weapons Systems 1982–1983*.

112. "The Arms Race in Space," *SIPRI Yearbook 1978*, p. 116.

113. "Improved U.S. Warning Net Spurred," *Aviation Week and Space Technology*, June 23, 1980, pp. 38ff.

114. John Hambre et al., *Strategic Command, Control and Communications: Alternative Approaches for Modernization* (Washington, D.C.: Congressional Budget Office, 1981), p. 10.

115. "SLBM Detection System," *Jane's Weapon Systems 1982–1983*, p. 501.

116. "U.S. Upgrading Ground Sensors."

117. "SLBM Detection Systems," *Jane's Weapon Systems 1982–1983*, p. 501.

118. "AN/FPS-85," *Jane's Weapons Systems 1982–1983*, p. 506; "The Arms Race in Space," *SIPRI Yearbook 1978*, p. 114–24; Hambre et al., *Strategic Command Control*.

119. Owen Wilkes, *Spacetracking and Spacewarfare* (Oslo: International Peace Research Institute, 1978), p. 27.

120. Ibid.

121. "AN/FPS–85"; Wilkes, *Spacetracking and Spacewarfare*, p. 27.

122. U.S. Air Force, "SAC Fact Sheet."

123. "The Arms Race in Space," *SIPRI Yearbook 1978*, pp. 114–24.

124. U.S. Air Force, "SAC Fact Sheet."

125. Defense Marketing Service, *Code Name Handbook 1981* (Greenwich, Conn.: DMS, 1981), p. 168; U.S. Congress, House Committee on Appropriations, *Department of Defense Appropriations for 1981, Part 8*, p. 241.

126. U.S. Air Force, "SAC Fact Sheet"; U.S. Congress, Senate Committee on Armed Services, *Department of Defense Authorization for Appropriations for Fiscal Year 1980, Part 6*, p. 3021.

127. U.S. Air Force, "SAC Fact Sheet."

128. The United States has not ratified the 1974 Threshold Test Ban Treaty. Both the United States and the Soviet Union have said they would abide by its provisions. See Walter Pincus, "White House Reassesses Opposition to Ratify Nuclear Test Treaty," *Washington Post*, June 25, 1983, p. A14.

129. U.S. Congress, Senate Committee on Appropriations, *Department of Defense Appropriations for Fiscal Year 1972, Part 1*, (Washington, D.C.: U.S. Government Printing Office, 1971), p. 672.

130. "Forum: The Explosion of October 16," *Bulletin of the Atomic Scientists*, February 1965.

131. See Jeffrey Richelson, "PD–59, NSDD–13 and the Reagan Strategic Modernization Program," *Journal of Strategic Studies* 6, no. 2 (1983): 125–46.

132. Larry Booda, "Satellite Planned to Detect Space Blasts," *Aviation Week and Space Technology*, November 14, 1960, p. 29. Of course, prior to that time the United States monitored Soviet nuclear explosions. The first Soviet atomic explosion was detected by a reconnaissance aircraft outfitted with air-sampling equipment that was flying a routine mission. VELA represents the beginnings of the present worldwide detection system.

133. Ibid.

134. Philip Klass, "Clandestine Nuclear Test Doubted," *Aviation Week and Space Technology*, August 11, 1980, pp. 67–72.

135. David Baker, *The Shape of Wars to Come* (New York: Stein & Day, 1982), pp. 147–48.

136. Ibid.

137. Ibid., p. 149.

138. Klass, "Clandestine Nuclear Test Doubted."

139. Sidney Singer, "The VELA Satellite Program for Detection of High Attitude Nuclear Detonations," *Proceedings of the IEEE* 53 (December 1965): 1935–48.

140. Klass, "Clandestine Nuclear Test Doubted"; Eliot Marshall, "Navy Lab Concludes VELA Saw a Bomb," *Science*, August 29, 1980, pp. 996–99.

141. Ibid.

142. Ibid.

143. Ibid.

144. "Industry Observer," *Aviation Week and Space Technology*, December 13, 1982, p. 13; "Washington Round-Up," *Aviation Week and Space Technology*, December 6, 1982, p. 19.

145. "Washington Round-Up," *Aviation Week and Space Technology*, December 6, 1982, p. 19; U.S. Congress, House Committee on Appropriations, *Department of Defense Appropriations for 1983, Part 5* (Washington, D.C.: U.S. Government Printing Office, 1982), pp. 16, 75.

146. U.S. Congress, House Committee on Appropriations, *Department of Defense Appropriations for 1983, Part 5*, p. 16; U.S. Congress, House Committee on Appropriations, *Department of Defense Appropriations for 1984, Part 8*, p. 337; U.S. Congress, House Committee on Armed Services, *Department of Energy National Security and Military Applications of Nuclear Energy Authorization Act of 1984* (Washington, D.C.: U.S. Government Printing Office, 1983), pp. 383–84.

147. "Navstar Bloc 2 Satellites to Have Crosslinks, Radiation Hardening," *Defense Electronics*, July 1983, p. 16.

148. U.S. Congress, House Committee on Armed Services, *Department of Energy National Security and Military Applications*, pp. 383–84, 392; RCA Astro-Electronics Briefing Slides, "Defense Meteorological Satellite Program," no date.

149. Air Force Technical Applications Center Regulation CENR 55-3, "Aerial Sampling Operations," October 22, 1982.

150. Ibid.

151. Henry R. Myers, "Extending the Nuclear Test Ban," *Scientific American* 226, no. 1 (January 1972): 13–23; Lynn R. Sykes and Jack F. Evernder, "The Verification of a Comprehensive Nuclear Test Ban," *Scientific American* 247, no. 11 (October 1982): 47–55.

152. "The Comprehensive Test Ban," *SIPRI Yearbook 1978 World Armaments and Disarmament* (New York: Crane, Russell, 1978), p. 335.

153. Ibid.

154. Ibid.

155. Ibid., p. 340.

156. Private information.

157. Desmond Ball, *A Suitable Piece of Real Estate: American Installations in Australia* (Sydney: Hale and Iremonger, 1980), pp. 84–85.

158. Ibid.

159. Ibid.

160. U.S. Congress, House Committee on Armed Services, *Department of Energy National Security and Military Applications*, pp. 384, 392.

161. Steven R. Taylor, "The Regional Seismic Test Network," *Energy and Technology Review*, May 1983, pp. 20–29.

162. Ibid.
163. Ibid.
164. Ibid.
165. Ibid.
166. Department of Defense, *Justification of Estimates for Fiscal Year 1984* (Washington, D.C.: DOD, 1983, pp. 257–61.

9 HUMAN AND OTHER SOURCES

It has often been noted that the increasing capability to collect intelligence via technical means has reduced the reliance on the human agent and other sources. However, it is not the case that human and other sources, whether open or clandestine, are inconsequential. Such sources can be used to fill gaps left by technical collection systems—in some cases important gaps. Sometimes gaps will result because of the inherent limitations of technical systems: With proper security, many discussions will be immune to interception; also, technical systems cannot photograph planning or policy documents locked in a vault. Additionally, technical systems are expensive and can be employed against a limited number of targets. Thus, information on lower priority targets may be desired, but only if it can be acquired without the introduction of a new or enhanced technical collection system or the diversion of an operating system away from higher priority targets.

A high priority for U.S. intelligence is to understand the decision processes involved in foreign, military, and economic policymaking in the Soviet Union. This includes the processes of the Politburo, the Defense Council, the entire military command (most especially that involved in military R&D), the GOS-PLAN, the KGB and the theater command structures.[1] An understanding of both the processes and people can lead to a more accurate estimation of the likely course of action in a given circumstance. Some data on such matters may be obtained by technical means, but there will be gaps that may be filled only by other sources.

A further objective of intelligence activities is the acquisition of planning documents, technical manuals, contingency plans, and weapons systems blue-

171

prints. As Amrom Katz noted, "the analysts . . . want the designer's plan, note-
books, tests on components, tests of materials, conversation between the designer and the customer."[2] Although in most cases the analyst must settle for
images and electronic data concerning test activities, it is often the designers'
documentation that constitutes the "best evidence."

Certain stages of military R&D are simply not available for technical monitoring. Once plans have reached the testing stage, a variety of U.S. technical collection systems can be employed. But when the weapon is being designed, its characteristics debated, technical collection can be of very limited utility. It is desirable to know about the characteristics of weapons systems when they have
reached the testing stage, but it is also important to know whatever one can
about what is going on in the design bureaus. It is always possible that by the
time some weapon reaches the testing stage it will be too late to develop a counter to it prior to its becoming operational.

In some countries—both Allied and Third World—U.S. intelligence requirements may focus primarily on domestic political conflict and economic activity.
The information desired may concern the activities of a nation's Communist or
Socialist party or the country's economic prospects in the short term. In such
cases, the information might be better acquired by penetrations of the Communist party or Ministry of Commerce and Trade than by sporadic signals intelligence. In many cases, open source information will be more valuable than anything that can be obtained by signals interception,

Significant intelligence concerning the political, military, and economic
affairs of other nations can be obtained through a variety of sources other than
technical collection, open source and human source collection being the most
well known of these methods. Specifically, open source collection includes the
acquisition of any verbal, written, or electronically transmitted material that it
is legal to acquire. Thus, open source collection includes the acquisition of newspapers, magazines, and unclassified journals as well as the monitoring of the public radio and television media. Human intelligence (HUMINT) collection covers
the intelligence obtained by clandestine agents and attachés as well as by the
interviewing of defectors, émigrés, and travelers.

Two additional sources of intelligence should be noted. An important part of
the HUMINT activities conducted by the Central Intelligence Agency and other
intelligence agencies is acquired by electronic surveillance and mail openings.
The electronic surveillance usually takes the form of bugging or phone tapping.
Although strictly a "technical collection" activity, bugging and phone tapping
are so distinct from satellite or aircraft signals interception as to merit separate
consideration. Further, such operations are conducted as part of overall CIA and
military service HUMINT activities. Finally, another significant aspect of intelligence collection revolves around "material exploitation"—the acquisition and
analysis of foreign weapons, communications, and other systems. Such acquisition and analysis yields information on weapons systems such as firearms that

cannot be acquired by overhead photography and more detailed information on systems such as tanks—information that can be used to design countermeasures.

OPEN SOURCE COLLECTION

Open source collection involves one of three activities: collection of legally available documents; open observation of foreign political, military, or economic activity; and the monitoring and recording of public radio and television broadcasts. In more open societies, a variety of open source information concerning political, military, and economic intelligence is available—newspapers, magazines, trade journals, academic journals, and government documents. These published sources may yield intelligence concerning the internal disputes plaguing a Western Communist party, French nuclear strategy, Japanese willingness to restrict imports, or scientific advances in East Germany.

Thus, the statement of Roscoe Hillenkoeter, the Director of Central Intelligence in 1948, that "80 percent of intelligence is derived from such prosaic sources as foreign books, magazines, technical and scientific surveys, photographs, commercial analysis, newspapers and radio broadcasts, and general information from people with a knowledge of affairs abroad" remains true today.[3]

Of course, in a closed society much less information will be available. Most particularly, direct reporting on internal political and military affairs will be absent. Further, all reporting will be conducted under the direction of government propaganda guidelines. However, even in a closed society such as the Soviet Union, there is a significant amount of intelligence that can be gleaned from legally obtainable documents.

The obtainable material will include newspapers, magazines, collected speeches, academic journals, and even official documents on military affairs. These latter documents, while generally devoid of information concerning specific weapons systems, do discuss in detail Soviet views concerning operational tactics and grand strategy.

The Soviets publish eleven major military journals and newspapers—including *Communist of the Armed Forces, Military-Historical Journal*, and *Military Herald.* Additionally, there are a significant number of minor and more specialized publications and as many as 500 books on military affairs published each year.[4]

The most important military newspaper is *Krasnaya Zvezda* (Red Star), published by the Main Political Administration of the Soviet Army and Navy (MPA). The MPA is responsible for ensuring the ideological conformity of Soviet military personnel and is outside the normal military chain of command; thus, *Krasnaya Zvezda* is somewhat more open about military shortcomings such as incompetence and corruption.[5] It can also provide information on Soviet military operations. For example, an early 1983 article by Lt. Col. Artemko entitled

"An Assault Landing Force Capturing It's Objective" discussed a particular military operation in Afghanistan.[6]

Civilian newspapers and collected speeches can provide a variety of information. Even in the Soviet Union, conflict at the higher levels can be detected by material, usually speeches, appearing in the press. The signs are more obscure than in Western society, but they do exist. There is a Soviet language of conflict indicating both ideological and practical disputes. The subject of these disputes might involve agricultural or economic policy, military strategy, or foreign policy. The signs of conflict might be a dropped signature, a pruned speech, or more direct indications. Andrew Cockburn relates the following set of events:

> In the fall of 1969, just as the talks were beginning in Helsinki, *Pravda*, the official organ of the Communist Party, reported a speech by the Foreign Minister, Andrei Gromyko, in which he had mentioned that "some people" were not convinced of the correctness of undertaking such negotiations. In the spring of 1973, Defense Minister Grechko had been promoted to the ruling Politburo at the same time as Gromyko, who had been prominently associated with the SALT I treaty signed in 1972, and Brezhnev's ally, Yuri Andropov. In January 1974, *Pravda* began publishing extracts of Grechko's speeches rather than the full versions, something that does not happen to members of the Politburo who are in good standing with the inner leadership.
>
> In 1974 the dispute erupted into what, by Soviet standards, was a public slanging match. A frequently expressed precept of Soviet military doctrine had been that the best way to preserve peace was to prepare for war. In June 1974 *Pravda* reported a remark by Brezhnev that conveyed a different notion: the best way to keep the peace was by "waging peace" – meaning detente, SALT negotiations, and so forth. Shortly after, *Krasnayazvezda* featured articles by both Grechko and Kulikov rejecting this concept and reaffirming the concept of military preparedness as the best way of preventing war.[7]

Additionally, the relative power of members of the ruling elite in Soviet society can be detected by following Soviet reporting. Hence, the first indication of Yuri Andropov's accession to the post of General Secretary was the public announcement that he had been designated to head the funeral procession for Leonid Brezhnev.

In some situations local newspapers can reveal useful data concerning local conditions, transfers of individuals, and, in wartime, casualty rates. In World War II the Office of Strategic Services (OSS) went to great trouble to obtain local newspapers because "there was a fairly constant ratio of enlisted men to officers killed. By underground means we obtained small-town newspapers. We read them carefully. By 1943 we were able to make an estimate of the strength of the German army that turned out to be curiously exact."[8] Even newspaper obituaries in peacetime can be of value, as they might indicate where someone worked as well as his position.

Academic journals can also be quite revealing. Journals of the social science research institutes—the USA and Canada Institute, for example—might indicate the subjects of particular concern to the leadership; that is, those about which it is considered most important to influence opinion. Technical journals are of more importance. Although the areas that are considered to be secret military research are much broader than in the West, there is still much available. For one thing, Soviet researchers, like researchers elsewhere, are interested in publishing their results—even if in watered-down form. Additionally, such publication is a necessary part of scientific communication which allows cumulative work in any field of research. Hence, some indication of the work being done at research institutes with military functions can be determined by examining the articles appearing in technical journals and the authors' names and affiliations.

In any case, examination of journals in fields such as chemistry, physics, biology, optics, or mathematics can indicate the state of Soviet knowledge in particular fields—fields that either have a military application or, at the very least, affect Soviet economic capability. Noting the authors and their affiliations will indicate which ones may be also working at nearby research institutes involved in military projects.

In addition, charting the frequency with which researchers publish may yield insights into the formation of new research groups, new weapons systems, or new directions for research. Thus, the first indication to Soviet intelligence that the United States was at work on producing an atomic bomb was the noted absence of publications by top U.S. nuclear physicists such as Hans Bethe, Eugene Wigner, and Edward Teller.[9] Recently, it has been noted that the Soviet Union once had a large number of research groups that published extensively on the theory of x-ray lasers until 1977. The sudden end to the published reports has led to speculation that the program has moved into direct military applications.[10]

Examination of the technical literature might also provide clues to the occurrence of events of interest to the intelligence community. Thus, on the basis of articles in Soviet technical journals, historian Zhores Medvedev has concluded that a serious nuclear accident took place in the Soviet Union in the late 1950s.[11] More recently, there have been charges that an anthrax outbreak in Sverslodk resulted from biological warfare experiments in violation of Soviet treaty commitments. It can confidently be assumed that U.S. intelligence analysts have examined both local newspapers and Soviet biological and chemical journals to detect information that would cast light on what actually happened.

The utility of open source information in producing intelligence estimates concerning the Soviet Union was the subject of the following exchange between a member of the House Permanent Select Committee on Intelligence (Rep. Anderson) and two Soviet experts (Richard Pipes and Raymond Garthoff).

Mr. Anderson. If I may, I would like to return to this question of how you can use open sources in the NIEs. How big a volume of this Soviet material is there? How many journals and how many newspapers are we talking about?

Mr. Pipes. It is a very large immense body of literature but a trained person can scan it quite rapidly, because so much of it is unimportant. This applies not only to strategic weapons. I am speaking in general terms. For example, a few years ago I did a sort of study of Soviet policy vis-à-vis the Third World. I had to wade through many articles, but they began to fall into certain patterns. You go through an article very rapidly to look at the key sentences as to what the policy will be, or the controversies, such as they were. When the volume is extremely large, you can develop analysts who go through it quickly, and then if they are well trained, their eyes will alight on what are the critical things. They can look at an article and say, now, this is something new, and they then can study the text more closely, whereas much of the text is repititious.

Mr. Anderson. But it would be fair to describe it as a full-time job for more than one person.

Mr. Pipes. Oh, heavens yes. This is a full-time job for many people.

Mr. Garthoff. But with one or two exceptions, there are about a dozen serious Soviet military journals which are available on subscription . . . there are a number of people working with these materials. As we were both saying earlier, the main problem is in the attention to be given to and in the thorough use of the material. The basic job of acquiring and of going through these materials and translating many of them is being done on a regular basis, and there are many people in the Government and a few outside who do follow these things fairly closely. So it is more a question of the weight to be given to it and the utilization of it—it is not a matter of ignoring it totally in the process.

Mr. Pipes. In London there is a small outfit called the Central Asian Research Center, which publishes a periodical called "The Soviet Union and China in the Third World." This is an invaluable source because they go through all the Soviet and Chinese literature dealing with the Third World. Now, this operation is carried on by a handful of people. It is a marvelous source of information on Soviet intentions, because you can tell a great deal about what the Russians intend to do from their pronouncements, from the quantity of aid they give to a country, and so on.

Take a methodological example. You trace over the years the amount of economic aid given by the Soviet Union to various countries, divide it by the number of its inhabitants, and you get a pecking order of its importance to the Soviet Union. Afghanistan and Yemen have the highest ratings. You could have almost predicted the Soviet involvement in Afghanistan on that basis. Similarly, for some reason, Morocco has a very high rating at present. I am just giving this as an illustration of what you can get by looking at the available material and analyzing it intelligently. Of course, this is more difficult in the military field than in the political one, but in the political field you have an enormous volume of material available which, if intelligently used, gives you a very good idea of their intentions, and then, if you superimpose or add it to the military information you have from intelligence sources, you obtain a very good picture of what the Russians are up to.[12]

Simple observation can also be of intelligence value. Noting the public appearances of Soviet leaders can indicate their relative positions at any given moment—either by their order of appearance or by their repeated absence. In December 1983, Western embassies monitored the passage of a high-speed motorcade that moved to and from the Kremlin during the morning and evening rush hours along the route from the city center to a special Kremlin hospital in an attempt to determine if Soviet President Yuri Andropov had returned to work.[13] The first signs of Andropov's death came on February 9, 1984 from a variety of public signs: changes in the programming of the state radio and television (from jazz to classical music) as well as scores of lit windows (rather than the normal three or four) in the offices in the headquarters of the KGB, Soviet general staff, and Ministry of Defense. Half the lights on the sixth and eight floors of the KGB were visible, as were those on three full floors of the Ministry of Defense. Additionally, there was an unusual amount of movement by cars belonging to the KGB.[14]

Open source collection also involves the information that can be acquired by open discussion between U.S. diplomatic and military personnel (attachés) with foreign officials. Thus, a significant open source collection role of diplomats and military attachés is the maintenance of contact with foreign officials to obtain information on foreign government policies, capabilities, and likely reaction to U.S. initiatives.

As evidenced in the case of Andropov's death, monitoring of radio and television broadcasts can also be a valuable source of information. Through the Foreign Broadcast Information Service (FBIS, discussed in Chapter 2) in cooperation with the British Broadcasting Corporation's Monitoring Service (discussed in Chapter 10) the United States obtains a vast amount of information concerning political, military, and economic events throughout the world. This monitoring also allows the United States to assess the impact of its own propaganda efforts.

FBIS monitoring stations are located at Abidjan. Ivory Coast; Amman, Jordan; Asuncion, Paraquay; Athens, Greece; Bangkok, Thailand; Chiva Chiva, Panama; Hong Kong; Key West, Florida; London; Nicosia, Cyprus; Okinawa; Seoul; Tel Aviv; Vienna; and Washington, D.C.[15] The results of the FBIS's monitoring operations are contained in the daily (Monday through Friday) summaries of broadcasts published for the different regions of the world.

HUMAN SOURCES

As noted above, human sources include clandestine agents and attachés as well as defectors, émigrés, and travelers. In some cases, information cannot be obtained by either open source or technical collection. The inability to obtain information by technical collection might be due either to the absence of the appropriate "system target connection"—for example, the inability of a photographic reconnaissance satellite to photograph pages of a weapons system manual—or to rigorous technical surveillance countermeasures to prevent electronic surveillance.

In any case, there will be numerous types of documents or information that require the use of clandestine agents. In the case of the Soviet Union or China, the minutes of Politburo meetings, war-planning documents, and the blueprints of new weapon systems cannot be obtained by technical means or found in the open press. If such information is to be obtained at all, which is unlikely, clandestine agents must do the job.

The Soviet Bloc, China, and Vietnam are not the only areas of the world where clandestine agents might be the best or only source of information. The plans of Colonel Khadafi or those of a guerrilla group or underground political party may be accessible only through infiltration of an agent into the higher levels of the relevant group. Such an agent might be able to cast light on a situation uncovered by a technical collection system such as overhead photography—for example, the massing of Libyan troops near Chad's border.

Recruiting of such an agent and turning him or her into a productive source involves three steps: identification, recruitment, and acquisition and transmission of information. Identification in the case of the Soviet Bloc might result, at least in part, from constant monitoring of Soviet Bloc personnel both inside and outside Russia—diplomats, officials, intelligence personnel, all overseas workers and students. Monitoring can determine which individuals would be the most valuable sources as well as those most vulnerable to exploitation.

Agents are of three basic types. There is the mole or penetration agent—somebody recruited prior to attaining an official position with the expectation that he or she will eventually attain a position of importance in the diplomatic, intelligence, or military area. This type of agent seems to be the exclusive preserve of the Soviet Union. The Soviet Union has recruited several moles (Kim Philby being the most prominent) whereas the United States, apparently, has not achieved similar success. Another type of agent is one who is "turned" or "defects in place"—that is, someone recruited after attaining an important position. Such agents may be turned for a variety of reasons, ideological and monetary being two. Alternatively, he or she might be blackmailed into providing information. The blackmail can be either impromptu—the seizing on illegal action or impropriety (adultery, embezzlement) that can be held over his or her head—or the result of entrapping the desired agent. Third, the agent may be a walk-in, someone who volunteers without any recruiting pitch.

One major source of potential agent material is foreign students studying in the United States. Foreign students of both Third World and Soviet Bloc countries are likely to be prime recruiting targets. It is often noted that Soviet Bloc students in the United States are studying scientific and technical subjects with military applications while U.S. students in the Soviet Union are studying topics such as Russian literature and history. This exchange clearly works to the Soviet's advantage in terms of technology acquisition, but it also potentially gives the United States a large recruiting base for obtaining agents in the Soviet military R&D establishment, including the design bureaus.

Agents might also be recruited from among émigrés and then returned to Soviet or other territory. The United States began attempts to infiltrate agents into the Soviet Union and Eastern Europe in the years immediately following World War II. In the early 1950s agents were parachuted into border areas of the Soviet Union or landed by sea from boats or submarines. Some Baltic agents were landed on the coast of their homeland from souped-up torpedo boats that could outrace their Soviet equivalents.[16]

Most agents were equipped with radios and sent in by air, some to make contact with resistance groups in the Baltic states and in the Ukraine (where they survived until the mid-fifties), others to become observers at selected transportation points to give notice of unusual movement or to collect or measure earth and water samples near suspected uranium-processing plants. A few tried to legalize themselves for permanent residence in urban areas. At the same time, hundreds of agents were sent into areas near Eastern European military bases. Border crossing became a common activity, agents being sent in to observe specific airfields or factories, to recruit new agents, to establish themselves in strategic locations, to act as couriers, and to service dead drops.[17]

Attempts to infiltrate agents into Soviet Bloc countries apparently ceased before the mid-1950s, the entire program having produced little in the way of useful information. Richard Bissell, former CIA Deputy Director for Plans, stated:

> I don't think clandestine collection is ever going to be a useful activity in a totalitarian society. The reason is only partly the difficulty of infiltrating agents into the country. The key difficulty is that even if you get an agent in place in Russia, say—and supposing he's well trained, of Russian nationality and speaks the language fluently, and knows his way around—this agent will still have no way of acquiring information of much value. Where can he get it? Unless he's a high up Russian, and he never was, he can only see as much as the ordinary Russian, which is hardly anything. The ordinary Russian isn't privy to what is said in councils of state, he doesn't know the design of a warhead or an intercontinental ballistic missile. He doesn't know if there is an airbase a hundred miles down the road.[18]

In more recent years the CIA has apparently had some successes with defectors-in-place and turned agents in the Soviet Bloc. Both Peter Popov, in the late 1950s, and Oleg Penkovskiy, in the early 1960s, were Soviet GRU (Chief Intelligence Directorate of the General Staff) officers who passed great quantities of material to the CIA and British intelligence, including information on the structure and operations of the GRU, Soviet strategic capability, and nuclear targeting policy. Among the information passed by Penkovskiy was a copy of the official Soviet MRBM (Medium Range Ballistic Missile) manual. Popov provided information that might have reduced defense R&D expenditures by one-half billion dollars. The information included specifications of Soviet conventional weapons including tanks, tables of equipment for Soviet tank, and mechanized and rifle divisions as well as a description of Soviet army tactics in the utilization of atomic weapons.[19]

A Colonel in the GRU, Anatoli Filatov, approached the CIA in the mid-1970s with a proposal of collaboration. Aleksandr Dmitrevich Ogordnik, a Soviet Ministry of Foreign Affairs employee, made contact with the CIA in Bogota, Columbia in 1974. In 1975 he was transferred to the Ministry's Global Affairs Department and gained access to a variety of KGB documents. For months he passed hundreds of such documents to the United States until he was detected in late 1977.[20]

In the late 1970s and early 1980s the CIA obtained information from a Colonel in the Polish military who was stationed at Polish Army headquarters. By the time General Wojciech Jaruzelski sent his tanks and troops into the streets, the Agency had had a complete copy of his operations plan for a full month.[21] In the fall of 1980, when labor unrest in Poland first aroused fear of a Soviet invasion, the Colonel reported that the Polish army had no intention of initiating or joining an operation that might end in violence and bloodshed. According to one U.S. official, "It was precisely because of this guy that we knew the Poles weren't going to act in December." Without Polish help, the Russians would have needed forty divisions to invade. Having only twenty-seven divisions ready for action, the Soviets could not be seriously considering invasion as an option.[22]

Subsequently, in late March and early April 1981 the Colonel reported that the KGB had instigated disturbances in the Polish industrial city of Bydgoszcz. The Colonel reported further that Jaruzelski had refused the KGB's gambit and declined to ask for Soviet aid, deciding instead to wait for the guidance of the Polish Communist Party Congress in July. The Colonel also reported Jaruzelski's hardening attitude and growing confidence among both the Polish and Soviet military that Polish security forces could handle the situation on their own.[23]

Within the Soviet Union an agent, possibly aboard an incoming civilian airliner bound for Moscow, photographed a new Soviet strategic bomber, the Ram-P, along with two TU-144 supersonic transports at the Ramenskoye flight test center on November 25, 1981.[24]

Outside the Soviet Union there is still a Soviet target: the Soviet Embassy. According to Rositzke,

> even a one- or two-year penetration of a Soviet embassy can provide classified information going far beyond the parochial concerns of the embassy itself; broad policy reports from the Soviet foreign office; party correspondence from the Central Committee, new directives from KGB or GRU headquarters in Moscow. All roads do not lead to Moscow, but in a highly centralized and disciplined bureaucracy most spokes lead to the hub.[25]

In nontotalitarian societies the United States is confronted with an easier task in running productive clandestine agents. A significant aspect of a clandestine human source program will involve seeking to penetrate the society at different levels—that is, recruiting agents at key spots in the nation's political, military, economic, administrative, labor, and social institutions, regardless of whether particular institutions are generally favorable or hostile to the United States. Further, Marchetti and Marks note that the CIA tries to penetrate, in addition to a nation's foreign and defense ministries, a nation's communications systems—sometimes with the help of U.S. companies such as IT&T.[26] Such infiltration can provide a steady flow of intelligence on all aspects of the targeted society.

In countries with strong Communist or revolutionary parties, penetration of such institutions might be a prime objective. Thus, when Philip Agee was attached to the CIA's Quito station in 1960, Priority A was to "collect and report intelligence on the strength and intentions of Communist and other political organizations hostile to the U.S., including their international sources of support and guidance and their influence in the Ecuadorean government."[27] This intelligence was to be collected by "agent and/or technical penetration of the highest possible level of the Communist Party of Ecuador (PCE), the Socialist Party of Ecuador (PSE-revolutionary), the Communist Youth of Ecuador (JCE), the Revolutionary Union of Ecuadorean Youth (URJE) and related organizations."[28]

Priority B involved collecting and reporting intelligence concerning the stability of the Ecuadorean government and the strength and intentions of dissident political groups. This intelligence was to be collected by agents and other sources maintained at high levels of the government, its security services, and the ruling political organization. Additionally, agents maintained in opposition political parties and among military leaders favorable to the opposition would also provide relevant intelligence.[29]

Although collection priorities in many Third World countries may be similar today and, in any case, likely to include such targets, events of the last fifteen years have significantly expanded the range of targets to include international terrorist organizations, the Islamic movement, OPEC and its member governments, relations between African governments and Cuba, and conflicts among Asian Communist nations. Thus, beginning with the Nixon administration, the CIA established "a large and highly productive network of sources among PLO leaders and guerrillas in Lebanon." The sources provided information on political and military developments in the Middle East, especially Lebanon. It also constituted a pipeline of information about terrorist organizations and militant Shiite Moslem groups.[30]

For purposes of intelligence, collection agents are generally natives of the country recruited by CIA intelligence officers. In other situations, the intelligence objective may allow for intelligence officers to operate under commercial cover to acquire information directly. Thus, the Navy's human intelligence activities in the 1969-1977 period was conducted by Task Force (TF) 157, which has apparently been absorbed by TF 168.

TF 157 was created in 1968 by Chief of Naval Operations Admiral Thomas Moorer to give the Navy a clandestine collection capability.[31] Throughout its existence, TF 157 carried out a wide variety of functions. It operated under the cover of the Naval Administrative Services Command and Pierce Morgan Associates with offices in Alexandria, Virginia.[32]

TF 157's major and official function, for which it employed fifty to seventy-five agents, was to monitor and collect information on Soviet shipping. It reported on routine cargo but also watched for the covert shipment of military goods and nuclear weapons, focusing on choke points such as the Straits of Gibraltar. It also had the responsibility of picking up intelligence operatives for Taiwan and secretly ferrying them inside mainland China, where they would implant sensitive seismic monitors and radio equipment. Such operations were halted after President Nixon's trip to China in 1972.[33]

The unit also set up a highly secret communications channel which was used to set up Henry Kissinger's secret 1971 visit to China. Other alleged projects included assessment of Soviet weapons capability for SALT, communications monitoring, and intelligence gathering for recovery of downed airplanes and sunken ships.[34] The unit operated through a variety of companies (at least ten) to shield the operations of the Task Force.[35]

Bobby Ray Inman, when he was Director of Naval Intelligence in 1977, decided to close down TF 157 due to questionable business deals and inadequate intelligence production. TF 157 officially ceased operations on September 30, 1977.[36]

The present TF 168 has several Forward Area Support Teams through which it operates worldwide: TF 168.1 (Pacific), TF 168.2 (Atlantic), TF 168.3 (Mediterranean), TF 168.4 (Europe), TF 168.5 (Naval Scientific and Technical Officer, Far East), and TF 168.6 (Panama).[37] The Army, via the Intelligence and Security Command (INSCOM), is also involved in human intelligence collection activities throughout the world. The 470th Military Intelligence (MI) Group (Panama), 501st MI Group (Korea), 500th MI Group (Japan), and 60th MI Group (Munich) all are responsible for managing a variety of intelligence and security activities including HUMINT, counterintelligence, signals intelligence, communications security, and reconnaissance.

In West Germany INSCOM clandestine collection activities coordinated by the 66th MI Group are actually run by the case officers of the 430th MI Detachment. The Detachment has four operational bases within West Germany—at Frankfurt, Berlin, Munich, and Bremerhaven—from which intelligence collection operations are run against Soviet and East European targets in East and West Germany, Czechoslovakia, and other Warsaw Pact countries (excluding the Soviet Union). The agents run are never Americans or Germans. Rather, a British or Turkish businessman living in Germany who travels to Eastern Europe may be recruited as an agent.[38]

Human sources also involve defectors, émigrés, and travelers who are not regular agents. The United States attaches major importance to the intelligence information that can be obtained via defectors. Thus, it has a coordinated Defector Program managed by the CIA's Interagency Defector Committee (IDC) with an IDC within every American embassy.[39] Whatever country the embassy may be located in, the primary targets will be the officials of the Soviet Bloc and Cuban embassies.

In some cases, the defectors might be Soviet Bloc high officials such as scientists, diplomats, or intelligence officers. Several Soviet Bloc intelligence officers have defected over the course of the last thirty years. These defectors can provide valuable information concerning the organizational structure, personalities, methods of operation, and foreign agents of their and other Soviet Bloc intelligence services. In the aftermath of the declaration of martial law in Poland, several Polish Ambassadors defected to the West, bringing with them their inside knowledge of personalities, procedures, policies, and relations with the Soviet Union.

Defectors, especially from Soviet Bloc intelligence units, are subject to detailed and extensive debriefings and possibly interrogations. One objective is to obtain every item of useful information possessed by the defectors. Another objective is to establish the defectors' bona fides—to ensure that they are who they say they are and that their information is not being planted as part of a disinformation campaign. Some of the conflicts that have plagued the U.S. intelligence community have revolved around questions concerning the legitimacy of certain defectors.[40]

A defector may be able to settle disputes concerning the meaning of data acquired via technical collection systems. Thus, one defector was asked to

> look at an elaborate analysis of something our cameras detected by chance when there was an abnormal opening in clouds that normally covered a particular region. Learned men had spent vast amounts of time trying to figure out what it was and concluded that it was something quite sinister, an Air Force officer said "Viktor took one look at it and convincingly explained why what we thought was so ominous was in fact comically innocuous."[41]

Emigrés—those legally permitted to leave the Soviet Union or other country— may also provide useful information. Many of these émigrés, many who move to the United States or Israel, have held positions in scientific research institutes or social science institutes such as the USA and Canada Institute or IMEMO (the Institute of World Economy and International Affairs). The former group can offer information concerning research in their specific fields while the latter can offer information and insights into both the Soviet policymaking apparatus and the perceptions and personalities of the leadership. Thus, several émigrés have produced analyses concerning the formation of Soviet defense, arms control, and foreign policy.[42]

Neither defectors nor émigrés need be high-level officials to provide valuable strategic or tactical information. A cipher clerk has access to extremely sensitive information. A workman at a military base may be able to provide information concerning the functions of structures identified by satellite photography— whether a structure is a command and control bunker or a repair facility will have important implications for targeting. Marchetti and Marks give the following account of the case of a defecting Soviet lieutenant.

> Although a comparatively low-level Soviet defector of this sort would seem to have a small potential for providing useful intelligence, the CIA . . . had so little success in penetrating the Soviet military that the lieutenant underwent months of questioning. Through him, agency analysts were able to learn much about how Soviet armor units and the ground forces in general, are organized, their training and tactical procedures, and the mechanics of their participation in the build-up that preceded the invasion of Czechoslovakia.[43]

Emigrés who were ordinary citizens can provide information concerning events of local interest. Initial reports of the 1979 anthrax incident circulated internally among dissidents and were carried abroad by émigrés.[44]

Processing of defectors and émigrés is anything but an ad hoc procedure. The CIA and the Air Force Intelligence Service's Special Activities Center maintain extensive facilities in the United States and abroad for such activities. The CIA's defector reception center at Camp King near Frankfurt, West Germany handles escapees from the Soviet Union and Eastern Europe.[45] At Lindsey Air Station in Wiesbaden, West Germany the Air Force 7113th Special Activities Squadron maintains a computerized list of questions that they ask individuals who come across the border.[46]

The CIA's Domestic Contact Service (DCS) seeks to interview some businessmen and tourists, either because of specific contacts they may have had during their foreign travels or because of the sites of their travels—for example, North Korea or Cuba. The information sought may include the health and attitudes of a national leader or the military activities in a particular region. In some instances, the DCS, upon hearing that a particular person plans to visit a particular location, will get in touch in advance and ask the traveler to seek out information on certain targets. However, the DCS has been reluctant to assign specific missions. Since the travelers are not professional agents, they might wind up being arrested as a result of taking their espionage roles too seriously.[47]

The same attachés who provide open source information also constitute human sources who may provide information that is not legally available to the general public in the nation in which they are stationed. The information might come from confidential conversations with government officials or private citizens, from specially arranged visits to military facilities, or from clandestine photography. The latter may result from on-the-ground photography by the attaché or assistants or from photographs taken from the embassy's aircraft. The United States maintains a fleet of airplanes to aid attachés in their observation duties. These planes allow the attaché to move around foreign countries as well as take photographs of the areas being overflown.

In the case of East Germany, the peculiar postwar arrangements include the presence of a U.S. Military Liaison Mission. The Mission is a fourteen-man team "that prowls East Germany conducting what amounts to legal espionage."[48] The team travels in Open sedans packed with telescopes, infrared cameras, and listening devices. Their most recent target is possible SS-21 or SS-22 missiles. In other cases, the team might take scrapings from a tank or other military vehicles for later analysis. In an effort to limit the effectiveness of their activities, East German military vehicles commonly tail them, and their cars are sometimes bumped or bracketed by trucks to keep them from probing in sensitive areas.[49]

Probably the strangest use of human resources is the reported use of psychics to conduct remote viewing operations against intelligence targets in the Soviet Union. Although this technique seems to be a long way from being considered a consistent and accepted intelligence collection method, both the CIA and the Defense Intelligence Agency (DIA) have evidenced strong interest in the general area of parasychology, particularly Soviet activities in that area.

The first CIA-DIA project, codenamed Scanate, involved providing a psychic with the latitude and longitude of a remote location and asking him to project his mind there and describe the scene. Another project, codenamed Grill Flame, involved two tests of remote viewing. In response to one set of coordinates, the psychic described an airfield, complete with details—including a large gantry and crane at one end of the field. The site was the Soviet nuclear testing area at Semipalatinsk, which possessed an airfield at the map coordinates but no gantry or crane according to what was then the most recent intelligence. However, the next set of reconnaissance photos showed a gantry and crane. In the second test, a psychic located within a few miles a Soviet bomber that the CIA knew had crashed in Africa.[50]

TECHNICAL SURVEILLANCE AND MAIL OPENING

An important aspect of political intelligence gathering is the technical surveillance and mail-opening operations conducted by the CIA and other intelligence units. Such operations can provide information in addition to or as a substitute for information provided by human sources. Technical penetration might in some cases be preferable to agent penetration. Technical penetration of a presidential residence offers twenty-four-hour coverage and can capture the exact conversation that occurs. Technical penetration of foreign embassies can provide information on plans, policies, and the activities of intelligence agents. Technical penetration does not require recruitment of an agent. On the other hand, it is often easier to detect than a human agent.

Two prominent forms of technical surveillance are "bugs" and telephone taps. A bug or audio device, which will transmit all conversations in a room, is planted by experts from the Science and Technology Directorate's Office of Technical Services. Planting of such a device is a complex operation involving such things as surveillance of the site, acquisition of building and floor plans, and determination of the color of the interior and texture of the walls. Activity in the room as well as the movements of security patrols are noted. When the information is acquired and processed it will be employed to determine the time of surreptitious entry and the materials needed to install the device in such a way as to minimize the probability of discovery.[51]

During the early 1970s one target of CIA audio devices was Nguyen Van Thieu, President of South Vietnam. Presents given to Thieu by the CIA—television sets and furniture—came equipped with audio devices, allowing the agency to monitor his personal conversations.[52] The CIA also attempted to install devices in the office and living quarters of the South Vietnamese observer at the Paris Peace Talks.[53]

An area in which audio devices have, at least in the past, produced much of the CIA's intelligence is Latin America. A report on clandestine collection activities in Latin America during the 1960s revealed that the CIA had managed to place audio devices in the homes of many key personnel, including cabinet ministers.[54]

Telephone taps also provided much of the CIA's intelligence, according to the report. During E. Howard Hunt's tenure in Mexico City, the CIA bugged or tapped several Iron Curtain embassies.[55] Both Hunt and Philip Agee have written about CIA technical operations in Uruguay. During Hunt's tenure, the CIA station conducted technical penetrations of embassies and the living quarters of key personnel. During Agee's tenure, seven telephones were being monitored. Included were the Soviet and Cuban Embassies, Consulates, and Commercial Offices.[56]

When a bug or tap is successfully placed, the information acquired from the source is clearly identified in the initial transmittal back to the Directorate of Operations. To hide the source from even the analysts in the Directorate of Intelligence, the Directorate of Operations will then bury the information in a report from a real agent—"a reliable source in the foreign ministry," for example.[57]

Technical surveillance operations might also employ lasers. A laser beam can be directed at a closed window from outside and used to detect the vibrations of the sound waves resulting from a conversation inside the room. The vibrations can be transformed back into the words spoken. According to Marchetti and Marks, such a device was successfully tested in West Africa but never seemed to function properly elsewhere except the United States.[58] However, the technical problems might have been overcome by now, and it may be employed on a more extensive basis.

For many years, until forced to stop by fear of public revelations, both the CIA and the FBI conducted mail openings on a widespread basis in the United States. Between 1952 and 1972, the CIA ran a mail-opening program, HTLINGUAL, targeted against mail being sent to and from the Soviet Union. The operation, which took place mainly at La Guardia and Kennedy International Airports in New York, involved over 215,000 letters. The CIA maintained a watch list that singled out certain groups for special attention—including many with no intelligence connection.[59]

Although the CIA and other agencies might have ceased their domestic mail-opening activities, a special Army unit, the Army Special Operations Field Office in Berlin, is involved in opening mail flowing between East and West Europe. The exact extent of the Office's activities is not clear—including the extent, if any, to which the mail of U.S. citizens is being opened.[60]

The Office was the subject of an early Carter administration Presidential Directive, PD/NSC-9 of March 30, 1977, the contents of which are considered Top Secret. PD/NSC-9 is listed as one of the references for Department of Defense (DOD) Directives 5240.1, 5240.1-R, and 5240.1-TS, all titled "Procedures Governing the Activities of DOD Intelligence Components that Affect U.S. Persons."[61]

DOD 5240.1-R specifies that

> DOD intelligence components are authorized to open mail to or from a United States person that is found outside United States postal channels only pursuant to the approval of the Attorney General.
>
> Heads of DOD intelligence components may authorize the opening of mail outside U.S. postal channels when both the sender and intended recipient are other than United States persons if such searches are otherwise lawful and consistent with any Status of Forces Agreement that may be in effect.[62]

In addition to its mail-opening operations, the Special Operations Field Office is also involved in wiretap operations.[63]

MATERIAL EXPLOITATION AND RECOVERY OPERATIONS

An important source of information comes from the acquisition of new or used foreign weapon systems, communication, and other devices of military significance. As noted earlier, in many cases information on small systems cannot be obtained by overhead reconnaissance or signals intelligence. In any case, possession of the actual system adds significant new information to whatever is already possessed. The acquisition and analysis—material exploitation—of such systems, a function of all the military scientific and technical intelligence units, allows scientists to determine not only the capabilities of the system but how such capabilities are achieved. Such knowledge can then be exploited to improve U.S. systems as well as to determine countermeasures to be employed against foreign systems.

Acquisition of systems is a high-priority intelligence objective and attained by a variety of methods. In Indonesia in the 1960s the CIA conducted an operation known as HABRINK. In one phase of the operation, CIA operatives entered a warehouse holding SAM-2 missiles, removed the guidance system from one, and took it with them. The acquisition allowed U.S. Air Force scientists to equip B-52s with appropriate countermeasures.[64] HABRINK also obtained the designs and workings of numerous Soviet weapons—the surface-to-surface Styx naval missile, W-class submarine, Komar guided-missile patrol boats, a RIGA-class destroyer, a Sverdlov cruiser TU-16 (BADGER) bomber, and a KENNEL air-to-surface missile.[65]

In a more recent version of HABRINK, the CIA purchased from retired officers of the Indian army and air force details on weapons furnished to India by the Soviet Union. The Indian officers involved included an Army Major General and Lt. Colonel and an Air Vice Marshal. Another source from which the CIA can apparently purchase some Soviet weapons is the Rumanian government.[66]

As noted in Chapter 3, the DIA and CIA also planned an operation in Iran to steal a Russian-made antiaircraft gun and armored personnel carrier that the Soviets had sold to the Iranian army in 1978.[67]

The United States can acquire advanced Soviet aircraft from the defection of pilots or by purchasing it. Once obtained, the aircraft is examined thoroughly by Foreign Technology Division (FTD) officers and scientists. Thus, when a MIG-25 pilot defected from Russia in 1976 with his plane, landing in Japan, a high priority of U.S. intelligence and the FTD was the examination of the airplane. Before being returned to the Soviet Union, the entire MIG-25 was disassembled at Hyakuri Air Base in Japan. The engines, radar, computer, electronic countermeasures, automatic pilot, and communications equipment were placed on blocks and stands for mechanical, metalurgical, and phogographic analysis.[68]

Examination of the plane, as well as debriefing of the pilot, sharply altered Western understanding of the plane and its missions. Among the discoveries was a radar more powerful than that ever installed in any interceptor or fighter and the use of vacuum tubes rather than transistors,[69] Vacuum tubes, although they represent a more primitive technology than transistors, are resistant to the electromagnetic pulse (EMP) created by nuclear detonations.

The MIG-25 was far from the first MIG obtained for purposes of exploitation. In early 1951 the Allied Air Force Commander in Korea was asked to make every effort to obtain a complete MIG-15 for analysis. As a result of the request, a MIG that was shot down and crashed off Korea was retrieved within a short time. Portions of another MIG were recovered by helicopter. The FTD (then the Air Technical Intelligence Center) personnel landed, ran up to the crashed plane, threw grenades into it to separate assemblies small enough to carry, and left under hostile fire. In 1953 a defecting North Korean pilot flew an intact MIG-15 to South Korea.[70]

Aircraft may be purchased either directly from a nation (a former Soviet client state), through an intermediary, or on the international arms market. The United States has apparently purchased at least one MIG-23 from Egypt.[71] And in the fall of 1983 Vought Aero Products offered to sell twenty-four MIG-21 fighters to the Navy. Since the fighters were to be new and the only MIGs available on the international arms market were used, Vought's source would seem to be China – the only nation still making MIG-21s.[72]

The offered MIG-21s and the purchased MIG-23 provide an example of another exploitation of such weapons systems: use in mock combat. The United States maintains OpFors (Opposition Forces) detachments to engage in such combat and allow U.S. forces to determine how they would perform against Soviet equipment as well as to gain an internal view of the operations of the Soviet equipment. Thus, at Nellis Air Force Base (AFB), MIG aircraft are tested against U.S. fighters – including those, such as the F-19 fighter, equipped with stealth technology. In addition, U.S. fighters are tested against Soviet air defense radars and electronic warfare equipment.[73] Similarly, at another facility Army OpFors personnel engage in mock combat with Soviet tanks and armored personnel carriers.

In other instances, material exploitation follows from the completion of a recovery operation in which a crashed plane or sunken ship is retrieved, usually from the ocean. In 1970 the United States recovered a nuclear weapon from a Soviet aircraft that crashed in the Sea of Japan; in 1971 the Navy recovered electronic eavesdropping equipment from a sunken trawler; and in 1972 a joint U.S.-British operation recovered electronic gear from a Soviet plane that had crashed earlier that year into the North Sea.[74]

A continuous recovery operation, possibly still ongoing, was Operation SAND DOLLAR. SAND DOLLAR involved the recovery of Soviet test warheads that landed in the ocean. By international agreement, the Soviet Union is required to specify the impact areas for such tests. U.S. radars (now COBRA DANE and COBRA JUDY) tracked the warheads to determine the precise impact point. What were apparently civilian drilling ships were then sent to the Pacific test range after the tests had been completed to recover nosecones the self-destructing warheads of which had not detonated as expected. Ships were guided to the proper location by computers coordinated with U.S. satellites and the objects were located by sonar and magnetometer devices. Scientists at the FTD who analyzed the captured nosecones learned how the Soviets designed and constructed each part.[75]

By far the best-known recovery operation was PROJECT JENNIFER, in which the Glomar Explorer was sent to the Pacific in an attempt to recover an entire Soviet submarine. The location of the Soviet Golf-II submarine northwest of Hawaii was determined by the Sound Surveillance System (SOSUS) network. The sub had gone down in the spring of 1968 carrying missile, torpedoes (possibly nuclear tippable), and coding material. An initial survey of the Russian submarine site in the Pacific was said to be made by a Navy deep-sea reconnaissance ship, the Mizar, a few small objects being recovered with a magnetic trawl.[76] Based on the initial survey, approval was given to arrange for the construction of a ship that could recover the submarine. Arrangements were made with Howard Hughes's Summa Corporation to construct such a ship: the Glomar Explorer. Completed in 1973, the ship conducted recovery operations during the summer of 1974.

The initial version of the story stated that the submarine was raised intact from the ocean floor some 750 miles northwest of Oahu but that halfway up the 16,500-foot ascent, two-thirds of the submarine broke away, damaging the claws and sinking to the bottom. According to the story, the submarine was to be raised by a specially designed claw through an opening in the bottom of the ship to a "pool" area. The two-thirds of the submarine lost supposedly contained all the missiles and coding material. Possibly two nuclear tippable torpedoes were saved.[77]

There is, however, reason to believe that the initial story was designed to allow the Soviets either to believe or pretend to believe (and save face) that the United States did not recover sensitive material. It has been pointed out that the length of the entire submarine was longer than the length of the opening through which it was to be raised—an especially curious fact since the ship was explicitly designed for that recovery operation. Hence, it has been suggested that the initial survey indicated the submarine had broken in two and that the operation raised each part, recovering all missile and coding material.[78]

Material exploitation represents far more than the result of chance defections and intelligence collection opportunities. Rather, it is a major and coordinated part of CIA, Army, Navy, and Air Force intelligence activities, the military services having a particular stake in the development of countermeasures to Soviet weapons systems.

Proposals for Naval foreign material exploitation projects are submitted to the Chairman of the Navy Foreign Material Program (NFMP) Committee. The proposal identifies and describes as completely as possible the foreign equipment/material involved and its location as well as the objectives of the exploitation project and the anticipated technical gain to the U.S. Navy as a result of the effort. The proposal then must describe the work effort to be performed, the resources required, the planned timetable for completion, and the estimated total cost of the exploitation.[79] An example of an NFMP proposal is shown as Figure 9-1.

Figure 9-1. Navy FMEP Proposal.

CLASSIFICATION UNCLASSIFIED

MANAGEMENT PLAN—PROJECT: CLUSTER BILL (fictitious)

PROJ./PROG. MGR./COORDINATOR: Mr. D. L. Jones CODE 342B. EXT. 123-4567	PROGRAM: Foreign Material Exploitation ELEMENT No.: 64761N BUDGET ACT. ______	Date 7 September 72

DESCRIPTION: CLUSTER BILL— The exploitation of the BIRDLEGS RADAR which is installed in the Soviet BIG BIRD bomber and provides acquisition and guidance data to the AS-O air-to-surface anti-shipping missile.

No.		FY 72 J A S O N D J F M A M J	FY 73 J A S O N D J F M A M J	FY 1 2 3 4	FY 1 2 3 4	FY 1 2 3 4
1	Photos/Sketches/ schematics	$4K				
2	Markings data coverage	$0.5K				
3	Initial evaluation	$6K				
4	Repairs/Parts Procurement	$34K				
5	Test Operations/Analysis		$78K			
6	Teardown Inspection		$7K			
7	Systems Evaluation		$28K			
8	Vulnerabilities Analysis		$36K			
9	Reports		$15K			
(Items may be broken down into subelements as appropriate)						
Funds Total — 208.5K	RDT&E	PRIOR 100.5K	108K			
KEY:						

Remarks: (Use additional pages as required; continue remarks on plain sheets) (For progress reports, shade areas to indicate progress)

Source: Naval Material Command Instruction C3882.IA, "Prosecution of the Navy Foreign Material Program (NFMP) in the NMC (U)," February 1, 1977.

NOTES TO CHAPTER 9

1. Roy Godson, "Clandestine Collection against the Soviet Union and Denied Areas," in Roy Godson, ed., *Intelligence Requirements for the 1980s: Clandestine Collection* (New Brunswick, N.J.: Transaction, 1982), pp. 1–16.

2. Amrom Katz, "Technical Collection Requirements for the 1980's," in Godson, ed., *Intelligence Requirements for the 1980's*, pp. 101–117.

3. Roscoe H. Hillenkoetter, "Using the World's Information Sources," *Army Information Digest* 3 (November 1948): 3–6.

4. Andrew Cockburn, *The Threat: Inside the Soviet Military Machine* (New York: Random House, 1983), p. 22; Jonathan Samuel Lockwood, *The Soviet View of U.S. Strategic Doctrine* (New Brunswick, N.J.: Transaction, 1983), pp. 3–9.

5. Cockburn, *The Threat*, p. 22.

6. Philip Jacobson, "The Red Army Finally Gets a Chance to Test Its Stuff," *Washington Post* February 13, 1983, pp. C1, C4.

7. Cockburn, *The Threat*, p. 67.

8. Richard Dunlop, *Donovan: America's Master Spy* (Chicago: Rand McNally, 1982), p. 366.

9. David Holloway, "Entering the Nuclear Arms Race: The Soviet Decision to Build the Atomic Bomb, 1939–1945," *International Security Studies Program Working Paper No. 9.*

10. William J. Broad, "X-Ray Laser Weapon Gains Favor," *New York Times*, November 15, 1983, pp. C1–C2.

11. Zhores Medvedev, *Nuclear Disaster in the Urals* (New York: Vintage, 1981).

12. U.S. Congress, House Permanent Select Committee on Intelligence, *Soviet Strategic Forces* (Washington, D.C.: U.S. Government Printing Office, 1980), pp. 30–32.

13. John F. Burns, "2 Moscow Meetings May Lift the Veil on Andropov," *New York Times*, December 24, 1983, p. 2.

14. Dusko Doder, "Unusual Activity in Moscow," *Washington Post*, February 10, 1984, pp. A1, A27.

15. Military Communications, Electronics Board, *Joint Department of Defense Plain Language Address Directory* (Washington, D.C.: Department of Defense, August 9, 1982), p. II–15.

16. Thomas Bell Smith, *The Essential CIA* (privately printed in 1975).

17. Harry Rositzke, "America's Secret Operations: A Perspective," *Foreign Affairs*, January 1975, pp. 334–51.

18. Leonard Mosely, *Dulles: A Biography of Eleanor, Allen and John Foster and Their Family Network* (New York: Dial, 1978), p. 324.

19. William Hood, *Mole* (New York: Norton, 1982); Oleg Penkovskiy, *The Penkovskiy Papers* (New York: Doubleday, 1965); John Prados, *The Soviet Estimate: U.S. Intelligence Analysis and Russian Military Strength* (New York: Dial, 1982), p. 148; Harry Rositzke, *The CIA's Secret Operations* (New York: Reader's Digest Press, 1977), pp. 68–69.

20. John Barron, *The KGB Today: The Hidden Hand* (New York: Reader's Digest Press, 1983), pp. 428–30.
21. "A Polish Agent in Place," *Newsweek*, December 20, 1982, p. 49.
22. Ibid.
23. Ibid.
24. "Soviet Strategic Bomber Photographed At Ramenskoye," *Aviation Week and Space Technology*, December 14, 1981, p. 17.
25. Harry Rositzke, *The CIA's Secret Operations*, p. 82.
26. Victor Marchetti and John Marks, *The CIA and the Cult of Intelligence* (New York: Dell, 1980), p. 169.
27. Philip Agee, *Inside the Company: A CIA Diary* (New York: Stonehill, 1975), p. 114.
28. Ibid.
29. Ibid.
30. Philip Taubman, "P.L.O. Pullout From Beirut Hurt U.S. Intelligence Links," *New York Times*, December 6, 1983, pp. A1, A21.
31. Joe Trento, "FBI Probing Ex-Spy's Role in Task Force," *Wilmington News Journal*, October 5, 1980, pp. 1, 6; Bob Woodward, "Pentagon to Abolish Secret Spy Unit," *Washington Post*, May 18, 1977, pp. 1, 5.
32. Ibid.
33. Seymour Hersh, "The Man with the Contacts," *New York Times Magazine*, June 14, 1981, p. 58.
34. Woodward, "Pentagon to Abolish Secret Spy Unit."
35. Philip Taubman, "Ex-Covert Agents Win Benefits Case," *New York Times*, November 30, 1982, p. A17.
36. Joe Trento, "CIA Fears Former Agents Will Spill Secrets to Block Probe," *Wilmington News Journal*, September 13, 1981, pp. 18.
37. Private information.
38. Private information.
39. E. Howard Hunt, *Undercover: Memoirs of an American Secret Agent* (New York: Berkley, 1974), p. 80.
40. See David Martin, *Wilderness of Mirrors* (New York: Harper & Row, 1979).
41. John Barrow, *MIG Pilot* (New York: Avon, 1981), p. 186.
42. See, for example, Vladimir Petrov, "The Formation of Soviet Foreign Policy," *Orbis* (Fall 1973): 819–50.
43. Marchetti and Marks, *The CIA and the Cult of Intelligence* (1980), p. 166.
44. Godson, *Intelligence Requirements for the 1980's.*
45. Marchetti and Marks, *The CIA and the Cult of Intelligence* (1980), p. 166.
46. Private information.
47. Marchetti and Marks, *The CIA and the Cult of Intelligence* (1980), p. 207.
48. James M. Markham, "On the Prowl in East Germany: A Team of G.I. Spies," *New York Times*, April 21, 1984, p. 2.
49. Ibid.
50. Jack Anderson, "Psychic Studies Might Help U.S. Explore Soviets," *Washington Post*, April 23, 1984, p. B14; Anderson, "Pentagon, CIA Cooperating on Psychic Spying," *Washington Post*, May 3, 1984, p. B15; Anderson, " 'Voodoo Gap' Looms as Latest Weapons Crisis," *Washington Post*

April 24, 1984, p. C13. In a case such as this, one cannot rule out the possibility of such reporting being the result of CIA disinformation.

51. Marchetti and Marks, *The CIA and the Cult of Intelligence*, p. 170.

52. John Stockwell, *In Search of Enemies: A CIA Story* (New York: Norton, 1978), p. 107.

53. Thomas Powers, *The Man Who Kept the Secrets: Richard Helms and the CIA* (New York: Knopf, 1979), p. 198.

54. Marchetti and Marks, *The CIA and the Cult of Intelligence*, p. 170.

55. Hunt, p. 80.

56. Ibid., p. 126; Agee, pp. 346–47.

57. Marchetti and Marks, *The CIA and the Cult of Intelligence*, p. 172.

58. Ibid., p. 171.

59. Morton Halperin, Jerry J. Berman, Robert L. Borosage, and Christine M. Marwick, *The Lawless State* (New York: Penguin, 1976), pp. 140–42.

60. Private information.

61. DOD Directive 5240.1, November 30, 1979; DOD 5240.1-R, "Procedures Governing the Activities of DOD Intelligence Components that Affect United States Persons," December 1982.

62. Ibid.

63. Defense Audit Service, *Report on the Review of Accounting Systems for Wiretap and Eavesdrop Equipment* (Washington, D.C.: Defense Audit Service, September 29, 1980), p. 3.

64. Barron, *The KGB Today*, pp. 233–34.

65. Ibid.; "Statement of Facts, United States of America v. David Henry Barnett," K 80–0390, United States District Court, Maryland, 1980.

66. William J. Eaton, "CIA Reportedly Caught Buying Indian Military Secrets," *Los Angeles Times*, December 15, 1983, p. 4; Cockburn, *The Threat*, p. 8.

67. "What the U.S. Lost in Iran," *Newsweek*, December 18, 1981, pp. 33–34.

68. John Barron, *MIG Pilot* (New York: Avon, 1981), pp. 169–86.

69. Ibid.

70. Foreign Technology Division, *FTD 1917-1967* (Dayton, Ohio: FTD, 1967), p. 24.

71. "Washington Roundup," *Aviation Week and Space Technology*, May 14, 1984, p. 17.

72. "Periscope," *Newsweek*, May 21, 1984, p. 17.

73. Wayne Biddle, "General Killed in Nevada Crash Flew Soviet Jet," *New York Times*, May 31, 1984, pp. 1, 22; "Washington Roundup," *Aviation Week and Space Technology*, May 7, 1984, p. 13.

74. Clyde W. Burleson, *The Jennifer Project* (Englewood Cliffs, N.J.: Prentice-Hall, 1977), p. 47.

75. Roy Varner and Wayne Collier, *A Matter of Risk* (New York: Random House, 1977), p. 26.

76. Ibid.

77. Ibid.

78. Ibid.

79. Naval Material Command Instruction C3882.1A, "Prosecution of the Navy Foreign Material Program (NFMP) in the NMC(U)," February 1, 1977.

10 COOPERATIVE ARRANGEMENTS AND OVERSEAS BASES

An important aspect of U.S. intelligence operations is the cooperative and liaison arrangements that exist between the United States and certain foreign nations. These arrangements involve technical collection as well as human intelligence operations and the sharing of the information acquired. The most visible aspect of cooperation is the maintenance of U.S. bases on foreign territory, most especially Central Intelligence Agency and National Security Agency (NSA) installations in countries such as Australia, Britain, China, Norway, and Turkey.

THE UKUSA AGREEMENT

The U.S.-British military alliance in World War II necessitated a high degree of cooperation with respect to intelligence activities. It was imperative that the United States and Britain, as the main Allied combatants in the European and Pacific theaters, establish a coordinated effort in the acquisition of worldwide intelligence and its evaluation and distribution. Of all the areas of intelligence collaboration, it was in the area of signals intelligence (SIGINT) that the most important and vital cooperation took place.

Cooperation began in the spring of 1941 when four U.S. representatives (two from the Navy and two from the Army) delivered a model of the Japanese PURPLE machine—used by Japan to encipher diplomatic communications to British codebreakers at Bletchley Park. In return, the British gave the U.S. representatives an assortment of advanced cryptological equipment, including the Marconi–Adcock high-frequency direction finder.[1]

Further cooperation involved both the exchange of personnel and a division of labor. A small U.S. mission was sent to the Combined Bureau at Singapore for the purpose of cooperation in signals intelligence and a British naval officer trained in Japanese and experienced in cryptanalysis was introduced into the U.S. signals intelligence station on Corregidor in the Philippines. A secret channel of communication was established between Corregidor and Singapore for the direct exchange of cryptanalytical material. Meanwhile, it was agreed that the British would break Tokyo-London traffic while the Americans broke Tokyo-Washington traffic. The results of the U.S. codebreaking effort that were considered useful to Britain in its war with Germany were passed to London via the British ambassador in Washington.[2]

U.S. entry into the war expanded the scope of the U.S.-British signals intelligence cooperation. Both U.S. and British commanders in the field (whether directing solely U.S. forces, solely British forces, or joint forces) required the most up-to-date intelligence available on the enemy order of battle and plan of action—exactly the type of information that could best be provided by intercepts of military wireless traffic. Thus, in addition to the intercepts of diplomatic traffic being widely exchanged, it was necessary to broaden the exchange of intercepted military traffic and make arrangements for a coordinated attack on such traffic. Britain's production of such intelligence was labeled ULTRA.[3]

Although ULTRA information was made available to U.S. and British military commanders via Special Liaison Units, the exact nature of its acquisition was obscured initially. It was not until April 1943 that the British revealed to U.S. military intelligence officials the secret—that Britain's codebreaking organization could break the ciphers produced by the German ENIGMA machine used for much German military communications.[4]

During the same visit to Bletchley Park at which British officials revealed the ULTRA secret to the U.S. military intelligence officials, a formal agreement of cooperation was concluded between Britain and the United States: the BRUSA Agreement. The agreement established high-level cooperation on SIGINT matters and covered the exchange of personnel, joint regulations for the handling of ULTRA material, and procedures for its distribution. The joint regulations included strict security regulations that applied to all British and U.S. recipients of ULTRA material.[5]

Along with increased cooperation between Britain and the United States, there was increased involvement by the Anglo-Saxon members of the British Commonwealth—Canada, Australia, and New Zealand—in a wide variety of intelligence activities. U.S.-Canadian cooperation began in October 1941 when the Canadians offered the U.S. Federal Communications Commission free access to the product of Canadian monitoring activities. In return, the United States provided Canada with technical Direction Finding (DF) data that were "invaluable for pinpointing the location of a transmitter."[6]

Canadian DF stations subsequently made significant contributions to the Allied North Atlantic SIGINT/ocean surveillance network.[7] The Canadian code-breaking agency was also successful in intercepting and decoding German espionage control messages to and from agents in South America, Canada, Hamburg, and Lisbon.[8] In addition, messages to and from the Vichy delegation in Ottawa were intercepted and decoded.[9] Further, the peculiarities of radio wave propagation resulted in Canadian monitoring facilities being able to intercept military transmissions originating in Europe that were inaccessible to equipment based in Britain.[10]

It was with respect to Japan, however, that SIGINT cooperation among all five nations reached its highest level. Monitoring stations in Canada, particularly the major one at Halifax, gathered large quantities of coded Japanese transmissions.[11] In April 1942 a combined allied signals intelligence agency for the Pacific, the Central Bureau of the Allied Intelligence Bureau, was activated in Melbourne with a U.S. Chief and Australian Deputy Chief.[12]

The extent of cooperation is particularly highlighted in the case of Australian intercept stations. There was an Australian Air Force intercept station at Darwin, a U.S. Army radio intercept station in Townsville, a Royal Australian Navy monitoring station at Darwin, and a British post in Brisbane for the interception and distribution of Japanese radio communications.[13] Additionally, a Canadian Special Wireless Group arrived in Australia on May 18, 1945 to take over from the Australians the task of intercepting and analyzing Japanese military Morse code signals.[14]

The intelligence relationship among Australia, Britain, Canada, New Zealand, and the United States that was forged by World War II did not end with the war. Rather, it became formalized and grew stronger. In 1946 William Friedman, America's premier cryptographer, visited the British cryptographers to work out methods of postwar consultation and cooperation. A U.S. Liaison Office was set up in London, and schemes were derived for avoiding duplication of effort. It was agreed that solved material was to be exchanged between the two agencies. In addition, an exchange program was started under which personnel from each agency would work two or three years at the other.[15]

Nineteen forty-seven saw an event that set the stage for post-World War II signals intelligence cooperation: the formulation and acceptance of the UKUSA Agreement, also known as the UK–USA Security Agreement or "Secret Treaty." The primary aspect of the agreement was the division of SIGINT collection responsibilities among the First Party (the United States) and the Second Parties (Australia, Britain, Canada, and New Zealand).[16] The specific agencies now involved are the U.S. National Security Agency, Australian Defence Signals Directorate (DSD), British Government Communications Headquarters (GCHQ), Canadian Communications Security Establishment (CSE), and New Zealand Government Communications Security Bureau (GCSB).[17]

Under the present division of responsibility, the Australian DSD is responsible for covering parts of the Indian Ocean, the South Pacific, and Southeast Asia.[18] The United Kingdom's GCHQ is responsible for Africa and the Soviet Union east of the Urals.[19] Canada is responsible for coverage of the northern Soviet Union and parts of Europe.[20] New Zealand is apparently responsible for a small portion of the southwest Pacific. The U.S.'s NSA and its military components are responsible for all other areas of interest.

Britain's geographical position gives it a significant capability for long-range SIGINT collection against certain targets in the Soviet Union.[21] Britain's historical role in Africa led to its assumption of SIGINT responsibility for that area. Canada's responsibility for the northern Soviet Union stems from its geographical position which gives it "unique access to communications in the northern Soviet Union."[22] Likewise, as noted earlier, the peculiarities of radio wave propagation mean that receivers in eastern Canada can intercept transmissions from portions of Europe that are inaccessible to U.K.-based equipment. The areas of responsibility of Australia and New Zealand clearly result from their geographical location.

The UKUSA relationship is more than an agreement to coordinate separately conducted intelligence activities and share the intelligence collected; the SIGINT aspect of the relationship is also more than that. Rather, it is cemented by the presence of U.S. facilities on British, Canadian, and Australian territory; by joint operations (U.S.-U.K., Australian-U.S., U.K.-Australian) within and outside UKUSA territory and, in the case of Australia, of U.K. and U.S. staff (and some NZ) at all DSD facilities.[23]

In addition to specifying SIGINT collection responsibilities, the Agreement also concerns access to the collected intelligence and security arrangements for the handling of data. Standardized codewords (e.g., UMBRA for signals intelligence), security agreements that all employees of the respective SIGINT agencies must sign, and procedures for storing and disseminating codeword material are all part of the implementation of the Agreement.[24] Thus, in a memo concerning the agreement dated October 8, 1948, the U.S. Army Office of the Adjutant General advised the recipients of the memo that

> the United States Chiefs of Staff will make every effort to insure that the United States will maintain the military security classifications established by the United Kingdom authorities with respect to military information of UK origin and the military security classifications established by the UK–US Agreement with respect to military information of joint UK–US origin.[25]

Similarly, in 1967, the "COMINT Indoctrination" declaration, which all British COMINT-cleared personnel had to sign, included in the first paragraph the statement,

> I declare that I fully understand the information relating to the manner and extent of the interception of communications of foreign powers by H.M. Gov-

ernment and *other cooperating Governments*, and intelligence produced by such interception known as Communications Intelligence (COMINT) is information covered by Section 2 of the Official Secrets Act 1911 (as amended).[26]

These requirements for standardized codewords (see Chapter 15), security arrangements, and procedures for the handling and dissemination of SIGINT material are apparently detailed in a series of "International Regulations on SIGINT" (IRSIG), which was in its third edition as of 1967.

Despite numerous references to the agreements in print, officials of some of the participating countries have refused to confirm not only the details of the agreement but even its existence. Thus, on March 9, 1977 the Australian Opposition Defense Spokesman asked the Prime Minister:

1. Is Australia a signatory to the UKUSA Agreement?
2. Is it a fact that under this agreement, NSA operates electronic intercept stations in Australia?
3. Does any other form of station operate in Australia under the agreement; if so, is it operated by an Australian or an overseas authority or is it operated under some sort of joint authority?
4. Will he identify the participating country or countries in any such arrangement?

The Prime Minister refused to answer and referred to a previous response wherein he said the government would not confirm or deny speculation in this area.[27] And the Australian D Notice, "Ciphering and Monitoring Activities," requests the media to refrain from publishing material on Australian collaboration with other countries in monitoring activities.

Similarly, a recent Freedom of Information Act request to the NSA asking for "all documents from 1947 outlining United States–United Kingdom–Australian–Canadian–New Zealand cooperation in Signals Intelligence" was responded to with the statement: "We have determined that the fact of the existence or non-existence of the materials you request is in itself a currently and properly classified matter."[28]

OCEAN SURVEILLANCE

The operation of the U.S. ocean surveillance information-gathering system has been discussed in Chapter 8. As part of this system there are several land-based SIGINT/ocean surveillance facilities operated by the United States, Britian, Australia, Canada, and New Zealand. The information acquired by these facilities, regardless of which nation actually maintains them, is fed into the regional Fleet Ocean Surveillance Information Centers (FOSICs) at London; Norfolk, Virginia; Makalapa, Hawaii; Rota, Spain; and Kamiseya, Japan.[29]

The land-based intercept direction-finding intercept system run by the U.S. Navy is, as noted previously, codenamed Classic Bullseye. Stations that are part of this network include a "joint" U.S.-British facility at Diego Garcia in the Indian Ocean; an Australian facility at Darwin; a joint Australian-British facility at Hong Kong; and U.S.-operated facilities at Edzell, Scotland and Brawdy, Wales.

Diego Garcia is a tiny atoll in Chayos Archipelago which became a British protectorate when Britain set up the British Indian Ocean Territory (BIOT) in November 1965. On December 30, 1966 the United States and Britain signed a fifty-year joint agreement with the title "Availability of Certain Indian Ocean Islands for Defense Purposes."[30]

In August 1974 the Diego Garcia station formally opened as part of the Classic Bullseye network. The station is manned by approximately 200 U.S. and thirty British personnel. Although it is theoretically a joint U.S.-British operation, day-to-day operations are "conducted simply on the basis of the U.S. military commander on the island informing his British counterpart."[31] In addition to fulfilling its Bullseye role, the Diego Garcia station also has a ground terminal for the Classic Wizard system.

A station at Hong Kong jointly operated by the United Kingdom and Australia was, until the mid-1970s, directed almost entirely against the People's Republic of China. Presently, however, it is involved in monitoring Soviet naval movements down the coast of Asia from major Soviet naval bases at Vladivostok and Petropavlosk-Kamchatka to Cam Ranh Bay in Vietnam.[32] Likewise, an Australian-New Zealand unit, the Australian-New Zealand Military Intelligence Service (ANZMIS), located in Singapore, monitors Soviet naval activities in the region. The information collected, including intercepts and photographs, is distributed to the United States, Britain, Singapore, and Malaysia.[33]

Several Australian-operated stations also contribute significantly to the Ocean Surveillance Information System (OSIS). These stations are located at Pearce, Western Australia; Cabarlah, Queensland; and Shoal Bay, New Territories. The Pearce station has as its primary purpose the monitoring of naval and air traffic over the Indian Ocean. In the early 1980s a Circularly Disposed Antenna Array (CDAA) codenamed Pusher was installed for the interception, monitoring, direction finding, and analysis of radio signals in the HF band from 1.5 to 30 MHz.[34]

The Cabarlah station on the east coast of Australia is operated by the DSD. Its main purpose is monitoring radio transmissions throughout the Southwest Pacific. Thus, the Cabarlah system was used to monitor Soviet intelligence-gathering trawlers that were watching the Kangaroo II naval exercise of October 1976.[35]

The most important station for monitoring the Southeast Asian area is the DSD station at Darwin (Shoal Bay). The Shoal Bay station originally had a very limited direction-finding capability. However, contracts signed in 1981 provided for the procurement of modern DF equipment to enable the station to "participate fully in the OSIS."[36]

In the Pacific area the United States also maintains bases in several countries—particularly Japan and the Philippines—that supplement the intelligence collected by the Australian and British stations. Thus, Soviet naval traffic entering either the Southwest Pacific or the South China Sea is monitored by stations on Guam and the Philippines.

Monitoring of the Atlantic-European ocean areas is conducted by stations on the U.S. east coast as well as Canadian stations at Halifax and U.S. stations in Edzell, Scotland and Brawdy, Wales. The Edzell station was opened in 1960 with a staff of nine. By 1976 it had a total of 1,500 military and dependents and was the home of a CDAA.[37] Additionally, a joint British-U.S. station on Ascension Island monitors naval traffic in the South Atlantic.

RADIO BROADCAST MONITORING

In addition to the highly formalized signals intelligence and ocean surveillance cooperative arrangements, there is a third highly formalized arrangement regarding intelligence collection. This is an agreement between the United States and Britain to divide up, on a geographic basis, the responsibility for the monitoring of *public* radio and television broadcasts—mainly news and public affairs broadcasts. These broadcasts can provide valuable political intelligence, particularly because in so many nations the media, particularly radio and television, are under government control. Monitoring of public radio broadcasts can yield intelligence concerning domestic political conflict and the propaganda line a government is taking internally as well as its pronouncements concerning foreign policy and international events. It also allows a country to judge the effectiveness of its propaganda operations.

The specific organizations involved in the arrangement are the British Broadcasting Corporation's Monitoring Service and the CIA's Foreign Broadcast Information Service (FBIS). Together, the organizations monitor most of the world's most significant news and other broadcasts. As noted, both the BBC Monitoring Service and the FBIS have a network of overseas stations, operated with varying degrees of secrecy to gather their raw material.[38]

BBC Monitoring Service and FBIS cooperation began in 1948 as an openly acknowledged arrangement. Thus, the BBC Annual Report for 1948-1949 noted,

> There (is) close cooperation between the BBC's Monitoring Service and its American counterpart the Foreign Broadcast Information Branch of the United States Central Intelligence Agency, and each of the two services maintained liaison units at each other's stations for the purposes of a full exchange of information.[39]

The CIA-FBIS liaison unit is located at Caversham Park.

The area of responsibility for the Monitoring Service is roughly equivalent to GCHQ's area of responsibility for SIGINT collection—Europe, Africa, and Western Russia. Thus, the Monitoring Service maintains a remotely controlled listening post on the rooftop of the Vienna embassy to monitor VHF radio and television broadcasts originating in Hungary and Czechoslovakia. It also maintains listening posts in Accra in Ghana and Abidjan in the Ivory Coast.[40] In 1976–1977 the Monitoring Service turned over responsibility for monitoring Far East broadcasts to the FBIS. To compensate, it had to provide additional coverage of Eastern Europe. In 1974–1975 it also had to step up its reporting of events in Portugal and Spain to meet CIA requirements.[41]

The value of the monitoring arrangement has been summed up by Ray Cline, former CIA Deputy Director for Intelligence:

> While radio broadcast monitoring is overt intelligence collection, it is a technically complex and costly undertaking. By roughly dividing the world between them and exchanging the materials recorded the U.S. and Great Britain have always saved themselves a great deal of money and trouble.[42]

OVERHEAD RECONNAISSANCE

Although none of the UKUSA countries other than the United States possess advanced means of airborne photographic intelligence collection, the United Kingdom has played a significant role in U.S. collection efforts. Britain and its Royal Air Force (RAF) became involved in the U.S. U-2 program soon after its inception. The involvement stemmed from the initial basing of a U-2 unit at Lankenheath. It was decided by the United States that the best way to maximize its chances of obtaining permission for an overflight of Soviet territory was to convert to joint Anglo-American control and make either the President's or the Prime Minister's approval sufficient to conduct an overflight.[43] The idea was accepted by Britain, and a number of RAF pilots were brought to the United States and trained, becoming part of the U-2 operation in Turkey. On at least two occasions, British Prime Minister Anthony Eden authorized the overflight of Soviet territory using RAF pilots.[44]

This cooperation helped facilitate the receipt of valuable intelligence by the British during the Suez invasion of 1956. On October 31, 1956 a U-2 flying out of Adana, Turkey passed over Egypt in the course of its sweep along the eastern Mediterranean. Normal practice involved making a 270-degree turn when passing over a target and flying over it for a second time before proceeding to the next part of the flight.[45]

The target involved was the principal military airport outside of Cairo. The first set of photographs taken showed Egyptian military aircraft intact on the ground; the second set showed hangars and installations burning fiercely. In the intervening ten minutes the RAF had destroyed them.[46] The CIA telephoned the pictures to the RAF and received the return message "WARM THANKS FOR THE PIX. IT'S THE QUICKEST BOMB DAMAGE ASSESSMENT WE EVER HAD."[47]

Britain has also provided base support for SR-71s in their photographic as well as electronics intelligence (ELINT) roles. The SR-71 is believed to have carried out missions over Southeast Asia, China, the Middle East, South Africa, and Cuba. One of the SR-71's earliest missions involved the photographing of sites that were feared to be Chinese Medium Range Ballistic Missile (MRBM) deployments. Missions from British air bases as an aspect of Anglo-American cooperation received the codename POPPY, and SR-71s from British bases in Cyprus obtained important photographic coverage of events in the 1967 and 1973 Arab-Israeli wars.[48] This cooperation paid off for Britain: Early in the Falklands crisis, the United States apparently flew a special SR-71 mission from California over Argentina and the Falklands at British request.[49]

Britain also aids U.S. satellite reconnaissance efforts. The Oakhanger Tracking Station (OTS), located at Borden Hauts near London, is part of the U.S. Air Force Satellite Control Facility (SCF). The SCF has five functions—tracking, telemetry, command, recovery, and radiometric testing—and consists of eleven remote tracking stations, including four double stations. The SCF performs these functions for a wide range of military satellites but is especially important with respect to photographic and ferret satellites since such low-attitude satellites require relatively frequent transmissions of command messages every revolution in addition to support from an average of 1.5 tracking stations for each earth orbit.[50] Funds have recently been requested by the Air Force in order to add a computer capability at OTS for a "new classified satellite program."[51]

HUMAN INTELLIGENCE COOPERATION WITH AUSTRALIA

Although there are formal arrangements among the UKUSA countries with respect to signals intelligence, ocean surveillance, and radio monitoring, no such agreement exists with respect to human clandestine intelligence collection activities. Thus, there is no overall arrangement for the division of human intelligence collection activity. However, there is significant cooperation among the United States and Australia.[52]

Both the British Secret Intelligence Service (SIS) and the U.S. CIA have sought Australian cooperation in areas where it has been easier for the Australian Secret Intelligence Service (ASIS) to deploy and operate. The ASIS has provided significant assistance in Chile, Thailand, Indonesia, and Cambodia. Thus, in 1976 William Colby, then the Director of the CIA, stated that

ASIS reporting has naturally been of most value in areas where our own coverage is limited, including the following:
(a) Reporting on Portuguese Timor and North Vietnam

(b) Reporting from Indonesian sources
(c) Operations and reporting on Chile; and
(d) Unique operations and reporting on Cambodia. . . .

During the period we were not present in Chile the service was of great help in assisting us to maintain coverage of that country's internal developments. For example, two of our Santiago Station assets were turned over to ASIS for handling and produced 58 disseminated reports during the period January, 1972 through July, 1973. The effective and professional handling of these assets by ASIS made possible continued receipt of this very useful information. The same basic comments apply to the case of Cambodia.

An ASIS station in Phnom Penh was approved by the Department of Foreign Affairs on February 5, 1965 and opened later in the year with one officer and one operational assistant. A second officer slot was added in 1970 but eliminated in 1972. The opening of the station coincided, approximately, with the withdrawal of the United States Mission in Cambodia.

The CIA had strongly supported the ASIS proposal to open a new station and, upon withdrawal, turned over to the ASIS a network of agents, some of whom were still operating when Australia withdrew from Cambodia in 1974, following the fall of the government. Information collected by the ASIS–CIA network was made available to the CIA.

The presence of the Australian Secret Intelligence Service in Chile can be traced back to a CIA request for ASIS support, received in early November 1970. It appeared to the U.S. government that the Allende government might sever diplomatic relations with the United States. The CIA, in anticipation of such a move, sought the opening of at least a limited ASIS network.

The proposal was supported by the Secretary of the Department of Foreign Affairs and approved by the Minister. The justification was not in terms of the ability of a Santiago station being able to produce intelligence important to Australia, but rather as reciprocation for the large amount of intelligence made available to Australia by the United States.

Actual agent-running operations did not begin until early 1972, after a five-month period during which embassy cover was established, the operational climate was assessed, and sufficient language fluency obtained. Details concerning three agents were passed to the ASIS by the CIA for approval. After the ASIS was satisfied that the agents were trustworthy, approval was given to begin operations.

In March 1973, the Minister requested a review of the station in Chile and in April decided that it should be closed. This decision was communicated to the CIA and active operations were halted on May 1, 1973, the agents being handed back to the CIA. For cover purposes, the ASIS officer remained in Santiago until July, and operational assistant until October 1973.

According to the findings of the Hope Report, ASIS activities in support of the CIA in Cambodia and Chile were strictly confined to intelligence gathering and did not involve covert action (destabilization) activities. Thus, according to Justice Hope, "at no time was ASIS approached by CIA, nor made aware of any plans that may have been prepared to affect the internal political situation in Chile. The ASIS station in Santiago was concerned only with intelligence gathering via the agents handed over to it."

In return for such help, the ASIS has received CIA human intelligence reports concerning areas of the world where the ASIS is represented. These reports, codenamed Remarkable, numbered 588 in 1974 and 794 in 1975.

THE ISRAELI CONNECTION

Besides the UKUSA countries, the nation with which the United States probably has the broadest set of intelligence-sharing arrangements is the state of Israel. Indeed, at present, there are over two dozen such arrangements, only some of which are known.[53] These arrangements involve U.S. agencies such as the CIA, the FBI, the Defense Intelligence Agency (DIA), the NSA, the Foreign Technology Division (FTD), and the Foreign Science and Technology Center (FSTC), and Israeli agencies such as the Mossad, Shin Bet, and AMAN.

Among the arrangements, one of the most important to the United States involves the U.S. receipt of Israeli intelligence concerning weapons systems, particularly Soviet weapon systems, captured in various wars or battles. This relationship has included U.S. access to the captured weapons systems themselves as well as access to data concerning their performance.

Such exchanges took place after the 1967 and 1973 Arab–Israeli wars. Israel furnished the United States with captured Soviet air-to-ground and ground-to-air missiles and with Soviet antitank weapons. Also furnished were Soviet 122- and 130-mm artillery pieces along with ammunition for evaluation and testing. After the 1973 war, the furnished material included a Soviet T–72 tank. Upon examination, it was discovered that the T–72 was equipped with a special type of air filter to defend against germ warfare.[54] Additionally, extensive joint analyses were done after the war: Eight volumes of between 200 and 300 pages each were produced. These analyses influenced subsequent developments in U.S. weapons tactics and military budgets.[55]

In early 1983 the Israeli government offered to share military intelligence gained during the war in Lebanon. This offer included details of an "Israeli invention" that was alleged by Prime Minister Menachem Begin to be the key to Israel's ability to destroy Syria's Soviet-made surface-to-air missiles during the war.[56]

However, Secretary of Defense Caspar Weinberger rejected a proposed agreement for sharing that information because he felt it would have trapped the United States into long-range commitments to Israel that he wanted to avoid. Administration officials argued that the "information was not worth the price being asked" and said that much of the information had already been learned through normal military contacts.[57]

As a condition for sharing the information, Israel insisted on sending Israeli experts to the United States with captured weapons and receiving whatever analyses came from U.S. research. Israel also insisted on the right to veto the transfer of information and analyses to third countries, including members of NATO, and on measures to ensure that sensitive data remained secret. The Israelis, according to diplomats, expressed fears that Soviet intelligence agents who have penetrated West European governments would find out what Israel had learned and would pass that information along to Arab allies of the Soviet Union.[58] Subsequently, an agreement was reached that continued the flow of information.[59]

A late 1983 reassessment of U.S. policy in the Middle East following on the deteriorating situation in Lebanon and continued Syrian intransigence resulted in National Security Decision Directive 111, which specified a "tilt" toward Israel and expanded U.S.-Israeli strategic cooperation.[60]

This cooperation will involve a higher degree of sharing of data from reconnaissance satellites, including data on Saudi Arabia and Jordan. Israeli access to such data has varied over time. William J. Casey, in his first three years as CIA Director (1981-1984) has provided Israeli intelligence with access to sensitive photographs and other reconnaissance information that the Israelis had been denied under the Carter administration. The head of AMAN from 1979 to 1983, Major General Yehoshua Saguy, said in early 1984 that the CIA was providing Israel with access to data from reconnaissance satellites—"not only the information but the photos themselves."[61] Under the Carter administration Director of Central Intelligence (DCI) Stansfield Turner refused to provide the satellite imagery that had been provided when George Bush was DCI in 1976 and 1977.[62]

Additionally, the United States will give Israel greater access to the intelligence take of Cyprus-based SR-71 flights. The United States has been sharing such data with Israel, Egypt, and Syria on a "highly selective basis" as a result of an agreement signed in 1974 after the October War of 1973. The information previously transmitted to Israel primarily concerned Egyptian or Syrian military developments but will now cover a "broader range."[63]

There will be limits to what the Israelis will receive, however. Thus, Israeli requests for a dedicated satellite and a system of ground stations that would "directly access" the KH-11 as it passes over the Middle East are "highly unlikely" to be granted. The Israelis already have ground receivers to "pull down" U.S. satellite transmissions in the area, but they lack the decryption mechanisms to make the signals intelligible.[64]

A third area of cooperation involves the large number of émigrés that arrive in Israel from the Soviet Union each year. Information obtained by interviews conducted by the Mossad is passed to the CIA.[65] Although it is unlikely that any startling revelations are produced, the collective data can be quite valuable.

In addition to intelligence exchanges, Israel has cooperated with the United States in regard to covert operations of varying kinds. In 1961 the Soviet Union introduced into the Middle East, amid great security, the MIG-21. The Mossad established contact with an Iraqi pilot who agreed to fly the plane to Israel for a half million pounds, undoubtedly provided by the CIA. The pilot landed in Israel via Turkey.[66]

More recently, Israel has been involved in supporting U.S. policy in Central America. At U.S. request, Israel has been supplying weapons captured by the PLO to Honduras for eventual use by Nicaraguan rebels. The arms shipments include artillery pieces, mortar rounds, mines, hand grenades, and ammunition. Israel has also consulted with Central American governments about intelligence operations.[67]

Liaison between the United States and Israel on intelligence matters dates back to the early 1950s during which

> the governments of Israel and the United States had agreed to exchange intelligence secrets. And most important of all as far as the Israelis were concerned, the Central Intelligence Agency along with the Federal Bureau of Investigation, had undertaken to supply the Israelis with some top secret equipment, including the most advanced computers for cryptanalysis, as well as to train selected Israeli officers in their use.[68]

The centerpiece of CIA-Mossad cooperation until 1975 was the CIA's Chief of the Counterintelligence Staff, James Jesus Angleton. Angleton had developed extensive contracts with future Israeli intelligence officials during his World War II European activities with the Office of Strategic Services (OSS). In 1957 Angleton set up a liaison unit to deal with the Mossad, which was made responsible for producing Middle East intelligence for both services. In addition, the CIA received intelligence from Mossad networks in the Soviet Union.[69]

After Angleton's dismissal, the liaison unit was abolished and the Israeli account was moved to the appropriate Directorate of Operations regional division. The CIA also began to operate more independently of the Mossad, befitting improved U.S. relations with Egypt. In the late 1970s the CIA began operating on the West Bank.[70]

COOPERATION WITH THE PEOPLE'S
REPUBLIC OF CHINA

As opposed to the long-standing arrangements with the UKUSA nations and Israel, U.S. cooperation with the People's Republic of China (PRC) is quite recent. In 1979 the United States and the People's Republic of China reached agreement on the establishment of two SIGINT stations—at Qitai's and Korla—in the Xinjlang Uighur Autonomous Region in Western China near the Soviet border. The stations were constructed by the CIA Directorate of Science and

Technology's Office of SIGINT Operations but manned by Chinese under the command of the General Staff's Technical Department, the PRC SIGINT agency. The information collected at the two sites includes data on the development of new Soviet missiles tested at Leninsk and Sary Shagan, as well as Soviet military communications, and is shared by both China and the United States.[71]

At the same time, the United States is providing the PRC with satellite reconnaissance photographs for mapping. According to one U.S. official, the Chinese reconnaissance satellite's "footprint is very small, and they want mapping support, especially of the Soviet Union."[72]

One other likely area of cooperation is with respect to the covert operations conducted by the CIA and the Chinese International Liaison Department — specifically, sending arms to Afghani rebels and to those opposing Vietnamese control of Cambodia.

ESTIMATES: COOPERATION AMONG THE ANGLO-SAXON COUNTRIES

The production of intelligence estimates with respect to Soviet guided missiles is another area in which there has been close U.S. and British cooperation. The two countries produced a joint estimate on the subject in 1949, the Joint Anglo-American Study, using information available through December 31, 1948. A second early study was a joint Army–Navy–Air Force examination of the Soviet missile program that was coordinated with the British in 1949.[73]

A 369-page estimate entitled *A Summary of Guided Missile Intelligence* and published in July 1953 was initially prepared by the U.S. Guided Missiles Working Group. The group consisted of Army, Navy, Air Force, and CIA guided-missiles intelligence specialists.[74] The initial document prepared by the U.S. Working Group was presented at the Joint US/UK Conference on Soviet guided missiles that took place in Washington, D.C. September 8–26, 1952. As a result of the conference, modifications in the original documents were made by the CIA.[75]

The estimate focused on a variety of subjects related to Soviet missiles: surface-to-surface missiles, surface-to-air missiles, air-to-surface missiles, air-to-air missiles, guided-missile testing facilities, guidance and control, propulsion and fuels, production, and Soviet guided-missile trends. A major focus of the document was Soviet exploitation of the German guided-missile program. The document also included a list of personalities known or suspected to be connected with Soviet guided missiles. The list included nationality, location, and specialty plus additional pertinent information.[76]

U.S.–Canadian joint estimates produced in the late 1950s focused on Soviet capabilities and likely actions in the event of a major Soviet attack on North America. Thus, *Soviet Capabilities and Probable Courses of Action Against*

North America in a Major War Commencing During the Period 1 January 1958 to 31 December 1958, as well as a similarly titled document for the period July 1, 1958 to June 30, 1959, prepared by the Canadian-U.S. Joint Intelligence Committee assessed the Soviet threat to North America. Factors considered included: Communist bloc political stability and economic support; the internal threat to North America; Soviet nuclear, radiological, biological and chemical weapons; aircraft, including bombers, transport aircraft, and tanker aircraft; guided missiles; naval weapons; electronics; ground, naval, and surface strength and combat effectiveness; Soviet worldwide strategy; and Soviet capabilities to conduct air and airborne missile, naval, amphibious, and internal operations against North America.[77]

More recently, the chiefs of the analytical branches of the Australian, British, Canadian, and U.S. intelligence communities would hold meetings every four years to discuss substantive methodological issues of interest. These meetings apparently are no longer being held.[78]

However, cooperation among those countries in the defense intelligence area remains strong. The DIA maintains liaison units at the Australian, British, and Canadian defense intelligence organizations.

In addition to continuous liaison, there are periodic conferences dealing with a wide range of scientific and defense intelligence matters. Thus, in 1974 the United States participated in the Annual Land Warfare Intelligence Conference, the International Scientific Intelligence Exchange, the Quadripartite Intelligence Working Party on Chinese Guided Missiles, and the Tripartite Defense Intelligence Estimates Conference. Held in London in May 1974, the Annual Land Warfare Intelligence Conference involved as participants the U.S., British, Canadian, and Australian defense intelligence organizations, members of which gathered to discuss the armaments used by Communist armies.[79]

The Third International Scientific Exchange, involving U.S., British, New Zealand, and Australian defense intelligence organizations, was held in Canberra from June 18 to 27. Initially established to discuss Chinese scientific development, particularly with respect to nuclear weapons, the 1974 meeting also focused on technical developments in India and Japan, nuclear proliferation in Asia, development and military applications of lasers, and application of peaceful nuclear explosives.

The Quadripartite Intelligence Working Party on Chinese Guided Missiles met in London in 1974. The panel, consisting of representatives from the U.S., British, Australian, and Canadian defense intelligence operations, focused on Chinese guided missiles and satellite launch vehicles.

The United States, New Zealand, and Australia constituted the participants in the Tripartite Defense Intelligence Estimates Conference. The 1974 conference, held in Wellington, New Zealand, involved "the exchange of military estimates and assessments" among the countries.[80]

OVERSEAS BASES

In addition to the bases already noted, the United States maintains a number of important facilities in several countries, including, as would be expected, Australia and Britain.

The United States maintains several military installations in Australia—the U.S. Naval Communications Station Harold E. Holt at North West Cape, the Joint Defense Space Research Facility at Pine Gap, and the Joint Defense Space Communications Station at Nurrungur being the most prominent.[81] All three installations are involved in U.S. intelligence and early warning operations.

Sometime in the late 1960s the Naval Communications Station Harold E. Holt became host to an operation of the Naval Security Group (NSG). The NSG equipment at the facility apparently includes a four-point log-periodic VLF electronic intelligence receiver for monitoring Soviet naval communications from Vladivostock and Khaborovsk.[82]

Probably the single most important U.S. facility in Australia is the Joint Defense Space Research Facility at Pine Gap near Alice Springs in central Australia. The facility is a CIA-run installation codenamed Merino that provides control signals and readout from the Rhyolite satellite stationed over the Pacific.[83]

Pine Gap consists of seven large radomes, a huge computer room, and about twenty support buildings. The radomes are made of perspex and mounted on concrete structures. They are designed to protect the enclosed antennas against dust, wind, and rain and to hide some of the operational elements of the antennas from Soviet satellite reconnaissance.

The first two radomes, which were installed in 1968, remain the largest in the complex. In March 1967 the first Chief of the Pine Gap facility stated that the largest dish is "about 100 feet" in diameter.[84] The second radome has a diameter of about 70 feet. These two radomes now form the western line of the antenna complex. Construction of the third and fourth radomes began in November 1968 and was completed in mid-1969.[85] The third radome, about 55 feet in diameter, is some 197 feet east of the largest radome; the fourth is less than 20 feet in diameter and is just north of the second radome. The fifth radome is less than 40 feet in diameter and was installed in 1971. The sixth dish is about the same size as the fifth and was installed in 1977. The seventh, which was built in 1980, houses a second communications terminal, designated SCT-8.[86]

On the northern edge of the complex is a high-frequency (HF) antenna that provides a direct communications link with the U.S. base at Clark Field in the Philippines. This is the only nonsatellite communications system linking the Pine Gap facility with terminals outside Australia, and before installation of the SCT-35 antenna in 1973 it was the primary communications link between Pine Gap and the United States.[87]

Pine Gap is strictly under U.S. (CIA) control. Further, very few Australians are permitted in the Top Secret sector of Pine Gap. The Signals Analysis Section of the computer room is staffed only by CIA and NSA analysts. It includes no U.S. contractor personnel and no Australian citizens.[88]

The NSA has four major independent establishments in Britain: at Chicksands in Bedfordshire; at Edzell (Tayside) in Scotland; at Menwith Hill, Harrogate; and at Brawdy, Wales. The installation at Brawdy is an NSG facility concerned with ocean surveillance.

The Chicksands facility is a major listening post run by the 6950th Electronic Security Group. An AN/FLR-9 antenna was installed at Chicksands at approximately the same time as one was installed at San Vito in 1964.[89] According to a former NSA officer, one of the prime tasks of Chicksands is to monitor the diplomatic communications of France and other European countries.[90] The Edzell outpost is an NSG facility apparently involved in both radio monitoring and ocean surveillance. Among the equipment at Edzell is a Circularly Disposed Antenna Array (CDAA) with eighty vertical supports, each ninety inches high.[91]

A major NSA station, codenamed STEEPLEBUSH, is located at Menwith Hill, eight miles west of Harrogate in Yorkshire. The station is 562 acres and consists of a large array of satellite-tracking aerials. Eight tracking dishes dominate the Menwith Hill site. Most of the time, they are pointed toward satellites operating in the highly elliptical orbit of the Soviet Molniya and U.S. Satellite Data System. Hence, the aerials might be intercepting signals from the former and transmitting or receiving signals to or from the latter.[92]

Menwith Hill is also a major communications intelligence collection site. According to Linda Malvern and Duncan Campbell, Menwith Hill has for fifteen years "sifted the communications of private citizens, corporations and governments for information of political or economic value to the U.S."[93] The British Post Office has built Menwith Hill into the heart of Britain's national communications system—and Britain occupies a nodal position in the communications of the world, especially those of Western Europe. The first stage of the Post Office microwave network was constructed around Menwith Hill and its operations; at least five high-capacity networks feed into the base from all parts of Britain through the nearby Post Office tower at Hunter Stones.[94]

One former British officer has stated that Menwith Hill intercepts telephone and other communications to and from Europe and the United States. One tap run from Menwith Hill allegedly involves 3,600 London-to-Paris telephone lines.[95] According to a former U.S. official, Menwith Hill provides ground station service for CIA and NSA intelligence satellites.[96] There is also a CDAA and a four-element VHF intercept antenna at Menwith Hill.

Finally, at Mildenhall Royal Air Force base there is an Electronic Security Squadron which provides personnel to operate the electronic intelligence gathering equipment that is on several aircraft stationed there. There are two U-2s, two SR-71s and two RC-135s.[97]

The United States has had significant intelligence links with Norway for many years—links dating back to World War II and the OSS's support of the Norwegian resistance against the Nazi occupation. At the end of 1944 the OSS sent a mission to impede German railroad movements. The operation was almost a complete failure and ten people were killed.[98]

In 1971 the Norwegian government allowed U.S. installation and operation of the Norwegian Seismic Array (NORSAR), a large seismic array designed to register underground nuclear explosions and determine their depth and energy yield. Data from the array are transmitted to the Seismic Data Analysis Center (SDAC) in Alexandria, Virginia.[99]

Norway is also involved in the U.S. ocean surveillance program, as one of the twenty-three Sound Surveillance System (SOSUS) sites is off the Norwegian coast. This array probably runs from the North Cape in Norway out to the Norwegian island territory of Swalbad, which juts toward the North Pole. This array probably allows monitoring of every submarine that arrives or leaves the Russian submarine base at Murmansk.[100]

The most important aspect of U.S.-Norwegian cooperation on intelligence matters is with respect to seven listening and intercept stations erected by the NSA and operated in cooperation with the Norwegian Security Service. These installations are located at Vadso, Kirkenes, Fauske (2), Namsos, Jessheim, and Randaberg and have CIA and NSA personnel on regular assignment.[101]

The equipment at Vadso includes HF listening equipment and VHF/UHF antennas. The HF equipment consists of a 450-foot diameter array of HF monopole antennas within which is a further array of monopoles. The array is of the Pusher type built by the Plessey Corporation for Britain's GCHQ (Government Communications Headquarters). The HF equipment can be used to monitor long-distance point-to-point radio communications, ship-to-ship, ship-to-shore, and air-to-ground communications. Four of the eight VHF/UHF antennas are pointed toward Murmansk and one toward the Barents Sea to monitor much telemetry from Soviet test launches.[102]

At Randaberg there are further circular arrays similar but not identical to the smaller Vadso arrays. These arrays are probably used mainly to intercept HF communications from Soviet ships, submarines, and long-range ocean surveillance aircraft in the Norwegian sea.[103] At Jessheim there is an array identical to the one at Vadso.[104]

A large radome at one of the two Fauske sites (Vetan) is situated in a valley surrounded by mountains—the typical layout for satellite ground control stations. This station is apparently either intercepting telemetry beamed down from a Russian military satellite to a ground station at Murmansk or is a ground station for an electronic reconnaissance satellite.[105]

Another key country for U.S. technical intelligence collection operations is Turkey. Intelligence collection sites in Turkey are those at Sinop and Samsun on the Black Sea coast in north central Turkey, Belbasi in central Turkey, Diyarbakir in southeastern Turkey, and Karamursel in northwestern Turkey.[106]

The Sinop facility is operated by INSCOM and collects data on Soviet air and naval activities in the Black Sea area. It also has HF receivers to record the countdown communications for missiles launched from Kapustin Yar and Tyuratam.[107]

Associated with Sinop is Samsun, a communications site manned by the Air Force Electronic Security Command (ESC).[108] The Diyarbakir site is operated by INSCOM and consists of an FPS-17 detection radar and FPS-79 tracking radar, both of which are targeted against missiles launched from Kapustin Yar and Tyuratam. The telemetry from such missiles is intercepted by the VHF-UHF-SHF receivers at the Karamursel and Samsun facilities.[109]

The Soviet Union's shooting down of KAL flight 007 cast further light on U.S. SIGINT activities conducted from bases in Japan. In addition to the Kadena Air Base (AB), Okinawa facility from which SR-71, U-2, and RC-135 aircraft fly reconnaissance missions, U.S. land-based SIGINT activities are conducted from Kadena AB (ESC), Misawa AB (ESC), Kamiseya (NSG and ESC), and Camp Fuchinobe (near Tokyo) to name just a few installations.[110]

The 6920th Electronic Security Group (ESG) at Misawa constitutes the largest U.S. SIGINT facility in Japan, with an AN/FLR-9 CDAA. At Kadena AB the 6990th ESG and a Naval Security Group detachment conduct both communications security (COMSEC) and SIGINT collection activities directed at Soviet and other targets.[111]

Some of the equipment at such facilities picks up radar signals from Soviet ground installations and aircraft, providing evidence of any Soviet air defense alert. Other receivers and antennas are then turned to pick up radio transmissions between Soviet air defense installations and interceptor aircraft, which are generally uncoded.[112]

NOTES TO CHAPTER 10

1. James Bamford, *The Puzzle Palace: A Report on NSA, America's Most Secret Agency* (Boston: Houghton Mifflin, 1982), p. 312.

2. Ronald Lewin, *The American Magic: Codes, Ciphers and the Defeat of Japan* (New York: Farrar, Strauss & Giroux, 1982), p. 46.

3. Ibid.

4. Bamford, *The Puzzle Palace*, p. 314.

5. Ibid.

6. Bob Elliot, *Scarlet to Green: Canadian Army Intelligence 1903-1963* (Toronto: Hunter Rose, 1982), p. 461.

7. F. H. Hinsley, E. E. Thomas, C. F. G. Ransom, and R. C. Knight, *British Intelligence in the Second World War*, vol. 2 (New York: Cambridge, 1981), p. 551n.

8. See p. xv of David Kahn's Introduction to Herbert O. Yardley, *The American Black Chamber* (New York: Ballantine, 1981); Robert Sheppard, "Lack of Quick RMCP Action Upset Gouzenko, Papers Say," *Toronto Globe & Mail*, October 17, 1981, p. 5; Elliot, p. 401.

9. Ibid.

10. Ibid., p. 460.

11. U.S. Congress, Joint Committee on the Investigation of the Pearl Harbor Attack, *Pearl Harbor Attack, Part 2* (Washington, D.C.: U.S. Government Printing Office, 1946), p. 947.

12. D. M. Horner, "Special Intelligence in the Southwest Pacific Area in World War II," *Australian Outlook* 32, no. 4 (1978): 310–27.

13. Desmond Ball, "Allied Intelligence Cooperation Involving Australia During World War II," *Australian Outlook* 32, no. 4 (1978): 299–309.

14. Elliot, *Scarlet to Green*, pp. 384–85.

15. Richard Clark, *The Man Who Broke Purple* (Boston: Little, Brown, 1977), p. 208.

16. Ball, "Allied Intelligence Cooperation."

17. See Jeffrey Richelson and Desmond Ball, *The Ties that Bind: The UK–USA Intelligence Network* (London: Allen & Unwin, 1985).

18. Committee for the Abolition of Political Police (CAPP), *Top Secret: A Closer Look at Australia's Secret Service* (North Balwyn: CAPP, 1977).

19. Duncan Campbell, "Threat of the Electronic Spies," *New Statesman*, February 2, 1979, pp. 140–44.

20. John Sawatsky, *Men in the Shadows: The RCMP Security Service* (New York: Doubleday, 1980), p. 92; Transcript of "The Fifth Estate – The Espionage Establishment," broadcast by the Canadian Broadcast Company, 1974.

21. Chapman Pincher, *Inside Story: A Documentary of the Pursuit of Power* (New York: Stein & Day, 1979), p. 157.

22. Sawatsky, *Men in the Shadows*, p. 92.

23. Desmond Ball, *A Suitable Piece of Real Estate: American Installations in Australia* (Sydney: Hale & Iremonger, 1980), p. 40.

24. Campbell, "Threat of the Electronic Spies."

25. Department of the Army, Office of the Adjutant General, "United States–United Kingdom Security Agreement" (Washington, D.C.: Department of the Army, October 8, 1948).

26. Private information (author's emphasis).

27. Paul Kelly, "NSA, The Biggest Secret Spy Network in Australia," *The National Times*, May 23–28, 1977.

28. Letter to the author from Eugene Y. Yeates, Director of Policy, National Security Agency, December 7, 1982.

29. U.S. Congress, Senate Committee on Appropriations, *Department of Defense Appropriations for Fiscal Year 1978, Part 5* (Washington, D.C.: U.S. Government Printing Office, 1977), pp. 600–601.

30. Desmond Ball, "The U.S. Naval Ocean Surveillance Information System (NOSIS)—Australia's Role," *Pacific Defense Reporter*, June 1982, pp. 40–49.

31. U.S. Congress, House Committee on Foreign Affairs, *Proposed Expansion of U.S. Military Facilities in the Indian Ocean* (Washington, D.C.: U.S. Government Printing Office, 1974), p. 33.

32. Ball, "The U.S. Naval Ocean Surveillance Information System."

33. Michael Richardson, "Australia and NZ use Singapore Base to Spy on Soviet Ships for CIA," *The Age*, April 12, 1984, p. 1.
34. Ball, "The U.S. Naval Ocean Surveillance Information System."
35. Ibid.
36. Ibid.
37. Bamford, *The Puzzle Palace*, p. 161.
38. Duncan Campbell and Clive Thomas, "BBC's Trade Secrets," *New States-man*, July 4, 1980, pp. 13–14.
39. Ibid.
40. Ibid.
41. Ibid.
42. Ray Cline, *The CIA Under Reagan, Bush and Casey* (Washington, D.C.: Acropolis, 1981), p. 189.
43. Leonard Mosely, *Dulles: A Biography of Eleanor, Allen and John Foster and Their Family Network* (New York: Dial, 1978), p. 369.
44. Ibid.
45. Ibid.
46. Ibid., pp. 417–18.
47. Ibid., p. 418.
48. John Prados, *The Soviet Estimates: U.S. Intelligence Analysis and Russian Military Strength* (New York: Dial, 1982), p. 176.
49. Duncan Campbell, "How We Spy on Argentina," *New Statesman*, April 30, 1982, p. 5.
50. U.S. Congress, House Committee on Armed Services, *Hearings on Military Posture and HR 1872 Book 1, Part 3* (Washington, D.C.: U.S. Government Printing Office, 1979), p. 1375.
51. *Defense Electronics*, October 1982, p. 154.
52. This section is based on *The Fifth Report of the Royal Commission on Intelligence and Security* (Canberra: Australia Government Printer, 1977) (Classified Version).
53. Richard Halloran, "U.S. Offers Israel Plan on War Data," *New York Times*, March 13, 1983, pp. 1, 13.
54. Stanley Blumberg and Gwinn Owens, *The Survival Factor: Israeli Intelligence from World War I to the Present* (New York: Putnam, 1982), p. 271.
55. Halloran, "U.S. Offers Israel Plan on War Data," *Washington Post*, October 15, 1982, p. A18.
56. Edward Walsh, "Begin Offers to Give War Intelligence to U.S.," *Washington Post*, October 15, 1982, p. A18.
57. Richard Halloran, "U.S. Said to Bar Deal with Israel," *New York Times*, February 10, 1983, pp. A1, A7.
58. Ibid.
59. Bernard Gwertzman, "Israelis to Share Lessons of War with Pentagon," *New York Times*, May 22, 1983, pp. 1, 11.
60. Bernard Gwertzman, "Reagan Turns to Israel," *New York Times Magazine*, November 27, 1983, pp. 62ff.

61. Bob Woodward, "CIA Sought 3rd Country Contra Aid," *Washington Post*, May 19, 1984, pp. A1, A13.
62. Ibid.
63. "U.S. to Share More Recon Data, Tightens Air Links With Israel," *Aerospace Daily*, December 8, 1983, pp. 193–94.
64. Ibid.
65. "Is the CIA Hobbled?" *Newsweek*, March 5, 1979, pp. 18–20.
66. Blumberg and Owens, *The Survival Factor*, p. 271.
67. Philip Taubman, "Israel Said to Aid Latin Arms to U.S.," *New York Times*, July 21, 1983, pp. A1, A4.
68. Stewart Steven, *The Spymasters of Israel* (New York: Macmillan, 1979), p. 37.
69. Judith Perera, "Cracks in the Special Relationship," *The Middle East*, March 1983, pp. 12–18.
70. Ibid.
71. "Spying on Russia, with China's Help," *U.S. News and World Report*, June 29, 1981, p. 10.
72. "Washington Round-up," *Aviation Week and Space Technology*, March 19, 1984, p. 15.
73. Prados, *The Soviet Estimates*, p. 57.
74. U.S. Guided Missile Working Group, *A Summary of Soviet Guided Missile Intelligence* US/UK GM4–52 (Washington, D.C.: CIA, July 20, 1953), cover page *Declassified Documents Reference System 1975–51I.*
75. Ibid.
76. Ibid.
77. Canadian–US Joint Intelligence Committee, *Soviet Capabilities and Probable Courses of Action Against North America in a Major War Commencing During the Period 1 January 1958 to 31 December 1958* (Washington, D.C.: Central Intelligence Agency, March 1, 1957) in *Declassified Documents Reference System*, 1981–169A.
78. Ray Cline, "A CIA Reminiscence," *Washington Quarterly*, Autumn 1982, pp. 88–92.
79. Joint Intelligence Organization (JIO), *Fourth Annual Report 1974* (Canberra: JIO, 1974), p. 36.
80. Ibid.
81. Ball, *A Suitable Piece of Real Estate*, pp. 50–58.
82. Ball, "American Bases," *Current Affairs Bulletin*, October 1978.
83. Ball, *A Suitable Piece of Real Estate*, p. 66.
84. *Northern Territory News*, March 23, 1967, p. 1.
85. Robert Cooksey, "Pine Gap Base Almost Visited," *The Age*, September 23, 1969, p. 7.
86. *Hansard (Australian House of Representatives)*, May 3, 1979, p. 1892; *The Age*, February 9, 1981.
87. Australian House of Representatives, Answer to Question No. 3418, November 25, 1981.
88. Ball, *Secret Satellites Over Australia*, forthcoming.

89. "Memorandum to Bill Moyers, Subject: President's Weekly Report," (Washington, D.C.: Department of Defense, May 12, 1964).

90. Duncan Campbell, "Target Britain," *New Statesman* October 31, 1980, pp. 6–9.

91. Duncan Campbell and Linda Malvern, "America's Big Ear on Europe," *New Statesman*, July 18, 1980, pp. 10–14.

92. Ibid.

93. Ibid.

94. Ibid.

95. Ibid.

96. Ibid.

97. Campbell, "Target Britain."

98. Konrad Ege, "U.S. Intelligence in Norway," *Counter Spy* 4 no. 1 (1980): 33–42.

99. Ibid.

100. Ibid.

101. F. G. Samia, "The Norwegian Connection: Norway (Un)Willing Spy for the U.S.," *Covert Action Information Bulletin* 9 (June 1980): 4–9.

102. Owen Wilkes and Nils Peter Gleditsch, *Intelligence Installations in Norway: Their Number, Function and Legality* (Oslo: PRIO, 1978), pp. 11–20.

103. Ibid.

104. Ibid.

105. Ibid.

106. U.S. Congress, House Committee on International Relations, *United States Military Installations and Objectives in the Mediterranean* (Washington, D.C.: U.S. Government Printing Office, 1977), pp. 37–39.

107. SIPRI, *World Armaments and Disarmament: SIPRI Yearbook 1980* (London: Taylor & Francis, 1980), p. 296.

108. U.S. Congress, House Committee on International Relations, *United States Military Installations*, pp. 37–39.

109. VHF–Very High Frequencies, UHF, Ultra High Frequencies, SHF, Super High Frequencies; SIPRI, *World Armaments and Disarmament*, p. 296.

110. Richelson and Ball, *The Ties that Bind*, Appendix A.

111. Ibid.

112. "How the U.S. Listened In," *Newsweek*, September 12, 1983, p. 25.

11 COUNTERINTELLIGENCE AND COVERT ACTION

In addition to the collection of positive intelligence, there are two other types of activities that fall within the responsibilities of most intelligence communities: counterintelligence and covert action.

Counterintelligence is a term often associated with the catching of spies. In fact, it is necessary to distinguish between offensive counterintelligence and defensive counterintelligence. It is not a distinction that can be perfectly made, but it is one with validity. Defensive counterintelligence is basically concerned with the catching of agents and intelligence officers. Offensive counterintelligence is a more involved activity.

Although it is generally not noted, counterintelligence activity forms the basis for many spy novels as well as many nonfiction accounts. The most prominent spy novelist whose novels focus on counterintelligence activity is John Le Carré. Indeed, all his best-known novels—*The Spy Who Came in from the Cold; Tinker, Tailor, Soldier, Spy; The Honorable Schoolboy;* and *Smiley's People*—are actually counterintelligence novels.

Covert action is a nation's attempt to influence the course of political life in a foreign nation without its role being revealed, at least in theory. As will be discussed below, covert activities may involve high-visibility operations seeking to bring about major changes or low-visibility operations seeking only to exert some undefined influence on the course of events. In either case, their intended covert nature has resulted in their implementation generally being made the responsibility of a nation's intelligence services.

219

COUNTERINTELLIGENCE

Counterintelligence was defined by President Carter's Executive Order 12036 as both "information gathered" and "activities conducted" the purpose of which is "to protect against espionage and other clandestine intelligence activities, sabotage, international terrorist activities, sabotage or assassination conducted for or on behalf of foreign powers, organizations or persons, but not including personnel, physical documents or communications security."[1] Thus, as defined in Executive Order 12036, counterintelligence incorporates a wide range of activities not strictly in the counterintelligence tradition. The definition above essentially stresses the counter aspect and lets intelligence represent activities below the conventional military level. Some would also consider counterdeception and counter-illicit technology transfer to be part of the list of counterintelligence subcategories.[2] Such a view essentially mixes traditional counterintelligence with positive intelligence designed to counter any form of hostile activity short of conventional military operations (e.g., terrorist attacks, sabotage) as well as with a framework of analysis (counterdeception) for the analysis of positive intelligence.

The more traditional notion of counterintelligence and the one that will be used here focuses on counterintelligence as being information gathered and activities conducted with the purpose of disrupting and neutralizing the activities of hostile intelligence services. In this view there are four basic functions of a counterintelligence unit:

1. penetration of hostile intelligence services;
2. evaluation of defectors and possible agents;
3. research and collection on hostile and friendly
   intelligence services; and
4. disruption and neutralization.

At the very least, the goal of the counterintelligence unit is to protect the integrity of the larger intelligence apparatus from penetration, disruption, or disinformation via planted defectors or double agents. At the limit of a counterintelligence unit's ambition is the complete penetration and disruption of the activities of a hostile intelligence service—as a means of blocking or neutralizing its activities.

Penetration means the placing or recruiting of agents inside hostile intelligence services. Such penetration may be accomplished via a mole—somebody recruited prior to entry into the intelligence service—or via a turned agent or "defector in place"—someone recruited after having attained an intelligence post. In the latter case, recruitment may be voluntary, for either ideological or financial reasons, or coerced. Coercion or blackmail might be based on threats to family, evidence of misbehavior (sexual or financial), or simply direct threats to the subject.

Numerous examples exist of penetration of various levels of a nation's intelligence and security apparatus. In World War II, by all standard accounts, the British Security Service was able to capture or turn every German agent sent into England. This operation, run by the "Double-Cross Committee" allowed British intelligence to determine the intelligence goals of the Germans as well as to plant false information concerning future Allied plans, force strengths, and the effectiveness of German bombing activities.[3]

The United States has had some success in the penetration of Soviet intelligence, specifically the Chief Intelligence Directorate of the General Staff (GRU). As noted earlier, in the late 1950s and 1960s it recruited first Peter Popov and then Oleg Penkovskiy, both Colonels in the GRU.[4] In addition to providing detailed information concerning the structure of the GRU, they provided information on its physical layout and the identities and personalities of GRU agents.

Soviet penetrations of Western intelligence have been more extensive, particularly in the case of West Germany and Britain. For example, the head of West Germany's BFV (Federal Office for Protection of the Constitution—i.e., counterintelligence and security) and the head of counterintelligence of the BND (Federal Intelligence Service) were both Soviet agents.[5]

In Britain the most notable penetrations into the Secret Intelligence Service (SIS) involved George Blake and H.A.R. "Kim" Philby.[6] Blake provided details of British–U.S. intelligence operations and operatives in Germany and the Middle East, including "Operation Gold," the Berlin Tunnel. Blake's revelations concerning the identities of British agents in the Middle East might have cost forty of them their lives. Philby provided a massive amount of information, including U.S.–British plans for covert action directed against the Soviet Union and East European countries. Included was a plan for the overthrow of the government of Albania. The information contributed to the virtual and complete neutralization of the commando forces sent into that country.

Not surprisingly, little is known concerning the details of present Central Intelligence Agency operations seeking to penetrate hostile intelligence services; although one can assume that such attempts are being made, the only information available is about one operation that apparently went wrong. This most peculiar counterintelligence operation concerned a Soviet defector to the United States.[7] In 1959 Captain Nikolai Fedorovich Artamonov, the youngest commanding officer of a destroyer in Soviet naval history, defected to Sweden. Information about Artamonov was transmitted to the United States by the CIA Station Chief in Sweden.

Artamonov was subsequently recruited by the Office of Naval Intelligence (ONI) to come to the United States. In his debriefing he provided the ONI with information on Soviet use of AGIs, Soviet nuclear strategy, and Soviet destroyer tactics against submarines. Subsequent to the debriefing, he was given a new name, Nicholas Shadrin, and a position as a translator in the Naval Scientific and Technical Intelligence Center (now the Naval Intelligence Support Center). In 1966 two events of importance occurred. Shadrin went to work for the Defense Intelligence Agency and was also approached by a Soviet intelligence officer who tried to recruit him. Shadrin did not close the door on the officer but reported it to the FBI. After initial hesitation, Shadrin was persuaded to become a double agent, to "accept" the Soviet offer and feed the KGB CIA-doctored information.

Among the reasons for U.S. pressure on Shadrin to accept the double agent role is that his recruiter, "Igor," was allegedly a Soviet "defector in place" whose assigned mission was the recruitment of Shadrin. Successful completion of his mission, said Igor, would help propel him to Chief of the KGB's American Department.

After several years of working for the KGB, Shadrin began to make trips abroad to meet his controller. He never returned from a December 18, 1975 meeting in Vienna. The general belief is that "Igor" was a plant and Shadrin was captured and taken back to the Soviet Union or killed in Vienna. An alternative explanation is that Shadrin was the bogus defector and disappearance simply represented his return to the Soviet Union.

Counterintelligence operations in which the United States seeks to convince the Soviet and other hostile intelligence services that military personnel are cooperating with them are run by the Army's Intelligence and Security Command (INSCOM) as well as by Navy and Air Force intelligence units. Such operations might serve to spread tactical disinformation and provide information concerning hostile intelligence service targets. The INSCOM agents involved in such operations bear codenames such as Royal Miter, Lancer Flag, and Hole Punch.

Evaluation of defectors and possible agents is a second important aspect of the counterintelligence mission. The inability of the CIA's counterintelligence staff to determine conclusively the bona fides of several important defectors has been a vital factor in much of the conflict that has torn the U.S. intelligence community over the last twenty years. In addition to the problems of defector exaggeration and boasting and the creation of new stories when the truth has been depleted, there is the possibility that the defector is actually a plant—a hostile counterintelligence operation directed at the intelligence service and nation. Among the false information that such a defector might sow is the allegation that there is a mole high up in the service. Such an allegation can lead to huge expenditures of resources chasing false leads. More damaging still, it can damage the careers and reputations of effective intelligence officers and cause a decline in morale in the service.

This was the case in the controversy that stemmed from the defection in 1962 of Anatoli Golitsin and has been resurrected in recent years by the apparent suicide of a highly placed CIA official and the realization that a Soviet U.N.

employee supposedly working for the United States had been under Soviet control all along. The severity of the controversy was in part due to the persistence in pursuing the mole by James Jesus Angleton, the Chief of the CIA's Counterintelligence Staff.

Golitsin defected to the CIA from Helsinki, Finland. He identified himself as a Major in the First Chief Directorate of the KGB, working primarily against targets in the NATO alliance. He was brought to Washington and was given the cover name John Stone.[8] The information Stone provided in his debriefing caused a sensation. According to Stone, the KGB had already planted an agent within the highest echelons of U.S. intelligence. This penetration agent would be assisted by "outside" men—other Soviet-controlled agents masking themselves as defectors or double agents—who would supply pieces of disinformation designed to bolster an "inside" man's credibility. The inside agent in turn would be in a position to help confirm the authenticity of the outside agent.

During his debriefing sessions with Angleton in 1962, Stone had called particular attention to a trip made by V.M. Kovshuk to the United States in 1957 under diplomatic cover, using the alias Komarov. Stone identified Kovshuk as the then-reigning head of the all-important American Embassy section of the KGB and stressed that only an extremely important mission would account for his leaving his post in Moscow to come to the United States. He suggested that Kovshuk's mission might have involved contacting or activating a high-level Soviet penetration agent within the CIA who had been recruited years before in Moscow.

Stone further cautioned that the KGB, realizing that he knew about Kovshuk's mission, would almost certainly attempt to discredit or deflect the CIA from the information he was providing. He warned Angleton that Soviet disinformation agents could be expected to make contact with the CIA for this purpose. Six months later, Yuri Nosenko defected to the CIA. Nosenko's information ran counter to that of Stone in many instances and tended to downplay the possibility of a Soviet penetration of the CIA. The explanation Nosenko gave concerning Soviet detection of a CIA agent in the GRU, Lieutenant Colonel Peter Semyonovich Popov, stressed Soviet security measures. There were several problems with Nosenko's story and bona fides that made him and his explanations suspect. Indeed, the extent of doubt about Nosenko led to his being incarcerated by the CIA for a period of three years until freed by Director Richard Helms.[9]

From the very beginning, Nosenko's story was confirmed by an FBI source codenamed FEDORA. FEDORA was a Soviet intelligence agent working under diplomatic cover at the United Nations; he had contacted FBI officials in March 1962 with information about Soviet espionage operations, just weeks after Golitsin's defection. He claimed to be an officer of the KGB's First Chief Directorate who was disaffected with the Soviets and offered to supply the FBI with secret information on Soviet missile capability and nuclear development plans.

FEDORA also confirmed that Nosenko was indeed a Lieutenant Colonel in the KGB (a point of dispute), with access to extraordinarily valuable information, and had indeed received a recall telegram from Moscow ordering him back on February 4 (Nosenko's claimed reason for defecting). FEDORA also apparently told the FBI that Daniel Ellsberg had delivered a copy of the Pentagon Papers to the Soviet Embassy.[10]

FEDORA's veracity eventually came to be doubted by the FBI. Nosenko, for example, had admitted that he was not a Lieutenant Colonel but a Captain. Nor did Daniel Ellsberg deliver a copy of the Pentagon Papers to the Soviet Embassy or any Soviet agent. The acid test in the view of the FBI was what FEDORA, now identified as Soviet U.N. diplomat Victor Lessiovski, would do when his retirement time came in 1981. Lessiovski's return to the Soviet Union seemed to confirm that he had been under Soviet control all along.[11]

As noted earlier, the Operational Approval Branch of the CIA Counterintelligence Staff "casts a vote" with regard to the recruitment of new agents. In addition to employing its data to determine if a potential recruit is actually an attempted plant, the Branch also attempts to employ its past experience to produce a judgment concerning the potential agent's likely reliability, integrity, and capability.

The third counterintelligence function is a research and collection one. It is fundamental to the performance of the counterintelligence mission that there exists a store of knowledge concerning the personalities, past operations, structure, and activities of hostile intelligence services. Only with such knowledge can one effectively conduct penetration and disruption and neutralization activities. More than any other aspect of intelligence work, counterintelligence is an area that requires significant knowledge. Thus, as one analyst has recently written:

> The recent flurry in the press about Anthony Blunt, fourth and fifth men, Kim Philby etc. illustrates a counterintelligence case which began in the mid-1930s and is still front page news, and still an active counterintelligence case behind the scenes almost fifty years later. The fictionalized middle-aged ladies with instant recall of the personal idiosyncracies of some hostile official are, in fact, essential in real life.[12]

The workings of foreign intelligence services is a subject of numerous studies. The CIA's Counterintelligence Staff prepares reports ranging from 50 to 100 pages on the intelligence communities of Cuba, the Soviet Union, China, Czechoslovakia, and other nations, including all Communist communities as well as friendly services, such as those of Israel. Each report bearing the title *Foreign Intelligence and Security Services; (Country Name)* details the origins of the intelligence services, their structure, function and mode of operation, and the arrangements for control by higher authority.

Thus, the forty-seven-page study *Foreign Intelligence and Security Services: Israel*, published in March 1979, focused in its first section on the background and development of services, objectives and structure, the relationship between the government and the services, and professional standards. The second, third, and fourth sections each focused on one of the three major Israeli intelligence and security units—the Mossad, Shin Bet, and Military Intelligence. In each case, the report examined the function, organization, administrative practice (including training), and methods of operation of the services. Additionally, liaison with other Israeli and foreign services was considered. The final four sections examined the Foreign Ministry's Research and Political Planning Center, the National Police, key officials, and comments on principal sources.[13] The study's Contents is shown as Table 11-1.

Likewise, the Air Force Office of Special Investigations (AFOSI) prepares studies on the Soviet Intelligence Services, Bulgarian Intelligence Services, and so on, usually based on the relevant CIA reports. In addition to focusing on the intelligence communities of a particular country, other AFOSI reports focus on the hostile intelligence establishment in third countries. Thus, "Hostile Intelligence Establishment in Thailand" would focus on the local organization and operations of all hostile intelligence services in Thailand—Soviet, Chinese, East European.[14] The report would examine the embassy intelligence structures, commercial covers, particular agents, methods of operations, and the means of communication.

The ultimate objective of any of the above activities is the disruption and neutralization of hostile counterintelligence activity. Disruption and neutralization can take many forms: successfully foiling a covert action operation, discovering a fake defector, detecting and disrupting the financial arrangements for an espionage operation, causing a rift between allied intelligence services, having a false defector feed information to the hostile service that will incriminate key personnel.

Whether the United States is immediately concerned with penetration, disruption, or simply counterintelligence collection, significant amount of U.S. counterintelligence activity involves the surveillance of hostile intelligence personnel in third countries—the KGB in France, England, or Argentina; the Cuban DGI in Venezuela, Mexico, and Spain; the Libyan intelligence service in Italy and France; the Syrian intelligence service in Saudi Arabia.

Collected information goes to Counterintelligence Staff analysts for inclusion in their data base, on which the Foreign Intelligence and Security Services (FISS) reports are based. In third countries, the counterintelligence effort will be directed at penetration of the hostile intelligence services as well as the disruption of any of their activities considered inimical to U.S. interests. This might involve preventing successful active measures operations—whether a coup, forgery, or political funding is involved—or preventing the recruiting of an agent of influence or agent in the nation's Defense Ministry. Such disruption might involve direct action by the CIA or simply informing the appropriate security authorities so they can take action.

Table 11-1. Table of Contents for Foreign Intelligence and Security Services: Israel.

SECRET
NOFORN/NOCONTRACT/ORCON

TABLE OF CONTENTS

		Page
A.	General	1
	1. Background and development of services	1
	2. Objectives and structure	3
	3. Political aspects	5
	a. Relationship between the government and the services	5
	b. Relationship between the services and the populace	6
	4. Professional standards	6
	a. Integrity	6
	b. Efficiency	7
	c. Security	7
	d. Morale and disciplinary methods	9
B.	Mossad—Secret Intelligence Service	9
	1. Functions	9
	2. Organization	10
	3. Administrative practices	13
	a. Training	14
	b. Funds and salaries	14
	4. Methods of operation	15
	a. Relationship with other services	17
	b. Liaison with foreign services	18
C.	Shin Beth—Counterespionage and Internal Security Service	19
	1. Functions	19
	2. Organization	19
	3. Administration practices	22
	4. Methods of operation	23
D.	Military Intelligence	24
	1. Functions	24
	2. Organization	24
	a. Air Force Intelligence	30
	b. Naval Intelligence	30
	3. Administrative practices	33
	4. Methods of operation	34
	5. Relations with other services	35
E.	Research and Political Planning Center	36
F.	The National Police	36
G.	Key officials	39
H.	Comments on principal sources	40
	1. Source materials	40
	2. Supplementary overt publications	40

FIGURES

Fig. 1	Soviet Agent Israel Beer (*photo*)	8
Fig. 2	Organization of Israeli Intelligence and Security Services, 1977 (*chart*)	9
Fig. 3	Organization of Mossad, 1977 (*chart*)	11

Table 11–1. continued

TABLE OF CONTENTS *(continued)*

FIGURES *(continued)*

		Page
Fig. 4	Eliahu Ben Shaul Coben's transmitter on display in Damascus, 1965 (*photo*)	12
Fig. 5	Johann Wolfgang Lotz illustrates the use of a transmitter during his trial in Cairo, July–August 1965 (*photo*)	13
Fig. 6	Organization of Shin Beth, 1977 (*chart*)	20
Fig. 7	Organization of Military Intelligence, 1977 (*chart*)	25
Fig. 8	Organization of Naval Intelligence, 1974 (*chart*)	31
Fig. 9	Organization of Israeli National Police, 1977 (*chart*)	37
Fig. 10	Israeli National Police headquarters, Jerusalem, November 1972 (*photo*)	38
Fig. 11	Israeli Border Guard post under construction at Kefar Rosenweld Zarit, June 1970 (*photo*)	39

COVERT ACTION

The functions of the CIA as defined in the National Security Act of 1947 did not explicitly include what has come to be known as covert action. However, as noted earlier, the fifth function of the CIA was to "perform other such functions and duties related to intelligence affecting the national security as the National Security Council may from time to time direct," a phrase that has subsequently been interpreted as authorizing covert action operations.

Whatever the validity of the above provision as legislative authorization for covert action operations, the CIA received presidential authorization to engage in psychological and covert operations in late 1947 in response to situations in Western Europe, most particularly in Italy. Countries such as Italy, France, and Greece were suffering from the devastation of World War II and had large Communist parties that had effectively opposed the Fascist regimes of Vichy and Mussolini. It appeared to the United States that a combination of economic deprivation and Communist political efforts could produce a general Communist victory, peaceful or otherwise, in those European countries. In this atmosphere it was decided to seek to support the non-Communist left as a buffer or block to Communist victory.

The vehicle for such activity was to be a unit of the CIA authorized by National Security Council Directive 10: the Office of Special Projects, soon retitled the Office of Policy Coordination (OPC) and placed under joint CIA-State Department control.[15] Subsequently, the OPC was merged with the CIA's Office of Special Operations to become the Directorate of Plans (now Operations).

Eventually, the scope of U.S. covert action moved beyond the geographical area of Europe and beyond the functional area of political support operations. U.S. covert actions have been directed at all major areas of the world—Eastern Europe and Russia, Africa, the Middle East, Asia, and Latin America. These covert actions have involved the entire range of possible covert actions: (1) political advice and counsel; (2) subsidies to an individual; (3) financial support and technical assistance to political parties; (4) support to private organizations, including labor unions and business firms; (5) covert propaganda, (6) private training of individuals and exchange of persons; (7) economic operations; (8) paramilitary or political action operations designed to overthrow or support a regime; and (9) assassinations.[16]

Many of these operations, such as paramilitary or political action operations, have been high-visibility operations designed to achieve a specific objective: for example, the overthrow of a regime or defeat of an insurgent force. Many behind-the-scenes political support and propaganda activities were also designed to achieve a specific objective: the defeat or victory of a political candidate or party. Such low-visibility operations were conducted for an extensive period of time in Italy. Other low-visibility operations involving propaganda and support to individuals or organizations were less directed to attainment of a specific objective than to the long-term enhancement of U.S. objectives and the provision of a counter to similar Soviet activities. A high-visibility operation might also be conducted without clear expectation of its ultimate results; thus, U.S. aid to guerrillas opposing Soviet troops in Afghanistan is given with the intention of generally degrading the Soviet world political, economic, and military position without the specific expectation of an eventual Soviet defeat.

The initial U.S. covert actions taken in Europe were low-visibility operations with a specific goal: prevention of a Communist victory in Italy. On December 20, 1947 a special procedures group was set up to organize propaganda in Italy, and it continued to initiate projects until its functions were taken over by the OPC. Ten million dollars was taken in secrecy from the economic stabilization fund and used to pay for local election campaigns, anti-Communist propoganda, and bribes. The covert operations was coupled with lobbying by Americans of Italian descent and dire threats by Truman about reductions in aid if the Communists won. In the 1948 election the Christian Democrats gained an overall majority of forty seats.

The funding operation in Italy was repeated in later years. In 1958 the U.S. Ambassador to Italy, Claire Boothe Luce, lobbied for covert funding, arguing such actions were needed to prevent a Communist electoral victory. As a result, William Colby was transferred from Stockholm to Rome to distribute twenty-five million dollars among the Christian Democrats, centrist parties, and other organizations including the Roman Catholic Church. Such support continued until 1967, when the funding program ended. Attempts by U.S. Ambassador Graham Martin in 1970 to have the funding restored were unsuccessful.

In France CIA covert action had two objectives: the reduction of Communist party influence, especially in the unions, and the influencing of French opinion behind the European Defense Community. The CIA assisted in the moderate Force Ouvriere's splitting away from the Communist-dominated CGT labor union. Aid was also given to the Catholic CFTC labor union and several other non-Communist groups.[17]

With respect to Eastern Europe and the Soviet Union, the CIA-supported resistance groups sabotaged and assisted in developing escape and evasion networks. The earliest operation involved the establishment of guerrilla networks in countries surrounding the Soviet Union in case of Soviet invasion. Additionally, the OPC supported Polish resistance groups operating south of Warsaw while pumping money and arms into Lithuania and the Ukraine to assist resistance groups. These operations ended by the mid-1950s, the one in the Ukraine being demolished by 1953.[18]

The CIA has been involved in numerous covert actions in Latin America, frequently of the high-visibility variety and with a very specific objective: a change of government or the death of a leader. The earliest major operation took place with respect to Guatemala in 1954. The United States created, trained, funded, and directed a paramilitary force that succeeded in overthrowing the government of Jacobo Arbenz. The regime was considered to be Communist dominated and had alienated the United Fruit Company with its social welfare legislation, including minimum wage rates, strict tax laws, and land redistribution.[19]

Probably the best known of the CIA covert actions are the ones directed at Cuba. These operations included attempted assassinations of Fidel Castro, the Bay of Pigs invasion, sabotage/economic warfare, and a variety of propaganda activities. The first CIA official to suggest the assasination of Fidel Castro was Colonel J. C. King, Chief of the Western Hemisphere Division of the Directorate of Plans.[20]

One of the first assassination attempts involved Robert Maheu, an official of Hughes's Summa Corporation. Maheu recruited Johnny Rosselli to kill Castro, the "hit" being timed to coincide with the Bay of Pigs invasion of April 17, 1961. The plot, along with the invasion, never came to fruition. A second intrigue, the "CIA Miami Plot," centered on a former Cuban Treasury Ministry employee, Louis Toroella. Toroella had been brought to Florida for training and by the time of the Bay of Pigs had been infiltrated back to Santiago in an underground network condenamed AM/BLOOD. On September 24 the Cuban government announced that it had discovered the AM/BLOOD plot.[21]

The CIA continued, however, to try to assassinate Castro despite a finding by the CIA's Board of National Estimates in a study entitled "If Castro Were to Die" that "his loss now, by assassination or by natural causes, would have an unsettling effect, but would accomplish nothing unless action were taken to capitalize on it."[22] On August 24, 1962 it was planned to assassinate Castro on his way to dinner with Russian, Czech, Polish, and Chinese advisers. The plan was approved by the Miami station (JM/WAVE) but aborted due to boat failure.[23]

In some instances, the assassination plots took on exotic overtones. One proposal involved rigging an exotic-looking seashell with an explosive device and leaving it on Varadino Beach so that it could be detonated remotely when Castro swam by, but the Technical Services Division rejected the idea as impractical. Second, a skindiver's suit was dusted inside with a fungus that would produce a chronic skin disease and the breathing apparatus was contaminated with turbercle baccilus. The suit was to be presented to Castro as a gift.[24]

In September 1963 Major Roland Cubela, a Castro official, offered to kill Castro for the CIA. Designated AM/LASH, Cubela was meeting CIA officials in Paris concerning his proposal at the very time that John Kennedy was assinated.[25]

In addition to attempts to assassinate Castro, a general campaign was directed against the Castro regime. After the Bay of Pigs, President Kennedy revised the Cuban project, issuing several National Security Action Memorandums (NSAMs). NSAM 55 instructed the Joint Chiefs of Staff to "know the military and paramilitary forces and resources available" and to take stock of their readiness, adequacy, and room for improvement. NSAM 57 directed that any future operations of a size requiring logistical support from the military should come under the command of the Pentagon.[26]

Operations against Cuba were conceived from the ideas of Colonel Edwin Lansdale, who suggested trying to crack the Castro regime from within. Lansdale suggested developing leadership elements among the exiles as "a very necessary political base" while putting together the "means to infiltrate Cuba successfully" and organizing "cells and activities inside Cuba." Landsdale's goal was to have "the people themselves overthrow the Castro regime rather than the U.S."[27]

On November 30, 1961, a memorandum instructed that the program "use our available assets . . . to help Cuba overthrow the Communist regime. It was to be called . . . Operation Mongoose."[28] Operation Mongoose's first planned mission to demolish a railroad yard and bridge on Cuba's north coast was to look like an "inside job." The mission, however, was aborted when the boat carrying the saboteurs was spotted.[29] As part of the economic warfare against Cuba, CIA agents in Europe pressured European shippers to turn down Cuban consignments. According to Hinckle and Turner, "In Frankfurt, Germany a ball bearing manufacturer was persuaded to send off-center bearings to Cuba; in England Leyland buses on order by Cuba were sabotaged on the docks."[30]

In January 1963 Operation Mongoose was terminated. Subsequent operations involved an attack by CIA-financed commandos on an 8,000-gallon oil tank at the Cuban port of Casilda, the tank being set on fire, and a partially successful attack on the Matahambre copper mine.[31]

On June 19, 1963, Kennedy authorized an escalated program of sabotage. Targets included petroleum facilities, railroad and highway transportation, and electric power communications facilities in Cuba. The Movement for the Recovery of the Revolution (MRR) was revived and soon received $250,000 a month to launch a campaign known as Second Naval Guerrilla. The purpose of the campain was to attack Cuban shipping and mount commando raids on shore installations. The CIA would supply the funding, logistical support, intelligence data, and guidance. The MRR would function independently but submit each operation to the CIA for approval.[32] On October 24, 1963 thirteen sabotage/ economic warfare operators were authorized, including attacks on an electric plant and a sugar mill, to be carried out by the end of January 1964.

During 1969 and 1970 the CIA employed futuristic weather modification technology as well as covert agents to ravage Cuba's sugar crop and undermine the economy. While planes from the China Lake Naval Weapons Center in California overflew the island, seeding rain clouds with crystals that precipitated torrential rains over nonagricultural areas and left the cane fields arid, a U.S. intelligence officer passed a vial of African swine fever virus to a terrorist group. The vial was taken by fishing trawler to Navassa Island, which had been used in the past by the CIA as an advance base, and was smuggled into Cuba. According to Hinckle and Turner, six weeks later Cuba suffered the first outbreak of the swine fever in the Western Hemisphere; pig herds were decimated, causing a serious shortage of pork, the nation's dietary staple."[33] The United Nations Food and Agricultural Organization called it the "most alarming event" of the year and futilely tried to track down "how the disease had been transmitted."[34]

In addition to the high-visibility operations with both specific and nonspecific objectives, low-visibility operations were also waged by the CIA against Cuba. Forgeries of various kinds were employed. The Cuban Consul in Buenos Aires, career diplomat Vitalio de la Torre, resigned unexpectedly after having held his post through the Prio and Batista regimes. He took eighty-two documents from the Cuban Embassy safe and turned them over to the Cuban Revolutionary Council (CRC) in Miami. The documents detailed a master plan, allegedly devised in Cuba, for the overthrow of the Frondizi government by means of infiltration of business and politics and the training of guerrillas.[35]

The CRC held onto the documents so as to use them to maximum advantage during Frondizi's state visit to the United States. The week before the Argentine Chief of State left, however, La Nacion of Buenos Aires ran a long article accompanied by photocopies of the documents resulting in a clamorous protest against Cuba. The Cubans claimed that the documents had been forged by Cuban exiles working in collusion with the CIA—which was, in fact, the case. The forgery was the beginning of a campaign aimed at documenting that Castro was exporting the revolution by subverting Organization of American States (OAS) nations, goal being to get Cuba dismissed from the OAS.[36]

Prior to the Reagan administration, the most recent dramatic instance of CIA covert action in Latin America occurred in Chile. The 1973 coup against Salvador Allende ended a long series of CIA covert action operations that sought to prevent Allende from coming to power or remove him once he did. The CIA worked clandestinely in 1958 and 1964 to block Allende's election to the presidency. In 1964 the CIA spent three million dollars in support of Chile's social democratic Christian Democratic party.[37] The Christian Democratic party's candidate, Eduardo Frei, was victorious with 56 percent of the total vote.

In the next presidential election, Allende was again a candidate, competing with a Christian Democrat and a right-wing candidate, and the CIA was again attempting to prevent his election. In this case, despite a variety of media and propaganda operations as well as continued support of the Christian Democratic candidate, Allende emerged as the plurality winner in the election with 36.3 percent of the total. Since Allende failed to obtain a majority, the final choice was to be determined by a joint vote of the 50 Senators and 100 members of the Chamber of Deputies. Traditionally, Congress confirmed the plurality winner as president.

In the wake of Allende's victory, the U.S. government explored a variety of options to block his accession to power. On September 15, 1970 President Nixon informed CIA Director Richard Helms that an Allende regime in Chile was unacceptable to the United States and instructed the CIA to play a direct role in organizing a military coup in Chile to prevent his accession to the presidency. The subsequent campaign proceeded on two tracks. Under Track I, (which was approved by the interagency 40 Committee responsible for supervising operations), the CIA employed a variety of covert political, economic, and propaganda tactics to manipulate the political scene. This track included the allocation of $25,000 to bribe members of the Chilean Congress—money that was apparently never spent.[38] Other CIA funds were employed in a strident propaganda campaign. In addition, efforts were made to create financial and political panic sufficient to produce a military coup. Helms's instructions from Nixon had been to "make the economy scream," and multinationals were approached to take such actions as cutting off credit to Chile, stopping the shipment of spare parts, and causing runs on financial institutions.[39]

Track II involved direct efforts to produce a military coup; neither the State Department nor the 40 Committee was informed about these activities. Helms was told that at least ten million dollars would be available to do the job.[40] The CIA proceeded to make twenty-one contacts in two weeks with key Chilean military personnel to assure them that the United States would support a coup d'état.[41] The main obstacle to such a coup was Chief of Staff General Rene Schneider, a strong supporter of the Chilean military's tradition of non-involvement in political affairs. Fearing the weight Schneider's dissent would carry, the CIA passed three submachine guns and ammunition to Chilean officers planning to abduct the General. In the third kidnap attempt, October 22, 1970, General

Schneider was shot and subsequently died. The Senate Committee later found that the guns used in the abortive kidnapping were probably not those supplied by the CIA.[42]

Allende was confirmed as President on October 24, 1970. Track II however, continued. The CIA was told to "stay alert and to do what we could to contribute to the objectives and purposes of Track II."[43] In the aftermath of Allende's inauguration, the CIA operated in several key areas. It spent an additional 1.5 million dollars in support of the opposition newspaper *El Mercurio*.[44] Financial support was given to labor unions and trade associations with the intention of encouraging economic disorder which would in turn cause political disorder. It has been suggested that the economically crippling truckers' strikes of 1972 and 1973 were CIA-supported.[45]

Probably the most successful U.S. covert action operation, in the short term, was Operation AJAX. AJAX was the U.S.-British response to the 1951 nationalization of the Anglo-Iranian Oil Company by Prime Minister Mossadegh and the subsequent failure of the Shah's military to remove Mossadegh, resulting in the Shah's flight in exile. AJAX—the plan for toppling Mossadegh—was first proposed to the British government by the Anglo-Iranian Oil Company nine months after the nationalization.[46]

The Secret Intelligence Service (SIS) then approached the CIA with the plan in November 1952. The plan ultimately involved the organization of pro-Shah gangs with clubs, knives, and occasionally a rifle or pistol.[47] CIA representative Kermit Roosevelt was approached by the Anglo-Iranian Oil Company and met the SIS spokesman for AJAX, the Deputy Director of SIS, General John Sinclair.[48] It was explained to Roosevelt that AJAX involved the overthrow of Mossadegh and that the British desired to begin the operation immediately.[49]

SIS officials traveled to Washington in December 1952 and February 1953.[50] The first meeting involved purely operational discussions; the February 1953 delegation attended a series of formal planning meetings at which CIA Director Allen Dulles was also present.[51] At these meetings the British "described the high capability of their principal agents, repeated their assessment of the Army—and of the loyalty of the people at large."[52] Dulles gave his support to AJAX, and plans were developed to attain the AJAX objective with the British government and SIS as the "driving force."[53]

While the SIS was the driving force, Kermit Roosevelt was selected as overall Commander of the operation, at British suggestion.[54] In conducting the operation, Roosevelt relied on both U.S. and British agents turned over to Roosevelt by the SIS to implement the operation.[55] Indeed, the majority of agents was probably British. Thus, in a letter to Leonard Mosely, Kim Philby remarked, "What is not so generally known is that the British were also heavily involved and felt some resentment when the Americans (a) blew the affair, and (b) grabbed all the credit."[56]

Two prominent cases of covert action in Africa are those of Zaire and Angola. Covert action in Zaire stemmed from the June 30, 1960, independence of the Belgian Congo under a democratic coalition government headed by "militant nationalist" Patrice Lumumba.[57] Shortly after the independence, the Congolese Army mutinied; Belgian troops reoccupied part of the country, helping to organize the secession of Katanga province. The Prime Minister, Lumumba, and the Chief of State, Joseph Kasavubu, called in U.N. forces to help reorganize the army and remove the Belgians. The United Nations, with U.S. approval, delayed, and secessionist and political pressures against the Lumumba government began to mount.[58]

U.S. policymakers viewed Lumumba's threats to expel the U.N. force except for African left-nationalist contingents and to invade Katanga with Afro–Asian and Soviet military assistance with alarm. On August 18 the Station Chief for the Congo cabled CIA headquarters that:

> Embassy and Station believe Congo experiencing classic Communist take government . . . whether or not Lumumba is actually Commie or just playing Commie games to assist his solidifying power, anti-west forces rapidly increasing power Congo there may be little time left in which to take action to avoid another Cuba.[59]

In light of these reports, President Eisenhower approved an agenda of covert action measures, possibly including assassination.[60] The CIA station began "covert operations through certain labor groups" and "the planned attempt to arrange a vote of no confidence in Lumumba" in the Congolese Senate.[61] On August 25 the Special Group decided that "planning for the Congo would not necessarily rule out consideration of any particular kind of activity which might contribute to getting rid of Lumumba," and a series of assassination plots were encouraged, developed, and put into effect.[62]

More recently, the CIA has been heavily involved in the Angolan civil war. In January 1975 Portugal set up a transitional tripartite coalition in Angola. The parties were the National Front for the Liberation (FNLA) (backed by the People's Republic of China—PRC—and Zaire), the Soviet-backed Popular Movement for the Liberation of Angola (MPLA), and Jonas Savimbi's National Union for the Total Independence of Angola (UNITA). In late January a CIA proposal to bolster the FNLA with $300,000 in political action funds was approved by the 40 Committee and President Ford.[63]

On July 17 the 40 Committee approved a $14 million, two-stage program of arms and other aid to Roberto and Savimbi with an additional $10.7 million being approved in early September.[64] Weismann suggests the covert action program had a threefold objective: to avoid a precedent of "Soviet expansion," to work with the "moderate" anti-Communist leaders of Zaire and Zambia, and to prevent Soviet- and MPLA-assisted black extremists from making gains in Namibia, Rhodesia, and the rest of southern Africa.[65]

The breakdown of covert action expenditures by the middle of the fall of 1975 (in millions) was: [66]

Political action support	5.80
Other propaganda	0.50
Travel miscellaneous	0.90
Arms and equipment	10.00
Communication gear	0.35
Shipping of arms and equipment	5.40
	22.95

As noted, among the lower visibility operations are the propaganda and media operations activities. At its peak the CIA's Propaganda Assets Inventory contained over 800 news and public information organizations and individuals.[67] Among these propaganda assets were the well-known "Radio Free Europe" and "Radio Liberty" as well as the lesser-known "Radio Free Asia," which began broadcasting to mainland China in 1951 from Manila. It went off the air in 1955. "Free Cuba Radio" did not have its own station but purchased airtime from Florida and Louisiana stations—WMIE and WGBS in Miami, SKSF in Key West, and WWL in New Orleans.[68]

CIA propaganda operations also include the subsidization of anti-Castro publications in the United States: *Advance, El Mundo, El Prensa, Libre, Bohemia,* and *El Diario de las Americas.* Also, AIP, a radio news agency in Miami, produced programs that were sent free to more than 100 small stations in Central and Latin America.[69]

The CIA also subsidized numerous social democratic magazines throughout Europe and elsewhere, the purpose of which was simply the projection of the center-left alternative. Thus, CIA conduits provided support to *Prevves* (France), *Forum* (Austria), *Der Monat* (West Germany), *El Mundo Nuevo* (Latin America), *Quiet and Thought* (India), *Argumenten* (Stockholm).[70]

In Saigon the CIA set up and financed the Vietnam Council on Foreign Relations, modeled after the U.S. version. It published a slick, expensively produced magazine that was distributed during the Vietnam War to the offices of all senators and representatives in Washington.[71]

The CIA has also been active in regards to book publishing. Nearly a dozen U.S. publishing houses have printed at least twenty of the more than 200 English-language books financed or produced by the CIA since the early 1950s. In many cases, the publisher was aware of the Agency's involvement. The CIA's relationship with Frederick Praeger, the book publisher, has been reported in the past. Praeger was only one of a number of publishing concerns, including some of the most prominent in the industry, that printed or distributed more than 1,000 volumes produced or subsidized in some way by the CIA over the last three decades.[72] Some publishing houses were simply CIA "proprietaries."

These included Allied Pacific Printing of Bombay and the Asia Research Centre in Hong Kong.[73]

The general types of covert action, as well as the specifics, undertaken by an administration is a function of several factors, including the international situation and the administration's (President's) view of the world. Thus, covert action beyond propaganda and media operations was generally deemphasized during the Carter administration. Such operations as did take place involved Afghanistan, Iran, and Libya.

The Reagan administration has taken a much more aggressive approach to the use of covert action. In contrast with the Carter years, where the House Intelligence Committee was informed of two or three major covert operations—that is, operations costing between $5 and $7 million or designed to undermine a foreign government—each year, the total under the Reagan administration has been seven to eight. Covert action is considered simply another option, perhaps one of the most desirable options, in the conduct of foreign affairs.

The most well known of these operations is the one directed at the Sandinista regime in Nicaragua. The operations involved the expenditure of approximately $180 million to supply some 10,000 opposition troops to conduct air strikes and commando raids against installations within Nicaragua and coordinating propaganda activities aimed at destabilizing the Sandinista regime.[74] A less known Central American operation involves covert support for El Salvadoran political parties via a propaganda and disinformation campaign aimed at "convincing the civilian population that the guerrillas, not the Army, are the real bad guys."[75]

The Reagan administration has continued Carter administration support to Afghan rebel groups, supplying more than $100 million in arms and ammunition through contacts in Pakistan and conduits in the Middle East. Nearby, the CIA is providing support to Iranian exiles in Turkey and France who seek to overthrow Ayatollah Khomeini.[76]

The CIA provides intelligence as well as overt aid training to the forces fighting Libyan forces in Chad. In addition, training, arms, and financial assistance are given to military forces in Ethiopia, Angola, and the Sudan. Two other planned operations were canceled due to congressional opposition—a plan to provide arms for anti-Libyan forces in Mauritius and for Kaddafi opponents inside Libya itself.[77]

In Thailand the CIA has been aiding Thai military forces with communications training and intelligence gathering for raids against heroin production and processing centers in Thailand and Burma. Additionally, the CIA is working with the PRC to supply arms to the forces of the former Cambodian ruler Pol Pot, who is conducting hit-and-run attacks against the present Hanoi-supported regime.[78]

NOTES TO CHAPTER 11

1. Jimmy Carter, "Executive Order 12036, United States Intelligence Activities," *Federal Register* 43, no. 18 (January 1978): 3675.
2. For example, William Harris, "Counterintelligence Jurisdiction and the Double Cross System by National Technical Means," in Roy Godson, ed., *Intelligence Requirements for the 1980s: Counterintelligence* (New Brunswick, N.J.: Transaction, 1980), pp. 53–82.
3. John Masterman, *The Double Cross System* (New Haven: Yale University Press, 1972).
4. William Hood, *Mole* (New York: Norton, 1982); Oleg Penkovskiy, *The Penkovskiy Papers* (Long Island: Doubleday, 1965).
5. Heinz Hohne, *The General Was a Spy* (New York: Coward, McCann, Geohegan, 1971).
6. E. H. Cookridge, *George Blake: Double Agent* (New York: Ballantine, 1970); Bruce Page, David Leitch, and Philip Knightley, *The Philby Conspiracy* (New York: Signet, 1969).
7. Henry Hurt, *Shadrin: The Spy Who Never Came Back* (New York: McGraw-Hill, 1981).
8. Edward J. Epstein, *Legend: The Secret World of Lee Harvey Oswald* (New York: McGraw-Hill, 1978), p. 27.
9. Thomas Powers, *The Man Who Kept the Secrets: Richard Helms and the CIA* (New York: Knopf, 1979).
10. "Tale of a Double Agent," *Newsweek*, September 14, 1981, p. 25.
11. Ibid.
12. Kenneth E. de Graffeneid, "Building for a New Counterintelligence Capability: Recruitment and Training," in Godson, *Intelligence Requirements for the 1980s*, pp. 261–71.
13. CIA, "Foreign Intelligence and Security Services: Israel," *Counter Spy* 6, no. 3 (May–June 1982): 34–57.
14. Fleet Marine Force Pacific Order 3850.1B, "Counterintelligence Contingency Materials," March 14, 1983.
15. Memorandum for the National Security Council from Sidney W. Souers, Subject: Establishment of a Special Services Unit in CIA, June 2, 1948; "A Report to National Security Council by the Executive Secretary on Office of Special Projects," *Declassified Documents Reference System* 1978–189C.
16. Marchetti and Marks (1983), p. 334.
17. Trevor Barnes, "The Secret Cold War: The CIA and American Foreign Policy in Europe, 1946–1956, Part I," *Historical Journal* 24, no. 2 (1981): 399–415.
18. Ibid.; Trevor Barnes, "The Secret Cold War: The CIA and American Foreign Policy in Europe, 1946–1956, Part II," *Historical Journal* 25, no. 3 (1982): 649–70.

19. See Stephen Kinzer and Stephen Schlesinger, *Bitter Fruit* (Boston: Hough-
     ton Mifflin, 1982); Richard Immerman, *CIA in Guatemala: The Foreign
     Policy of Intervention* (New York: Columbia University Press, 1982).

20. Warren Hinckle and William Turner, *The Fish is Red: The Story of the
     Secret War Against Castro* (New York: Harper & Row, 1981), p. 106.

21. Ibid., p. 108.

22. Ibid.

23. Ibid., p. 191.

24. Ibid., p. 219.

25. Ibid., p. 101.

26. Ibid., p. 111.

27. Ibid.

28. Ibid., p. 121.

29. Ibid., p. 122.

30. Ibid., p. 143.

31. Ibid., pp. 144, 148.

32. Ibid., p. 293.

33. Ibid., p. 293.

34. Ibid., p. 129.

35. Ibid.

36. Ibid.

37. U.S. Congress, Senate Select Committee to Study Governmental Opera-
     tions with Respect to Intelligence Activities, *Covert Action* (Washington,
     D.C.: U.S. Government Printing Office, 1976), pp. 1, 15.

38. Ibid., pp. 23, 33.

39. Ibid., pp. 25–26.

40. Ibid.

41. U.S. Congress, Senate Select Committee, *Covert Action*, p. 26.

42. U.S. Congress, Senate Select Committee to Study Governmental Opera-
     tions with Respect to Intelligence Activities, *Alleged Assassination Plots
     Involving Foreign Leaders* (Washington, D.C.: U.S. Government Printing
     Office, 1976), p. 226.

43. Ibid., p. 254.

44. U.S. Congress, Senate Select Committee, *Covert Action*, p. 29.

45. Ibid., pp. 30–31.

46. M. Richard Shaw, "British Intelligence and Iran," *Counter Spy* 6, no. 3
     (May–June 1982): 31-33.

47. Ibid.

48. Kermit Roosevelt, *Countercoup: The Struggle for Control of Iran* (New
     York: McGraw-Hill, 1979), p. 3.

49. Ibid., p. 107.

50. Ibid., p. 119; Shaw, "British Intelligence and Iran."

51. Ibid.

52. Roosevelt, *Countercoup*, p. 121.

53. Shaw, "British Intelligence and Iran."

54. Roosevelt, *Countercoup*, p. 120.

55. Ibid., p. 46.

56. Leonard Mosely, *Dulles: A Biography of Eleanor, Allen and John Foster and Their Family Network* (New York: Dial, 1978), p. 492.

57. Stephen R. Weissman, "CIA Covert Action in Zaire and Angola: Patterns and Consequences," *Political Science Quarterly* 94, no. 2 (1979): 263–86.

58. Ibid.

59. Ibid.

60. Ibid.

61. Ibid.

62. Ibid.

63. Ibid.

64. Ibid.

65. Ibid.

66. Ibid.

67. John Crewdson, "Worldwide Propaganda Network Built by the CIA," *New York Times*, December 26, 1977, pp. 1, 37.

68. Ibid.

69. Ibid.

70. John M. Crewdson, "The CIA's 3-Decade Effort to Mold the World's Views," *New York Times*, December 25, 1977, pp. 1, 12.

71. Ibid.

72. Ibid.

73. "America's Secret Warriors," *Newsweek*, October 10, 1983, pp. 38ff.

74. Ibid.

75. Ibid.

76. Ibid.

77. Ibid.

78. Ibid.

12 ANALYSIS AND ESTIMATES

The U.S. intelligence community produces a vast amount of finished intelligence of numerous varieties. National intelligence is the intelligence produced for the use of national decisionmakers and comes in several forms: current intelligence, estimates, analysis, and reports. Current intelligence focuses on a situation of immediate concern. Estimates are concerned with both summarizing a present state of affairs and projecting into the future. Other reports may be concerned solely with summarizing a particular state of affairs, whether it be a political, military, or economic situation.

Similar intelligence is produced by various agencies in support of national intelligence production or for the use of departmental officials—distinguishable both on substantive and on current/estimate/report dimensions. As should be clear from Chapters 2 through 6, there are numerous analytical units throughout the U.S. government.

This chapter examines the intelligence product of the intelligence community as a whole (i.e., national intelligence) as well as of a variety of significant analytical units. The analytical units examined include the Central Intelligence Agency, the Defense Intelligence Agency (DIA), the Bureau of Intelligence and Research (INR), the military service scientific and technical intelligence units, and those belonging to selected unified and specified commands.

NATIONAL INTELLIGENCE

National intelligence produced by the U.S. intelligence community comes in several forms. These include the *President's Daily Brief,* the *National Intelli-*

241

gence Digest, the *Weekly Watch Report*, the *National Intelligence Situation Report*, National Intelligence Estimates, Special National Intelligence Estimates, National Intelligence Analytical Memorandums, and Interagency Intelligence Memorandums.

The *President's Daily Brief* (PDB) is published on a daily basis. The PDB has a circulation limited to the President and a select number of his principal advisers (the Vice President, Secretaries of State and Defense, and the Assistant to the President for National Security Affairs in the Carter administration) and contains information from the more sensitive U.S. sources. The PDB is designed to be read in ten to fifteen minutes at the beginning of the day.[1] It provides whatever significant information has been acquired during the previous day and commentary as to its significance. According to Cord Meyer, a former CIA official, in the hands of the CIA Director, the PDB

> is a powerful tool for focusing the attention of the President on potential crisis areas and for alerting him to situations that may require rapid policy adjustment. Occasionally, when fresh intelligence sheds new light on a complex problem an annex is attached to the PDB to give the President more extensive background for the decisions he has to make.[2]

The second daily national current intelligence publication is the *National Intelligence Digest* (NID). The NID was the idea of former CIA Director William Colby who had repeatedly recommended during the mid-1960s that the CIA's daily intelligence report be issued in newspaper format to emphasize the more important items and to offer its readers the choice between a headline summary and reading in depth.[3] Colby's interest was sufficient to lead him to join, on every evening he could, the editorial conference as to what subjects would be carried in the next day's edition.[4] Since Colby's departure, what was the Daily has become the Digest and has assumed a more conventional format.

The NID is somewhat longer than the PDB and serves a somewhat larger audience – about two hundred top-level foreign policy officials in Washington plus a limited number of U.S. Ambassadors and CIA Station Chiefs.[5] For security reasons, it does not contain some of the more sensitive items contained in the PDB.[6]

Despite deletion of such items, the Digest may be classified TOP SECRET RUFF UMBRA, indicating the presence of intelligence derived from satellite photography as well as signals intelligence, as was the issue of November 12, 1975.[7] That issue contained the following front-page headlines: "Motion to Impeach President Gaining Support in Argentina;" "Disorders Seen in Aftermath of Whitlam Firing;" "Military Leader Warns Turkey on Violence;" "Morocco, Spain Discuss Sahara;" and "Israel is Exaggerating Gravity of Deteriorating Trade Situation." In the article on the Whitlam firing it was stated that

> Australia may be entering a period of unprecedented disorder in the wake of Governor-General Kerr's sacking of former Prime Minister Whitlam. Inflam-

matory remarks by Whitlam could turn scattered demonstrations and work stoppages supporting him into a nationwide general strike, despite calls for restraint by some trade union leaders.[8]

During the early years of the Reagan administration, Director of Central Intelligence (DCI) William Casey initiated publication of the *Weekly Watch Report* (WWR).[9] The WWR apparently is restricted to items concerning "front-burner" situations.

A fourth current intelligence product is the *National Intelligence Situation Report* (NISR). NISRs are issued only in the midst of a crisis. During a major crisis, NISRs are issued at frequent intervals and are prepared by a community task force, usually under the DCI or a National Intelligence Officer. This coordination is an attempt to provide crisis managers with a single "authoritative" report that summarizes all important developments during the reporting period, preventing the White House and other authorities from being inundated with redundant or conflicting reports from different agencies.[10]

The best-known national intelligence products are the National Intelligence Estimates (NIEs) and Special National Intelligence Estimates (SNIEs). As their name implies, these documents attempt to project into the future existing military, political, and economic trends and to estimate for policymakers the likely implications of these trends. As defined by the House Committee on Foreign Affairs, an NIE is "a thorough assessment of a situation in the foreign environment which is relevant to the formulation of foreign, economic, and national security policy, and which projects probable future courses of action and developments."[11]

NIEs cover a wide variety of topics, both geographic and functional. In 1961 there was a World Wide Series (00), Communist State Series (10), Western and Southern Europe Series (20), Middle East Series (30), Far East Series (40), Southeast Asia Series (50), North and West Africa Series (60), South and East African Series (70), Caribbean Area Series (80), and American Series (90).[12]

Thus, NIEs issued in the 1960–1962 period were NIE 100-2-60, *Sino-Indian Relations*, NIE 10-61, *Authority and Control in the Communist Movement*, NIE 24-61 *The Outlook for Italy*, NIE 36-61, *Nasser and the Future of Arab Nationalism*, NIE 41-61, *Prospects for Japan*, NIE 51-62, *The Prospects for Burma*, NIE 60-62, *Guinea and Mali*, NIE 76-60, *Probable Trends in the Horn of Africa*, NIE 85-62, *The Situation and Prospects in Cuba*, and NIE 99-61, *Trends in Canadian Foreign Policy*.

Some of the NIEs—for example, those concerning the Soviet Union and China—are issued on an annual or biannual basis; others—for example, *The Prospects for Burma*—are issued less frequently. The NIEs concerning the Soviet Union are, of course, the most significant ones and constitute the NIE 11 series.

In the 1960–1962 period at least fourteen NIEs were issued in the 11 series. Their titles are given in Table 12–1. Included were NIEs on the Soviet space program, air defense, offensive capabilities, foreign policy, and the economy. Among

Table 12-1. NIE-11 Series, 1960-1962.

NIE Number	Title
11-1-62	Soviet Space Programs
11-2-61	The Soviet Atomic Energy Program
11-3-61	Sino-Soviet Air Defense Capabilities through Mid-1966
11-4-60	Soviet Policy and Courses of Action
11-4-61	Main Trends in Soviet Capabilities and Policies 1961-66
11-5-61	Soviet Technical Capabilities in Guided Missiles and Space Vehicles
11-6-60	Strength of the Armed Forces of the U.S.S.R.
11-7-60	Soviet Capabilities and Intentions with Respect to the Clandestine Introduction of Weapons of Mass Destruction in the U.S.
11-8-61	Soviet Capabilities for Long Range Attack
11-8-62	Soviet Capabilities for Long Range Attack
11-9-62	Trends in the Soviet Foreign Policy
11-11-62	Trends in the Soviet Economy
11-12-62	Soviet Policy Toward Africa

Source: National Security Council Information Liaison, "National Intelligence Estimates," May 25, 1962, LBJ Library Vice Presidential Security Files, Boxes. Folder of NSC Records of Actions 1962.

the NIEs was one that probably was done on an infrequent basis: NIE 11-7-60, *Soviet Capabilities and Intentions with Respect to the Clandestine Introduction of Weapons of Mass Destruction Into the U.S.*[13]

Among the NIEs now declassified is NIE 11-4-57, *Main Trends in Soviet Capabilities and Policies 1957-1962*, superseding NIE 11-4-56. The Estimate, sixty-one pages and six chapters in length, consists of chapters on internal political developments, and trends in the Soviet economy, in Soviet science and technology, in Soviet military posture, in Soviet relations with other Communist states, and in Soviet foreign policy.[14]

Subsequently, the NIE 11 series has undergone some revision from its 1961 structure. As of the mid-1970s the 11 series consisted of twelve Estimates including ones on Soviet general purpose forces, military R&D, the economy, political-military operations outside the Soviet Union and the Warsaw Pact, Soviet space programs, and Soviet foreign policy. The two major Estimates were 11-3, *Soviet Strategic Defensive Forces*, and 11-8, *Soviet Strategic Offensive Forces and Capabilities*[15], which are now done as part of one volume, 11-3/8, on Soviet strategic capabilities. It reads as a systematic, blow-by-blow description of Soviet weapons military doctrine. Each chapter deals with a different category of Soviet weaponry. For instance, one chapter might deal with long-range missiles, another with bombers, and another with defensive radars and antiaircraft missiles. Along with the description of current Soviet forces, parts of the text will also summarize the intelligence community's projection for future Soviet force levels in a given year and the time at which the Soviets are expected to be able to deploy a weapon incorporating a certain type of technology.[16]

The importance and frequency of the NIEs have varied from administration to administration. In 1961 there were more than twenty-five issued. The yearly total rose to fifty in the late 1960s before falling to eleven or twelve a year during the final years of the Carter administration. The decline was largely due to CIA Director Stansfield Turner's view that "national estimates are [not] a very efficient way of preparing finished intelligence."[17]

Under the Reagan administration and CIA Director William Casey, the number of NIEs rose to thirty-eight in 1981 and sixty in 1982.[18] The 1981 NIEs included estimates on the balance of power in the Middle East, Soviet strategic offensive and defensive capabilities, the strategic implications of Soviet economic problems, Soviet dependence on Western technology and trade for its military buildup, the likely impact and effectiveness of allied trade sanctions against the U.S.S.R., the European peace movement, the Mexican financial crisis, the Iran-Iraq War, international terrorism, Soviet and Cuban involvement in Central America, prospects for free elections in El Salvador, involvement of external powers in the Salvadoran conflict, and the prospects for conflict in South Africa.[19]

In addition to the regularly scheduled NIEs, the President and members of the National Security Council may call for production of SNIEs when some unforeseen development requires production of an additional estimate. Thus, as indicated in Tables 12-2 and 12-3, at least six SNIEs were written during the 1961 Berlin crisis and seven or more during the period 1960-1962 concerning Southeast Asia.[20] During the Cuban missile crisis of 1962, at least two SNIEs were prepared: SNIE 85-3-62, *The Military Build-Up in Cuba*, and SNIE 11-19-62, *Major Consequences of Certain U.S. Courses of Action on Cuba*. SNIE

Table 12-2. SNIEs Concerning the 1961 Berlin Crisis.

Number and Date	Title
SNIE 2-61, June 13	Soviet and Other Reactions to Various Courses of Action Regarding Berlin
SNIE 2-2-61, July 11	Soviet and Other Reactions to Possible U.S. Courses of Action with Respect to Berlin
SNIE 2-3-61, July 18	Probable Soviet Reactions to a Western Embargo
SNIE 2-4-61, August 31	Reaction to Certain U.S. Measures in the Berlin Crisis
SNIE 2-5-61, September 14	Soviet Reactions to Certain U.S. Courses of Action
SNIE 2-6-61, October 19	Probable Soviet and Other Reactions to Certain U.S. Military Measures in the Berlin Crisis

Source: National Security Council Information, "National Intelligence Estimates," May 25, 1962, LBJ Library Vice Presidential Security Files, Box 5. Folder of NSC Records of Actions 1962.

Table 12-3.   SNIEs 1960–1962 on Southeast Asia.

Number and Date	Title
SNIE 10-61, February 21, 1962	Communist Objectives, Capabilities and Intentions in Southeast Asia
SNIE 13-3-61, November 30, 1961	Chinese Communist Capabilities and Intentions in the Far East
SNIE 10-2-61, June 27, 1961	Likelihood of Minor Communist Military Intervention in Mainland Southeast Asia
SNIE 58-62, January 11, 1962	Relative Military Capabilities of Opposing Forces in Laos
SNIE 58/1-62, January 31, 1962	Same Title as 58-62
SNIE 10-3-61, October 10, 1961	Probable Communist Reaction to Certain SEATO Undertakings in South Vietnam
SNIE 53 2-61, November 19, 1961	Bloc Support of the Communist Effort against the Government of Vietnam
SNIE 10-4-61, October 5, 1961	Probable Communist Reaction to Certain U.S. Actions in South Vietnam
SNIE 52-61, December 13, 1961	Thailand's Security Problems and Prospects

Source: National Security Council Information Liaison, "National Intelligence Estimates," May 25, 1962, LBJ Library Vice Presidential Security Files, Box 5. Folder NSC Records of Actions 1962.

11-19-62 thus covered the status of the Soviet buildup (with regard to MRBMs, aircraft, antiaircraft sites, cruise missile sites, and cruise missile patrol boats); the purpose of the buildup; and the likely effects and Soviet actions in response to U.S. acquiescence, warning, a naval blockade, or use of military force.[21]

A more recent SNIE was *Soviet Support for International Terrorism and Revolutionary Violence* of May 27, 1981, completed "after several versions were drafted alternatively by CIA, DIA and CIA again."[22]

A more recent form of national intelligence is the Interagency Intelligence Memorandum (IIM), coordinated like an NIE, among different agencies, but designed to provide basic information rather than estimates. Recent IIMs include NI-IIM 10025 of December 1981, "INF Support: Theater Nuclear Forces," and NI-IIM 10002 of March 1981, "SALT Support: European Theater Nuclear Forces."[23]

A fourth type of noncurrent national intelligence is the National Intelligence Analytical Memorandum (NIAM).[24] NIAMs, as their title indicates, include more detailed analyses of political, military, or economic situations than do IIMs.

CENTRAL INTELLIGENCE AGENCY

In addition to providing much of the analytical capability for the production of national intelligence products, the CIA also produces a wide variety of studies on political, economic, social, and military matters.

The major focus of the CIA analyses and reports is, of course, the Soviet Union. It is particularly with regard to the Soviet Union that CIA reports touch all aspects of a nation's activities. CIA reports on the Soviet Union show particular concern about both civilian and military decisionmaking. Thus, the CIA's Directorate of Intelligence has produced codeword level reports entitled *The Soviet Defense Council and Military Policy Making* (April 1972), *The Soviet Decision Making Process for the Selection of Weapons Systems* (June 1973), and *The Politburo and Soviet Decisionmaking* (April 1972).[25]

With regard to Soviet military activities, one area of CIA concern has been the amount of money spent on defense—a concern resulting in *A Dollar Cost Comparison of Soviet and US Defense Activities, 1966-1976* (January 1977), *Estimated Soviet Defense Spending in Rubles 1970-1975* (May 1976), and *Soviet and U.S. Investment in Intercontinental Attack Forces, 1960-1980 and Outlook for the Future* (August 1981).[26]

Other reports on Soviet military matters have focused on Soviet manpower issues (*Soviet Military Manpower Issues in the Eighties*, May 1980), political control of the armed forces (*Political Control of the Soviet Armed Forces*, July 1980), attack submarine threats (*The Soviet Attack Submarine Force and Western Lines of Communication*, April 1979), and topics that would be more suited to DIA or service intelligence analysts—for example, *Soviet Military Aircraft Maintenance* (October 1979), and *Soviet Naval Mine Counter-Countermeasures* (June 1980).[27]

Scientific intelligence reports on the Soviet Union have included *Soviet Research on Excimer Lasers, Soviet and East European Parapsychology Research* (April 1977), and *New Soviet Large-Scale Scientific Computer* (April 1979).[28] Both broad trends in the Soviet economy and the situation in particular industries are the subjects of Intelligence Directorate Studies, e.g., *The Soviet Economy in 1976-1977 and Outlook for 1978* (1978), *Soviet Long Range Energy Forecasts* (June 1978), and *The Soviet Tin Industry: Recent Developments and Prospects Through 1980* (1977).[29]

Soviet grain production, with its impact on Soviet internal and external developments, has been the subject of numerous reports. Included among them are *Biological and Environmental Factors Affecting Soviet Grain Quality* (1978), *USSR: The Long Term Outlook for Grain Imports*, and *USSR: The Impact of Recent Climate Change on Grain Production* (1976).[30] Likewise, Soviet demographics—shifts in population proportions among the multiple Soviet nationalities, especially declines in the proportion of Great Russians and White Russians—might have a major impact on Soviet military and economic policy. Thus, the Intelligence Directorate has produced reports such as *USSR: Some Implications of Demographic Trends for Economic Policies* (1977).[31]

The basic thrust of CIA research with regard to the Soviet Union is duplicated with respect to the People Republic of China (PRC). Its reports on the PRC include *Defense Modernization in China* (October 1980), *China's First Nuclear Powered Ballistic Missile Submarine* (April 1981), *China: Agricultural*

Performance (1975), *China: International Trade 1976-1977* (1978), and *China: Gross Value of Industrial Output 1965-1977* (1978).[32]

Although the Soviet Union and the PRC receive the majority of the CIA's analytical attention, the rest of the world is also covered with respect to political, economic, military, social, agricultural, and demographic trends and issues. Reports on Allied and Third World countries have included *Korea: The Economic Race Between the North and South, Kampuchea: A Demographic Catastrophe, The Refugee Resettlement Problem in Thailand*, and *Pakistan: The Ethnic Equation.*[33]

Other analyses focus not on individual nations but on regional or international issues or problems such as international energy levels, markets, or regional politics. Reports produced since 1977 in these areas include *Central America: Short Term Prospects for Insurgency, World Shipbuilding: Facing Up to Oversupply, World Steel Market: Continued Trouble Ahead*, and *The International Energy Situation: Outlook to 1985.*[34]

In addition, the CIA offices produce a variety of current intelligence items. These reports have included the *Scientific Intelligence Weekly Review, Middle East and South Asia Review, Military Weekly Review, Weapons Intelligence Summary*, and others.[35]

Articles in the *Scientific Intelligence Weekly Review* included "Haiti: Nationwide Spread of African Swine Fever Disastrous for Agricultural Economy" (June 15, 1979), and "Dominican Republic: First Occurrence of Sugar Cane Rot in Western Hemisphere" (December 11, 1978). Articles in the *Middle East and South Asia Review* have included "Iran: the Prospects for Responsible Government" (October 20, 1978) and "The Tudeh Party: the Lazarus of Iranian Politics" (October 20, 1978). An article in the February 2, 1979 *Military Weekly Review* was entitled "Iran: Navy Expansion Program Endangered."[36]

There has probably been a restructuring of this current intelligence product in accord with the 1981 reorganization of the Directorate of Intelligence. Whatever the restructuring with regard to the above current intelligence reports, the Directorate still produces the *CIA Weekly Review*, classified TOP SECRET UMBRA. Among the items in the November 7, 1975 issue was the SECRET NOFORN item entitled "Australia Impasse Continues," discussing the conflict between the government of Prime Minister Gough Whitlam and the Liberal party.[37]

DEFENSE INTELLIGENCE AGENCY

As with the CIA, the DIA produces a wide variety of intelligence products— current intelligence, estimates, general intelligence, scientific and technical intelligence. The DIA also coordinates the counterintelligence products of the military departments.

Paralleling the NIEs and SNIEs are the Defense Intelligence Estimates and Special Defense Intelligence Estimates. These estimates often cover similar topics to those covered by the NIEs and SNIEs; they, however, have more of a military slant. Being departmental estimates, they are produced without interdepartmental coordination.

Current intelligence products include the *Weekly Intelligence Summary* (WIS), which contains items on foreign defense personnel as well as military hardware. The July 4, 1975 WIS contains an item entitled "New Australian Defense Minister is Whitlam's Man," classified SECRET NOFORN, which called the Minister, William L. Morrison, "an articulate, if sometimes blustery, opposition spokesman on foreign affairs" and noted that he had routine access to sensitive U.S. and Australian intelligence, including information on U.S. military facilities." It also noted that "Morrison may have an unsettling impact on the top management of the Defense Department in view of his long-standing enmity with the Defense Permanent Secretary Sir Arthur Tange."[38]

A more recent issue, July 23, 1982, had articles entitled "New Philippine Defense Attache Team is Assigned" and "Tracked Multiple Rocket Launchers Noted in Beijing Military Region." The first article, classified SECRET/NOFORN, noted that the attachés "will undoubtedly report on, and possibly operate against, anti-Marcos Philippine activists in the U.S." The second reported that "eighteen tracked MRL's were sighted with the 359th Artillery Regiment of the 79th Infantry Division, 27th Army, at Xingtai, Hebei on 18 May." The total title to the article was itself classified SECRET/WNINTEL/NOFORN— an indication that the information was obtained either by a clandestine human source or overhead photography, almost certainly the latter. A third article, also with a classified title, concerned the testing of a possible Soviet chemical weapon launcher and included apparent satellite photography of the test area.[39]

Altogether, the July 23, 1982 issue contained twenty-one articles on five different regions of the world: the Soviet Union/Eastern Europe, Asia, Western Europe, Africa, and Latin America. The table of contents for the issue is shown as Table 12-4. Other WIS articles have included "Soviet Space and Missile Wrap-up" (December 15, 1978), "Chinese Navy Adopts New Training Practices," "Flexibility of Soviet Air Defense Forces Increased" (March 5, 1982), and "Chinese IRBM Training Activity" (January 18, 1980).[40]

A second current intelligence product is the daily *Defense Intelligence Commentaries*, a newsletter-like publication containing articles on several subjects. These articles are more analytical and more personal than those appearing in the WIS. Articles, in recent *Defense Intelligence Commentaries* have included: "Soviets Have SS-20 Reload and Refire Capability" (December 2, 1982), "Israeli Press Claims of Lebanese Army Atrocities May Be Effort to Direct Attention from Inquiry on Phalange" (December 2, 1982), "Interest in Commercial Ties with US Points to Iraq Desire for Improved Relations (November 9,

Table 12-4. Table of Contents for WIS 29-82.

SECRET   23 JULY 1982

CONTENTS

USSR-EASTERN EUROPE   *Page*

Soviet FOXBAT Is Upgraded (U)   1
First VICTOR III SSN Deployed to Indian Ocean (S)   1
USSR Builds Aircraft Takeoff Ramp (S/WNINTEL/NOFORN)   2
Soviets Upgrade GSFG VHF Jamming and Communications Capability (C)   3
Possible Soviet Chemical Weapon Launcher Is Tested (S/WNINTEL/NOFORN)   4

ASIA

Additional FITTER Aircraft Identified in Vietnam (S/NOFORN)   7
South Korean Army Implements Force Realignment (U)   9
New Philippine Defense Attache Team Is Assigned (U)   10
Tracked Multiple Rocket Launchers Noted in Beijing Military Region (C)   11
Pakistani Naval Training Program Is Implemented (C)   12
New Self-Propelled Artillery Observed in China (S/WNINTEL/NOFORN)   13
Chinese Officials Comment on Nuclear Arsenal (S/WNINTEL/NOFORN)   14
Brunei Prepares for Independence (U)   15

WESTERN EUROPE

Swedish Defense Industry Develops New Weapons (U)   17
Switzerland Considers Tank Acquisition Options (C/NOFORN)   18
Defense Budget Problems Projected for the Netherlands (C/NOFORN)   19

AFRICA

Libya Is Seeking To Purchase New Weapons (U)   23
Strategic Value of Simonstown Naval Base May Decline (U)   23

LATIN AMERICA

USSR Continues Arms Deliveries to Cuba (U)   27
Brazil Will Begin Production of EMB-120 Aircraft (C)   27
Defense Plans Are Being Formulated For Falkland Islands (U)   28

1982), and "Cubans Are Worried About Sandanista Regime's Problems," (October 22, 1982).[41]

Other DIA current intelligence products include the *Defense Intelligence Notice* (DIN), the *Special Defense Intelligence Notice* (SDIN) and the *Periodic Intelligence Summary*. Each DIN normally addresses a single development, situation, event, or activity that is felt to have a possible impact on future planning and operations. The primary objective of the DIN is to report an event, to explain why it occurred, and to make an assessment of its impact on the United States.[42]

The SDIN, like the DIN, is intended to inform the Joint Chiefs of Staff (JCS), the unified and specified commands, the military services, and selected agencies of particular events of importance. The events that are the subject of a SDIN, however, are required to have an immediate and significant effect on current planning and operations.[43]

The *Periodic Intelligence Summary* is intended to provide the JCS, the military services, and military commanders worldwide with periodic intelligence concerning actual or training exercises that could have an immediate actual (or simulated) effect on U.S. plans and operations. Information, if applicable, is included in following format:

1. Situation summary/highlights
2. Political developments
3. Military activity
   a. Air
   b. Ground
   c. Navy
   d. Missile
   e. other
4. Outlook.[44]

Other DIA products include the Defense Intelligence Projections for Planning (DIPPs) that summarize the state of the Soviet and Chinese armed forces and project future trends and force levels. Each set consists of seven volumes. Volume I examines Ballistic Missile Forces. Volume II in the PRC DIPP is concerned with Strategic Bomber Forces and in the Soviet DIPP with Long Range Aviation. In both DIPPs Volume III is devoted to Aerospace Defense Forces. Volume III contains at least four sections, the third and fourth IIIC being concerned with Surface-to-Air Missile Forces and IIID with Ballistic Missile Defenses. Volume IV on General Purposes Forces, has at least five sections including A on Ground Forces, B on General Purpose Naval Forces, D on Military Transport Aviation, and E on Military Helicopter Aviation. The Volume V is entitled *Space Systems for the Support of Military Operations.* Volume VII is entitled *Military Manpower Implications.*[45]

Other estimated projections may be done on either a regular or occasional basis. Some of these are: *Projected Space Programs – USSR* (1982), *ASW Weapons and Decoys (Current and Projected)–ECC* (1976), and *Combat Vehicle Systems (Current and Projected)–Eurasian Communist Countries* (1976).[46]

Within the general intelligence category, the DIA publishes a variety of general intelligence products. These include: Area Handbooks, Order of Battle Studies, Military Intelligence summaries, Defense Intelligence Studies, Targeting/Installation Documents, Lines of Communication Studies, and Tactical Commanders Terrain Analysis studies.[47] Examples of such reports include *Soviet Strategic Surface-to-Surface Missile Order of Battle* (September 1978), *Electronic Order of Battle Volume I: USSR and Mongolia* (March 1979), *Ground Order of Battle: PRC* (January 1980), *Military Intelligence Summary: Volume VII, People's Republic of China and Eastern Asia* (January 1980), *Naval Forces Intelligence Study: People's Republic of China* (March 1981), *Handbook on the*

Chinese Armed Forces (July 1976), and *Soviet Kola Peninsula Missile Submarine Base: Two Decades in the Making* (August 1978).[48]

All such studies are intended to form an extensive data base relevant to assessing foreign military capabilities in general or with regard to specific matters (e.g., seizure of the Falklands) and for use in U.S. military operations. Order of Battle Studies specify in as much detail as possible the organization and armaments of a foreign nation's military establishment or a component of that establishment. Targeting/Installation Documents will be used by operations planners in assessing the requirements for destroying or damaging an airfield, a port facility, or a missile base. Lines of Communications Studies describe the means by which military forces are supported and supplied and thus are used in designing plans to sever those lines.

In addition, the DIA produces thousands of reports on military and military-related scientific and technical matters that are not part of the series mentioned above. The subjects of these reports include strategy, politico-military relations, scientific and technical matters, weapons systems, intelligence, geopolitics, C^3, and R&D.

DIA reports on strategy include *Luring Deep: China's Land Defense Strategy* (September 1980) and *Detente in Soviet Strategy* (September 1975). Political-military subjects were the focus of *China's Urban Militia: Military Arm or Political Tool?* (June 1974) and *USSR: The Unity and Integration of Soviet Political, Military and Defense Industry Leadership* (March 1977).[49]

Scientific and technical reports concern general assessments, computer technology, microelectronics, and medical activities. Included in these reports are *Long Range Scientific and Technical Assessment: The People's Republic of China* (October 1973) and *Psychopharmacological Enhancement of Human Performance – USSR.*[50]

As might be expected, reports on specific weapons systems constitute the bulk of DIA reports. The reports vary from a focus on an entire class of weapons to reports of more than 100 pages on a single weapon system. Such reports include *Ballistic Missile Payloads (Current and Projected) – USSR and China, Antisatellite Systems – USSR* (October 1977), *Over the Horizon Radars for Air Defense* (December 1979), *Typhoon/Oscar – A Special Report, Soviet ALFA Class SSN Study* (December 1979), *Backfire Weapon System* (July 1980), and *SS-11 ICBM System* (February 1979).[51]

Reports concerning C^3 have focused on Warsaw Pact and Soviet C^3 capabilities as a whole as well as on the command structures for particular military regions. Reports have included *Warsaw Pact Forces Command, Control and Communications* (August 1980), *New Military Command Structure for Soviet Forces Opposite China*, and *Soviet Command, Control and Communications.*[52]

Another major area of DIA analysis is with respect to R&D weapons acquisition. The concern is with the decisionmaking acquisition process, the role of the design bureaus, and design and testing philosophy. Among the DIA studies dealing with these subjects is a 1972 study entitled *Soviet Military Research and Development—an Overview* and the more recent (1980) five-volume study entitled *U.S. and Soviet Weapon System Design Practice*.[53]

BUREAU OF INTELLIGENCE AND RESEARCH

As noted in Chapter 5, the State Department's INR contributes to national intelligence production and provides the Secretary of State, and the rest of the State Department, with intelligence support. In the latter role it provides both current and long-term intelligence.

Daily current intelligence is contained in the *Morning Summary*—intended to inform the Secretary and principal deputies of current events and intelligence and provide concise commentaries concerning their significance.[54] The first part of the summary consists of short "list and comment" reports based on newly available information. The second part usually consists of four one-page essays drafted by INR analysts.[55]

Also, within the current intelligence description is a series of regional and function summaries published up to six times a week. In 1983 these included *Arab-Israeli Highlights* (six times); *Afghanistan Situation Report* (twice); *African Trends, East Asia and Pacific Weekly Highlights*, and *Inter-American Highlights* (all once a week); and *Central American Highlights, Global Issues Review, Politico-Military Analyses, Science and Technology*, and *Soviet Weekly*. These publications consist of short essays or brief analyses, usually followed by summaries of significant intelligence reports.[56]

Single-subject reports are published under three titles: *Current Analyses, Assessments and Research*, and *Policy Assessments. Current Analyses* are papers that analyze recent or ongoing events and assess prospects and implications in the next six months.[57] Recent analyses have included "Soviet Exercise 'ZAPAD-81' Implications for CBMs" (September 28, 1981), "Soviets Seek Restraints on Use of Space Shuttle" (May 7, 1981), and "Moscow's Response to NATO Ministerial Ministry Defends TNF Position" (May 20, 1981).[58]

Assessment and Research (AR) papers are studies that either assess past trends or project the course of events more than six months in the future. They are reports in which the analyst has done substantial background or in-depth research.[59] Recent AR papers include "Central Issues in Soviet Nuclear Strategy" (January 12, 1981), "Soviet Activities in Africa in the 1980's" (May 21, 1981), and "Soviet Support for Insurgencies" (March 3, 1981).[60] Policy Assessments are papers that analyze the context or results of past policies or assess comparative policies or policy options.[61]

The focus of the *Current Analyses, Assessment and Research*, and *Policy Assessments* papers is not exclusively, or even predominately, the Soviet Union. As noted earlier, non-Soviet Bloc economic intelligence is the primary responsibility of the State Department and hence the INR. Economic intelligence reports have concerned natural resources, trade within and among various blocs, prospects for various commodity markets, and the economic/agricultural situation within specific countries. Thus, the INR has produced reports entitled "The Majors' Declining Share of Oil Distribution" (February 26, 1980), "The Revised Outlook for Oil Demand" (September 22, 1981), "The International Sugar Agreement Besieged" (March 5, 1981), "Dim Prospects for Coffee Exporters" (September 14, 1981), "Trade Patterns of the West" (July 17, 1980), "Trade of NATO Countries with Communist Countries 1976-1979" (December 1, 1980), "Energy Food/Population Balances in the Maghreb Countries" (July 21, 1982), and "El Salvador: Brighter Prospects for Land Reform" (May 17, 1983).[62]

MILITARY SERVICE SCIENTIFIC AND TECHNICAL INTELLIGENCE CENTERS

As noted in Chapter 4, each military service has at least one scientific and technical (S&T) intelligence organization. Included in this category are the Air Force Systems Command's Foreign Technology Division (FTD), the Naval Intelligence Command's Naval Intelligence Support Center (NISC), and the Army Foreign Science and Technology Center (FSTC).

As with the CIA, DIA, and INR, the product of these organizations is divided among current intelligence products and more in-depth studies and analyses. Thus, the FSTC publishes several current intelligence reports, the *Biweekly Scientific and Technical Intelligence Summary* (BSTIS), the *Army Scientific and Technical Intelligence Bulletin* (ASTIB), and the *Weekly Wire*.[63]

Similarly, the FTD publishes, on a weekly basis, the *Foreign Technology Bulletin*, a classified magazine with articles of a current intelligence nature. Among the articles that have appeared in the bulletin are: "SS-17 Accelerometer Quality Assessment" (August 17, 1979); "Further Data on the Soviet 270-Liter Cold Cathode Electric Discharge Laser" (August 31, 1976); "PRC S&T Intelligence Organization Identified" (June 28, 1977); "Soviet Tactical and Strategic Photoreconnaissance and Aerial Film Technology" (June 29, 1976); and "Chinese CSSC-2 (Silkwork) Coastal Defense Missile" (July 31, 1980).[64]

In-depth studies by the FTD include studies of Soviet space activities (*Soviet Space Program*, October 1974), electromagnetic combat (*Electromagnetic Combat Threat Environment Description*, 4 vols., 1981), the use of lasers for air defense (*Soviet Laser Tactical Air Defense Design Study*, November 1981), Soviet aircraft (*Backfire-B*, June 1979; *The MIG-19*, 1972), design and acquisition procedures (*Soviet Aircraft Design and Acquisition*), and exploitation reports (e.g., the *Gram Troy Exploitation Report*, December 27, 1977).[65]

Studies by the FSTC have focused on subjects directly and indirectly related to the Army mission. FSTC studies have included: *Microelectronics Technology and Applications – Eurasian Communist Countries and Japan* (December 1974), *Chinese Land Defenses Force* (June 1973), *Soviet Twin 57-min Self Propelled Antiaircraft Gun ZSU-522-2* (June 1976), *Soviet Large Helicopter Mil Mi-12* (June 1972), *USSR Ground Forces R&D Overview 1975* (June 1975), *An Outstanding Weapons System for Soviet Air Defense Traps* (1972), and *Chemical Warfare Capabilities – Warsaw Pact* (October 31, 1979).[66]

NISC products include reports on sea-based weapons and aircraft; all varieties of surface ships and submarines; ASW tactics, strategy, and intelligence; Naval orders of battle; and amphibious warfare. NISC reports have included *Combat Swimmer Systems and Capabilities – Selected Communist Countries* and *Communist Military Sealift and Afloat Logistic Support Forces* (March 1977).[67]

UNIFIED, SPECIFIED, AND THEATER COMMANDS

Among the major functions of the intelligence components of the unified and specified commands is the preparation of current and other intelligence specifically geared to the needs of the command and its Commander in Chief (CINC). Included in these requirements is intelligence relating to the nuclear targeting responsibilities of the command.

Among the regular publications of the Strategic Air Command (SAC) intelligence component is the *SAC Intelligence Quarterly*. As with FTD's *Foreign Technology Bulletin*, the *SAC Intelligence Quarterly* is a classified journal containing several articles of current intelligence interest. Issues of the *Quarterly* have included articles on Soviet tactical and strategic aircraft ("Comparison Between Soviet and USAF Tactical Fighter Training," July 1978 and "Backfire Deployment Status," April 1978); Soviet strategic rocket forces ("Modernization of the Soviet Strategic Rocket Forces," July 1978); SAC reconnaissance ("SAC Reconnaissance and the SA-5," April 1978); Soviet civil defense ("Soviet Civil Defense, Personnel Shelters," October 1978); and Soviet surface-to-air missiles ("SA-10 Missile System," July 1981).[68]

NORAD's intelligence component also produces a variety of intelligence products. NORAD's main current intelligence vehicle is the *NORAD Weekly Intelligence Review*, which has included articles such as "Soviet Missile/Space Launch Activity for January 1977" (February 11, 1977), "Impact of Marshal Ogarkov's Appointment on Automated Decision-Making" (February 18, 1977), and "Soviet Army Employs Smoke in Tactical Doctrine," (November 26, 1976).[69]

The major NORAD intelligence product is the *NORAD Intelligence for Planning* volume, which has sections on Soviet spacecraft, antisatellite systems, bombers, and strategic offensive systems. The volume is kept up to date by revision. Other intelligence products include Capabilities Assessments Briefs – for example, *Soviet Naval Capabilities Against North America* (January 1977) and

Table 12-5.   General Intelligence Production Responsibilities.

Unit	Military Capabilities				Military Geography and Transportation	Targets
	Ground	Air	Navy	Missiles		
DIA[a]	All strategic including space OB.				NIS data base. Assists Commands as resources permit.	National data base BE, TDI, CPFL, physical vulnerability studies. Evaluation of target lists.
SAC				Produces intelligence on communist countries, world wide. Maintains EOB data base on USSR and Mongolia.		SLOP-NSTL targets weapons applications. Field AIF inputs.
USEUCOM	Monitors theater military capabilities. Performs timely analysis of all-source intelligence to determine foreign military, political, psychosocial and economic capabilities and vulnerabilities and to provide imminence of hostilities intelligence. Insures production of counterintelligence to satisfy command requirements. Produces intelligence in support of operational planning requirements. Monitors support of the DoD OB System. Produces ELINT of both tactical and technical significance and fuses ELINT with all-source intelligence to provide timely theater defense analysis. Produces unique intelligence in support of electronic warfare operations. Produces EOB on Alabania, Bulgaria, Czechoslovakia, East Germany, Hungary, Poland, Romania, Yugoslavia, Western Europe, Africa and the Middle East (less India and Pakistan). Arranges for production of required intelligence by supporting CONUS production agencies.				Assures production of studies to support JCS-approved contingency plans as required to supplement national intelligence products, and monitors theater MGID production in support of NATO.	Field AIF inputs into DIA Data Base. Verification of targets selected from DIA data base for inclusion in theater OPLANS. Monitors and insures production of target intelligence and target materials in support of USCINCEUR/ SACEUR.
USAREUR	Monitors theater ground military capabilities. Produces ground intelligence to support operational planning requirements. Performs timely analysis of all-source intelligence to determine foreign military, political, psychosocial and economic capabilities and vulnerabilities and to provide imminence of hostilities intelligence. Produces GOB, including technical information, on Albania, Bulgaria, Czechoslovakia, East Germany, Hungary, Poland, Romania, Yugoslavia and				Produces Military Geographic Information and Documentation (MGID) in conformance with NATO Standardization Agreements (STANAGs).	Field AIF inputs into DIA data base. Produces tactical target intelligence in support of USCINCEUR/SACEUR.

	the Soviet Group of Forces in Eastern Europe. Monitors and is responsive to current and general intelligence requirements on ground forces in North Africa and the Middle East. Monitors GOB on Western Military Districts of the USSR and technical intelligence on the USSR for military equipment and weapons in the hands of troops. Produces AAAOB on Czechoslovakia, East Germany and Poland. Produces MOB (including Tactical Missile/Rocket OB) on Czechoslovakia, East Germany, Hungary and Poland.		
USNAVEUR	Monitors theater naval capabilities. Produces naval intelligence in support of operational planning requirements. Performs timely analysis of all-source intelligence to determine foreign military, political, phychosocial and economic capabilities and vulnerabilities and to provide imminence of hostilities intelligence. Produces European, Middle East and African NOB. Produces installations, biographic and OB digitized data bases (including AOB, GOB, EOB, AAOB and Aerospace OB) for the USEUCOM area in support of the Naval Intelligence Processing System (NIPS).	Produces port, urban amphibious, weather and country intelligence studies for approved plans.	Field AIF inputs into DIA data base. Produces target intelligence and target materials and performs mission planning in support of USCINCEUR/SACEUR.
USAFE	Monitors theater aerospace capabilities. Performs timely analysis of all-source intelligence to determine foreign military, political, phychosocial and economic capabilities and vulnerabilities and to provide imminence of hostilities intelligence in support of operational planning requirements. Directs the multisensor exploitation activities of the European Special Activities Facility. Produces AOB on Eastern European Communist countries. Provides NATO with AOB to 75 degrees East. Produces NATO releasable MOB (including SAGMOB) on Albania, Bulgaria, Czechoslovakia, East Germany, Hungary, Poland, Romania and Yugoslavia.	Evasion and Escape for approved plans.	Field AIF inputs into DIA data base. Provides weapons application data, target intelligence and target materials in support of USCINCEUR/SACEUR.

(*Table 12–5. continued overleaf*)

Table 12-5. continued

Unit	Military Capabilities				Military Geography and Transportation	Targets
	Ground	Air	Navy	Missiles		
PACOM	Manages theater military capabilities production.					Manages PACOM target materials program. Monitors production of target intelligence by IPAC.
IPAC	Produces EOB on PACOM area. Produces Theater Intelligence. Supports DoD GOB Inputs to S. Vietnam, Cambodia, and Laos GOB.	Air defense analyses; Supports DoD AOB; produces SEA AAAOB.			Detailed studies in support of JCS-approved contingency plans as required to supplement DIA finished intelligence. Studies include terrain, urban area, transportation, and cross-country movement.	Field AIF inputs into DIA data base; verification of targets selected from DIA data base for inclusion in theater OPlans; development of intelligence on CINCPAC OPlan and on DIA data base (AIF) installations in PACOM.
PACAF		Produces theater air intelligence.			Evasion and escape for approved plans.	Confirmation of targets assigned by PACAF. Field AIF inputs.
PACFLT			Monitors theater naval intelligence		Port, amphibious, POL, weather and country studies for approved plans.	Confirmation of targets assigned to PACFLT.
ALCOM	Monitors Soviet strategic and general purpose forces East of 100° E longitude.		Monitors and reports on Soviet Fishing Fleet Activity in Alaskan Waters north of 45° N and east of 170° E.			
USARAL	Monitors theater Soviet Far East ground.					
Alaskan Air Command		Monitors theater Soviet Far East air.				

SOUTHCOM	Manages theater military capabilities production.		Detailed studies to support JCS-approved contingency plans as required to supplement DIA finished intelligence.	
LANTCOM	Manages theater military capabilities production. Supports DoD OB system. Maintains EOB in Latin America and Caribbean. Inputs to specific Caribbean GOB; to specific Caribbean, Latin American and African NOB.		Detailed studies to support JCS-approved contingency plans as required to supplement DIA finished intelligence.	Field AIF inputs. Confirmation of demph targets selected from DIA data base for inclusion in theater OPS plans.
LANTFLT		Supports DoD NOB with inputs as above.	Port, amphibious, weather, and country intelligence studies for approved plans.	
ARLANT	Produces Caribbean.		Lines of communications studies, terrain, urban areas, telecom, drop zones, and TacCTAs to support contingency plans.	Field AIF inputs.
AFLANT	AOB, Caribbean	MOB, Caribbean		
CONAD	Supports DoD OB system. Supports production on LRA activity.	Monitors and supports production on ICBM's. (Supports production on Foreign Space Objects).		
MIL	Maritime Shipping / Certain SIGINT products.		Oceanographic.	Field AIF inputs.

a. DIA has sole responsibility for the production of intelligence on the topics of military economics, military material production, and telecommunications.

b. Navy makes inputs to DOD NOB on certain East European countries.

Soviet Capabilities in Space (August 1975)—and Intelligence Memos—for example, the four-page *Soviet Fighter Design Philosophy.*[70]

Among the large number of theater command intelligence units are the Intelligence Center Pacific, the Fleet Intelligence Center(s), and the European Defense Analysis Center. The Intelligence Center Pacific, in addition to its current intelligence product, has produced reports on the surveillance of PRC naval activities (*Clipper Troop West (CTW) Surveillance Operations Against PRC Broad Ocean Area (BOA) Task Group*, March 1981); the Chinese-Vietnamese conflict (*PRC-SRV Conflict*, July 1979); Soviet Far Eastern military capabilities and activities (*Soviet Far East Logistics*, September 1978 and *Soviet Far East Sea and Airborne Landing Capabilities*, 1979); and nuclear targeting issues (*Targeting Potential Soviet Attack Corridors*, 1981).[71]

The Fleet Intelligence Center (Europe and Atlantic) produces a *Monthly Intelligence Digest* with articles such as "Update of Soviet Development and Use of Facilities at Berbera, Somalia" (December 1976), and "SA-8 Missile System Review" (November 1976). Longer studies have included *Soviet Naval Air Long Range Reconnaissance* and *U.S. Sixth Fleet Missile Threat Guide* (February 1974).[72]

The European Defense Analysis Center (EUDAC) is, as noted earlier, the ELINT (electronics intelligence) Center for the European Command. In addition to its current intelligence product, its reports have included the *Analysis of AN-12/CUB ECM Capabilities Against the NATO Air Defense System* (February 1975); *Detection Ranges for Soviet Ground Based Radar in the Forward Areas* (May 1, 1980); *Fencer Aircraft in the Forward Area* (September 1979); and *Soviet Intelligence Collection Flights Over the Forward Area* (July 1, 1979).[73]

Table 12-5 summarizes the General Intelligence Production responsibilities of a variety of unified, specified, and theater commands.

NOTES TO CHAPTER 12

1.   Cord Meyer, *Facing Reality: From World Federalism to the CIA* (New York: Harper & Row, 1981), p. 352; Zbigniew Brzezinski, *Power and Principle: Memoirs of the National Security Adviser 1977-1981* (New York: Farrar, Straus & Giroux, 1983), p. 224.

2.   Meyer, *Facing Reality*, p. 352.

3.   William Colby with Peter Forbath, *Honorable Men: My Life in the CIA* (New York: Simon & Schuster, 1978), p. 354.

4.   Ibid.

5.   Meyer, *Facing Reality*, p. 353.

6.   Ibid.

7.   Brian Toohey and Dale Van Atta, "How the CIA Saw the 1975 Crisis," *National Times*, March 28–April 3, 1982, pp. 16ff.

8.   Ibid.

9.   "America's Secret Warriors," *Newsweek*, October 10, 1983, pp. 38ff.

10. Meyer, *Facing Reality*, p. 357.

11. U.S. Congress, House Committee on Foreign Affairs, *The Role of Intelligence in the Foreign Policy Process* (Washington, D.C.: U.S. Government Printing Office, 1980), p. 235.

12. National Security Council Information Liaison, "National Intelligence Estimates," May 25, 1962, LBJ Library Vice Presidential Security Files Box 5. Folder NSC Records of Actions 1962.

13. Ibid.

14. NIE 11-4-57, *Main Trends in Soviet Capabilities and Policies 1957-1962, Declassified Documents Reference System*, 1979-128A.

15. Lawrence Freedman, *U.S. Intelligence and the Soviet Strategic Threat* (London: Macmillan, 1977), pp. 34-35.

16. Bruce Berkowitz, "Intelligence in the Organizational Context: Coordination and Error in National Estimates" (University of Minnesota, 1983). (Mimeo.)

17. Philip Taubman, "Casey and His CIA on the Rebound," *New York Times Magazine*, January 16, 1983, pp. 21ff.

18. Robert C. Toth, "Casey Shapes Up CIA, Survives as Top Spy," *Los Angeles Times*, January 3, 1983, pp. 1, 18.

19. Taubman, "Casey and His CIA."

20. National Security Council Information Liaison, "National Intelligence Estimates."

21. *Declassified Documents Reference System*, 1975-48E, 1976-15B.

22. U.S. Congress, House Permanent Select Committee on Intelligence, *U.S. Intelligence Performance on Central America* (Washington, D.C.: U.S. Government Printing Office, 1982), p. 7.

23. U.S. Congress, Senate Committee on Armed Services, *Department of Defense Authorization for Appropriations FY 1983, Part 7* (Washington, D.C.: U.S. Government Printing Office, 1982), p. 4393.

24. AR 381-19, "Military Intelligence; Intelligence Support," July 19, 1981.

25. List of CIA documents on Soviet decisionmaking in possession of the author.

26. Private information.

27. Private information.

28. Private information.

29. Private information.

30. Private information.

31. Myron Smith, ed., *The Secret Wars: Intelligence, Espionage and Covert Operations* (Santa Barbara: ABC-Clio, 1980), p. 122.

32. Private information.

33. Jeffrey Richelson and Desmond Ball, *The Ties that Bind: The UKUSA Intelligence Network* (London: Allen & Unwin, 1985), ch. 6.

34. Smith, *The Secret Wars*, p. 122.

35. United States of America v. Lee Eugene Madsen, Criminal No. 79-130F, District Court for Eastern District of Virginia; U.S. Congress, Senate Select Committee on the Intelligence, *National Security Secrets and the Admin-*

istration of Justice (Washington, D.C.: U.S. Government Printing Office, 1978), p. 4.

36. Private information.

37. "Australia Impasse Continues," *CIA Weekly Review*, November 7, 1975, p. 22.

38. "New Defense Minister is Whitlam's Man," *Weekly Intelligence Summary*, July 4, 1975, pp. 10–11.

39. *Weekly Intelligence Summary* 29–82, July 23, 1982.

40. Private information.

41. Private information.

42. Joint Chiefs of Staff, *Joint Reporting Structure (JRS) Volume II–Joint Reports, Part 10–Intelligence* (Washington, D.C.: JCS, 1980), pp. 10-1-10-2.

43. Ibid., pp. 10-2-1 – 10-2-2.

44. Ibid.

45. Private information. (Volume 6 title unavailable.)

46. Private information.

47. "I Marine Amphibious Force Order P 3800.1A," (Camp Pendleton, Cal.: I Marine Marine Amphibious Force, May 9, 1977).

48. Private information.

49. Private information.

50. Private information.

51. Private information.

52. Private information.

53. Private information.

54. *INR: Intelligence and Research in the Department of State* (Washington, D.C.: Department of State, 1983), p. 6.

55. Ibid.

56. Ibid.

57. Ibid.

58. Private information.

59. *INR*, p. 7.

60. Private information.

61. *INR*, p. 7.

62. Bureau of Intelligence and Research, "Available Reports 1980 to Present." (Mineo: Department of State 1983.)

63. *U.S. Army Foreign Science and Technology Center* (Charlottesville, Virg.: FSTC, n.d.), p. 11.

64. Private information.

65. Private information.

66. Private information.

67. Private information.

68. Private information.

69. Private information.

70. Private information.

71. Private information.

72. Private information.

73. Private information.

13 MANAGEMENT AND DIRECTION

Given the number of intelligence agencies, offices, and units, the conflicting and diverse supervisory executive departments, and the wide range of intelligence activities, it is clear that the U.S. intelligence community requires a system of coordination and control to guide its work. Furthermore, the highly sensitive nature of some of these activities requires approval by high-level officials. Thus, it is not surprising that over the last thirty years an elaborate system of directives, committees, offices, plans, and programs has been established.

This system can be divided into three basic categories: Executive Orders, Presidential directives and agency or departmental regulations. These establish the basic missions and structure of the intelligence community. There are also the individuals, committees, and offices that implement as well as formulate directives, seek to resolve conflicts, provide advice and counsel, and establish collection and analysis priorities. Finally, there are the plans, programs, and requirements documents that establish objectives or specify resource allocation for the attainment of specific collection or analysis tasks.

ORDERS, DIRECTIVES, AND REGULATIONS

The orders, directives, and regulations that guide the activities of the intelligence community all begin as presidential orders and directives. Presidential orders and directives represent the apex of the system and come in two varieties—unclassified Executive Orders and often classified National Security Decision Directives (NSDDs). The title of the second type of document changes with administration.

263

Thus, Reagan's National Security Decision Directives were Presidential Directives (PDs) in the Carter administration, National Security Decision Memorandums (NSDMs) in the Nixon-Ford administration, and National Security Action Memorandums in the Kennedy-Johnson administration.

Executive Orders governing the intelligence community are reissued with each new administration although they often overlap in content. The three latest were issued on February 18, 1976 by President Ford ("United States Foreign Intelligence Activities"), on January 24, 1978 by President Carter ("United States Intelligence Activities"), on December 4, 1981 by President Reagan ("United States Intelligence Activities").

The Reagan Executive Order Number 12333 is divided into three parts: Goals, Direction, Duties, and Responsibilities with Respect to the National Intelligence Effort; The Conduct of Intelligence Activities; and General Provisions.[1] Part 1 authorizes the establishment of National Foreign Intelligence Advisory Groups, specifies the agencies and offices that constitute the intelligence community, defines their general functions, and lists the duties and responsibilities of the senior officials of the community.

Part 2, on the conduct of intelligence activities, establishes procedures concerning and restrictions on the collection of information abroad and in the United States concerning U.S. persons. It also establishes (or continues) procedures concerning assistance to law enforcement authorities, human experimentation, and contracting as well as prohibiting assassinations. Part 3 deals with congressional oversight, implementation, and definitions.

Changes in the contents of the Executive Orders governing the intelligence community over the last ten years have been the product of three factors: differing modes of National Security Council (NSC) organization, revelations concerning abuses by the intelligence community, and differing attitudes concerning "domestic" intelligence activities. Thus, the Ford Executive Order Number 11905 imposed restrictions on physical and electronic surveillance activities, experimentation, and assistance to law enforcement authorities in response to the 1974-1975 revelations concerning Central Intelligence Agency, Federal Bureau of Investigation, and National Security Agency (NSA) activities. It also specified, for the first time, that "no employee of the United States Government shall engage in, or conspire to engage in, political assassination."[2]

The Carter Executive Order Number 12036 was predominantly concerned with restrictions and oversight.[3] The Reagan Executive Order loosened some of those restrictions, allowing the collection of significant foreign intelligence within the United States by the CIA so long as the collection effort is not undertaken for the purpose of acquiring information concerning the domestic activities of U.S. persons.

In addition to an Executive Order governing the intelligence community, each President has also issued an order concerning National Security Information. These orders deal with classification levels and authority, downgrading and declassification, safeguarding classified information, and implementation of their provisions. The most recent of these orders is Executive Order 12356 of April 2, 1982. This order reversed trends that began in the Nixon administration which sought to lower classification levels on many documents and reduce the absolute quantity of classified material. The new order no longer requires a balancing of national security considerations with the public interest in access to information and allows "reclassification" of previously declassified material if such material is considered "reasonably recoverable."[4]

The usually classified Presidential directives that deal with intelligence matters tend to deal with more specific and often sensitive areas of intelligence operations—particular changes in intelligence community organization and procedures, sensitive covert action or clandestine collection activities, and space reconnaissance.[5] Carter administration PDs concerning intelligence included PD-9 of March 30, 1977, "Army Special Operations Field Office in Berlin"; PD-17 of August 4, 1977, "Reorganization of the Intelligence Community"; and PD-19 of August 25, 1977, "Intelligence Structure and Mission (Electronic Surveillance Abroad and Physical Searches for Foreign Intelligence Purposes).[6] Additionally, PD-37, "National Space Policy," apparently contained substantial portions concerning U.S. employment of reconnaissance satellites.[7]

At least four Reagan NSDDs concern intelligence matters. NSDD-17 deals with covert operations in Central America.[8] NSDD-19 of January 12, 1982 is entitled "Protection of Classified National Security Council and Intelligence Information," and NSDD-84 of March 11, 1983, "Safeguarding National Security Information," specifies new security requirements for individuals to obtain access to codeword information.[9] NSDD-42, "National Space Policy," signed in mid-1982, is certain to contain significant portions concerning satellite reconnaissance.[10]

Both Executive Orders and Presidential Directives deal with subjects in fairly general terms. Implementation requires more detailed directives. The directives that emanate from the presidential level are of two basic types: (1) National Security Council Intelligence Directives (NSCIDs) and their descendants and (2) Departmental Directives and their descendants.

NSCIDs offer guidance to the entire intelligence community, and the Director of Cental Intelligence (DCI) in particular, concerning specific aspects of U.S. intelligence operations. The NSCID numbering system is unlike that for NSDMs, PDs or NSDDs, which are temporally numbered. In general, a NSCID number is assigned to a particular topic, and subsequent revisions of the NSCID bear the same number. At the same time, the topic assigned to a particular number may change over time, one topic being subsumed under another.

NSCIDs were first issued in 1948 and have been updated numerous times since then. Sometimes revisions have been of selected documents; other times the entire group has been revised. The most recent mass revision seems to have been the one that produced an entire new set of NSCIDs on February 17, 1972,

Table 13-1.   NSCIDs Issued on February 17, 1972.

Number	Title
1	Basic Duties and Responsibilities
2	Coordination of Overt Activities
3	Coordination of Intelligence Production
4	The Defector Program
5	U.S. Espionage and Counterintelligence Activities Abroad
6	Signals Intelligence
7	?
8	Photographic Interpretation
9	?
10	?

Note: Titles of NSID 7, 9, and 10 not known.

many of which might still be in effect. The number and names of these NSCIDs are listed in Table 13-1.

NSCID No. 1, "Basic Duties and Responsibilities," was first issued in 1948 with subsequent updates in 1952, 1958, 1961, 1964, and 1972. NSCID No. 1 of February 17, 1972 assigned four major responsibilities to the DCI:

1. planning, reviewing, and evaluating all intelligence activities and the allocation of all intelligence resources;
2. producing national intelligence required by the President and national consumers;
3. chairing and staffing all intelligence committee advisory boards; and
4. establishing and reconciling intelligence requirements and priorities with budgetary constraints.

NSCID No. 1 also (1) instructs the DCI to prepare and submit to the Office of Management and Budget (OMB) a consolidated intelligence budget, (2) authorizes the issuance of Director of Central Intelligence Directives as a means of implementing the NSCIDs, and (3) instructs the DCI to protect sources and methods.[11]

NSCID No. 2 of February 17, 1972 concerns the coordination of overt collection activities. Originally titled "Coordination of Collection Activities Abroad" when first issued in 1948, the Directive divided collection activities among the Department of State (cultural, political, and sociological intelligence), Army (military intelligence), Navy (naval intelligence), and Air Force (air intelligence) while assigning the collection of economic, scientific, and technical intelligence to each agency according to its own needs.[12]

NSCID No. 2 of February 17, 1972 makes the DCI responsible for planning the utilization of collection and reporting capabilities of the various government departments and the CIA responsible for conducting, as a service of common concern, radio broadcast monitoring. The Department of State is charged with overt collection of political, sociological, economic, scientific, and technical information; militarily pertinent scientific and technical intelligence; and economic intelligence.[13]

NSCID No. 3 deals with the coordination of the production of intelligence. It was first issued on February 13, 1948 and subsequently revised in 1958, 1961, and 1972. The 1972 version makes the Department of State responsible for the production of political and sociological intelligence on all countries and for economic intelligence on countries of the "Free World." It makes the Department of Defense (DOD) responsible for the production of military intelligence and scientific and technical and economic intelligence pertinent to the missions of DOD components. The CIA is given responsibility for economic and scientific and technical intelligence plus "any other intelligence required by the DCI."[14] In practice, this has meant the CIA is heavily involved in the production of political and military intelligence, especially strategic intelligence. In addition, atomic energy intelligence is decreed to be the responsibility of all National Foreign Intelligence Board (NFIB) agencies.[15]

Originally, NSCID No. 4 concerned Priority National Intelligence Objectives (PNIOs)—a system for prioritizing collection efforts. Thus, NSCID No. 4 of August 20, 1956, entitled "National Intelligence Objectives," authorized the DCI to prepare, in collaboration with other agencies concerned, "a comprehensive outline of national intelligence objectives applicable to foreign countries and areas to serve as a guide for the coordinated collection and production of National Intelligence." In addition, the DCI was authorized, in collaboration with other agencies concerned and under the guidance of the NSC staff, to select from time to time items of the outline as priority items.[16]

The system of PNIOs has been eliminated; hence, NSCID No. 4 no longer concerns that system. NSCID No. 4 of February 17, 1972 bore the title "The Defector Program" and presumably concerned the inducement of defections and the responsibility of the CIA and other agencies in the program.[17]

NSCID No. 5 of February 17, 1972 is entitled "U.S. Espionage and Counterintelligence Activities Abroad." That version is the successor to versions issued in 1951, 1958, and 1961. The Directive authorizes the DCI to "establish the procedures necessary to achieve such direction and coordination, including the assessment of risk incident upon such operations as compared to the value of the activity, and to ensure that sensitive operations are reviewed pursuant to applicable direction."[18]

NSCID No. 6, "Signals Intelligence," serves as the charter for the NSA. The February 17, 1972 version was still effective as of the time of the Reagan transition. NSCID No. 6 defines the nature of SIGINT (Signals intelligence) activities and directs the Director of the NSA (DIRNSA) to produce intelligence "in accordance with objectives, requirements and priorities established by the Director of Cental Intelligence and the United States Intelligence Board."[19] It further authorizes the DIRNSA "to issue direction to any operating elements engaged in SIGINT operations such instructions and assignments as are required. All instructions issued by the Director under the authority provided in this paragraph shall be mandatory subject only to appeal to the Secretary of Defense." [20]

The most recent available version of NSCID No. 7 was among the original NSCIDs issued in 1948. Thus, NSCID No. 7 of February 12, 1948, "Domestic Exploitation," stated that "the Central Intelligence Agency shall be responsible for the exploitation on a highly selective basis within the U.S. of business concerns, non-governmental organizations and individuals as sources of foreign intelligence information." [21] Subsequent guidance on the subject of domestic exploitation has been contained in NSCID No. 2, the topic of NSCID No. 7 being changed. The most recent evidence suggests NSCID No. 7 concerns "critical information." [22] It might deal with the classification system as well as with conditions and procedures for its distribution among U.S. agencies and foreign countries.

The original NSCID No. 8 was issued on May 25, 1948 and was entitled "Biographical Data on Foreign Scientific and Technological Personalities" but by 1961 dealt, instead, with "Photographic Interpretation." [23] NSCID No. 8 of February 17, 1972 continues the National Photographic Interpretation Center (NPIC) as a service of common concern to be provided by the DCI. Additionally, it specifies that the Director of NPIC is to be selected by the DCI with the concurrence of the Secretary of Defense. [24]

The present topic of NSCID No. 9 is not known. The original NSCID No. 9 was that of July 1, 1948, "Communications Intelligence" it served as the basis for the subsequent NSCID No. 6 of September 15, 1952, "Communications Intelligence and Electronics Intelligence." [25] Information concerning NSCIDs 10, 11, 12, 15, and 16 goes back to 1953 or earlier. NSCID No. 10 of January 18, 1949, "Collection of Foreign Scientific and Technological Data," designated the Department of State as having primary responsibility for collection abroad for all government agencies of information in the basic sciences. [26] NSCID No. 11 of January 6, 1950 was titled "Security of Information on Intelligence Sources and Methods" and made the DCI responsible for protecting intelligence sources and methods from unauthorized disclosure—a provision that is presently contained in NSCID No. 1. [27]

NSCID No. 12 of January 6, 1950, "Avoidance of Publicity Concerning Intelligence Agencies of the U.S. Government," directed all departments and agencies of the intelligence community to take steps to prevent the unauthorized disclosure "for written or oral publication" of *any* information concerning intelligence or intelligence activities. [28] NSCID No. 15 of June 13, 1951, "Coordination and Production of Foreign Economic Intelligence," has been incorporated in NSCID No. 3. The CIA was authorized and directed to review continuously foreign economic intelligence requirements and the coordination of foreign economic research and product as a common concern to supplement other agencies. [29]

Finally, NSCID No. 16 of March 3, 1953, "Foreign Language Publications," instructed the DCI to ensure coordination of the procurement of foreign-language publications for intelligence purposes.[30]

The NSCIDs state, in general terms, the responsibilities of the DCI and other components of the intelligence community. One provision of NSCID No. 1 authorizes the DCI to issue more detailed directives—Director of Central Intelligence Directives (DCIDs)—in pursuit of the implementation of the various NSCIDs. DCIDs are keyed to the NSCIDs from which they follow by the DCID numbering system. Thus, DCID 1/5 is the 5th DCID issued pursuant to NSCID No. 1.

DCIDs in the DCID 1/ series have covered "Priority National Intelligence Objectives" as well as the "Terms of Reference of the Watch Committee." With the abolition of the PNIO system and the intelligence-monitoring Watch Committee, these Directives are no longer in effect. More recent DCIDs in the 1/ series include 1/2, 1/3, 1/4, 1/5, 1/7, 1/10, 1/11, 1/13, 1/14, 1/16, and 1/19.

DCID 1/2 of January 21, 1972 lists U.S. intelligence objectives and priorities that were to serve as guidance for planning and programming for the subsequent five years. It identifies intelligence targets in terms of information needed "to enable the U.S. intelligence community to provide effective support for decision-making, planning and operational activities of the United States government."[31] DCID 1/3 if May 18, 1976, entitled "Committees of the Director of Central Intelligence," outlines the basic composition and organization of the committees and authorizes the DCI to designate their Chairmen.[32] DCID 1/4 of the same date establishes the Intelligence Information Handling Committee, and DCID 1/5, also of May 18, concerns "Data Standardization for the Intelligence Community."[33] DCID 1/7 of May 4, 1981, "Control of Dissemination of Intelligence Information," imposes restrictions on the dissemination of intelligence to immigrant aliens and foreign governments.[34]

DCID 1/10 of January 18, 1982 is entitled "Security Policy Guidance on Liaison Relationships with Foreign Intelligence Organizations and Foreign Security Services."[35] DCID 1/11 of August 23, 1974 spells out the mission, functions, and composition of the Security Committee, and DCID 1/17 of May 18, 1976 does the same for the Human Resources Committee.[36] Another NFIB committee, the Committee on Imagery Requirements and Exploitations (COMIREX), is the main subject of DCID 1/13, "Coordination of the Collection and Exploitation of Imagery Intelligence."[37]

Security standards are the subject of DCIDs 1/14, 1/16, and 1/19. DCIDs 1/14 and 1/19 are concerned with the protection of Sensitive Compartmented Information. DCID 1/14 of May 13, 1976 is entitled "Minimum Personal Security Standards and Procedures Governing Eligibility for Access to Sensitive Compartmented Information." DCID 1/19, "Uniform Procedures for Administrative Handling and Accountability of Sensitive Compartmented Information (SCI)," focuses on physical security requirements.[38] DCID 1/16 of June 6, 1978 deals with the "Security of Foreign Intelligence in Automated Data Processing Systems and Networks."[39]

DCID 2/1 of March 8, 1960 concerns the "Coordination of Overt Collection Abroad." That DCID superseded 2/1 of October 1948 as well as 2/3, "Domestic Exploitation of Non-Governmental Organizations and Individuals," and 2/5, "Procurement of Foreign Publications."[40] DCID 2/3 of June 26, 1959 authorized the CIA to determine the foreign intelligence potential of nongovernmental organizations and individuals. It also authorized establishment of a committee of USIB agencies under CIA leadership to meet periodically and discuss problems. More recent DCIDs, 2/2 and 2/6, established the Committee on Exchanges and the Critical Collection (now Intelligence) Problems Committee.[41]

DCIDs in the 3/ series have involved implementation of NSCID No. 3, "Coordination of Intelligence Production." These Directives have dealt with the production of National Intelligence Estimates as well as the establishment of numerous NFIB committees to facilitate production of intelligence in specific areas. Early versions of DCID 3/1 (July 8, 1948), 3/2 (September 13, 1948) and 3/5 (September 1, 1953) were entitled, respectively, "Standard Operating Procedures for Departmental Participation in the Production and Coordination of National Intelligence"; "Policy Governing Departmental Concurrences in National Intelligence Reports and Estimates"; and "Production of National Intelligence Estimates."[42]

Later DCIDs in the 3/ series have defined the mission and functions of the Economic Intelligence Committee (3/1), the Joint Atomic Energy Intelligence Committee (3/3), the Guided Missile and Astronautics Intelligence Committee (3/4), and the Scientific and Technical Intelligence Committee (3/5).[43]

DCID 5/1 of May 1976 is entitled "Coordination of U.S. Clandestine Foreign Intelligence Activities Abroad"; DCID 5/2, also of May 1976, is entitled "U.S. Clandestine Foreign Intelligence and Counterintelligence Liaison."[44] DCIDs 4/1 and 4/2 of May 1976 are entitled, respectively, "Interagency Defector Committee" and "The Defector Program Abroad."[45] DCID 6/1 focuses on the functions, composition, and mission of the SIGINT Committee. The Committee was first established by DCID 6/1 on May 12, 1962.[46]

Several older DCIDs are no longer part of the series in which they were originally issued—having been revised and subsumed as part of other series—especially those dealing with protection of sources and methods (1/1) and intelligence production (3/1).

DCID 7/1 of October 1, 1953, "Domestic Exploitation of Non-Governmental Individuals Approaching Intelligence Agencies," instructed all intelligence agencies to establish a Washington, D.C. office for receiving nongovernment visitors who offer positive foreign intelligence. NSCID No. 7 seems to involve "Critical Information" since DCID 7/1 of August 1976 is entitled "Handling of Critical Information."[47]

DCID 11/2 of November 15, 1954, "Control and Dissemination and Use of Intelligence and Intelligence Information," focused on the markings relevant to restricted distribution of intelligence information. Labels authorized were NO DISSEM ABROAD (No Dissemination Abroad even to U.S. Installations), NSC Participatory Agencies Only, FOUO (For Official Use Only), NO FORN (Not Releasable to Foreign Nationals), NO FORN EXCEPT BRITISH AND CANA-DIAN, and RELEASABLE TO THE U.K.[48]

Finally, DCID 15/1 of September 14, 1954, "Production and Coordination of Foreign Economic Intelligence," defined the responsibilities of the previously created Economic Intelligence Committee.[49] It also made the CIA responsible for Soviet Bloc economic intelligence and the State Department responsible for the remainder of the economic intelligence effort. Economic intelligence was defined to include intelligence on economic doctrines, political and social aspects of economic organizations (including trade unions), and the relationship between political and economic policies.

In addition to DCIDs, the DCI issues supplemental Communications Intelligence Security Regulations.[50]

As discussed above, the Director of the NSA is the individual responsible for the supervision of all U.S. signals and intelligence activities. In this role the DIRNSA is authorized to issue Signals Intelligence Directives (SIDs). These have included SID 3, "SIGINT Security" (August 1972); SID 4 on "SIGINT Support to Military Commanders" (July 1, 1974); SID 18 "Limitations and Procedures in Signals Intelligence Operations of the U.S.S.S." (May 18, 1976); SID 40, "ELINT Operating Policy" (October 1970); SID 701, "Sanitizing and Declassifying ADP Storage Devices" (September 30, 1976); SID 702, "Automatic Data Processing Systems Security" (September 1980); and SID 1045, "SIGINT Tasking for USM-45, Misawa" (January 16, 1980)."[51]

SIDs may be issued by the Director of NSA solely on his or her authority and in implementation of NSCID No. 6 or in response to a DCID. SID 702, for example, was issued to implement DCID 1/16.[52]

Departmental regulations and directives on intelligence matters of greatest significance are those of the DOD Directives, which concern both intelligence policies and the operations of specific intelligence units. Hence, DOD Directive 3310.1, "International Intelligence Agreements," specifies that

1. The Deputy Under Secretary of Defense (Policy) (DUSD(P)) is the principal within the Department of Defense responsible for oversight, coordination, and policy review of intelligence matters relating to agreements with foreign parties.
2. The Director, Defense Intelligence Agency (DIA), shall exercise, for the Department of Defense, approval authority (which may not be further delegated) to negotiate and conclude non-SIGINT intelligence agreements. . . .[53]

Other DOD Directives with respect to intelligence policy include "Department of Defense Human Resources Intelligence Collection Training" (S-3115.6, January 7, 1965); "Signals Intelligence" (S-3115.7, January 25, 1983); "Implementation of National Security Council Intelligence Directive No. 7" (S-5100.19, March 19, 1959); "Intelligence Activities Utilizing Human Sources" (S-5105.29, December 1, 1978); "The Security, Use and Dissemination of Communications Intelligence (COMINT)" (S-5200.17, January 26, 1965); "Security Classification Concerning Airborne Radar Imaging Systems" (5210.57, September 26, 1973); and "Protection of Classified National Security Council and Intelligence Information" (5230.21, March 15, 1982).[54]

These Directives may represent initial DOD implementation of an NSCID, DCID, or NSDD. Thus, S-5100.19 represents initial implementation of NSCID No. 7, 3310.1 represents implementation of DCID 1/10, and 5230.21 represents implementation of NSDD-19.

Other DOD Directives specify the mission and functions of the Defense Special Plans Office (C-5155.1, April 24, 1982); The National Security Agency and Central Security Service (S-5100.20, December 23, 1971); the Defense Intelligence Agency (5105.21, May 19, 1977); the Defense Special Missile and Astronautics Center (S-5100.43, April 27, 1974); the Defense Mapping Agency (5125.40), August 10, 1978); and the Armed Forces Medical Intelligence Center (6420.1, December 9, 1982).[55]

Directive 6420.1 specifies that

> The Director, Armed Forces Medical Intelligence Center, shall:
> 1. have sole responsibility within the Department of Defense for the production of required medical scientific and technical intelligence (S&TI) and general medical intelligence (GMI);
> 2. provide timely medical intelligence support to the following:
>   (1) DOD Components
>   (2) national-level intelligence production agencies
>   (3) other federal agencies as required;
> 3. organize and execute all medical aspects of the DOD Foreign Material Exploitation Program (FMEP);
> 4. exploit foreign medical material obtained in support of DOD FMEP;
> 5. plan, coordinate, and provide intelligence studies in accordance with DOD S&TI production policies and procedures;
> 6. prepare medical intelligence under DIA technical direction for submission to the DOD GDIP [General Defense Intelligence Program];
> 7. manage the medical intelligence data base and the medical portion of the DOD S&TI data base;
> 8. provide quick response capability in medical intelligence for DOD and other government agencies, as required;
> 9. assist in debriefing personnel on matters related to medical intelligence;
> 10. sponsor medical intelligence training for selected reserve military units and individual mobilization designees;

11. maintain coordination and liaison with members of the intelligence community on matters involving medical intelligence;

12. provide the medical intelligence adviser to the Military Services;

13. comply with medical intelligence collection management and production tasking policies and procedures established by DIA and the Executive Agent;

14. provide coordinated collection requirements for medical intelligence in accordance with DOD Directive 5000.11 (reference (b)), for the DOD intelligence community; and

15. administer contracts funded outside the GDIP when there is a technical or administrative advantage in doing so.[56]

Military service and command regulations also state intelligence policies as well as define the mission and functions of service intelligence units. Among Air Force Regulations (AFRs) governing intelligence policy are those listed in Table 13-2 and include those entitled "Security Policy for USAF Sensitive Reconnaissance Programs," "The Medical Intelligence Program," "USAF Participation in the Defector Program," and "Protection of Classified National Security Council and Intelligence Information"—the latter implementing DOD Directive 5230.21.[57]

AFRs governing the activities of specific intelligence units include AFR 23-30 of August 13, 1982, "Electronic Security Command," as well as those dealing with the Air Force Technical Applications Center (AFR 23-44, May 18, 1983) and the Air Force Intelligence Service (AFR 23-45, June 10, 1974).[58]

Table 13-2. Selected Air Force Regulations (AFRs) Concerning Intelligence.

AFR	Title	Date
55-29	Security Policy for USAF Sensitive Reconnaissance Programs	December 17, 1979
200-1	Air Force Intelligence Mission and Responsibilities and Functions	May 17, 1971
200-3	The Medical Intelligence Program	July 9, 1965
200-7	Sensitive Compartmented Information (SCI)	June 28, 1982
200-9	Disclosure of Classified Military Information to Foreign Government and International Organizations	
200-26	USAF Participation in the Defector Program	February 1, 1980
205-19	Control of Dissemination of Intelligence Information	May 12, 1983
205-50	Protection of Classified National Security Council and Intelligence Information	December 20, 1982

Source: *AF Regulation 0-2* (Washington, D.C.: Department of the Air Force, May 25, 1983) pp. 27, 77-80.

Table 13-3. Selected Army Regulations (ARs) Concerning Intelligence.

AR	Title
10-61	Intelligence Operations Detachment, U.S. Army Organization and Function
381-3	Signals Intelligence Operations
381-5	Signals Intelligence Activities
10-50	Medical Intelligence and Information Agency, Army Organization and Functions
381-14	Counterintelligence
381-15	Foreign Intelligence Collection Activities Program
381-47	Offensive Counterintelligence
381-8	Reconnaissance/Mapping Imagery Recorder Data
381-12	Subversion and Espionage
381-19	Support Operations
10-53	Army Intelligence and Security Command Organization and Functions

Source: DA PAM 310-1, *Consolidated Index of Army Publications and Blank Forms* (Washington, D.C.: Department of the Army, September 1, 1983).

The Foreign Technology Division's activities are governed by Air Force Systems Command Regulation 23-2, which is the subject of AFR 23-8 of June 4, 1979.[59] Similar Army Regulations (ARs) governing intelligence units and activities are listed in Table 13-3.

The most detailed regulations and directives are those issued by the intelligence units themselves. These directives seek to implement the broader DOD and military service Directives by adopting the guidelines, restrictions, and procedures mandated by those broader Directives and by specifying the internal structure and organization of the unit and the functions of the subunits.

Thus, INSCOM (Intelligence and Security Command) Regulation 10-2, "Organization and Functions, UNITED STATES ARMY INTELLIGENCE AND SECURITY COMMAND," of April 1, 1982 is 131 pages and enumerates the functions of each of the Deputy Chiefs of Staff and their division, branches, and offices that make up the organization.[60] Likewise, the Air Force Technical Application Center (AFTAC) publications index lists hundreds of regulations covering administrative practices, organization and mission, personnel operations, equipment maintenance, R&D, security, and supply.[61] Among the regulations are R55-3, "Aerial Sampling Operations," and R55-22, "Vela Satellite Data Collection, Analysis and Reporting Instruction."[62] Similarly, the DIA Index of Administrative Publications covers thirty-eight categories in thirty-four pages that list administrative, intelligence collection and production, and counterintelligence regulations.[63]

INDIVIDUALS, COMMITTEES, AND OFFICES

No matter how thorough the documents and directives described above or the plans described below are in stating the responsibilities and subjects for collection and analysis, they will for several reasons be insufficient as complete guides. First, every document will leave some room for interpretation. Second, attainment of the objectives specified will require cooperation and coordination on a regular basis. Hence, it is necessary to maintain a structure that facilitates such cooperation and coordination. Third, it is necessary to see that the members of the intelligence community are performing their activities within the restrictions imposed on them—that activities planned to attain specified objectives are acceptable to higher authority. Finally, changing circumstances will require an alteration in preconceived plans and priorities.

At the top of the individual, committee, and office control system is the President and those National Security Council (NSC) committees charged with the supervision of intelligence activities. Under the Carter administration there were two such committees: the Special Coordination Committee (SCC) and the Policy Review Committee (PRC). The SCC had jurisdiction over covert operations and counterintelligence matters, and two components of the PRC were concerned with intelligence. PRC–Intelligence (PRC-I) was concerned with the preparation of a consolidated national intelligence budget and resource allocation for the entire intelligence community. PRC–Space was concerned with space matters, possibly having some responsibility for space-based reconnaissance.[64]

The SCC and PRC were two more of a long line of NSC committees responsible for supervising intelligence activities. Until the Nixon administration such committees were exclusively concerned with covert operations. The first of these committees was established in 1948 by NSC 10/2 and known as the 10/2 Panel. In subsequent years, as it was re-created and its membership and functions altered or maintained, it was renamed the 10/5 Panel (NSC 10/5, October 23, 1951), the Operations Coordinating Board (NSC 5412, NSC 5412/1 of March 12-15, 1954), the 5412 Group or Special Group (NSC 5412/2 of December 28, 1955) and the 303 Committee (NSAM 303 of June 2, 1964).[65] In 1959 the Special Group became responsible for the approval of the sensitive air and naval reconnaissance missions conducted on the Soviet periphery.[66]

With the signing of National Security Decision Memorandum 40, "Responsibility for the Conduct, Supervision and Coordination of Covert Action Operations," on February 17, 1970, it was required that "the Director of Central

Intelligence shall obtain policy approval for all major and/or politically sensitive covert action operations through the 40 Committee."[67] The memorandum also called for an annual review of all covert action programs previously approved.[68]

In addition to the 40 Committee, the Nixon administration created a second committee for the supervision of intelligence activities in general known as the National Security Council Intelligence Committee (NSCIC). Creation of the NSCIC acknowledged that there were several issues in addition to covert operations and sensitive reconnaissance missions that required high-level attention. These issues included the need to make the intelligence community more responsive to policymakers, the establishment of intelligence priorities, and the allocation of resources.[69] Given the expense of technical collection systems and the competing claims for their time, a higher degree of coordination was required.

The basic two-committee system was continued by the Ford administration and, as already noted, the Carter administration. In Executive Order 11905 President Ford established the Committee on Foreign Intelligence (CFI) and the Operations Advisory Group (OAG). The CFI was chaired by the DCI with the Deputy Secretary of Defense for Intelligence and the Deputy Assistant to the President for National Security Affairs as members. The CFI was given control over budget preparation and resource allocation for the National Foreign Intelligence Program (NFIP) and was charged with establishing (1) policy priorities for collection and production of national intelligence and (2) policy for the management of the NFIP.[70] Supervision of covert operations was the function of the Operations Advisory Group, which consisted of the Assistant to the President for National Security Affairs, the Secretary of State, the Secretary of Defense, the Chairman of the Joint Chiefs of Staff (JCS), and the DCI, the Chairman being determined by the President.[71] Membership of the OAG represented an upgrading in the status of the covert operations supervision mechanism. Previously, membership on such committees involved officials at the Under Secretary and Deputy Secretary level.

This upgrading was maintained in the Carter Executive Order 12036 and extended to both committees. The SCC consisted of the Assistant to the President for National Security Affairs as Chairman, the Secretary of State, Secretary of Defense, the DCI, the Chairman of the JCS, the Attorney General, and the Director of the OMB. The PRC-I consisted of the same group except that the Vice President and Secretary of the Treasury were members instead of the Attorney General and Director of the OMB.[72]

Under the Reagan administration the Senior Interagency Group–Intelligence (SIG-I) is given the responsibility to advise and assist the NSC with respect to intelligence policy and intelligence matters. The SIG-I is chaired by the DCI, and its members include the Assistant to the President for National Security Affairs, the Deputy Secretary of State, the Deputy Secretary of Defense, and the Chairman of the JCS.

In addition to the statutory members, provision is made for attendance by departments and agencies with a direct interest in the activities under consideration, including cases involving sensitive intelligence collection activities. The functions of SIG-I require it to:

1. establish requirements and priorities for national foreign intelligence;
2. review such National Foreign Intelligence Program and budget proposals and other matters as are referred to it by the Director of Central Intelligence;
3. review proposals for sensitive foreign intelligence collection operations referred by the Director of Central Intelligence;
4. develop standards and doctrine for the counterintelligence activities of the United States; resolve interagency differences concerning the implementation of counterintelligence policy; and develop and monitor guidelines, consistent with applicable law and Executive Orders, for the maintenance of central counterintelligence records;
5. consider and approve any counterintelligence activity referred to the Group by the head of any organization in the intelligence community;
6. submit to the NSC an overall annual assessment of the relative threat to United States interests from intelligence and security services of foreign powers and from international terrorist activities; including an assessment of the effectiveness of United States counterintelligence activities;
7. conduct an annual review of ongoing sensitive national foreign intelligence collection operations and sensitive counterintelligence activities and report thereon to the NSC; and
8. carry out such additional coordination review and approval of intelligence activities as the President may direct.[73]

Subordinate to SIG-I are several Interagency Groups, including the Interagency Group for Counterintelligence (IG-CI) and the Interagency Group for Countermeasures (IG-CM). The IG-CI is chaired by the Director of the FBI and includes representatives of the Secretary of State, Secretary of Defense, DCI, Assistant to the President for National Security Affairs, Chairman of the JCS, and the NSA as well as representatives of any other intelligence community organization directly involved in the activities to be discussed. The IG-CI is responsible for developing policy and recommendations for counterintelligence and counter-hostile covert action activities.[74]

The IG-CM is chaired by the Deputy Secretary of Defense and is responsible for the development of countermeasures policy for dealing with technical intelligence threats as well for developing policy concerning protective security programs.[75] Subsequent to the initial establishment of NSC SIGs an SIG-Space was established.[76] As with PRC-Space, this committee might have some role in approval of space reconnaissance activities.

Responsibility for approval and supervision of covert operations in the Reagan administration lies with the National Security Planning Group—a group that consists of the President, the Secretaries of State and Defense, the DCI, the Assistant for National Security Affairs, and advisers Edwin Meese, Michael Deaver, and James Baker.[77] Inclusion of the President makes it the highest level committee ever employed for this purpose. It is this group that has been directly supervising and approving funding for U.S. covert action operations in Nicaragua.[78]

Responsibility for management of the intelligence community emanates in two different but not totally distinct directions from the President and the NSC. One direction is toward the DCI, the other toward the Secretary of Defense.

The DCI is the statutory head of the intelligence community. Executive Order 12333 instructs him to:

1. act as the primary adviser to the President and the NSC on national foreign intelligence;
2. develop such objectives and guidance for the Intelligence Community as will enhance capabilities for responding to expected future needs for national foreign intelligence;
3. promote the development and maintenance of services of common concern by designated intelligence organizations on behalf of the Intelligence Community;
4. ensure implementation of special activities;
5. . . . coordinate foreign intelligence and counterintelligence relationships between agencies of the Intelligence Community and the intelligence or internal security services of foreign governments;
6. ensure the establishment by the Intelligence Community of common security and access standards for managing and handling foreign intelligence systems, information, and products;
7. ensure that programs are developed which protect intelligence sources, methods, and analytical procedures;
8. establish uniform criteria for the determination of relative priorities for the transmission of critical national foreign intelligence, and advise the Secretary of Defense concerning the communications requirements of the Intelligence Community for the transmission of such intelligence;
9. establish appropriate staffs, committees, or other advisory groups to assist in the execution of the Director's responsibilities;
10. have full responsibility for production and dissemination of national foreign intelligence, and authority to levy analytical tasks on departmental intelligence production organizations, in consultation with those organizations' policymakers;
11. ensure the timely exploitation and dissemination of data gathered by national foreign intelligence collection means;
12. establish mechanisms which translate national foreign intelligence objectives and priorities approved by the NSC into specific guidance for the Intelligence Community, resolve conflicts in tasking priority . . . and

provide for the development of plans and arrangements for transfer of required collection tasking authority to the Secretary of Defense when directed by the President;

13. develop, with the advice of the program managers and departments and agencies concerned, the consolidated National Foreign Intelligence Program budget;

14. monitor National Foreign Intelligence Program implementation, and, as necessary, conduct program and performance audits and evaluations; and

15. together with the Secretary of Defense, ensure that there is no unnecessary overlap between national foreign intelligence programs and Department of Defense intelligence programs consistent with the requirement to develop competitive analysis, and provide to and obtain from the Secretary of Defense all information necessary for this purpose.[79]

The responsibilities of the Director as stated in Executive Order 12333, previous Executive Orders, and the National Security Act of 1947 has not been matched by the power to fulfill these responsibilities. As Richard Helms noted in 1969, while the DCI was theoretically responsible for 100 percent of U.S. intelligence activities, he controlled less than 15 percent of the intelligence community's assets while almost 85 percent was controlled by the Secretary of Defense and JCS.[80] And, until the signing of PD-17 in the Carter administration, the DCI had neither budgetary nor day-to-day management control. Management control of the National Reconnaissance Office (NRO) and NSA remained with the Secretary of Defense. The DCI did receive full and exclusive authority to approve the NFIP budget—which includes the Department of Defense portion that encompasses the General Defense Intelligence Program, Air Force Special Reconnaissance Activities, Navy Special Reconnaissance Activities, the Consolidated Cryptographic Plan, and the Defense Foreign Counterintelligence Program.[81] As discussed in greater detail in Chapter 16, the DCI's role and attempts to enhance his power has been a source of major conflict throughout the last thirty years.

Four organizations established to help the DCI fulfill his responsibilities are the Intelligence Community Staff (ICS), the National Intelligence Council, the National Foreign Intelligence Council (NFIC), and the National Foreign Intelligence Board (NFIB). The present ICS is the descendant of the National Intelligence Programs Evaluation Staff created in 1963 as well as the more recent Resource Management Staff.[82] The ICS is the principal support element of the DCI on matters relating to the NFIP budget prior to its presentation to the President, for its presentation to Congress, and for reprogramming NFIP funds and monitoring the implementation of the programs.[83]

As part of its review function, the ICS recently set up a Community Counterintelligence Staff drawn from the FBI, CIA, and Department of Defense to make regular overall assessments of intelligence threats and U.S. countermeasures.[84] It has also reviewed technical collection programs to evaluate their efficiency and provide data for resource allocation decisions. Thus it has conducted studies to evaluate the utility of photo reconnaissance signals and other intelligence collection systems in producing high-level intelligence.

The ICS also took over some of the collection tasking work performed in the Carter administration by the National Intelligence Tasking Center (NITC) via its Collection Tasking Staff.[85] The present organization of the ICS is shown as Figure 13-1. In addition to providing secretariat staff for various community boards and committees and dealing with budget and program issues, it also serves as home for the support elements for eight NFIB committees.

The National Intelligence Council is the DCI's principal means of producing National Intelligence Estimates (NIEs), Special National Intelligence Estimates (SNIEs), and Interagency Intelligence Memorandums (IIMs). The Council consists of a Chairman, seventeen National Intelligence Officers responsible for specific geographic or substantive areas (e.g., Warning, Soviet Union, Strategic Programs, Europe, Latin America, East Asia), and an Analytical Group consisting of approximately fifteen analysts.[86]

The NIOs are specifically tasked with

1. becoming knowledgeable of what substantive intelligence questions policymakers want addressed;
2. drawing up the concept papers and terms of reference for the NIEs;
3. participating in the drafting and draft review of the NIEs;
4. chairing coordination sessions and making judgments on substantive questions in debate; and
5. ensuring that the final texts accurately reflect the substantive judgments of the DCI.[87]

While the ICS and National Intelligence Council are subordinate to the DCI, the NFIB and NFIC provide "advice and counsel" to the DCI and are his principal means of coordinating intelligence community activities and attaining consensus on major issues.

The NFIB is the successor to the United States Intelligence Board (USIB), which was abolished on February 18, 1976. The USIB was formed in 1958 by the merger of the Intelligence Advisory Committee and the Communications Intelligence Board. The DCI serves as Chairman and members include the Directors of the NRO, NSA, and Bureau of Intelligence and Research (INR) and representatives for the FBI, Department of Energy, and Treasury Department as well as the Deputy Director of the CIA for the CIA. The Assistant Chiefs of Staff for Intelligence of each military service sit as observers.[88]

Working through thirteen committees, the NFIB

lists the targets for American intelligence and the priority attached to each one, coordinates within the intelligence community the estimates of future events and enemy strengths, controls the classification and security systems for most of the U.S. government, directs research on the various fields of

Figure 13–1.   Intelligence Community Staff.

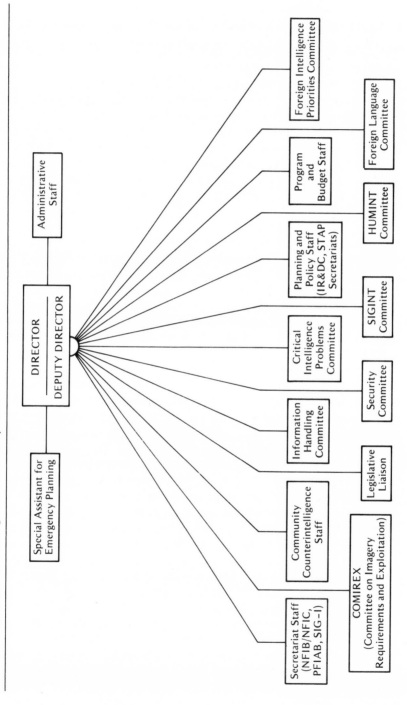

technical intelligence, and decides what classified information will be passed on to foreign friends and allies.[89]

The committees also serve as a means of informing the members of the intelligence community on particular matters (e.g., weapons and space systems) and providing support to agencies outside the intelligence community.

The present committees are the SIGINT Committee, the Technology Transfer Intelligence Committee, Economic Intelligence Committee, Security Committee, Human Resources Committee, Critical Intelligence Problems Committee, Scientific and Technical Intelligence Committee, Intelligence Information Handling Committee, Joint Atomic Energy Intelligence Committee, the Weapons and Space Systems Intelligence Committee, the Foreign Language Training Committee, the Foreign Intelligence Priorities Committee, and the Committee on Imagery Requirements and Exploitation.[90] Previous committees that have been abolished or absorbed include the Technical Surveillance Countermeasures Committee, the Watch Committee, and the Committee on Exchanges.[91]

The SIGINT Committee was formed in 1962 by the merger of the COMINT and ELINT Committees. It reviews and validates all proposed requirements before they are levied on the NSA.[92] The Technology Transfer Intelligence Committee (TTIC) was created in 1981 to deal with what was perceived to be a growing hemorrhage of critical technology to the Soviet Union. The TTIC draws on scientific and technical analysts through the military technical intelligence centers and elsewhere in the intelligence community. The TTIC also ensures that intelligence information collected on technology transfer is consistent with the DCI's priorities and guidance and meets the needs of community production organizations. The TTIC has two subcommittees. The Subcommittee on Exchanges, which used to be the Committee on Exchanges until the formation of the TTIC, advises U.S. government departments and agencies on technology transfer and foreign intelligence involved in exchange programs and commercial transactions with nationals from designated foreign countries. The Subcommittee on Export Control provides foreign intelligence support on export control issues to various U.S. government agencies.[93]

The Economic Intelligence Committee was established in 1948 as a subsidiary of the Intelligence Advisory Committee and has continued as a subsidiary of the USIB and NFIB. The Subcommittee on Requirements and Coordination of the EIC produces the Economic Alert List (EAL) which highlights the current economic information needs of all agencies participating in the Combined Economic Reporting Program (CERP).[94] The Security Committee oversees the establishment of security procedures concerning personnel, facilities, documents, dissemination, the release of intelligence to foreign governments, and intelligence stored or processed by computers.[95]

The Human Resources Committee was first proposed in 1973 by DIA Director Lt. General Donald V. Bennett to coordinate various human source collection programs, both overt and clandestine. It was established (as the Human Sources Committee) over opposition from the Director of the CIA. In 1974 it was accorded permanent status.[96]

The Joint Atomic Energy Intelligence Committee was created to "foster, develop and maintain a coordinated community approach to the problems in the field of atomic energy intelligence, to promote interagency liaison, and to give added impetus and community support to the efforts of individual agencies."[97]

The Critical Intelligence Problems Committee was created in 1958 — as the Critical Collection Problems Committee (CCPC) — to examine, as its name suggests, particularly difficult collection problems regardless of the technique involved. Thus, in 1971 one subject considered by the CCPC was narcotics intelligence.[98]

According to a DCID of April 6, 1983, the Committee is to identify:

1. the specific intelligence requirements and shortfalls associated with the critical intelligence problem under review;
2. current and programmed collection, processing, and production resources directed against the critical intelligence problem;
3. options for adjustments in collection, processing, and production efforts which could be accomplished within existing resources, and the associated impact such adjustments would have on the Intelligence Community's ability to respond to other priority intelligence needs; and
4. recommendations for new initiatives which could increase collection, processing, and production efforts against the critical intelligence problem, noting which options would require reprogramming of supplemental funding actions.[99]

The Scientific and Technical Intelligence Committee serves as the supervisory committee over all civilian and military scientific and technical intelligence production as well as a means of coordinating such production and the necessary acquisition. The Intelligence Information Handling Committee is responsible for all aspects of information handling — supervising research and development of information-handling systems, developing rules and procedures for the exchange of information between agencies, and establishing education and training programs in information science.[100]

The Weapons and Space System Intelligence Committee was created, as the Guided Missile Intelligence Committee, in 1956. In addition to producing analyses of the technical characteristics of Soviet and other foreign missile systems it assigns designators and codenames for such systems.[101] It also serves as the means for disseminating intelligence to the rest of the intelligence community on weapons and space systems and promoting liaison among intelligence units on weapons and space system matters. The Committee on Imagery Requirements and Exploitation (COMIREX) was created in 1964 succeeding the Committee on Overhead Reconnaissance (COMOR) as the USIB committee responsible for approving reconnaissance targets and priorities. COMIREX also has responsibility for the distribution of imagery obtained from overhead reconnaissance programs.[102]

A Reagan administration creation is the NFIC. The Council evolved out of the NFIB and deals with priorities and budgets. It focuses on management issues while the NFIB concentrates on analytical and substantive issues. As with the NFIB, the DCI is designated Chairman, the Deputy DCI being Vice Chairman and CIA representative. Membership includes those agencies represented on the NFIB as well as the intelligence chiefs of the military services and senior representatives of the Secretary of Defense, the Attorney General, the Secretary of Commerce, and the Assistant to the President for National Security Affairs.

Another recently created council that is outside the NFIB structure is the Intelligence Producers Council (IPC) created by a DCID on March 30, 1983. In addition to the Chairman of the council, its members include senior representatives of the CIA, DIA, INR, and NSA, with senior representatives of the military intelligence services attending, on some occasions, as observers. The functions of the IPC include monitoring the intelligence producer's needs for intelligence information and participating in assessments and evaluations of present and proposed intelligence community collection and processing systems and activities as well as identifying means to improve intelligence production programs.[103]

The Secretary of Defense exerts control over intelligence matters through several channels: two executive committees, two Undersecretaries and the JCS.

The executive committees responsible to the Secretary are both concerned with reconnaissance matters. The National Reconnaissance Executive Committee (NREC) was created in 1965 to eliminate feuding between the Air Force and the CIA over control of the NRO. It is chaired by the DCI and also includes the Assistant to the President for National Security Affairs and a DOD representative. A second executive committee, probably called the National Executive Committee for Special Navy Activities, supervises sensitive undersea intelligence programs. As with the NREC, it is chaired by the DCI and reports to the Secretary of Defense.[104]

Subordinate to the Deputy Under Secretary of Defense for Policy (DUSD(P)) are several offices with the responsibility of establishing policies for and supervising intelligence activities. These include the Office of Intelligence and Space Policy, the Special Advisory Staff, and the Office of Counterintelligence and Investigative Programs.[105]

Particularly interesting is the Special Advisory Staff, the Director of which is

responsible for serving as the principal assistant to the DUSD (Policy) for all matters relating to the conduct of sensitive intelligence, intelligence-related and reconnaissance activities. In this regard, the Director, Special Advisory Staff will formulate policy positions which will strongly influence the deployment of U.S. reconnaissance assets, the movement of personnel in support of special operations, and the allocations of DOD fiscal and physical resources to operations within and outside DOD.[106]

Also subordinate to the DUSD(P) is the Defense Counterintelligence Board (DCIB) created by DOD Directive 5240.2 in December 1979 to advise on counterintelligence matters. The Board is chaired by the Director of Counterintelligence and Security Policy and has eight other members: the Assistant General Counsel (Intelligence, International, and Investigative Programs), the Inspector General for Defense Intelligence, and representatives of the DIA, the NSA, the INSCOM, the Defense Investigative Service, the Air Force Office of Special Investigations, and the Naval Investigative Service.[107]

Subordinate to the Undersecretary for Research, Development, and Engineering is a Deputy Secretary for C^3I with an Assistant Deputy Undersecretary for Intelligence. In turn, the Assistant Deputy Under Secretary is responsible to the Director of Intelligence Resources, the Director, National Intelligence Systems, and the Director, Tactical Intelligence Systems.[108]

The Deputy Under Secretary for C^3I also serves as the Chairman of the National Communications Security Committee (NCSC). The NCSC was established by a Presidential Directive in October 1952, at which time it was designated the United States Communications Security Board (USCSB). With the approval of the National Communications Security Directive of June 1979, the USCSB was renamed the National Communications Security Committee with a representative of the Secretary of Defense as Chairman and composed of representatives designated by State, Treasury, the Attorney General, the Secretary of Transportation, the Secretary of Energy, the Secretaries of the Army, Navy, and Air Force, the DCI, and the Director of the NSA. The Directive further states that representatives of Commerce, the JCS, the General Services Administration, the Federal Communications Commission, the Manager of the National Communications System, the Defense Communications Agency, the DIA, the Defense Logistics Agency, and the Federal Emergency Management Agency may participate as observers in all aspects of the Committee's work.[109]

The Committee was made responsible for developing for approval by the Secretary of Defense broad communications security objectives, policies, and implementation procedures; providing guidance and assistance to the departments and agencies of the federal government in their communications security activities; conducting an annual review of the status and objectives of the communications security activities of the departments and agencies; and making recommendations concerning those activities to the Secretary of Defense.[110]

Under the authority of the JCS, and ultimately the Secretary of Defense, management and control of some intelligence activities is conducted through the JCS as well as the Director of the DIA (DDIA). Within the J-3 (Operations) section of the JCS is a Reconnaissance, Space, Electronic Warfare and C^3CM Directorate with a Reconnaissance Operations Division as well as a Reconnaissance

Plans and Programs Division. The functions of the Reconnaissance Operations Division include performing flight—following functions on reconnaissance missions to ensure that all incidents or significant activities are "promptly brought to the attention of appropriate authorities"—as well as providing a visual display of all current peacetime military reconnaissance missions for the JCS and National Command Authorities.[111]

As part of its responsibilities, the Division runs the Joint Reconnaissance Center (JRC), set up in 1959 after an American RB-47 aircraft was shot down in the Baltic in June of that year.[112] The JRC keeps watch over sensitive airborne (e.g., U-2 and SR-71) and ship-based reconnaissance missions.[113] The JRC contains representatives from the DIA, the NSA, the State Department, the CIA, the OSD, and the four services.[114]

The Reconnaissance, Plans, and Programs Division is responsible for reviewing, evaluating, and submitting for approval to the JCS the air and sea reconnaissance plans, programs, and schedules originated by the commanders of the unified and specified commands, the military services, and other government agencies.[115]

JCS management responsibilities are also fulfilled by the DDIA. In addition to the management role exercised through the DIA's internal organization, the DDIA also chairs the Military Intelligence Board. The additional Board membership includes the Assistant Chief of Staff for Intelligence, Army; the Director of Naval Intelligence; the Assistant Chief of Staff, Intelligence, Air Force; and the Director of Intelligence, Marine Corps. The Board serves to provide a forum for the defense intelligence community to discuss coordination and cooperation in a variety of areas.

Within the individual services, most management responsibility is exercised by the previously discussed offices of the Assistant Chief of Staff (or Naval Operations) for Intelligence. The Navy does maintain a two-man (one military officer, one civilian assistant) Naval Reconnaissance Center. The Center provides information and guidance to Fleet Commanders with regard to the conduct of reconnaissance missions in accordance with JCS guidance as well as participating in the planning of reconnaissance and surveillance operations "in satisfaction of Navy and National requirements." Through liaison with the JRC, it monitors on a daily basis worldwide reconnaissance activity.[116]

Subordinate to the Under Secretary of the Air Force is the Defense Support Project Office (DSPO), which is responsible for providing central management for the Defense Reconnaissance Support Program (DRSP)—a program directed at providing space reconnaissance data in support of operational military forces. Subordinate to the Director and Deputy Director of the DSPO is the DSPO Staff Director, who supervises a small staff of Army, Navy, and Air Force personnel divided into offices for Program Management, Operations and Plans, and Program Control.[117]

Subordinate to the Air Force's Deputy Chief of Staff for Plans and Operations is the Special Projects Office (not to be confused with the NRO subsidiary of the same name), divided into Test, Tactical, Strategic, and Administration Branches. The office's responsibilities include monitoring and validating requirements for classified programs, presumably including reconnaissance programs.[118]

Finally, the Army Space Program Office, subordinate to the Army Material Development and Readiness Command (DARCOM), might be the Army point of contact to the TENCAP (Tactical Exploitation of National Capabilities) program (discussed below).[119]

Outside the intelligence community per se are two presidential advisory committees: the President's Foreign Intelligence Advisory Board (PFIAB) and the Intelligence Oversight Board (IOB). The PFIAB was originally known as the President's Board of Consultants on Foreign Intelligence Activities when established in the Eisenhower administration. Its designation as the PFIAB came during the Kennedy administration. In May 1977 President Carter abolished it, but it has been reinstituted by President Reagan. The Board has the authority to review the performance of all agencies in regard to intelligence collection, analysis, and execution. It has a full-time staff and consultants to conduct special inquiries. The IOB is a three-member committee, the function of which is to ensure the "legality and propriety" of intelligence activities.[120]

PROGRAMS, PLANS, AND REQUIREMENTS DOCUMENTS

In any given year there must be a specific allocation of resources (collection systems) to targets in order to produce the intelligence required by decision-makers and other government officials. Two programs govern the allocation of resources: the NFIP and the Tactical Intelligence and Related Activities (TIARA) program.

The NFIP encompasses all national foreign intelligence activity. One aspect of the NFIP is the Central Intelligence Agency Program. There are five DOD components to the NFIP: the Consolidated Cryptographic Program (CCP), the General Defense Intelligence Program (GDIP), Navy Special Reconnaissance Activities, Air Force Special Reconnaissance Activities, and the Defense Foreign Counterintelligence Program.[121]

The CCP is managed by the NSA and includes all SIGINT resources in the NFIP. The GDIP includes all non–SIGINT, nonreconnaissance programs. Specifically, the GDIP includes eight activities:

1. General military production
2. Imagery collection and processing
3. HUMINT

4. Nuclear monitoring
5. R&D and procurement
6. Field support
7. General support
8. Scientific and technical intelligence production

The Navy Special Reconnaissance Activities Program specifies the allocation of attack submarines (SSNs) and other craft for the performance of intelligence gathering in the Arctic and near (or in) Soviet territorial waters. The Air Force Special Reconnaissance Activites Program is also known as the National Reconnaissance Program, the program that dictates the activities of the NRO.

The TIARA program is composed of three programs: Tactical Intelligence, Reconnaissance, Surveillance, and Target Acquisition; the DRSP; and the Tactical Cryptologic Program (TCP).[122] The DRSP is a subset of the Military Space Program and to some extent involves use of national collection systems (e.g., the KH-11) to acquire tactical intelligence. Although no dedicated tactical space reconnaissance systems exist at present, the proposed Integrated Tactical Surveillance System (ITSS) would constitute such a system.

The number of individual programs that constitute a military service's portion of a TIARA may be quite large. Thus, the Navy's portion of TIARA consists of the following thirty-three programs: AN/SKR-7, Battle Group Passive Horizon System, Beartrap, Classic Wizard, Combat Direction Finding, Combat Underwater Exploitation System, Cryptologic Direct Support, Cryptologic Training, Defense Meteorological Satellite Program (DMSP), Fleet Intelligence Support Center (Western Pacific), Guardian Bear, ITSS, Intelligence Engineering, Intelligence Staff Support, Joint Tactical Fusion Program, Naval Intelligence Processing System, Naval Space Surveillance System, Ocean Surveillance Information System, Outboard, Over the Horizon Targeting, Photo Reconnaissance Squadrons–Tactical Air Reconnaissance Pod System, Prairie Wagon Augmentation, Rapidly Deployable Surveillance Systems (RDSS), Reserve Intelligence Program, Tactical Air Reconnaissance System (RF/A-18), Shore-Based Electronic Warfare Squadrons (VQ), Fixed Undersea Surveillance System (SOSUS), Surface Towed Array Surveillance System (SURTASS), Tactical Intelligence Support, Tactical Cryptologic Shore Support, Tactical Cryptologic Technical Development, Training, and TENCAP.[123]

Based on such national plans, plans are established at lower levels to specify allocations of resources to targets/activities and objectives. Thus, the Air Force recently established the Air Force Intelligence Plan with three subsidiary plans: the Signals Intelligence Baseline Plan, the Imagery Architecture Plan, and the Air Force Intelligence Communications Plan.[124]

Prior to allocation of resources to collection tasks, there needs to be (at least in theory) appropriate guidance telling intelligence officials which items or subjects are of greatest priority to their customers. Guidance documents are of varying levels of specificity, and several guidance documents might emerge from the same source. In the Ford administration the DCI alone had a Directive (a matrix of 120 countries against 83 topics, with numerical priorities assigned from one to seven for each country); Perspectives defining the major problems that policymakers would face over the next five years; Objectives detailing resource management, and Key Intelligence Questions (KIQs) identifying topics of particular interest to national policymakers.[125]

The KIQs were introduced by William Colby during his tenure as DCI. They were designed to get all of the intelligence agencies to respond to policymakers' needs rather than just to their own operational requirements.[126] They were also designed "to replace an enormous paper exercise called the requirements process with a simple set of general questions about the key problems we should concentrate on."[127]

As the process is described by Colby,

> once each KIQ was formulated, the various agencies discussed what each would do to answer the question. This was followed by a statement of the resources that each agency would apply, so that an initial judgment would be made as to whether too many or too few were involved in the resolution of each KIQ.[128]

In Fiscal Year 1975 there were sixty-nine KIQs covering military, political, and economic topics. KIQ 57 asked: "What are the principal objectives of the major economic powers (especially France, West Germany, Japan, the U.K., Italy, Canada and Brazil) in forthcoming multi-lateral trade (GATT) and financial negotiations (IMF)?" KIQ 59 asked: "What are the policies, negotiating positions and vulnerabilities of the major petroleum exporters with respect to the production and marketing of oil, and how are their policies affected by the prospects for development of non–OPEC energy sources?"[129]

The KIQs never apparently had the desired affect of directing the intelligence collection units toward collection in response to the concerns of national leaders. Thus, the Church Committee concluded that the "DIA and DDO invoked the KIQs to justify their operations and budgets, however they did not appear to be shaping the programs to meet KIQ objectives."[130]

Under the Carter and Reagan administrations the KIQs have been replaced by the NITs—National Intelligence Topics. These documents were issued by the NSC Policy Review Committee and were intended to "articulate National level policymakers' intelligence requirements which are reflective of current national policy."[131] Along with "U.S. Foreign Intelligence Requirements Categories and Priorities," a basic requirements document that is reissued annually and periodically updated, the National Intelligence Topics are intended to "provide all elements of the intelligence community with guidance for the conduct of collection, analysis, and production management activities."[132]

NOTES TO CHAPTER 13

1. Ronald Reagan, "United States Intelligence Activities," Executive Order 12333, *Federal Register* 46, no. 235 (December 5, 1981): 59941–54.
2. Gerald Ford, "United States Foreign Intelligence Activities," Executive Order 11905, *Weekly Compilation of Presidential Documents* 12, no. 8 (1976): 234–43.
3. Jimmy Carter, "United States Intelligence Activities," Executive Order 12036, *Federal Register* 43, no. 18 (January 24, 1978), pp. 3675–98.
4. Ronald Reagan, "National Security Information," Executive Order 12356, *Federal Register* 47, no. 66 (April 6, 1982), pp. 14874–84.
5. In some cases, the titles themselves are classified.
6. Lawrence J. Korb, "National Security Organization and Process in the Carter Administration," in Sam C. Sarkesian, ed., *Defense Policy and the Presidency: Carter's First Years* (Boulder, Colo.: Westview, 1979), pp. 111–39.
7. Judging from the fact that approximately four of the Directive's seven pages are deleted from the sanitized version available in the U.S. National Archives.
8. "National Security Council Document on Policy in Central America and Cuba," *New York Times*, April 7, 1983, p. 16; Raymond Bonner, "President Approved Policy of Preventing 'Cuba-Model States," *New York Times*, April 7, 1983, pp. 1, 16.
9. NSDD–19 is reference (a) of Department of Defense Instruction 5230.21 of March 15, 1982, "Protection of Classified National Security Council and Intelligence Information."
10. U.S. Congress, House Committee on Science and Technology, *National Space Policy* (Washington, D.C.: U.S. Government Printing Office, 1982), p. 13.
11. NSCID No. 1, "Basic Duties and Responsibilities," February 17, 1982, *Declassified Documents Reference Service* 1976–167G.
12. NSCID No. 2, "Coordination of Collection Activities Abroad," January 13, 1948, *Declassified Documents Reference System* 1976–165F.
13. NSCID No. 2, "Coordination of Overt Collection Activities," February 17, 1972, *Declassified Documents Reference System* 1976–253D.
14. NSCID No. 3, "Coordination of Intelligence Production," February 17, 1972, *Declassified Documents Reference System* 1976–253E.
15. Ibid.
16. NSCID No. 4, "National Intelligence Objectives," August 29, 1956, *Declassified Documents Reference System* 1976–252C.
17. U.S. Congress, House Permanent Select Committee on Intelligence, *Annual Report* (Washington, D.C.: U.S. Government Printing Office, 1978), p. 70.
18. NSCID No. 5, "U.S. Espionage and Counterintelligence Activities Abroad," February 17, 1972, *Declassified Documents Reference System* 1976–253F.

19. Department of Justice, *Report on Inquiry into CIA-Related Electronic Surveillance Activities* (Washington, D.C.: Department of Justice, 1976), p. 77.
20. Ibid., p. 78.
21. NSCID No. 7, "Domestic Exploitation," February 12, 1948, *Declassified Documents Reference System* 1976–166A.
22. U.S. Congress, House Permanent Select Committee on Intelligence, *Annual Report*, p. 71.
23. NSCID No. 8, "Photographic Interpretation," February 17, 1972, *Declassified Documents Reference System* 1976–253G.
24. Ibid.
25. NSCID No. 9, "Communications Intelligence," July 1, 1948, *Declassified Documents Reference System* 1976–166C; NSCID No. 6, "Communications Intelligence and Electronics Intelligence," September 15, 1952, *Declassified Documents Reference System* 1976–167D.
26. NSCID No. 10, "Collection of Foreign Scientific and Technological Data," January 18, 1948, *Declassified Documents Reference System* 1976–166D.
27. NSCID No. 11, "Security of Information on Intelligence Sources and Methods," January 6, 1950, *Declassified Documents Reference System* 1976–166E.
28. NSCID No. 12, "Avoidance of Publicity Concerning the Intelligence Agencies of the U.S. Government," January 6, 1950, *Declassified Documents Reference System* 1976–166F.
29. NSCID No. 15, "Coordination and Production of Foreign Economic Intelligence," June 13, 1951, *Declassified Documents Reference System* 1976–251E.
30. NSCID No. 16, "Foreign Language Publications," March 7, 1953, *Declassified Documents Reference System* 1976–252A.
31. Department of Justice, *Report on Inquiry into CIA-Related Electronic Surveillance Activities*, p. 91.
32. DCID 1/3, "Committees of the Director of Central Intelligence," May 18, 1976.
33. DCID 1/4, "Intelligence Information Handling Committee," May 18, 1976; U.S. Congress, House Permanent Select Committee on Intelligence, *Annual Report*, p. 70.
34. Enclosure 1 of DOD Instruction 5230.22, April 1, 1982, "Control of Dissemination of Intelligence Information."
35. Reference (d) to DOD Directive 1/11, "Security Committee," August 23, 1974, *Declassified Documents Reference System* 1980–133A; DCID 1/17, "Human Resources Committee," May 18, 1976.
36. DCID 1/11, "Security Committee," August 23, 1974, *Declassified Documents Reference System* 1980–133A; DCID 1/17, "Human Resources Committee," May 18, 1976.
37. DCID 1/13, "Coordination of the Collection and Exploitation of Imagery Intelligence," February 2, 1973, *Declassified Documents Reference System* 1980–132D.

38. U.S. Congress, House Permanent Select Committee on Intelligence, *Security Clearance Procedures in the Intelligence Agencies* (Washington, D.C.: U.S. Government Printing Office, 1979), pp. 25–29; U.S. Congress, House Permanent Select Committee on Intelligence, *Espionage Laws and Leaks* (Washington, D.C.: U.S. Government Printing Office, 1979), p. 276.

39. Working Group on Computer Security, *Computer and Telecommunications Policy* (Washington, D.C.: National Communications Security Committee, July 1981), p. 158.

40. DCID 2/1, "Coordination of Overt Collection Abroad," March 8, 1960, *Declassified Documents Reference System* 1980–131D.

41. U.S. Congress, House Permanent Select Committee on Intelligence, *Annual Report*, pp. 30, 32.

42. John Prados, *The Soviet Estimate: U.S. Intelligence Analysis and Russian Military Strength* (New York: Dial, 1982), pp. 306–307.

43. U.S. Congress, House Permanent Select Committee on Intelligence, *Annual Report*, pp. 35, 49; DCID 3/3, "Production of Atomic Energy Intelligence," April 23, 1965, *Declassified Documents Reference System* 1980–131G; DCID 3/4, "Production of Guided Missile and Astronautics Intelligence," April 23, 1965, *Declassified Documents Reference System* 1980–132G.

44. U.S. Congress, House Permanent Select Committee on Intelligence, *Annual Report*, p. 70.

45. Ibid., pp. 42, 70.

46. DCID 6/1, "SIGINT Committee," May 31, 1962, *Declassified Documents Reference System* 1980–131D.

47. U.S. Congress, House Permanent Select Committee on Intelligence, *Annual Report*, p. 71; DCID 7/1, "Domestic Exploitation of Non-Governmental Individuals Approaching Intelligence Agencies," October 1, 1953, *Declassified Documents Reference System* 1980–129D.

48. DCID 11/2, "Control of Dissemination and Use of Intelligence and Intelligence Information," November 15, 1954, *Declassified Documents Reference System* 1980–13A.

49. DCID 15/1, "Production and Coordination of Foreign Economic Intelligence," September 14, 1954, *Declassified Documents Reference System* 1980–129E.

50. U.S. Congress, House Permanent Select Committee on Intelligence, *Security Clearance Procedures*, p. 29.

51. U.S. Congress, House Permanent Select Committee on Intelligence, *Annual Report*, pp. 70, 72; Working Group on Computer Security, pp. 110, 157.

52. Working Group on Computer Security, p. 22.

53. DOD Directive 3310.1, "International Intelligence Agreements," October 22, 1982.

54. *DOD Directives System Quarterly Index*, March 31, 1983 (Washington, D.C.: DOD, 1983), pp. 24, 27, 51, 61, 63, 65.

55. Ibid., pp. 47, 48, 51, 52, 75.

56. DOD Directive 6420.1, "Armed Forces Medical Intelligence Center," December 9, 1982.
57. *AF Regulation 0-2* (Washington, D.C.: Department of the Air Force, May 25, 1983), pp. 27, 77-80.
58. Ibid., pp. 11-12.
59. AFSC Regulation 23-2, "Foreign Technology Division-Organization and Mission-Field," June 4, 1979.
60. Obtained under the Freedom of Information Act.
61. Air Force Technical Applications Center Regulation 0-2, "Numerical Index of Center Publications," May 4, 1983.
62. Ibid., p. 5.
63. DIA Regulation No. 0-2, "Index of DIA Administratives Publications," December 24, 1981.
64. Korb, "National Security Organization and Process in the Carter Administration."
65. Emanuel Adler, "Executive Command and Control in Foreign Policy: The CIA's Covert Activities," *Orbis* 23 (Fall 1979): 671-96.
66. U.S. Congress, Senate Select Committee to Study Governmental Operations with Respect to Intelligence Activities, *Foreign and Military Intelligence, Book I* (Washington, D.C.: U.S. Government Printing Office, 1976), p. 53.
67. National Security Decision Memorandum 40, "Responsibility for the Conduct, Supervision and Coordination of Covert Action Operations," *Declassified Documents Reference System* 1976-297A.
68. Ibid.
69. U.S. Congress, Senate Select Committee, *Foreign and Military Intelligence*, Book I, p. 57.
70. Gerald Ford, "United States Foreign Intelligence Activities."
71. Ibid.
72. Jimmy Carter, "United States Intelligence Activities."
73. NSDD-2, "National Security Council Structure," January 12, 1982.
74. U.S. Congress, *Report of the Senate Select Committee on Intelligence* (Washington, D.C.: U.S. Government Printing Office, 1983), p. 23.
75. Ibid.
76. "Washington Round-Up," *Aviation Week and Space Technology*, February 28, 1983, p. 10.
77. "National Security Council Document on Policy in Central America and Cuba," *New York Times*, April 7, 1983, p. 16; Raymond Bonner, "President Approved Policy."; Leslie Gelb, "Shift is Reported on C.I.A. Action," *New York Times*, June 11, 1984, pp. 1, 4.
78. Ibid.
79. Ronald Reagan, "United States Intelligence Activities."
80. Victor Marchetti and John Marks, *The CIA and the Cult of Intelligence* (New York: Dell, 1980 edition), p. 90.
81. Caspar Weinberger, *FY 1983 Report of Secretary of Defense Caspar Weinberger* (Washington, D.C.: U.S. Government Printing Office, 1982), p. III-88.

82. U.S. Congress, Senate Select Committee, *History of the Central Intelligence Agency* (Washington, D.C.: U.S. Government Printing Office, 1976), p. 84.

83. Central Intelligence Agency, *CIA Fact Book* (Washington, D.C.: CIA, 1979).

84. U.S. Congress, *Report of the Senate Select Committee on Intelligence*, p. 23.

85. U.S. Congress, House Committee on Foreign Affairs, *The Role of Intelligence in the Foreign Policy Process* (Washington, D.C.: U.S. Government Printing Office, 1980), p. 72.

86. Ibid., pp. 73, 135; Stephen J. Flanagan, "The Coordination of National Intelligence," in Duncan Clarke, ed., *Public Policy and Political Institutions. United States Defense and Foreign Policy: Policy Coordination and Integration* (Greenwich, Conn.: JAI, forthcoming).

87. Ibid., p. 230.

88. Ibid., p. 235.

89. Marchetti and Marks, *The CIA and the Cult of Intelligence*, p. 73.

90. Letter to the author from Larry Strawderman, CIA Information and Privacy Coordinator, October 22, 1982.

91. National Academy of Sciences, *Scientific Communication and National Security* (Washington, D.C.: National Academy Press, 1983), p. 72; DCID 1/5, "Terms of Reference, Watch Committee of the USIB," *Declassified Documents Reference System* 1976–20C; Cornelius Roosevelt, "Conversation with Mr. James O. Golden, Moscow Episode," October 19, 1971, *Declassified Documents Reference System* 1979–214C.

92. U.S. Congress, House Permanent Select Committee on Intelligence, *Annual Report*, p. 55.

93. National Academy of Sciences, *Scientific Communication and National Security*, pp. 141–42.

94. Konrad Ege, "CIA Targets African Economies," *Counter Spy* 6 (July–August 1982): 30–38.

95. DCID 1/11, "Security Committee."

96. William Corson, *The Armies of Ignorance* (New York: Dial, 1977).

97. DCID 3/3, "Production of Atomic Energy Intelligence."

98. Department of Justice, *Report on Inquiry into CIA-Related Electronic Surveillance Activities*, pp. 72–73.

99. DCID, "Critical Intelligence Problems Committee," April 6, 1983.

100. DCID 1/4, "Intelligence Information Handling Committee."

101. Prados, *The Soviet Estimate*, pp. 59–61; U.S. Congress, House Committee on Appropriations, *Department of Defense Appropriations for 1978, Part 2* (Washington, D.C.: U.S. Government Printing Office, 1977), p. 224.

102. U.S. Congress, Senate Select Committee, *Supplementary Detailed Staff Reports on Foreign and Military Intelligence, Book IV*, p. 75.

103. DCID, "The Intelligence Producers Council," March 30, 1983.

104. U.S. Congress, Senate Select Committee, *Supplementary Detailed Staff Reports, Book IV*, p. 75; U.S. Congress Senate Select Committee, *Foreign and Military Intelligence, Book I*, p. 335.

105. *Organizational Directory, Office of the Under Secretary of Defense (Policy)*, September 1982.

106. Senior Executive Service Vacancy Announcement No. SES 3–83.

107. U.S. Congress, Senate Select Committee on Intelligence, *HR 6588 The National Intelligence Act of 1980* (Washington, D.C.: U.S. Government Printing Office, 1980), p. 88; DOD Directive 5240.2, "Department of Defense Counterintelligence," December 18, 1979.

108. *Department of Defense Telephone Directory April 1983* (Washington, D.C.: U.S. Government Printing Office, 1983), p. 0–3.

109. National Security Agency, *NSA Transition Briefing Book* (Ft. Meade, Md.: NSA, 1981), Attachment 2.

110. Ibid.

111. Joint Chiefs of Staff, JCS Publication No. 4, *Organization and Functions of the Joint Chiefs of Staff* (Washington, D.C.: JCS, 1980), Section III–3.

112. U.S. Congress, Senate Select Committee, *Foreign and Military Intelligence, Book I*, p. 52.

113. U.S. Congress, House Committee on Armed Services, *Inquiry into the U.S.S. Pueblo and EC-121 Plane Incidents* (Washington, D.C.: U.S. Government Printing Office, 1969).

114. Ibid., pp. 1635–39.

115. Joint Chiefs of Staff, JCS Publication No. 4, *Organization and Functions of the Joint Chiefs of Staff*, Section III–3.

116. Officer Billet Description/Requisition, Head, Naval Reconnaissance Center.

117. "Defense Support Project Office (DSPO) Organization" (obtained under Freedom of Information Act).

118. "Functional Responsibilities–AF/XO–SP Special Projects Office," "AF/XO–SP Organization," (obtained under FOIA).

119. "Army Space Program Office Organization Chart" (obtained under Freedom of Information Act).

120. Judith Miller, "Intelligence Advisory and Oversight Units Named," *New York Times*, October 21, 1981.

121. Weinberger, *FY 1983 Report of Secretary of Defense*, p. III–88.

122. Ibid.

123. "Navy's Portion of TIARA consists of 23 Programs," *Aerospace Daily*, April 8, 1983, p. 231.

124. William E. Parson, "Improving Intelligence Communications Programming," *Signal*, January 1983, pp. 74–75.

125. Richard Betts, "American Strategic Intelligence: Politics, Priorities and Direction," in Robert L. Pfaltzgraff, Jr., Uri Ra'anan, and Warren Milberg, eds., *Intelligence Policy and National Security* (Hamden, Conn.: Archon, 1981).

126. Ibid.

127. William Colby with Peter Forbath, *Honorable Men: My Life in the CIA* (New York: Simon & Schuster, 1978), p. 361.

128. Ibid.

129.   Philip Agee and Henry Kissinger, "What Uncle Sam Wants to Know About You: The KIQ's," in Philip Agee and Louis Wolf, eds., *Dirty Work: The CIA in Western Europe* (Secaucus, N.J.: Lyle Stuart, 1978), pp. 111–26.

130.   U.S. Congress, Senate Select Committee, *Foreign and Military Intelligence, Book I*, p. 91.

131.   U.S. Congress, House Committee on Foreign Affairs, *The Role of Intelligence in the Foreign Policy Process*, p. 112.

132.   Flanagan, "The Coordination of National Intelligence."

14 MANAGING INTELLIGENCE COLLECTION

Management of the three different types of collection—imagery, SIGINT, and HUMINT—reflects the commonality and diversity of the operations and collection systems the intelligence community employs. Both imagery and SIGINT are collected by satellite systems; both may involve operations (such as overflights) that can end in an international incident. At the same time, SIGINT is collected by land stations, ships, and submarines—which are not employed, to a significant extent, for the acquisition of imagery. And, of course, human collection is a quite different method of collection.

MANAGING SATELLITE RECONNAISSANCE

Basic decisions concerning satellite reconnaissance matters are the responsibility of the National Foreign Intelligence Board, two of its committees, and the National Reconnaissance Executive Committee (NREC). While the Board and its committees are concerned with collection priorities and their implementation, the NREC focuses on a different set of issues.

As notes in Chapter 13, it is chaired by the Director of Central Intelligence (DCI) and reports to the Secretary of Defense. If the DCI objects to a decision made by the Secretary, he may appeal directly to the President. When initially formed, the Committee consisted of the President's Science Adviser and an Assistant Secretary of Defense in addition to the DCI. Subsequently, the Assistant to the President for National Security Affairs replaced the Science Adviser.[1] The position of the Department of Defense (DOD) representative has changed as the upper echelons of the Department have been reorganized. In the Reagan administration the DOD representative is probably the Assistant Deputy Under Secretary of Defense (Intelligence).

According to one account, formation of the NREC was the product of several years of conflict between the Air Force and DCI John McCone. The original agreement concerning the National Reconnaissance Office (NRO) gave the Air Force responsibility for the launchers, bases, and recovery capability for reconnaissance systems but gave the Central Intelligence Agency responsibility for R&D as well as contracting and security. The arrangement, as the Air Force saw it, left the CIA in control of the overhead reconnaissance program.[2] Others have focused on an initial rivalry over reconnaissance systems, with Air Force attempts to unilaterally conduct the program producing a CIA counterattack.[3]

Air Force sensitivity was heightened by two other developments unrelated to intelligence. One was the introduction of the ICBM and the consequent downgrading of the Air Force's main weapon system, the strategic bomber. Second was the creation in 1958 of the civilian-controlled National Aeronautics and Space Administration (NASA) which denied the Air Force control of the entire U.S. aerospace effort. The Air Force and Strategic Air Command thus viewed any CIA control of reconnaissance R&D to be another intrusion on Air Force turf.[4]

More was at stake, however, than the Air Force's collective ego. Control of R&D meant control of the type of systems that would be produced. The Air Force and the military in general had a greater interest in tactical intelligence and detailed technical intelligence than did the CIA, the main concern of which was national intelligence. The Air Force, for example, would be far more interested in obtaining every detail possible concerning Soviet aircraft—details that would aid them in specifying or estimating the aircraft's performance and in designing countermeasures. Such requirements place a higher value on high-resolution photography than do requirements concerned primarily with the number of such aircraft.

A high-resolution system would also facilitate the provision of tactical intelligence, enhancing U.S. capability to determine the exact changes in the Warsaw Pact order of battle by providing more detailed imagery.

In 1965 an agreement was reached creating the NREC, chaired by the DCI but reporting to the Secretary of Defense, who had final authority subject only to the DCI's appeal to the President.[5] The Committee was given responsibility over NRO's budget, structure, and R&D.[6]

The Committee has therefore been at the center of several important decisions in recent years. In 1975 the Committee, with the concurrence of DCI William Colby, approved development and deployment of a SIGINT satellite codenamed ARGUS.[7] ARGUS was an intended follow-on to the Rhyolite satellite with an antenna twice the size of the Rhyolite antenna and an enhanced telemetry collection capability.[8] Secretary of Defense James Schlesinger ruled the system unnecessary, apparently preferring to maintain a peak level of photo reconnaissance coverage.[9] Colby appealed to President Ford, who ordered the National Security Council (NSC) to examine the issue. On the basis of that review, Ford sided with Colby. However, funding for the satellite was deleted by the congressional supervisory committee.[10]

During the Carter administration it was decided, on the basis of the KH-11's successful record, to end the film-return program in favor of total dependence on real-time satellites.[11] In that case, CIA Director Stansfield Turner and Secretary of Defense Harold Brown apparently agreed on the desirability of such a course of action, although there was probably significant conflict within the reconnaissance bureaucracy.

The choice by the NREC and Secretary of Defense of one satellite system over another obviously has significant implications with regard to the type of targets on which information is acquired and the detail of the information. Clearly, choice of a SIGINT system over a photo reconnaissance or a high-resolution over lower resolution area surveillance system automatically constrains coverage in one direction and enhances it in another.

But even without such sharp choices, there will be a wide range of options—a large number of targets from which to choose. And even as the United States moves away from a variety of imaging systems to sole reliance on the KH-11 and its successors (with resolution equivalent to today's close-look satellite), which will enhance coverage capability, significant choices among possible targets will still need to be made.

Overall responsibility for approval of intelligence collection requirements is the responsibility of the National Foreign Intelligence Board (NFIB), giving it ultimate jurisdiction over selection of targets for imagery and SIGINT systems.

Thus, in 1970 the Air Force requested permission from the Board—then the United States Intelligence Board (USIB)—to alter the targeting of a "very sophisticated satellite." This apparently involved maneuvering the satellite, and the Board, citing the great cost of the satellite and the possibility that maneuvering might lead to a malfunction, denied its request.[12] Ten years later, a KH-11 that was maneuvered to increase coverage of the Iran–Iraq war malfunctioned. Maneuvering of the satellite also led to a decrease in its lifetime to 550 days from the more usual 750.[13]

The actual job of translating general imagery collection priorities into the targeting of systems against installations is the responsibility of the NFIB's Committee on Imagery Requirements and Exploitation (COMIREX), particularly its Imagery Collection Requirements Subcommittee.[14] As presently constituted, the membership of COMIREX consists of representatives from all NFIB agencies plus the Assistant Chief of Staff for Intelligence, Army; the Director of Naval Intelligence; and the Assistant Chief of Staff, Intelligence, Air Force.[15]

COMIREX is faced with three basic questions with regard to the establishment of targets and priorities:

1. What installations/areas are to be subject to photo coverage?
2. What systems will be targeted on specific installations/areas?
3. What will be the frequency of coverage?

As the United States moves to a single type of satellite imaging system, COMIREX's decision problem will be eased in regard to question 2. However, there will still be significant areas of contention among consumers over priorities and targeting. Short of a U.S. decision to increase greatly the number of on-orbit KH-11s, at a cost of several billion dollars, only a fraction of the areas/installations about which information is desired can be targeted.

Deployment of such a system has been proposed in the past and still is considered desirable by some in the Department of Defense. In the aftermath of the 1967 Arab-Israeli war, studies were conducted on the type of imagery desired during such an event—studies that eventually produced the KH-11 concept. One possibility considered, labeled the KH-X, called for enough real-time satellites to give worldwide coverage in a single day. Besides the cost of such a system, another drawback was noted: The product of such a configuration would be immense and require a massive increase in the number of photo interpreters and analysts to process it. Otherwise, the quantity of output would swamp the National Photographic Interpretation Center (NPIC), CIA, and DIA.[16]

The main conflict over satellite imagery targeting and priorities is between those consumers with national intelligence responsibilities (i.e., the CIA) and the military, which is more concerned with tactical intelligence. The military, with its mission of being able to fight a war, wants as much warning as possible as well as the most up-to-date and detailed coverage concerning Warsaw Pact capabilities. Day-to-day coverage is thus seen as valuable on the tactical level—in revealing movements of troops or weapons and changes in capabilities; at the national level, in the absence of a crisis, it is of little interest. COMIREX serves as a means of prioritizing claims of the CIA, DIA, military services, and other consumers, attempting to distribute a strictly limited resource in such a way as to at least minimally satisfy the legitimate requests of several competitive bureaucracies.

COMIREX was established on July 1, 1967 by Director of Central Intelligence Directive 1/13 as the successor to the Committee on Overhead Reconnaissance (COMOR).[17] The Committee is staffed by personnel from the CIA and DIA. As its name indicates, COMIREX's responsibilities, unlike COMOR's, extended to the exploitation—the processing and distribution—of the imagery as well as its collection.

COMOR's responsibilities included coordination of collection requirements for the development and operation of all overhead imaging satellites. As these programs grew, the number of photographs substantially increased, resulting in serious duplication of imagery exploitation activities. One proposed and implemented solution was the replacement of COMOR by COMIREX.[18]

COMIREX has an additional responsibility: It administers a complex accounting system designed to evaluate how well, in technical terms, specific missions fulfill the various national and departmental requirements.[19]

Targeting of SIGINT satellites — Rhyolite, Chalet, and so forth — is the responsibility of the SIGINT Committee, discussed in the next section.

MANAGING SIGINT

Management of the United States Signal Intelligence System (USSS) is vested in the Director of the NSA by National Security Council Intelligence Directive (NSCID) No. 6. The most recent available version of NSCID No. 6, that of February 17, 1972, was still "in force" as of early 1981.[20] In addition to defining the components of SIGINT — COMINT (communications intelligence) and ELINT (electronics intelligence) — the Directive states:

> The Secretary of Defense is designated as Executive Agent of the Government for the conduct of SIGINT activities in accordance with the provisions of this directive and for the direction, supervision, funding, maintenance and operation of the National Security Agency. The Director of the National Security Agency shall report to the Secretary of Defense and shall be the principal SIGINT adviser to the Secretary of Defense, the Director of Central Intelligence, and the Joint Chiefs of Staff. The Secretary of Defense may delegate in whole or part authority over the Director of the National Security Agency within the Office of Secretary of Defense. . . .
>
> It shall be the duty of the Director of the National Security Agency to provide for the SIGINT mission of the United States, to establish an effective unified organization and control of all SIGINT collection and processing activities of the United States, and to produce SIGINT in accordance with the objectives, requirements and priorities established by the Director of Central Intelligence Board. No other organization shall engage in SIGINT activities except as provided for in this directive.
>
> Except as provided in paragraphs 5 and 6 of this directive (re unique responsibilities of CIA and FBI) the Director of the National Security Agency shall exercise full control over all SIGINT collection and processing activities. . . . The Director of the National Security Agency is authorized to issue direct to any operating elements engaged in SIGINT operations such instructions and assignments as are required. All instructions issued by the Director under the authority provided in this paragraph shall be mandatory, subject only to appeal to the Secretary of Defense. . . .
>
> The Armed Forces and other departments and agencies often require timely and effective SIGINT. The Director of the National Security Agency shall

The intelligence components of individual departments and agencies may continue to conduct direct liaison with the National Security Agency in the interpretation and amplification of requirements and priorities within the framework of objectives, requirements and priorities established by the Director of Central Intelligence.[21]

As indicated in the extract above, although the Secretary of Defense is the executive agent and the Director of the NSA is the program manager, requirements and priorities are to be established by the SIGINT Committee of the NFIB. Much of the SIGINT Committee's work in this area is the responsibility of its SIGINT Requirements Validation and Evaluation Subcommittee.[22]

The SIGINT Committee is the successor to a series of predecessors. As of 1950, prior to the creation of the NSA, the work was divided between the Armed Forces Security Agency Council's Intelligence Requirements Committee (AFSAC/IRC) and the United States Communications Intelligence Board's Intelligence Committee (USCIB/IC). The AFSAC/IRC consisted of representatives from the Office of Naval Intelligence (ONI), Army Intelligence, Air Force Intelligence, and the Armed Forces Security Agency (AFSA) and was responsible primarily for targeting and setting priorities for military traffic intercepts. The USCIB/IC was primarily concerned with nonmilitary traffic.

Following the creation of the NSA, NSCID No. 9 of December 9, 1952 reconstituted the USCIB to operate under the Special Committee of the NSC for COMINT consisting of the Secretary of State, Secretary of Defense, and Attorney General and assisted by the DCI. In 1958, when the USCIB and Intelligence Advisory Committee were merged into the USIB, two committees were created: the COMINT Committee (by DCID 6/1 of October 21, 1958) and the ELINT Committee (by DCID 6/2 of October 21, 1958). In 1962 the SIGINT Committee was formed by DCID 6/1 of May 31, 1962 merging both committees.[23] The SIGINT Committee became responsible for both COMINT and ELINT requirements and priorities.

Thus, prior to the Middle East war in 1973, the USIB SIGINT Committee recommended that the Middle East be a priority target for intelligence collection if hostilities erupted. The NSA was asked to evaluate the intelligence collected and to determine appropriate targets. Upon the outbreak of war, the NSA implemented the SIGINT Committee's guidance. Later that week, the Committee discussed and approved the DIA's recommendation to change the primary target of one collector.[24]

A second NFIB committee that might on occasion have input on the subject of SIGINT requirements is the Critical Intelligence Problems Committee (CIPC). Thus, on January 31, 1972 the DCI requested the CIPC—then the Critical Collection Problems Committee (CCPC)—to conduct a review of intelligence efforts against narcotics. In October 1972 the CCPC report noted in a section entitled "SIGINT Information on Narcotics and Dangerous Drugs" that

1. No SIGINT resources are dedicated solely to the intercept of narcotics information. . . .
5. The effective use of SIGINT information in support of ongoing operations while at the same time protecting the source has been a problem.
6. Successful usage of the SIGINT product is largely contingent upon close collaboration between the SIGINT producers and the appropriate customers.

The CCPC therefore recommended that the "NSA, in conjunction with interested customers, particularly BNDD and Customs, make appropriate determination of what COMINT support is required on the narcotics problem and that the requisite priorities be established through the SIGINT Committee."[25]

During 1975 the Board approved a new National SIGINT Requirements System which requires the NFIB to initiate a formal community review and approval of each requirement before its validation and placement on the National SIGINT Requirements List (NSRL). The NSRL is today the basic guidance document for the NSA and specifies SIGINT targets according to well-defined priorities, including cross references to the DCI and other national requirements.[26] The system does not, however, prevent the Director of the NSA from determining which specific communications to monitor and which signals to intercept in fulfillment of requirements. Nor does it prevent the Secretaries of State and Defense or military commanders from directly tasking the NSA in a crisis, informing the DCI and SIGINT Committee afterward.[27]

The yearly statements of objectives, requirements, and priorities are stated in the Consolidated Cryptologic Program (CCP) and Tactical Cryptologic Program (TCP), as noted in the previous chapter. The majority of U.S. signals intelligence activities is funded through the CCP. The TCP "was established in 1979 to correct the problem of disparate requirements competing for limited available funding within the NFIP which resulted in inadequate treatment of Service tactical support needs."[28]

MANAGING SENSITIVE RECONNAISSANCE MISSIONS

Reconnaissance conducted by satellite is relatively nonintrusive, not requiring actual violation of the target nation's airspace. Further, with exception of the Soviet Union, no nation possesses the means for destroying U.S. reconnaissance satellites. And, short of war, the costs to the Soviet Union of interfering in an obvious way with such satellites is likely to be far greater than the potential benefits.

When airborne overflights or air and sea missions close to a nation's borders are involved, the potential for an international incident is much greater. The early U.S. aircraft reconnaissance missions directed at the Soviet Union involved this risk—approaching or penetrating the margins of Soviet and East European territory to collect a variety of intelligence, including the signatures and operating frequencies of air defense systems. When the U-2 program was approved, it was clear that a series of overflights over the Soviet Union, China, and other locations further heightened the risk of an international incident.

This risk was very apparent to President Eisenhower. At a meeting of the NSC on February 12, 1959 he expressed reservations concerning continuation of the program on an extensive basis, noting that nothing would make him request authority to declare war more quickly than a Soviet violation of U.S. airspace.[29] In a meeting of the NSC on February 8, 1960 he noted that if a U-2 were lost "when we are engaged in apparently sincere deliberations," it could be put on display in Moscow and ruin the President's effectiveness.[30]

Eisenhower's 1960 fears were certainly heightened by the loss of an NSA RB-47 aircraft in the Soviet Baltic region in June 1959 due to hostile action.[31] This may have been the second such incident.[32] In any case, the President's alarm was validated a few months later with the shooting down of Francis Gary Powers's U-2.

In subsequent years numerous other incidents occurred involving air and sea missions, some of which have been mentioned previously. In 1961, during the Cuban missile crisis, a U-2 was shot down during a flight over Cuba. In 1967 the Israeli Air Force bombed the U.S.S. Liberty while it was collecting signals intelligence in the midst of the Six Day War. In 1968 the U.S.S. Pueblo was seized by the North Koreans during a SIGINT mission off the North Korean coast, and in 1969 an EC-121 SIGINT plane was shot down by the North Koreans while it patrolled off the same coast.[33] The North Koreans have also attempted to shoot down overflying SR-71s.[34]

The U-2 incident of May 1960 resulted in an immediate seven-month moratorium on further flights.[35] Given the development of satellite reconnaissance capabilities, no further U-2 flights over the Soviet Union were required, eliminating one source of a potential incident. However, at almost the same time U-2 overflights were ending, the Holystone submarine reconnaissance program was beginning. As noted earlier, the operation produced several near confrontations—colliding with a Soviet ship fifteen to thirty-five miles from the entrance to the White Sea, beaching for two hours on the coast, and surfacing underneath a Soviet ship in the midst of a Soviet fleet naval exercise. That a major incident did not occur was possibly the result of deliberate Soviet restraint, since they were apparently aware of the program from the beginning.[36]

Whether or not the Holystone program is still ongoing, it is highly likely that several other Special Navy programs are involved in operations that involve some risk of conflict, whether they involve intelligence collection on the Soviet/War-saw Pact periphery or recovery of Soviet warheads, ships, or other material. Additionally, SR-71 and U-2 overflights continue over North Korea, Libya, Cuba, Nicaragua, and other areas under codenames such as SENIOR YEAR, OLIVE HARVEST, and SENIOR CROWN. There are also the Air Force Technical Application Center (AFTAC) aerial sampling operations. Further, RF-4C Phantoms and EC-130s stationed in West Germany collect a variety of overhead intelligence. Overflights of the Berlin Corridor by EC-130s are conducted under the codenames CREEK MISTY AND CREEK FLUSH.[37] Finally, the employment of destroyers off the Nicaraguan coast has reintroduced ship-based SIGINT collectors.

The U.S. system for management of these missions reflects their many considerations or aspects. Many of the missions are conducted in support of and proposed by the unified and specified commands. Others are clearly designed to provide national intelligence. In either case, these missions, as discussed, represent the possible cause of an international incident; thus, they require national-level approval.

As noted in Chapter 13, special Navy reconnaissance missions are the initial responsibility of the National Executive Committee for Special Navy Activities, chaired by the DCI and reporting to the Secretary of Defense. Missions originating from the Commanders in Chief of the unified commands go through a chain of supervisory offices and divisions beginning with those directly responsible to the Joint Chiefs of Staff (JCS). The Reconnaissance Plans and Programs Division of the Reconnaissance, Space, Electronic Warfare, C^3 CM Directorate of the J-3 (Operations) section of the JCS is responsible for

1. receiving, reviewing, evaluating and submitting for approval to the Joint Chief of Staff the reconnaissance plans, programs and schedules originated by the commanders of the unified and specified commands, the Services and other governmental agencies;
2. preparing planning guidance for the execution of reconnaissance operations of special significance or sensitivity; and
3. coordinating U.S. peacetime military reconnaissance and certain sensitive operations associated U.S. military support with the appropriate Services and/or the commanders of unified and specified commands, other U.S. agencies and allied organizations.[38]

After various area Commanders in Chief (CINCPAC, CINCEUR) have their regular meetings on reconnaissance missions in their area, the proposals are forwarded to the Reconnaissance Plans and Programs Division. Previously, this function was performed by the Joint Reconnaissance Center but was apparently removed in the aftermath of the Pueblo and EC-121 incidents. After an individual mission deployment has been coordinated and staffed, it receives a formal input from each of the agencies affected, either approving the proposed mission, suggesting a modification, or recommending cancellation.[39] The mission, if approved by the JCS, then goes to the Joint Reconnaissance Committee (JRC), an interagency group largely controlled by the JCS.[40]

Missions approved by the JRC are then placed in the Joint Reconnaissance Schedule (JRS), a document "always several inches thick and filled with hundreds of pages of highly technical data and maps."[41] The JRS includes the missions emanating from the commands and all SR-71 and U-2 missions.

The Reconnaissance Operations Division is responsible for performing flight-following functions and ensuring that "all incidents or significant activities are promptly brought to the attention of appropriate authorities."[42] It is also responsible for displaying on a current basis all peacetime military reconnaissance and selected sensitive operations in order to provide the National Command Authorities and JCS with a visual display of reconnaissance missions.

As part of its responsibilities, the division runs the JRC, set up in 1959 after the RB-47 incident in June of that year. The Center keeps watch over sensitive airborne and ship-based reconnaissance missions that emanate from the unified and specified commands or the JCS, providing a means by which the JCS and national authorities can supervise and control the missions as well as allowing authorized agencies "to assemble data, conduct analyses, evaluate critical situations, and initiate implementing actions."[43]

Sensitive missions, whether they initially come before the Special Navy Committee or the Joint Reconnaissance Committee, ultimately require higher level approval. After the RB-47 incident the Special Group assumed ultimate responsibility for approval of sensitive missions. The group's primary concern then was, and in its various subsequent incarnations is, "the political sensitivity of these missions—not their technical aspects or even their intelligence value. The committee is supposed to warn if a flight over or a cruise off a particular country is too dangerous to be carried out at a particular time."[44]

The above description applied specifically to the 40 Committee. Subsequently, the Operations Advisory Group and Special Coordination Committee were responsible for approval of sensitive missions. In a break with tradition, the Reagan administration committee with that responsibility, the Senior Interagency Group-Intelligence (SIG-I), is not the committee responsible for supervision of covert action operations.

MANAGING HUMAN COLLECTION

Managing human source collection involves managing the collection of information from foreign service officers, clandestine agents, and defectors as well as nongovernment individuals. These diverse sources are reflected in the management arrangements for human source collection.

The titles of NSCID No. 4 of February 4, 1972, "The Defector Program," and two DCIDs—4/1, "The Interagency Defector Committee," and 4/2, "Defector Program Abroad"[45]—suggest the importance of defectors to U.S. security. None of these documents is public, even in part, but they must seek to establish guidelines concerning methods of inducement and procedures for handling defectors. It is also necessary to coordinate the CIA, Air Force Intelligence Service (AFIS), and other agencies that participate in the defector program.

NSCID No. 5, "U.S. Espionage and Counterintelligence Abroad," of February 17, 1972 gives the DCI primary responsibility for coordination of clandestine collection activities. Paragraphs 2a and 2b authorize the DCI to

> establish the procedures necessary to achieve such direction and coordination, including the assessment of risk incident upon such operations as compared to the value of the activity, and to ensure that sensitive operations are reviewed pursuant to applicable directives [and to] coordinate all clandestine activities authorized herein and conducted outside the United States and its possessions, including liaison that concerns clandestine activities or that involves foreign clandestine services.[46]

At the NFIB committee level, these responsibilities belong to the Human Resources Committee. The Committee was first proposed in 1970 by General Donald Bennett, Director of the DIA, as a means of providing a national-level forum to coordinate both overt and clandestine human source collection programs. Immediate formation of such a committee was prevented by objections from the CIA's Directorate of Plans. In addition to the bureaucratic "territorial imperative," the Directorate also sought to minimize the number of individuals with access to information concerning clandestine sources. DCI Richard Helms established an ad hoc task force to study the problem of human source collection. After a year of study the task force recommended the establishment of a USIB committee on a one-year trial basis—a suggestion endorsed by the President's Foreign Intelligence Advisory Board (PFIAB) in a separate study. In June 1974 it attained permanent status as the Human Sources Committee and in 1975 its name was changed to the Human Resources Committee.[47]

The Committee's functions, specified by DCID 1/7 of May 18, 1976 are

1. to examine problems and consider possible improvements in collection by human resources and . . . provide recommendations to the Director of Central Intelligence. . . ;
2. to encourage collaboration and coordination among human resource collection agencies with emphasis on the allocation of effort and responsibility for the satisfaction of intelligence requirements susceptible to human resource collection and on the evaluation of end products;
3. to assist in the review and evaluate the effectiveness of human resource collection and reporting activities and to make recommendations to the

Director of Central Intelligence for improvements or modifications thereof; and

4. to recommend or sponsor research, experimentation and training in techniques, procedures and equipment to increase the effectiveness of human resource collection.[48]

The Committee, when established, was specifically not given responsibility for reviewing the operational details or internal management of the individual departments or agencies. Departments and agencies were authorized to withhold "sensitive" information from the Committee and report directly to the DCI.[49]

As of 1975 the Committee had "only just begun to expand community influence over human collection," issuing a general guidance document called the Current Intelligence Reporting List (CIRL). The military made some use of this document but the Directorate of Operations instructed CIA stations that the list was provided only for reference and did not constitute collection requirements for CIA operations.[50]

During 1977 the Committee provided the U.S. Ambassador in Iran, William Sullivan, with a short prioritized list of items of national intelligence interest. The list was developed by the Committee with advice of the National Intelligence Officer for the Near East and South Asia. The Chairman of the Human Resources Committee, in his cover letter, expressed his hope that the list would "be of some use . . . as a coordinated interagency expression of the most important information Washington needs."[51]

In partial fulfillment of function 3, the Committee has conducted communitywide assessments of human source reporting in individual countries. It has not defined a national system for establishing formal collection requirements for the agencies employing human sources.[52]

In addition to the Human Resources Committee, the Intelligence Community Staff has played a role in HUMINT Tasking. During the 1970s it began to issue the National Human Intelligence Collection Plan. The Plan includes an advisory for HUMINT collectors, such as foreign service officers, who are outside the National Foreign Intelligence Program (NFIP). Its effect has been limited by being only one of several guidance documents levied on human source collectors.[53]

DCID 2/3 of July 25, 1963, entitled "Domestic Exploitation of Nongovernmental Organizations and Individuals" vests in the CIA responsibility for managing the domestic exploitation program. The CIA is instructed to determine the foreign intelligence potential of nongovernmental organizations and individuals, serve as coordinator for other government agencies, and disseminate to intelligence departments and agencies all foreign intelligence information obtained through the program.[54]

NOTES TO CHAPTER 14

1.   U.S. Congress, Senate Select Committee to Study Governmental Operations with Respect to Intelligence Activities, *Foreign and Military Intelligence, Book I* (Washington, D.C.: U.S. Government Printing Office, 1976), p. 73; Victor Marchetti and John Marks, *The CIA and the Cult of Intelligence* (New York: Dell/Laurel, 1983), p. 174.

2.   U.S. Congress, Senate Select Committee, *Foreign and Military Intelligence*, p. 74.

3.   See Jeffrey Richelson, "The Keyhole Satellite Program," *Journal of Strategic Studies* 7, no. 2 (1984): 121–53.

4.   U.S. Congress, Senate Select Committee, *Foreign and Military Intelligence*, p. 74.

5.   Ibid., p. 75.

6.   Ibid.; James Bamford, *The Puzzle Palace: A Report on NSA, America's Most Secret Agency* (Boston: Houghton Mifflin, 1982), p. 189.

7.   Philip Klass, "U.S. Monitoring Capability Impaired," *Aviation Week and Space Technology*, May 14, 1979, p. 18.

8.   Robert Linsdey, *The Falcon and the Snowman* (New York: Simon & Schuster, 1979), p. 347.

9.   Klass, "U.S. Monitoring Capability Impaired."

10. Ibid.

11. "Space Reconnaissance Dwindles," *Aviation Week and Space Technology*, October 6, 1980, pp. 18–20.

12. Marchetti and Marks, *The CIA and the Cult of Intelligence*, p. 73.

13. Philip Taubman, "Gulf War Said to Reveal U.S. Intelligence Lapses," *New York Times*, September 27, 1980, p. 3.

14. U.S. Congress, House Permanent Select Committee on Intelligence, *Annual Report* (Washington, D.C.: U.S. Government Printing Office, 1978), p. 54.

15. DCID 1/13, "Coordination of the Collection and Exploitation of Imagery Intelligence, February 2, 1973, *Declassified Documents Reference System* 1980–132D.

16. Author's interviews.

17. DCID 1/13, "Committee on Imagery Requirements and Exploitation," July 1, 1967, *Declassified Documents Reference System* 1980 132–B.

18. U.S. Congress, Senate Select Committee, *Foreign and Military Intelligence, Book I*, p. 85.

19. Ibid., p. 84.

20. National Security Agency, *NSA Transition Briefing Book* (Ft. Meade, Md.: NSA, 1981), p. 1.

21. Department of Justice, *Report on CIA-Related Electronic Surveillance Activities* (Washington, D.C.: Department of Justice, 1976), pp. 77–79.

22. U.S. Congress, House Permanent Select Committee on Intelligence, *Annual Report*, p. 55.

23. Bamford, *The Puzzle Palace*, p. 50; Department of Justice, *Report on CIA-Related Electronic Surveillance Activities*, p. 91; DCID 6/1, "Communica-

tions Intelligence Committee," October 21, 1958, *Declassified Documents Reference System* 1980–130C; DCID 6/2, "Electronics Intelligence Committee," October 21, 1958, *Declassified Documents Reference System* 1980–130D; DCID 6/1, "SIGINT Committee," May 1, 1962, *Declassified Documents Reference System* 1980–131D.

24. U.S. Congress, Senate Select Committee, *Foreign and Military Intelligence, Book I*, p. 85.

25. Department of Justice, *Report on CIA Related Electronic Surveillance Activities*, pp. 101–103.

26. U.S. Congress, Senate Select Committee, *Foreign and Military Intelligence, Book I*, p. 85; U.S. Congress, House Permanent Select Committee on Intelligence, *Annual Report*, p. 55; Stephen J. Flanagan, "The Coordination of National Intelligence," in Duncan Clarke, ed., *Public Policy and Political Institutions United States Defense and Foreign Policy: Policy Coordination and Integration* (Greenwich, Conn.: JAI, forthcoming).

27. U.S. Congress, Senate Select Committee, *Foreign and Military Intelligence, Book I*, p. 86.

28. National Security Agency, *NSA Transition Briefing Book.*

29. John Eisenhower, "Memorandum for the Record," February 12, 1959, *Declassified Documents Reference System* 1981–622A.

30. A. J. Goodpaster, "Memorandum of Conference with the President," February 5, 1960, *Declassified Documents Reference System* 1981–622B.

31. U.S. Congress, Senate Select Committee, *Foreign and Military Intelligence, Book I*, p. 1.

32. U.S. Congress, Senate Committee on Foreign Relations, *Executive Sessions of the Senate Foreign Relations Committee – XII* (Washington, D.C.: U.S. Government Printing Office, 1982), p. 130.

33. Bamford, *The Puzzle Palace*, pp. 184–85, 216–31; U.S. Congress, House Committee on Armed Services, *Inquiry into the U.S.S. Pueblo and EC-121 Plane Incidents* (Washington, D.C.: U.S. Government Printing Office, 1969).

34. "Radar Detector Aboard SR–71 Alerted Plane Missile Attack," *New York Times*, August 29, 1983, p. 3.

35. "Future of the Agency's U–2 Capability" July 7, 1960, *Declassified Documents Reference System* 1981–13A.

36. Hannes Adomeit, *Soviet Risk Taking and Crisis Behavior* (Winchester, Mass.: Allen and Unwin, 1982), p. 242.

37. Peter Pringle and William Arkin, *SIOP* (London: Sphere, 1983), ch. 3.

38. Joint Chiefs of Staff, JCS Publication 4, *Organization and Functions of the Joint Chiefs of Staff* (Washington, D.C.: JCS, 1980), Section III–3.

39. Ibid.

40. Marchetti and Marks, *The CIA and the Cult of Intelligence* (1983), p. 283.

41. Marchetti and Marks, *The CIA and the Cult of Intelligence* (1980), p. 293.

42. Joint Chiefs of Staff, JCS Publication 4, *Organization and Functions of the Joint Chiefs of Staff*, Section III–3.

43. Ibid.

44. Marchetti and Marks, *The CIA and the Cult of Intelligence* (1983), p. 283.

45. U.S. Congress, House Permanent Select Committee on Intelligence, *Annual Report*, p. 54.

46. NSCID No. 5, "U.S. Espionage and Counterintelligence Directives Abroad," February 17, 1972, *Declassified Documents Reference System* 1976–253F.

47. U.S. Congress, Senate Select Committee, *Foreign and Military Intelligence, Book I*, p. 85.

48. DCID 1/17, "Human Resources Committee," May 18, 1976.

49. U.S. Congress, Senate Select Committee, *Foreign and Military Intelligence, Book I*, p. 86.

50. Ibid.

51. Scott Armstrong, "Intelligence Experts Had Early Doubts About Shah's Stability," *Washington Post*, February 2, 1982, pp. 1, 9.

52. U.S. Congress, Senate Select Committee, *Foreign and Military Intelligence, Book I*, p. 87.

53. Flanagan, "The Coordination of National Intelligence."

54. DCID 2/3, "Domestic Exploitation of Nongovernmental Organizations and Individuals," July 25, 1963, *Declassified Documents Reference System* 1980–131E.

15 MANAGING INFORMATION ACCESS AND ANALYSIS

The U.S. intelligence collection effort produces an enormous volume of information, particularly from the variety of technical collection systems. The National Security Agency (NSA) alone generates several tons of paper on a daily basis.[1]

Collection, however, is only an intermediary step in the intelligence process between the statement of requirements and the production of finished intelligence. Thus, the information collected must be channeled to those who are responsible for processing and analysis—the National Photographic Interpretation Center (NPIC), the Defense Intelligence Agency (DIA), the State Department's Intelligence and Research Bureau (INR), the Central Intelligence Agency's Directorate of Intelligence, and the Foreign Technology Division (FTD), among others. The same information, either in its raw or processed/analyzed form, must also be made available to a wide variety of individuals—policymakers, policy implementers, strategists, contractors, and consultants—who need the information to perform their jobs. At the same time, much of the information needs to be protected since its disclosure could reveal the specific targets of the collection effort as well as the capabilities of collection systems—disclosures that could lead to effective countermeasures and precautions and the denial of such information in the future. Much information is also made available to U.S. allies under treaty or other arrangements for intelligence sharing. Hence, it is necessary to establish guidelines for the classification and distribution of as well as access to intelligence information, with respect to both U.S. citizens and foreign governments.

Although the numerous analytical intelligence units have substantially distinct functions, it is still necessary to manage the analytical process on a communitywide basis. Aside from the avoidance of undesired duplication where the potential for such duplication exists, it is necessary to ensure that intelligence production is responsive to the requirements of national and departmental leaders. It is also necessary to have mechanisms to deal with analytical problems and ensure that there is an adequate degree of cooperation on a day-to-day basis among agencies working on similar problems. Further, it is necessary to coordinate the production of national estimates—a delicate process involving several agencies with differing perspectives.

MANAGING THE ACCESS TO INFORMATION

The basic means for managing or controlling access to intelligence information is the classification system which defines different levels of sensitivity and restricts access to those who have been cleared at that level. The best-known classifications are those used to restrict access to a wide range of national security information: Confidential, Secret, and Top Secret.

Confidential information is defined as information, "the unauthorized disclosure of which reasonably could be expected to cause damage to the national security."[2] Secret information differs from confidential information in that the expected damage would be "serious." In the case of Top Secret information, the damage would be "exceptionally grave"[3]

Information concerning nuclear weapons or nuclear energy has a specific set of classifications. The Department of Energy requires a Q clearance for access to information concerning nuclear weapons, and some Nuclear Regulatory Commission information is restricted to those with an L clearance. The clearances are comparable, respectively, to Top Secret and Secret clearances.[4] Within Q are several levels of access. A Critical Nuclear Weapons Design Information (CNWDI) clearance is required for access to such information in Department of Defense or Top Secret documents.

The classifications noted above apply to the vast bulk of nonintelligence national security information, but a different system is employed for the control of intelligence information. The first public hint of the existence of such categories occurred during the Senate hearing on the Gulf of Tonkin Resolution in 1964 when Chairman William Fulbright inquired into the source of a report that the North Vietnamese patrol boats were about to attack the Turner Joy on the night of August 4, 1964. Defense Secretary Robert McNamara, Fulbright, and Senators Frank Lausche and Albert Gore engaged in the following colloquy;

> McNamara: We have some problems because the [committee] staff has not been cleared for certain intelligence.

> Lausche: I do not understand that. The members of our staff are not cleared?

Fulbright: All of those who have worked on this matter, but he is talking of a special classification of intelligence communications. . . .

Gore: Mr. Chairman, could we know what particular classification that is? I had not heard of this particular super classification.

McNamara: . . . Clearance is *above* Top Secret for the particular information on the situation. (Emphasis added.)[5]

The "above Top Secret" category dealt with communications or signals intelligence (rather than intelligence communications), and McNamara revealed that it was called Special Intelligence or SI.[6] SI is but one of several above Top Secret categories used to restrict access to Sensitive Compartmented Information (SCI).

The institutionalization of such categories and clearances, particularly SI, can be traced to the successful interception and decryption of Japanese, German, and Italian signals during World War II by the United States and Great Britain. The machine by which the United States was able to decode Japanese diplomatic messages was known as PURPLE, and the intelligence provided by the decryption activity was known as MAGIC.[7] Distribution of MAGIC material was sharply restricted by George Marshall, who drew up a "Top List" of those authorized to have access. The list was restricted to President Roosevelt; the Secretaries of State, War, and the Navy; and the Directors of Military and Naval Intelligence.[8] Not among those on the list was the Commander of U.S. Naval Forces at Pearl Harbor, Admiral Husband Kimmel.

The British also instituted a codeword system to guard the fact that they were able to decrypt German and Italian military and intelligence communications.[9] The most sensitive military material was originally designated PEARL, ZYMOTIC, SWELL, and SIDAR. Later, the British settled on three codewords — ULTRA, PEARL, and THUMB — to indicate material of special sensitivity. Eventually, PEARL and THUMB were combined into a single classification: PINUP.[10]

Intercepts of German intelligence communications by the British Radio Security Service were given the labels ISOS and ISK depending on whether they were intercepts of Enigma-generated or hand-generated cipher systems.[11] This information, when passed on to the United States, became ICE and PAIR.[12]

In addition to intercepting Japanese diplomatic communications, the United States also spent considerable effort in intercepting and trying to decipher Japanese military communications. The United States employed several codenames to represent the product of such activity. DEXTER was the codeword used for intercepts of the highest level traffic — for example, Admiral Yamomoto's travel plans. CORRAL indicated less sensitive intercepts. RABID was used to indicate Traffic Analysis intelligence.[13] With the signing of the BRUSA Communications Intelligence Agreement in 1943, which standardized signals intelligence procedures between the United States and Britain, ULTRA was made a prefix to each classification so that they became ULTRA DEXTER, ULTRA CORRAL, and ULTRA RABID.[14]

Although the outbreak of World War II required a significant expansion of those "in the know" concerning ULTRA, extraordinary security procedures were maintained and distribution restricted as much as possible, the source of ULTRA intelligence being disguised whenever possible. Thus, the British maintained a system of Special Liaison Units to facilitate the transmission of ULTRA from the Government Code and Cypher School in Bletchley to military commanders. It was required that those with knowledge of ULTRA remain outside of battle areas to avoid any chance of capture. On occasions where exceptions to the rule occurred and ULTRA-cleared personnel did risk capture, they carried cyanide pills to allow them to commit suicide to avoid interrogation.[15]

The restricted distribution of ULTRA by the United States is indicated by the fact that in 1943 there were only sixty-one individuals in the China–Burma– India theater, outside of the personnel in the Signals Intelligence Service and Radio Intelligence Units, who were ULTRA cleared. It was required that "requests for . . . additions [to the list] . . . be kept by each headquarters to the absolute minimum necessary for the efficient handling of the material."

The above Top Secret nature of the ULTRA material was clearly indicated by the same directive, which stated,

> The Assistant Chief of Staff, G–2 War Department, requires that all ULTRA DEXTER material be classified TOP SECRET and so marked in addition to the prescribed codewords. This classification will in no way be interpreted as releasing ULTRA DEXTER from the requirements defined herein or authorizing TOP SECRET control officers or other personnel to handle, see, or discuss ULTRA DEXTER in any form, unless they are also on the list of authorized ULTRA DEXTER recipients.[16]

At present, the United States maintains a large number of above Top Secret categories or compartments with respect to intelligence information. The information in these compartments is referred to as Sensitive Compartmented Information. As Secretary of Defense Robert McNamara testified in February 1968, "There are a host of different clearances. I would guess I have perhaps twenty-five. There are certain clearances to which only a handful of people in the government are exposed."[17]

The three major categories concerning intelligence information are SI, TK, and BYEMAN, the first two of which indicate that the information is the product of signals intelligence and/or overhead reconnaissance.

Just as there were different ULTRA levels (for the United States) there are different codewords that indicate the sensitivity of the SI information—specifically, UMBRA and SPOKE.[18] UMBRA is the successor to DINAR and TRINE as the indicator of the most sensitive SI material. SPOKE material is less sensitive, including, for example, intercepts of PLO communications.[19]

UMBRA is always written as TOP SECRET UMBRA. SPOKE is written as SECRET SPOKE. This use of Top Secret and Secret prefixes is motivated by several factors. Besides indicating the level of sensitivity of the information within the SI category, it allows the fiction that the classifications are special access categories within the Top Secret and Secret categories. The desire to create such an appearance was apparently motivated by the mistaken belief that Executive Orders required the use of only the Confidential, Secret, and Top Secret classifications.

Within the UMBRA category there are further designators employed by the NSA for especially sensitive intelligence. GAMMA is a designator that at one time was reserved exclusively for intercepts of Soviet communications until the NSA received orders in 1969 to use the same methods and procedures to monitor the communications of U.S. antiwar leaders. At one point, there were at least twenty GAMMA designations, including GILT, GOAT, GULT, GANT, GUPY, GABE, GYRO, and GOUT, each of which referred to a specific operation or method.[20] GAMMA GUPY referred to the interception of radio-telephone conversations that Soviet leaders were conducting as they were driven around Moscow in their limousines; GAMMA GOUT referred to the material obtained by interception of South Vietnamese government communications.[21]

At one time, there was a DELTA compartment of UMBRA which referred to intercepts relating to Soviet military operations, such as the location of Soviet submarines or Russian aircraft operations. DELTA categories included DACE, DICE, and DENT.[22]

TK is short for TALENT-KEYHOLE, the compartment for the product of overhead reconnaissance systems, both satellites and aircraft.[23] Within the TK category are codewords such as RUFF. Photographs obtained by satellite systems are designated TOP SECRET RUFF.[24] A report on the Soviet ICBM force and national C^3 network might be designated TOP SECRET RUFF UMBRA.

In some cases, it is felt that certain codeword information needs to or should be made available to a larger audience than the codeword (SCI) system permits. Secret or Top Secret documents, when authorized to contain such information, bear the additional control marking WNINTEL: Warning Notice – Intelligence Sources and Methods Involved.

The term Keyhole or KH is also used with a number to indicate the specific photographic satellites that produce a particular product. Thus, the KH–11, as noted in Chapter 7, is only one of a series of satellites designated Keyhole satellites. In practice, SI and TK clearances, representing the product of technical collection systems, are almost always awarded jointly. Hence, the term "SI-TK clearance" is more common than the terms "SI clearance" or "TK clearance."

SI-TK clearances give individuals access to the product of sensitive intelligence systems; they do not grant access to information concerning the systems themselves. Thus, information about the type of system, its location, name, orbit, or capabilities is not accessible to an individual simply on the basis of a SI-TK clearance. Clearances for such information are granted on a system-by-system basis, each system having a specific codeword. These codewords represent the compartments of the BYEMAN system.[25] RHYOLITE and CHALET represent the BYEMAN codewords for those systems. Likewise, the Keyhole satellites have BYEMAN codenames: As noted above, the KH-4 was also known as CORONA. When they were classified programs, the U-2 and SR-71 were codenamed IDEALIST and OXCART, respectively.

The SI, TK, and BYEMAN categories are the major classifications with respect to technical collection systems, but there are at least three other intelligence-related categories of importance. Special Navy clearances, designated M and N clearances, grant access to information concerning Special Navy operations such as HOLYSTONE, DESKTOP, JENNIFER, SAND DOLLAR, and PRAIRIE SCHOONER.

In the human intelligence area, the CIA Directorate of Operations maintains several dozen compartments for the transmission of human source reports. These compartments are informally designated "blue border" or "blue stripe" material for the blue stripes on the border of the cover sheet to any document containing such material.[26] Blue border compartments may be based on the source of the material or the subject matter involved. In World War II the Office of Strategic Services (OSS) had compartments such as Vessel and the Boston Series, and the CIA's Soviet Russia Division used compartments such as REDWOOD and REDCOAT.[27] Separate compartments might be created to segregate information about the source of the information from the information itself; hence, in *Tinker, Tailor, Soldier, Spy* there is source MERLIN and product WITCHCRAFT.[28]

The Department of Energy, in addition to Q clearances, also has special compartments. For example, SIGMA is used as designator for information on Soviet nuclear weapons.[29]

Compartments for either technical systems or human agent activities might also be established on an ad hoc basis. When a covert operation that is designated to produce a specific outcome by a specific time is involved, the project will obviously be short lived. In other cases, information on particularly sensitive situations and operations will be held outside channels. During the Cuban missile crisis, the CIA inaugurated a special daily Cuba situation report under the codeword PSALM.[30] In the 1970s the CIA, in a letter to TRW, the contractor for the PYRAMIDER agent communications satellite study, stated:

> This study effort is classified TOP SECRET and has been assigned a codeword designator. "PYRAMIDER."
>
> All contractor personnel working on this study effort must have a current TOP SECRET clearance and must be approved by Headquarters prior to being briefed on PYRAMIDER.
>
> Contractor personnel proposed for clearance access to this study must qualify by holding a currently valid BYEMAN security access approval.
>
> While this study effort will be conducted within the contractor facilities as TOP SECRET, and while only those personnel holding active BYEMAN

access approvals are eligible for consideration, the effort is not a BYEMAN study, but is to be conducted in all aspects of document control, physical security standards, communications within Headquarters, and the like, as if it were BYEMAN.

Security officers will assure documents within the contractor facility are stamped TOP SECRET/PYRAMIDER only, and are not entered into the BYEMAN system.

The highly sensitive nature of this effort cannot be emphasized enough. Personnel submitted for access approval will be submitted via cable message which shall fully outline their need-to-know. No Form 2018 will be submitted to Headquarters. A list of those persons approved for access to PYRAMIDER shall be maintained by Headquarters Security Staff. Cable messages shall be sent via secure TWX and shall be slugged PYRAMIDER on the second line. PYRAMIDER shall enjoy limited distribution within Project Headquarters.[31]

It should be noted that the term Sensitive Compartmented Information or Special Access Program may also refer to information about specially sensitive military plans, weapons systems, operations, or diplomatic negotiations. Probably the most notable nonintelligence Special Access Programs were the Manhattan Project and Operation Neptune (the invasion of France in 1944).[32] The initials WDD, standing for the Western Development Division of Air Research and Development Command in 1951, were classified Top Secret. WDD was involved in the initial U.S. effort to develop an ICBM.[33] Presently, within the Department of Defense (DOD) and the Department of Energy (DOE) are several programs designated as special access programs—for example, the DOD Continuity of Government Program and the DOE Nuclear Emergency Search Team, information on which is available only to those with a Q-1 clearance. A Defense Advanced Research Project Agency project directed toward the research, development, test, and evaluation of long-endurance vehicles known as TEAL RAIN has three access levels (General Administrative, Intermediate, System Application) and its own secrecy and debriefing oaths.[34]

Likewise, the Counterterrorist Joint Task Force was and the Stealth program is a special access program and information concerning the SIOP (Single Integrated Operational Plan) is designated SIOP-ESI (Extremely Sensitive Information).[35] Finally, when Multiple Protective Structures was the planned MX basing mode, the Air Force established a special compartment for Position Location Uncertainty (PLU) sensitive data requiring special access.[36]

The classification system described above, as well as personnel and security standards for access to and handling of intelligence information, is defined by a series of Executive Orders, National Security Decision documents (NSDDs), National Security Council Intelligence Directives (NSCIDs), Director of Central Intelligence Directives (DCIDs), and DOD Directives. Additionally, committees such as the National Foreign Intelligence Board (NFIB) Security Committee are concerned with security of information acquired as well as that of sources and methods.

As noted earlier, since the Eisenhower administration every administration has issued an Executive Order on National Security Information, the latest three being Executive Order 11652 of March 10, 1972, "Classification and Declassification of National Security Information and Material," with amendments during the Ford administration; Executive Order 12065 of June 28, 1978, "National Security Information"; and Executive Order 12356 of April 2, 1982, "National Security Information."[37]

Part 1 of Executive Order 12356 defines classification levels (Top Secret, Secret, Confidential) and specifies the officials (by position) who can classify (at different levels) or delegate authority to classify information as well as the identifications and markings that are to be shown on the face of all documents and basic rules concerning the duration of the classification.

In addition, Part 1 defines the types of information that shall be considered for classification as well as establishing limitations on classification. Information may be considered for classification if it concerns:

1. military plans, weapons, or operations;
2. the vulnerabilities or capabilities of systems, installations, projects, or plans relating to the national security;
3. foreign government information;
4. intelligence activities (including special activities), or intelligence sources or methods;
5. foreign relations or foreign activities of the United States;
6. scientific, technological, or economic matters relating to the national security;
7. United States Government programs for safeguarding nuclear materials or facilities;
8. cryptology;
9. a confidential source; or
10. other categories of information that are related to the national security and that require protection against unauthorized disclosure as determined by the President or by agency heads or other officials who have been delegated original classification authority by the President.

Section 1.6, which deals with limitations on classification, forbids classification meant to conceal violations of law, inefficiency, or administrative error as well as to prevent embarrassment to a person, organization or agency. It also prohibits classification of basic scientific research information "not clearly related to the national security." However, in a sharp reversal from such past orders, Part 1 of Executive Order 12356 contains the provision that

The President or an agency head or official designated under Sections 1.2 (a) (1), 1.2 (b) (1) or 1.2 (c) (1) may reclassify information previously declassified and disclosed if it is determined in writing that (1) the information requires protection in the interest of national security; and (2) the information may reasonably be recovered.

The remaining parts of the Order deal with derivative classification, declassification and downgrading, safeguarding and implementation, and review. Part 4, "Safeguarding," includes Section 4.2, "Special Access Programs," which states that

> agency heads designated pursuant to Section 1.2 (a) may create special access programs to control access, distribution and protection of particularly sensitive information classified pursuant to this order or predecessor orders. Such programs may be created or continued only at the written direction of these agency heads. For special access programs pertaining to intelligence activities (including special activities but not including military operational, strategic and tactical programs), or intelligence sources or methods, this function will be exercised by the Director of Central Intelligence.

Thus, this section authorizes the above Top Secret classification system for intelligence information.

The Reagan administration has issued two NSDDs concerning the control of intelligence information: NSDD-19 of January 12, 1982, "Protection of Classified National Security Council and Intelligence Information," and NSDD-84 of March 11, 1983, "Safeguarding National Security Information."[38]

NSDD-19 requires that all contacts with any element of the news media in which classified National Security Council (NSC) or classified intelligence information is to be discussed require advance approval by a senior official; that the number of officials with access to documents relating to NSC matters be kept to the minimum essential; and that in the event of unauthorized disclosure of such information, government employees who have had access to that information will be subject to investigation that will include the use of all legal methods.

NSDD-19 has led to the requirement that those granted access to classified NSC information sign a cover sheet acknowledging access and agreeing to "cooperate fully with any lawful investigation by the United States Government into any unauthorized disclosure of classified information contained therein."[39]

NSDD-84 specifies that all government officials and employees with access to SCI must sign a nondisclosure agreement that provides for prepublication review of any writings or speeches that deal with subjects relating to SCI—for example, START verification.

NSCID No. 1 of February 17, 1972, "Basic Duties and Responsibilities," specifies that the Director of Central Intelligence (DCI) is authorized to

> disseminate national intelligence and interdepartmental intelligence on a strictly controlled basis to foreign governments and international bodies upon his determination after consultation with the United States [now National Foreign] Intelligence Board, that such action would substantially promote

the security of the United States, provided that such dissemination is consistent with existing statutes and Presidential policy, including that reflected in international agreements.[40]

NSCID No. 1 also makes the DCI responsible for the development of policies and procedures for the protection of intelligence and of intelligence sources and methods from unauthorized disclosure—including personnel and physical security policies.

In carrying out the responsibilities stated in NSCID No. 1, the DCI has issued several DCIDs concerning the dissemination of intelligence information to foreign governments, personnel, and physical security policies as well as establishing a Security Committee.

DCID 1/7, "Control of Dissemination of Intelligence Information," contains several provisions concerning the release of intelligence information to foreign governments. Release of intelligence to foreign governments *in original form* requires originator approval. Any information contained in classified intelligence documents originated by one intelligence community component may be transmitted by another component provided it bears no restrictive markings prohibiting such transfer and

1. no reference is made to the source documents upon which the released product is based;
2. the information is extracted or paraphrased to ensure that the source or manner of acquisition of the intelligence cannot be deduced or revealed in any manner; and
3. foreign release is made through established foreign disclosure channels and procedures.[41]

The Directive also authorizes control markings in addition to the classification levels. ORCON is an abbreviation used to indicate that dissemination and extraction of information is controlled by the originator and is employed "when unique source sensitivity factors, known to the originator, require strict compliance with third agency rule procedures, in addition to continuing knowledge and supervision on the part of the originator as to the extent to which the original document and information contained therein is disseminated." NO CONTRACT indicates the document is not available to contractors or consultants, *regardless of their level of clearance.* PROPIN is short for "CAUTION–PROPRIETARY INFORMATION INVOLVED." It is used in conjunction with foreign intelligence obtained from various sources in the U.S. private business sector and indicates that a source has a proprietary interest in the information or that the information could be used to the source's detriment.

The most significant control marking with respect to foreign release is the NOFORN marking, which is short for "SPECIAL HANDLING REQUIRED– NOT RELEASABLE TO FOREIGN NATIONALS." According to DCID 1/7, examples of when the control marking may be used include: "(1) the possible compromise of the status of relations with collaborating foreign governments or officials [and] (2) jeopardizing the continuing viability of vital technical collection programs." Withholding of information from allied governments is also authorized for general security reasons (minimizing the number of individuals with access, especially nationals of foreign governments with lax security), because they reveal plans or activities directed at the government or its citizens (e.g., COMINT), because they reveal the conditions under which a country may be abandoned, and particularly, if they involve sensitive intelligence sources and methods (technical or human).

One document labeled SECRET NOFORN ORCON PROPIN is the 1977 CIA study entitled *Israel: Foreign Intelligence and Security Services.*[42] Its NOFORN control marking was assigned for a variety of reasons including (1) above. When the study became public, due to its being removed from the U.S. Embassy in Teheran in 1979, it caused acute embarrassment to both governments, as it alleged that Israeli intelligence agencies blackmailed, bugged, wiretapped, and offered bribes to U.S. government employees in an effort to gain sensitive information. Israeli spokesmen denounced such allegations as "ridiculous."[43] Such studies are conducted of all intelligence and security communities of interest to the CIA. All such studies are labeled NOFORN ORCON PROPIN.

As its title indicates, DCID 1/10 of January 18, 1982, "Security Policy Guidance on Liaison Relationships with Foreign Intelligence Organizations and Foreign Security Services," establishes procedures concerning liaison arrangements with organizations, including the exchange of information.

Personnel and physical security are the subject of DCID 1/14 of May 13, 1976, "Minimum Personnel Security Standards and Procedures Governing Eligibility for Access to Sensitive Compartmented Information," and DCID 1/19, "Uniform Procedures for Administrative Handling and Accountability of Sensitive Compartmented Information."

Under DCID 1/14 the "granting of access to SCI shall be controlled under the strictest application of the 'need-to-know' principle and all individuals who are given access are required, as a condition of gaining access, to sign an agreement that they will not disclose that information to persons not authorized to receive it."[44] The present nondisclosure agreement, shown as Table 15–1, specifies that the signee has been advised of the security procedures used to protect SCI material, that unauthorized disclosure will be a serious violation of the agreement that could result in loss of employment and criminal prosecution, that the government may seek a court injunction preventing the disclosure of such information and, most recently, that the signee

agree to submit for security review by the Department or Agency that last authorized ... access to such information, all information or materials, including works of fiction, which contain or purport to contain any Sensitive Compartmented Information or description of activities that produce or

TABLE 15-1.

SENSITIVE COMPARTMENTED INFORMATION
NONDISCLOSURE AGREEMENT

An Agreement Between _____ and the United States

(Name–Printed or Typed) (Last, First, Middle Initial)

1. Intending to be legally bound, I hereby accept the obligations contained in this Agreement in consideration of my being granted access to information protected within Special Access Programs, hereinafter referred to in this Agreement as Sensitive Compartmented Information. I have been advised that Sensitive Compartmented Information involves or derives from intelligence sources or methods and is classified or classifiable under the standards of Executive Order 12356 or other Executive order or statute. I understand and accept that by being granted access to Sensitive Compartmented Information special confidence and trust shall be placed in me by the United States Government.

2. I hereby acknowledge that I have received a security indoctrination concerning the nature and protection of Sensitive Compartmented Information, including the procedures to be followed in ascertaining whether other persons to whom I contemplate disclosing this information have been approved for access to it, and I understand these procedures. I understand that I may be required to sign an appropriate acknowledgment upon being granted access to each category of Sensitive Compartmented Information. I further understand that all my obligations under this Agreement continue to exist with respect to such categories whether or not I am required to sign such an acknowledgment.

3. I have been advised that direct or indirect unauthorized disclosure, unauthorized retention, or negligent handling of Sensitive Compartmented Information by me could cause irreparable injury to the United States or be used to advantage by a foreign nation. I hereby agree that I will never divulge such information to anyone who is not authorized to receive it without prior written authorization from the United States Government department or agency (hereinafter Department or Agency) that last authorized my access to Sensitive Compartmented Information. I further understand that I am obligated by law and regulation not to disclose any classified information in an unauthorized fashion.

4. In consideration of being granted access to Sensitive Compartmented Information and of being assigned or retained in a position of special confidence and trust requiring access to Sensitive Compartmented Information, I hereby agree to submit for security review by the Department or Agency that last authorized my access to such information, all information or materials, including works of fiction, which contain or purport to contain any Sensitive Compartmented Information or description of activities that produce or relate to Sensitive Compartmented Information or that I have reason to believe are derived from Sensitive Compartmented Information, that I contemplate disclosing to any person not authorized to have access to Sensitive Compartmented Information or that I have prepared for public disclosure. I understand and agree that my obligation to submit such information and materials for review applies during the course of my access to Sensitive Compartmented Information and thereafter, and I agree to make any required submissions prior to discussing the information or materials with, or showing them to anyone who is not authorized to have access to Sensitive Compartmented Information. I further agree that I will not disclose such information or materials to any person not authorized to have access to Sensitive Compartmented Information until I

have received written authorization from the Department or Agency that last authorized my access to Sensitive Compartmented Information that such disclosure is permitted.

5. I understand that the purpose of the review described in paragraph 4 is to give the United States a reasonable opportunity to determine whether the information or materials submitted pursuant to paragraph 4 set forth any Sensitive Compartmented Information. I further understand that the Department or Agency to which I have submitted materials will act upon them, coordinating within the Intelligence Community when appropriate, and make a response to me within a reasonable time, not to exceed 30 working days from date of receipt.

6. I have been advised that any breach of this Agreement may result in the termination of my access to Sensitive Compartmented Information and retention in a position of special confidence and trust requiring such access, as well as the termination of my employment or other relationships with any Department or Agency that provides me with access to Sensitive Compartmented Information. In addition, I have been advised that any unauthorized disclosure of Sensitive Compartmented Information by me may constitute violations of United States criminal laws, including the provisions of Sections 793, 794, 798, and 952, Title 18, United States Code, and of Section 783(b), Title 50, United States Code. Nothing in this Agreement constitutes a waiver by the United States of the right to prosecute me for any statutory violation.

7. I understand that the United States Government may seek any remedy available to it to enforce this Agreement including, but not limited to, application for a court order prohibiting disclosure of information in breach of this Agreement. I have been advised that the action can be brought against me in any of the several appropriate United States District Courts where the United States Government may elect to file the action. Court costs and reasonable attorneys fees incurred by the United States Government may be assessed against me if I lose such action.

8. I understand that all information to which I may obtain access by signing this Agreement is now and will forever remain the property of the United States Government. I do not now, now will I ever, possess any right, interest, title, or claim whatsoever to such information. I agree that I shall return all materials, which may have come into my possession or for which I am responsible because of such access, upon demand by an authorized representative of the United States Government or upon the conclusion of my employment or other relationship with the United States Government entity providing me access to such materials. If I do not return such materials upon request, I understand this may be a violation of Section 793, Title 18, United States Code, a United States criminal law.

9. Unless and until I am released in writing by an authorized representative of the Department or Agency that last provided me with access to Sensitive Compartmented Information, I understand that all the conditions and obligations imposed upon me by this Agreement apply during the time I am granted access to Sensitive Compartmented Information, and at all times thereafter.

DD FORM 1847-1
83 JAN

Table 15-1. continued

10. Each provision of this Agreement is severable. If a court should find any provision of this Agreement to be unenforceable, all other provisions of this Agreement shall remain in full force and effect. This Agreement concerns Sensitive Compartmented Information and does not set forth such other conditions and obligations not related to Sensitive Compartmented Information as may now or hereafter pertain to my employment by or assignment or relationship with the Department or Agency.

11. I have read this Agreement carefully and my questions, if any, have been answered to my satisfaction. I acknowledge that the briefing officer has made available Sections 793, 794, 798,

and 952 of Title 18, United States Code, and Section 783(b) of Title 50, United States Code, and Executive Order 12356, as amended, so that I may read them at this time, if I so choose.

12. I hereby assign to the United States Government all rights, title and interest, and all royalties, remunerations, and emoluments that have resulted, will result, or may result from any disclosure, publication, or revelation not consistent with the terms of this Agreement.

13. I make this Agreement without any mental reservation or purpose of evasion.

Signature	Organization
Printed/Typed Name (Last, First, Middle Initial)	SSN (See Notice Below)

Rank/Grade	Date (YY, MM, DD)	Billet Number (Optional)

FOR USE BY MILITARY AND GOVERNMENT CIVILIAN PERSONNEL

Witness and Acceptance:
The execution of this Agreement was witnessed by the undersigned who accepted it on behalf of the United States Government as a prior condition of access to Sensitive Compartmented Information.

Signature	Organization
Printed/Typed Name (Last, First, Middle Initial)	Date (YY, MM, DD)

FOR USE BY CONTRACTORS/CONSULTANTS/NON-GOVERNMENT PERSONNEL

Witness
The execution of this Agreement was witnessed by the undersigned.

Signature	Organization
Printed/Typed Name (Last, First, Middle Initial)	Date (YY, MM, DD)

Acceptance:
This Agreement was accepted by the undersigned on behalf of the United States Government as a prior condition of access to Sensitive Compartmented Information.

Signature	Organization
Printed/Typed Name (Last, First, Middle Initial)	Date (YY, MM, DD)

Notice: The Privacy Act, 5 U.S.C. 552a, requires that federal agencies inform individuals, at the time information is solicited from them, whether the disclosure is mandatory or voluntary, by what authority such information is solicited, and what uses will be made of the information. You are hereby advised that authority for soliciting your Social Security Account Number (SSN) is Executive Order 9397. Your SSN will be used to identify you precisely when it is necessary to certify that you have access to the information indicated above. While your disclosure of SSN is not mandatory, your failure to do so may delay the processing of such certification.

relate to Sensitive Compartmented Information or that (the signee) contemplates disclosing to any person not authorized to have access to sensitive compartmented information or that (the signee has) prepared for public disclosure.[45]

DCID 1/14 also specifies that, except under special circumstances (which include liaison arrangements), individuals to be given SCI access and their families must be U.S. citizens. It also requires that intended recipients undergo a Special Background Investigation (SBI) before being awarded SCI access—an investigation that is more extensive than the Background Investigation required for Secret or Top Secret clearances. After the initial SBI, a periodic reinvestigation every five years (or less) is required. Additionally, DCID 1/14 requires all departments with personnel who have SCI access to institute security programs that involve security education, security supervision, and security review. As of 1979, 115,000 individuals had SCI clearances, including 13,000 contractor employees.[46]

DCID 1/19 concerns physical security issues such as the establishment of vault facilities for holding SCI information and of intrustion detection systems, communications, computer and data-processing security relating to the transmission of SCI information, other physical security systems, and the location of vault facilities in exposed or combat areas. Thus, DCID 1/19 requires that "all electronic equipment which is used to process or transmit Sensitive Compartment Information (SCI) shall meet national standards for TEMPEST."[47]

On the basis of the Executive Orders, NSDDs and the Departments of State, Defense, and Treasury (among others) 'and their subsidiary units produce directives and manuals to implement the Directives—hence, DOD Instruction 5230.22, "Control of Dissemination of Intelligence Information"; DIA Regulation 50-10, "Control of Dissemination of Foreign Intelligence"; and DIA Manual 50-3, *Physical Security Standards for Sensitive Compartmented Information Facilities.*[48]

There are two NFIB committees established by DCIDs that are concerned with the dissemination of intelligence information. DCID 1/11 establishes the Security Committee (SECOM).[49] Originally established in 1964 pursuant to NSCID No. 1 and National Security Action Memorandum 317, the SECOM's mission is to provide the means by which the DCI can

1. ensure the establishment of security policies and procedures including recommendations for legislation for the protection of intelligence sources and methods from unauthorized disclosure;
2. review and formulate personnel, physical and document security, policies, standards and practices and dissemination procedures applicable to all government departments and agencies as such policies, standards, practices and procedures relate to the sources and methods in consideration of the effectiveness, risks and costs factors involved;

3. review and formulate policies and procedures governing the release of intelligence to foreign governments and international organizations . . . [and] with respect to foreign disclosure, ensure that releases are in consonance with U.S. security policy . . . and that the intelligence itself is accorded a degree of protection equal to that afforded by the United States . . . ;

4. review special security and compartmentation procedures and develop proposals for any necessary changes to achieve optimum use of intelligence consistent with protection of sensitive intelligence sources and methods; and

5. ensure the development, review and maintenance of security standards and procedures for the protection of intelligence stored in or processed by computers.[50]

Hence, the Committee is involved in all aspects of security—dissemination and control as well as physical and personnel security. Thus, in 1980 the SECOM recommended that all officials with access to SCI material be polygraphed at regular intervals.[51]

A second committee, concerned primarily with intelligence handling and dissemination within the intelligence community, is the Intelligence Information Handling Committee, established by DCID 1/4 of May 18, 1976.[52] The Committee's responsibilities include developing intelligence community rules for the exchange of information between agencies; promoting and coordinating the development of intelligence community information-handling capabilities that "will provide on a timely basis required relevant multi-source information in response to authorized queries"; and formulating and recommending policies and procedures relating to the procurement, indexing, flow, storage, exchange, and release of intelligence documents.

MANAGING THE ANALYTIC PROCESS

Management of the analytic process has two basic aspects. The most visible aspect is the management of the production of national intelligence—specifically, the National Intelligence Estimates (NIEs) and Special National Intelligence Estimates (SNIEs).

In addition to the NIEs, SNIEs, and Interagency Intelligence Memorandums (IIMs), the U.S. intelligence community, as is clear from Chapter 12, produces a vast amount of finished intelligence—military, economic, political, and scientific and technical. Although much of this intelligence is not "national" in the sense of being produced by interagency coordination or being produced for national policymakers, it is important to the attainment of national security objectives.

Extensive intelligence production on atomic energy problems; space and weapons systems; and economic, social, and political matters is necessary as input to national estimates as well as to inform officials in various departments who need detailed intelligence. Thus, it is necessary to ensure that departmental intelligence production is consistent with national priorities.

As with other types of intelligence activities, management of the analytical process is handled through NSCIDs, DCIDs, various committees, and requirements documents, NSCIDs No. 1 and No. 3 being the general guidance documents for all aspects of intelligence production.

Section 6 of NSCID No. 1 defines national intelligence as intelligence required for the formulation of national security policy, concerning more than one department or agency, and transcending the exclusive competence of a single department or agency. It authorizes the DCI to produce national intelligence and disseminate it to the President, the NSC, and other appropriate U.S. government components. Section 6 also stipulates that national intelligence will carry a statement of abstention or dissent of any NFIB member or intelligence chief of a military department.[53]

NSCID No. 3 of February 17, 1972, "Coordination of Intelligence Production," distinguishes between different types of intelligence—basic intelligence, current intelligence, departmental intelligence, interdepartmental intelligence, and national intelligence—and assigns responsibilities for the production of basic and current intelligence to the CIA and a variety of other agencies.

The Directive also specifies that

1. The Department of State shall produce political and sociological intelligence on all countries and economic intelligence on countries of the Free World.
2. The Department of Defense shall produce military intelligence. This production shall include scientific, technical and economic intelligence directly pertinent to the mission of the various components of the Department of Defense.
3. The Central Intelligence Agency shall produce economic, scientific and technical intelligence. Further, the Central Intelligence Agency may produce such other intelligence as may be necessary to discharge the statutory responsibilities of the Director of Central Intelligence.

It assigns to all NFIB members charged with the production of finished intelligence the responsibility for producing atomic energy intelligence. In addition, when an intelligence requirement is established for which there is no existing production capability, the DCI, in consultation with the NFIB, is responsible for determining which departments or agencies of the intelligence community can "best undertake the primary responsibility as a service of common concern."[54]

On the basis of NSCIDs No. 1 and No. 3, the DCI issues DCIDs in the 1/1 and 3/1 series to further implement the Directives. The original DCIDs governing the national intelligence process were issued in July and September 1948. DCID 3/1 of July 8, 1948, "Standard Operating Procedures for Departmental Participation in the Production and Coordination of National Intelligence," required, except under exceptional circumstances, that upon initiation of a report or estimate the CIA inform departmental intelligence organizations of

1. the problem under consideration;
2. the nature and scope of the report or estimate involved;
3. the scheduled date of issuance of the first draft;
4. the requirements for departmental contributions . . . ; and
5. the date upon which such departmental action should be completed.[55]

Under normal procedures the CIA was to prepare an initial draft and then furnish copies to departmental intelligence organizations with a request for review and preparation. If the comments received indicated differences of opinion, the CIA was instructed to arrange for an informal discussion with departmental personnel. The CIA was then to prepare a final draft and distribute it to departmental intelligence organizations for concurrence or statements of substantial dissent which would be incorporated in the final paper.

DCID 3/2 of September 13, 1948 complemented 3/1. Entitled "Policy Governing Departmental Concurrences in National Intelligence Reports and Estimates," the Directive specified three options for departmental intelligence organizations: concur, concur with comment, or dissent. The Directive further stated the considerations that should be involved in choosing among the options.[56]

Subsequently, DCIDs 3/1 and 3/2 were superseded by DCID 3/5 of September 1, 1953, entitled "Production of National Intelligence Estimates." The Directive reflected the changes that occurred in the intervening years—particularly the establishment of the Board of National Estimates (BNE) and the Intelligence Advisory Committee (IAC). It was required that by January 1 the BNE present to the IAC a production program for NIEs and SNIEs.[57]

In 1950 an Office of National Estimates (ONE) was established within the CIA's Directorate of Intelligence with the responsibility for drafting national and special national estimates. The Office consisted of a Board of National Estimates and its staff. The Board consisted of between seven and twelve senior officials with expertise in particular areas with the responsibility for managing the production of national estimates. Members of the Board were initially drawn from academia and subsequently from the CIA.[58]

The Board was serviced initially by fifty professional analysts, subsequently by thirty. In theory, the Board reacted to specific requests from the NSC. In emergencies this was often the case. Thus, as noted, several SNIEs were commissioned during the Cuban missile crisis. However, the subject of NIEs became routinized on the basis of the Board's judgment as to the requirements of policymakers.[59]

The process for drafting NIEs was that initially established by DCID 3/1: initial drafting by BNE/ONE, interagency review, revision, and submission to the USIB with dissenting footnotes, if any.[60] During the process, the BNE operated in collegial fashion, taking collective responsibility for the estimates produced and exercising collective judgment in approving it.

The ONE suffered a decline of prestige and influence during the Nixon administration for a variety of reasons, including Henry Kissinger's unhappiness with its product.[61] In June 1973 John Huizenga, the BNE Chairman, retired on an involuntary basis. DCI William Colby decided not to replace him and abolished ONE.[62] Colby gave two reasons for his decision:

> One, I had some concern with the tendency to compromise differences and put out a document which was less sharp than perhaps was needed in certain situations. Second, I believed that I needed the advantage of some individuals who could specialize in some of the major problems that we face around the world and look at these problems not just as estimative problems but as broad intelligence problems. They could sit in my chair, so to speak, and look at the full range of an intelligence problem: Are we collecting enough? Are we processing the raw data properly? Are we spending too much money on it? Are we organized right to do the jobs?[63]

Colby created the National Intelligence Officer (NIO) system in which specific individuals were held solely responsible for producing a particular estimate. NIOs are recruited mainly, but not exclusively, from the CIA and are specialists in a specific functional or geographic area. The number of NIOs has varied from thirteen to eight to the present seventeen. In addition to three at-large NIO's there are NIOs for Africa, East Asia, Europe, the Near East and South Asia, Latin America, the USSR, Counter-Terrorism, Foreign Denial, Science and Technology, Economics, General Purpose Forces, Strategic Programs, Warning and Narcotics. The NIO for Warning serves as the focal point for the receipt of all Indications and Warning intelligence for its evaluation. Initially, NIOs were purposely not given a staff but were expected to draw on the resources of the CIA, DIA, INR, and other analytical units to produce the required estimates.[64]

Subsequently, the NIO process was further revised with establishment on January 1, 1980 of the National Intelligence Council (NIC), giving the NIOs a collective existence.[65] The NIOs are specifically tasked with

1. becoming knowledgeable of what substantive intelligence questions policymakers want addressed;
2. drawing up the concept papers and terms of references for the NIE;
3. participating in the drafting and draft review of the NIE;
4. chairing coordinating sessions and making judgments on substantive questions in debate; and
5. ensuring that the final texts accurately reflect the substantive judgment of the DCI.[66]

In addition to NIEs, the NIOs are responsible for the SNIEs and IIMs.

Besides giving NIOs a collective identity, creation of the NIC also provided the NIOs with a staff—the NIC Analytical Group—so as to provide the Council with control over production resources.[67]

When created, the BNE/ONE was firmly a part of the CIA. Under DCI John McCone and BNE was attached to the DCI's office, responsible to him alone.[68] Under the Carter administration the NIOs became part of the National Foreign Assessment Center (NFAC) and hence under the direct control of the CIA's Deputy Director for National Foreign Assessment.

As noted earlier, one of the earliest Reagan administration actions concerning intelligence as the downgrading of the NFAC to its previous identity: the Directorate of Intelligence. With that change the NIOs were once again placed under the control of the DCI. According to the Director of the NFAC at that time, John McMahon, that was a decision that

> the Director and I debated long and hard because at the time that happened I was in charge of the national foreign assessments, and I did not want it to happen out of the symmetry of management. The Director wanted to have it because he felt that intelligence was so vital, so important that it should not be left to one person to manage and control. And so by having the NIOs separate and under himself, he could insure that he could get a balanced view coming out of the agency on one hand and the rest of the intelligence community and the NIOs on the other. And it was just his way of assuring that all alternative views . . . bubbled to the top.[69]

In addition to the NIC, several NFIB committees play a significant role in managing the intelligence production effort—the Economic Intelligence Committee, the Joint Atomic Energy Intelligence Committee, the Scientific and Technical Intelligence Committee, the Weapons and Space Systems Intelligence Committee, and the Intelligence Producers Council.

DCID 3/3, "Production of Atomic Energy Intelligence," governs the responsibilities of the Joint Atomic Energy Intelligence Committee. The Directive, pursuant to NSCID No. 3, notes that atomic energy intelligence is the responsibility of all NFIB committees and further declares that

> the mission of the Joint Atomic Energy Intelligence Committee (JAEIC) shall be to foster, develop and maintain a coordinated community approach to problems in the field of atomic energy intelligence, to promote interagency liaison and to give impetus and community support to the efforts of individual agencies.[70]

The JAEIC's specific responsibilities are officially classified but certainly must include assessing major developments in the nuclear weapons development of the nuclear powers, considering the possible impact of atomic power programs on proliferation in countries not yet possessing nuclear weapons, providing national decisionmakers with advice on the possible authorization of U.S. foreign sales in the nuclear energy area, providing warning of a country "going nuclear," and assessing the regional impact of such an event.

On February 28, 1950 the Committee issued a memorandum stating that the Committee, "after considering certain information which has become available, is of the opinion that this information should be interpreted as an indication that a Soviet bomb test may take place in Central Asia as early as March 1950."[71]

The Weapons and Space Systems Intelligence Committee (WSSIC) was created in 1956 as the Guided Missile Intelligence Committee and subsequently became the Guided Missile and Astronautics Intelligence Committee (GMAIC). According to DCID 3/4, "Production of Guided Missiles and Astronautics Intelligence," the Committee's membership consists of representatives of all NFIB agencies plus Army, Navy, and Air Force representatives. Its Chairman is named by the DCI with approval of the NFIB.[72] The CIA was made responsible for providing secretariat support. In addition to coordinating the guided missile and astronautics intelligence activities of the intelligence community, the WSSIC has performed technical studies on Soviet missiles as *inputs* to the NIEs. These papers have been coordinated in the same manner as NIEs but have been directed at informing the intelligence community.[73]

At one time, functions of the Economic Intelligence Committee were governed by DCID 15/1, "Production and Coordination of Foreign Economic Intelligence."[74] The Directive, as noted earlier, allocated primary production responsibilities for economic intelligence among the Department of State (INR) and the CIA, the former being responsible for economic intelligence for all non-Soviet Bloc countries, the latter with Soviet Bloc economic intelligence. The Economic Intelligence Committee was assigned responsibility for periodic review of the allocations and interpreting the provisions of the Directive in areas of common or overlapping interest.

As discussed earlier, the present Committee plays a significant role in establishing economic reporting requirements. It also probably plays a similar role in coordinating the production of economic intelligence, especially since the importance of economic intelligence relative to military and political intelligence has increased in recent years.

Management of intelligence productions is also partially a function of the requirements documents discussed in Chapter 13—documents such as the Key Intelligence Questions, Key Intelligence Requirements, and National Intelligence Topics. The same documents that state collection requirements when issued by the NSC, DCI or, Secretary of Defense also establish guidelines for forthcoming intelligence production, both for the NIOs and the various NFIB committees.

NOTES TO CHAPTER 15

1. James Bamford, *The Puzzle Palace: A Report on NSA, America's Most Secret Agency* (Boston: Houghton Mifflin, 1982).
2. Ronald Reagan, "National Security Information," Executive Order 12356, April 2, 1982, *Federal Register* 47 no. 66 (April 6, 1982): 14874–84.
3. Ibid.
4. DOD, *Department of Defense Industrial Security Manual for Safeguarding Classified Information*, DOD 5820.22-M (Washington, D.C.: DOD, July 1981).
5. Quoted in David Wise, *The Politics of Lying: Government Deception, Secrecy and Power* (New York: Vintage, 1973), p. 86.
6. Ibid.
7. Ronald Lewin, *The American Magic: Codes, Ciphers and the Defeat of Japan* (New York: Farrar, Straus & Giroux, 1982), p. 17.
8. Anthony Cave-Brown, *The Last Hero* (New York: Times Books, 1982), p. 193.
9. Bamford, *The Puzzle Palace*, p. 314.
10. Ibid.
11. Nigel West, *MI6: British Secret Intelligence Operations 1909–1945* (London: Weidenfeld & Nicholson, 1983), p. 163.
12. Cave-Brown, *The Last Hero*, p. 182; David Martin *Wilderness of Mirrors* (New York: Harper & Row, 1979), p. 15.
13. Bamford, *The Puzzle Palace*, p. 314.
14. Ibid.
15. F. W. Winterbotham, *The Ultra Secret* (New York: Harper & Row, 1974).
16. *Procedures for Handling ULTRA DEXTER Intelligence in the CBI* (Rear Echelon, HQ U.S. Army Forces, China, Burma, India Theater, March 22, 1944) RG 457, Modern Military Branch, Military Archives Division SRH-046, U.S. National Archives.
17. U.S. Congress, Senate Committee on Foreign Relations, *The Gulf of Tonkin: The 1964 Incidents* (Washington, D.C.: U.S. Government Printing Office, 1968), pp. 35–39.
18. Wise, *The Politics of Lying*, p. 83.
19. Jack Anderson, "Syrians Strive to Oust Arafat as PLO Chief," *Washington Post*, November 10, 1982, p. D–22.
20. Bob Woodward, "Messages of Activists Tapped," *Washington Post*, October 13, 1975, pp. 1, 14.
21. Seymour Hersh, *The Price of Power: Kissinger in the Nixon White House* (New York: Summit, 1983), p. 183.
22. Woodward, "Messages of Activists Tapped."
23. Hersh, *The Price of Power*, p. 92n.
24. James Ott, "Espionage Trial Highlights CIA Problems," *Aviation Week and Space Technology*, November 27, 1978, pp. 21–22.
25. Robert Lindsay, *The Falcon and the Snowman: A True Story of Friendship and Espionage* (New York: Simon & Schuster, 1979), pp. 214–45.

26. Philip Agee, *Inside the Company: A CIA Diary* (New York: Stonehill, 1975).

27. Ibid., p. 68; Cave-Brown, *The Last Hero*, p. 278.

28. John Le Carré, *Tinker, Tailor, Soldier, Spy* (New York: Knopf, 1974).

29. *Final Report of the DOD/DOE Long Range Resource Planning Group*, July 15, 1980, cover of Appendix B.

30. John Prados, *The Soviet Estimate: U.S. Intelligence Analysis and Russian Military Strength* (New York: Dial, 1982), p. 134.

31. Lindsay, *The Falcon and the Snowman*, p. 215.

32. Cave-Brown, *The Last Hero*, pp. 521–22.

33. Fred Kaplan, *The Wizards of Armageddon* (New York: Simon & Schuster, 1983), p. 116.

34. Defense Advanced Research Projects Agency, *TEAL RAIN Security Classification Guide (ARPA-T10 CG-39)* (Washington, D.C.: DARPA, March 6, 1979).

35. U.S. Congress, House Committee on Armed Services, *Leaks of Classified National Defense Information–Stealth Aircraft* (Washington, D.C.: U.S. Government Printing Office, 1980), p. 58; U.S. Congress, House Committee on Appropriations, *Department of Defense Appropriations for 1982, Part 5* (Washington, D.C.: U.S. Government Printing Office, 1981), pp. 643–45.

36. Office of Technology Assessment, *MX Missile Basing* (Washington, D.C.: U.S. Government Printing Office, 1981), p. 39.

37. Richard Nixon, "Classification and Declassification of National Security Information and Material," Executive Order 11652, *Federal Register 37* no. 48 (March 10, 1972): 5209–18; Jimmy Carter, "National Security Information," Executive Order 12065, *Federal Register 43*, no. 128 (July 3, 1978): 28950–61; Ronald Reagan, "National Security Information," Executive Order 12356, *Federal Register 47*, no. 66 (April 2, 1982): 14874–84.

38. DOD Instruction 5230.21, "Protection of Classified National Security Council and Intelligence Information," March 15, 1982; NSDD–84 is reprinted in *First Principles* 8, no. 4 (March/April 1983): 2–3.

39. NSDD–19, "Protection of Classified National Security Council and Intelligence Information," January 12, 1982; William Clark, "Implementation of NSDD–19 on Protection of Classified National Security Council and Intelligence Information," (Washington, D.C.: Office of the Assistant to the President for National Security Affairs, February 2, 1982).

40. NSCID No. 1, "Basic Duties and Responsibilities," February 17, 1972, *Declassified Documents Reference System* 1976–167G.

41. DCID 1/7, "Control of Dissemination of Intelligence Information," May 4, 1981, enclosure to DOD Directive 5230.22 April 1, 1982.

42. Reprinted in *Counter Spy* 6, no. 3 (May–June 1982): 30–58.

43. Scott Armstrong, "Israelis Have Spied on U.S. Secret Papers Show," *Washington Post*, February 1, 1982, pp. A1, A18; "Israel Calls Report of CIA Findings Ridiculous," *Washington Post*, February 3, 1982, p. 10.

44. DCID 1/14, in House Permanent Select Committee on Intelligence, *Security Clearance Procedures in the Intelligence Agencies* (Washington, D.C.: U.S. Government Printing Office, 1979), pp. 25–29.

45. "Sensitive Compartmented Information Nondisclosure Agreement," DD 1847-1, January 1983.

46. U.S. Congress, House Permanent Select Committee on Intelligence, *Pre-Employment Security Procedures of the Intelligence Agencies* (Washington, D.C.: U.S. Government Printing Office, 1980), p. 79.

47. Defense Intelligence Agency, *Physical Security Standards for Sensitive Compartmented Information Facilities* DIAM 50-3, (Washington, D.C.: DIA, 1980).

48. Ibid.; Department of Defense Instruction 5230.22, "Control of Dissemination of Intelligence Information," April 1, 1982; Defense Intelligence Agency Regulation 50-10, "Control of Dissemination of Foreign Intelligence," May 11, 1977.

49. DCID 1/11, "Security Committee," August 23, 1974, *Declassified Documents Reference System* 1980-133A.

50. Ibid.

51. Ronald J. Ostrow, "The Tests Urged for Officials with High Security Clearances," *Los Angeles Times*, October 8, 1981, p. 5.

52. DCID 1/4, "Information Handling Committee," May 18, 1976.

53. NSCID No. 1, "Basic Duties and Responsibilities."

54. NSCID No. 3, "Coordination of Intelligence Production," February 17, 1972, *Declassified Documents Reference System* 1976-253E.

55. DCID 3/1, "Standard Operating Procedures for Departmental Participation in the Production and Coordination of National Intelligence" July 8, 1948.

56. DCID 3/2, "Policy Governing Departmental Concurrences in National Intelligence Estimates," September 13, 1948.

57. DCID 3/5, "Production of National Intelligence Estimates," September 1, 1953.

58. Lawrence Freedman, *U.S. Intelligence and the Soviet Strategic Threat* (London: Macmillan, 1977), p. 31.

59. Ibid., p. 34.

60. Ibid.

61. Ibid., Chapter 3; Ray Cline, *Secrets, Spies and Scholars* (Washington, D.C.: Acropolis, 1976).

62. Freedman, "U.S. Intelligence and the Soviet Strategic Threat," p. 54.

63. Ibid.

64. U.S. Congress, House Select Committee on Intelligence, *U.S. Intelligence Agencies and Activities: Intelligence Costs and Procedures, Part 1* (Washington, D.C.: U.S. Government Printing Office, 1975), p. 389.

65. U.S. Congress, House Committee on Foreign Affairs, *The Role of Intelligence in the Foreign Policy Process* (Washington, D.C.: U.S. Government Printing Office, 1980), p. 135.

66. Ibid., p. 230.

67. Ibid., p. 73.

68. Freeman, *U.S. Intelligence and the Soviet Strategic Threat*, p. 31.

69. U.S. Congress, Senate Select Committee on Intelligence, *Nomination of John N. McMahon* (Washington, D.C.: U.S. Government Printing Office, 1982), p. 48.

70. DCID 3/3, "Production of Atomic Energy Intelligence," January 27, 1959, *Declassified Documents Reference System* 1980–130E.

71. Joint Atomic Energy Intelligence Committee Memorandum, *Declassified Documents Reference System* 1978–21D.

72. DCID 3/4, "Production of Guided Missile and Astronautics Intelligence," April 23, 1965, *Declassified Documents Reference System* 1980–132A.

73. Prados, *The Soviet Estimate*, p. 202.

74. DCID 15/1, "Production and Coordination of Foreign Economic Intelligence," September 14, 1954, *Declassified Documents Reference System* 1980–129E.

16 ISSUES

During the mid-1970s the U.S. intelligence community was placed under prolonged scrutiny by both Senate and House investigating committees. Both committees concerned themselves with more than simple questions of improper activity and went further than mere historical replay of events. They identified many of the issues that had been problems for the intelligence community throughout its existence.

These issues can be divided into two broad categories: management issues and policy issues. Management issues are concerned with the effective management of the intelligence community's diverse components and assets—a particularly important set of issues because, despite the vastness of the community, it cannot hope to satisfy totally the multitudes of competing claims and requirements of intelligence consumers. Hence, questions concerning things such as the control of reconnaissance assets, the role and powers of the Director of Central Intelligence (DCI), and the ability to ensure responsiveness to both national and tactical intelligence needs constitute some of the primary management issues.

Policy, or ethical, issues are those that involve questions of what activities the intelligence community should be performing and under what circumstances, the extent of public control that is appropriate, and U.S. involvement with foreign countries in conducting such activities. Thus, issues such as the propriety of covert action, secrecy, and the use of bases on foreign territory all qualify as policy issues.

MANAGEMENT ISSUES

The original intent behind the creation of the Central Intelligence Agency was to establish an organization that would coordinate the intelligence activities of the various other U.S. intelligence components and take the results of their work, both with regard to collection and analysis, to produce a common estimate.

Although the CIA soon grew beyond its intended coordinating role to become a primary actor in human and technical collection as well as analysis, it never truly attained the supreme coordinating role envisaged. This has resulted in part from the intelligence explosion that began in the mid-1950s and continues through the present day—an explosion that involved a quantum leap in technical intelligence collection techniques (from the U-2 to the KH-11 and Rhyolite satellites) as well as a proliferation in the number of intelligence collection and analysis units, particularly in the military services.

The explosion in technical collection capabilities has produced competition for limited funds to develop and produce such assets and for control over the associated programs among the CIA, the National Security Agency (NSA), the Navy, and the Air Force. Further, it has created competing demands between tactical and national-level users for the targeting of satellite and other collection systems.

These latter issues were in theory to have been resolved by the creation of organizations such as the National Reconnaissance Office (NRO), the National Reconnaissance Executive Commitee (NREC), the Committee on Imagery Requirements and Exploitation (COMIREX), and the SIGINT Committee.

Despite these mechanisms, however, basic conflicts have persisted, culminating in the struggle during the first years of the Carter administration for control of the NRO and NSA. DCI Stansfield Turner argued that economic and other nonmilitary information might be more important to the President and national decisionmaking than is tactical military intelligence. On the other hand, Secretary of Defense Harold Brown argued that without control of the NSA and NRO, the military would not be able properly to advise the President on military matters.[1]

Further, as noted above, satellite and other forms of technical collection are valuable methods for both strategic and tactical intelligence consumers and thus create competing demands. Thus, Marchetti and Marks note that "an American commander in Germany may desire data on the enemy forces that would oppose his troops if hostilities broke out, but the day-to-day movements of Soviet troops along the East German border are of little interest to high officials back in Washington."[2]

In addition, in many cases the distinction between "national departmental and tactical intelligence are out of date ... [resulting] in redundant acquisition of data at all levels."[3] Attempts in recent years to alleviate the problems have involved the creation of the Tactical Exploitation of National Capabilities (TEN-CAP) and National Exploitation of Tactical Capabilities (NETCAP) programs and installations such as the Tactical Fusion Center at Boerfink, Germany.

These programs will help to alleviate some of the problems involved in competing requirements for scarce resources, but they are unlikely fully to resolve the issues. Rather, they can be interpreted as an attempt to lessen the divisions and satisfy a large portion of the requirements within certain constraints, specifically the decision to maintain control of the NRO and NSA within the Department of Defense (DOD).

The control of reconnaissance assets is but one manifestation of the struggle over the powers of the DCI. Unfortunately, what could have been a turning point in the role in the mid-1950s never occurred due to the singular focus of Allen Dulles on covert operations.

From the very creation of the CIA, the DCI's role has been under challenges by other components of the intelligence community—initially being seen by some as more a servant or staff manager than an actual director or coordinator. Thus, when he first took office in 1951, Walter Bedell Smith was viewed as acting not with the advice of the Intelligence Advisory Committee (IAC) but rather at its direction. One of Smith's first innovations was to put the IAC in an advisory rather than supervisory role with respect to the DCI.

Smith's action was only a first step toward asserting the DCI's control over the intelligence community as a whole. He was succeeded as DCI in 1953 by Allen W. Dulles, brother of Secretary of State John Foster Dulles. Dulles, however, despite his long tenure as DCI (nine years) and unique level of influence, did little to enhance the Director's role, repeated urgings by presidential consultants notwithstanding. Dulles's primary, indeed possibly only, interests lay in the covert action and clandestine collection areas.

Thus, it was not surprising that in 1956, three years after Dulles's appointment as DCI, the President's Board of Consultants in Foreign Intelligence Activities (PBCFIA) stated:

Despite his title, the Director of Central Intelligence neither by law, directive nor otherwise, is the central director of the total intelligence effort of the government. Actually, his control of intelligence *operations* is restricted to those of the Central Intelligence Agency. On the other hand, he does have a broad responsibility for the correlation, evaluation and dissemination of intelligence related to the national security.

But the dominant responsibility for the production of "Departmental" intelligence ("subject to refinement through a continuous process of coordination by the Director of Central Intelligence") rests with the head of each of the separate Departments and Agencies represented in the Intelligence Community. In our judgment this arrangement, with its division of responsibility and despite the elaborate intelligence committee coordinating mechanism which exists, is not any longer adequate. Wherever their Department needs are judged by them to be paramount the separate elements of the Intelligence Community are inclined to operate independently. This has resulted in an undue amount of built-in duplication in our national intelligence effort. It has also generated competition and frictions, some long standing, which have impeded the real integration of intelligence activities.[4]

One means of enhancing the DCI's control suggested by the PBCFIA was the creation of a Chief of Staff or Executive Director to relieve Dulles of his management responsibilities. By 1958 the recommendation had been made several times to the President by the Board and discussed several times between the President and DCI Dulles without Dulles accepting the recommendation. Thus, President Eisenhower noted on December 16, 1958 "that there had already transpired considerable discussion but said he would talk to him once again."[5]

The issue still persisted near the end of Eisenhower's term in office when it finally became clear that Dulles would not accept such a recommendation. Thus, in a conference with members of the PBCFIA the President noted the "recommendation that the Board had made once concerning an Administrative Deputy to Mr. Allen Dulles. He said it became clear that he would have to make a choice either to keep Mr. Dulles without such a deputy or relieve him in order to carry out the reorganization. He thought that Mr. Dulles's value was such that he should not take this latter course."[6]

Dulles quite possibly missed a unique opportunity to gain for the DCI a more central role in the intelligence process. This failure has been noted by a former head of the PBCFIA, James Killian. In his memoirs Killian writes,

> I do feel that Eisenhower failed to recognize the administrative inadequacies of Allen Dulles. . . . At least he failed to take remedial measures. . . . I several times questioned Dulles's administrative competence, while recognizing his charismatic, even legendary, gifts as an intelligence expert. Each time, Eisenhower responded by asking me: "Whom I could get as a replacement whose competence would approach that of Dulles as an intelligence officer?" I now think the board was at fault in accepting Eisenhower's answer without explaining insistently our concern about Dulles's handling of his broader responsibilities. Some of the fissures that later showed up in the CIA might well have resulted from loose administration.[7]

Advances that did occur during Dulles's tenure in the administration of the community tended to stem from the PBCFIA. The 1958 merger of the IAC and the United States Communications Intelligence Board (USCIB) into the United States Intelligence Board (USIB), giving the DCI greater control over the SIGINT activities of the armed services, was the result of Board recommendations.[8]

However, it was not until Dulles's successor, John McCone, became DCI that significant management reforms were attempted. Both the Kennedy administration's desire for greater central organization and coordination of national security activities (particularly after the Bay of Pigs fiasco) and McCone's personal attitudes toward the DCI role contributed to these attempted reforms.

On January 16, 1962 President Kennedy sent a letter to McCone defining his role as DCI. It read, in part, as follows:

> In carrying out your newly assigned duties as DCI, it is my wish that you serve as the government's principal foreign intelligence officer, and as such that you undertake as part of your responsibility, the coordination and effective guidance of the total U.S. foreign intelligence effort. As the government's principal intelligence officer, you will assure the proper coordination, correlation and evaluation of intelligence from all sources and its prompt dissemination to me and to other recipients as appropriate. In fulfillment of these tasks, I shall expect you to work closely with the heads of all departments and agencies having responsibilities in the foreign intelligence field.[9]

Further, with the Dulles experience clearly in mind, the letter went on to say,

> As head of the CIA, while you will continue to have overall responsibility for the Agency, I shall expect you to delegate to your principal deputy, as you may deem necessary, as much of the direction of the detailed operation of the Agency as may be required to permit you to carry out your primary task as DCI.[10]

Even with the support of Kennedy's letter, McCone could only make a marginal dent in the established situation, for nothing in the letter required the military intelligence units to treat McCone as their director. Thus, institutions established by McCone, such as the National Intelligence Program Evaluation (NIPE) Staff, had only a small impact in rationalizing the national intelligence effort.

The years subsequent to McCone's tenure saw further efforts to enhance the role of the Director; such efforts were often consumated only on paper. Under Richard Helms the National Intelligence Resources Board was established, followed in 1971 by the Nixon-mandated National Security Council Intelligence Committee (NSCIC) and the Intelligence Resources Advisory Commiteee (IRAC)—the latter to advise in the allocation and use of intelligence resources and the formulation of the DCI's recommendations on the NFIP.[11]

However, the NSCIC met only once and Helms was more inclined simply to rubber stamp requests rather than risk conflicts. Thus, in 1969 he noted that although the "DCI is theoretically responsible for 100 percent of the nation's intelligence activities, he in fact controlled less than 15 percent of the community's assets and most of the other 85 percent belonged to the Secretary of Defense and the Joint Chiefs of Staff."[12]

Subsequent to Helms's dismissal in 1973, both of his successors, James Schlesinger and William Colby, began management reforms but neither held office long enough to make a significant impact. As noted previously, Admiral Stansfield Turner sought day-to-day as well as budgetary control of the NRO and NSA. This was part of a broader program to give the DCI and his staff the power fully to direct the activities of the entire intelligence community.

As also noted, Turner attained only a portion of his goals. However, he attained establishment of the National Intelligence Tasking Center (NITC), headed by a Deputy to the DCI and responsible for tasking the entire community. Offices under the NITC included those for photo, signals intelligence, and human source tasking.[13] The objective was twofold: (1) to provide stronger direction than was coming, in Turner's eyes, from NFIB collection committees such as COMIREX and the SIGINT Committee and (2) to create an organization that could rationalize the overall assignment of different collection systems (photo, SIGINT, human) to the entire target set.[14]

NITC's fate during the Carter administration was a perfect example of a major paper reform that resulted in only a marginal change. Actual activities were still directed by the DOD and individual service components, which largely ignored the NITC. At the beginning of the Reagan administration, the NITC was disestablished with no formal successor organization being created.

The problems involved in such management issues cannot be easily resolved; both those arguing for more central control and their opponents have valid concerns. Both can see in the other's framework a hindrance to making the intelligence community properly responsive.

Thus, at the national level it can be argued that the tremendous expenses and limited targeting capabilities of national collection systems require that they be employed for the benefit of national decisionmakers and that the only way of ensuring that this happen is their control by the national decisionmakers' intelligence adviser, the DCI. Likewise, it can be argued that the overall production of intelligence should be managed in such a way as to maximize benefit to the entire national security establishment rather than to one branch.

At the same time, departments and services can claim a legitimate need to direct and manage intelligence collection and production in response to their needs. Since their mission is considered of major importance in the overall national security position, they can argue that they are best able to judge the quality and quantity of intelligence needed and that their crucial needs might be overlooked by a DCI with no military forces to support directly.

POLICY ISSUES

Management issues received greatest attention during the Carter administration, but policy issues have come to the forefront during the Reagan administration. The questions of U.S. covert action activities and secrecy have been particularly prominent. Additionally, the issue of U.S. intelligence bases has continued to be an important issue in nations such as Australia and Greece.

The Reagan administration has seen a resurgence in covert action, particularly major paramilitary covert action. This is largely due to the proclivities of the administration, particularly its DCI William Casey, as well as the perceptions of its officials concerning threats to U.S. national security in Latin America and Africa. This resurgence comes after a relative lull in the Carter years, during which most covert action involved propaganda and political influence operations.

The covert action operation that has attracted the most attention has been the one directed at the Sandinista government in Nicaragua. It is also the operation that clearly highlights the issues involved in such activity.

The ostensible purpose of the operation—which includes support for the anti-Sandinista guerrilla forces, which in turn have raided both military targets in Nicaragua—is to eradicate (alleged) support of El Salvadoran guerrillas. Supposedly, exerting military and economic pressure will cause the Sandinistas to reevaluate their policies.

The issues involved in such activities are both ethical and practical. Under what circumstances, if any, are covert actions morally justified? Second, leaving aside the question of whether what is best for the United States is best for the covert action target, does the history of U.S. covert activities indicate that such activities are beneficial in the long run to U.S. national interests?

Several U.S. presidents have defended covert activities. President Ford argued that such activities were acceptable international conduct—in defending U.S. funding of political parties in Italy as well as destabilization activities in Chile—even offering the comment that the Chilean people were better off as a result of U.S. activities. More recently, President Reagan said he believed in "the right of a country when it believes its interests are best served to conduct covert activity."[15]

One might suggest that any covert activity under any circumstances is illegitimate—that it violates a nation's sovereignty. However, given a willingness to go to war against another nation, it seems peculiar to rule out a less violent form of activity, particularly if there is a strong possibility that such an action might prevent war. One might suggest the acceptability of covert action depends on the threat to the country practicing covert action as well as the type of action and nature of the target.

Hence, one might suggest that covert action is acceptable with respect to democratic nations only when there is a direct, immediate, and grave physical threat to national security—a set of circumstances extremely unlikely to occur. The term "physical threat" would suggest that the democratic country is close to launching some military attack on the United States or its possessions. The prospect of the loss of bases or cancellation of a defense or intelligence agreement would be insufficient.

Under such criteria covert actions directed against Italy or Australia would have been unacceptable. Likewise, no rationale concerning economic interests would justify covert action. Such criteria would also rule out low-visibility propaganda or political influence operations whether simply support for newspapers and magazines or black propaganda involving the planting of false stories.

One might even suggest that covert action is unacceptable when targeted against nondemocratic regimes except in exceptional circumstances. The planting of false or misleading stories is a type of action that seems particularly questionable since the target is likely to be a population and not a government. It seems particularly inappropriate for the U.S. to add further lies to those already transmitted by a population's government.

As an alternative to covert action, the United States might undertake a counter-covert action program designed to prevent Soviet or other hostile covert action activity. Such a program would seek to detect and expose (either to the target government or the world at large) or block such activity. Such an activity would avoid leaving the United States defenseless against such Soviet activity without requiring the commission of the same sins.

On the practical side of the question, the history of U.S. covert action does not support the view that such action serves long-term U.S. national interests. Certainly, it has served short-term interests of some segments of the United States. However, eventually—as in the case of Iran—the supported regime falls, its crimes being blamed (sometimes legitimately) on its U.S. sponsors.

A second issue of major importance to be highlighted in the Reagan administration concerns secrecy. Its most prevalent aspect is the secrecy requirements and agreements that are required of those gaining access to Sensitive Compartmented Information (SCI). However, this only highlights the entire issue of secrecy concerning intelligence activities.

There have been several moves in the administration to increase the ease of classifying information and maintaining its classification. Included is a variety of Executive Orders and National Security Decision Directives (NSDDs) as well as legislation such as the Intelligence Identities Protection Act.

There are many aspects of the secrecy issue. It is clear that there is a significant amount of information that can justifiably be classified. This includes aspects of nuclear targeting, C^3, COMSEC, and intelligence sources and methods. At the same time, it can be persuasively argued that there is a peculiar mystique concerning intelligence activities that leads to an overclassification above that which exists with respect to defense matters. There is a general attitude that intelligence matters should be covered in a blanket of secrecy to prevent any compromise. Thus, the very existence of the NRO is considered secret, as is the array of reconnaissance satellites in existence.

Further, in many cases the classified information is obviously available to the Soviet Union from its own technical intelligence collection systems, but not to the U.S. populace at large. It is characteristic that information concerning the orbital parameters of some satellite that is not made available to NASA for reproduction in its publicly available *Satellite Situation Report* is made available under treaty commitments to the United Nations for its Registry of Space Objects—a registry available to the representatives of every U.N. member but not to the press or public.

Such secrecy serves more to remove such matters from public scrutiny and supervision than to keep the information from hostile powers. Further, such secrecy actually hurts the chances of keeping truly important secrets secure: the broader the secrecy the greater the personnel and physical security requirements. Such requirements eventually necessitate a tradeoff. The measures that can be employed for 10,000 individuals and 100,000 documents cannot be employed for 100,000 individuals and 10,000,000 documents. Additionally, such secrecy creates an inevitable and unbridgeable gap between those responsible for classification and those researching and reporting on such matters. When the letterhead of the NRO is classified Secret, it is hard to take the classification system seriously.

The Reagan administration has not only sought to broaden the material that falls into the classified category but has taken extraordinary steps to ensure that such material stays secret for as long as government officials so desire. The most prominent of these efforts is NSDD–84, "Safeguarding National Security Information," signed on March 11, 1984. The document requires any government employee who is to be granted access to SCI to sign a nondisclosure agreement providing prepublication review of any material that "contains or purports to contain any Sensitive Compartmented Information or description of activities that produce or relate to Sensitive Compartmented Information."[16] The latter provision will rule out any unapproved discussion of verification, reconnaissance, or SIGINT.

Such a system will require a massive bureaucracy to implement, for 164,000 people have already signed the agreement, many of whom will have access to such information for only a brief period of time. Further, such a system would prevent short-term (and possibly long-term) commentaries by former government officials.

A third policy issue less visible in the United States is that of U.S. intelligence facilities abroad. The United States maintains a large number of bases in Europe and Asia for intelligence collection purposes. These bases include land-based intercept facilities as well as ground stations for reconnaissance satellites.

Recently, there have been discussions concerning U.S. bases in Greece and Australia. Two issues have been raised with respect to such bases. One concerns the advisability of maintaining such bases as opposed to relying more heavily on satellites, ships, and aircraft. The second concerns the question of what obligation (if any) the United States has in informing the populace concerning the nature of these activities and the risks they present.

With regard to questions of advisability, there are economic/feasibility and political/security considerations. Capabilities produced by land stations can be attained by other means, such as satellite-to-satellite cross links as exist with respect to the KH-11 and are planned for the Defense Support Program (DSP) and the Nuclear Detection System (NDS). In some cases, this may be done at substantially greater expense than otherwise possible. In other cases, land stations might be indispensable in attaining a specific level of capability. Thus, the Rhyolite satellite could only intercept a portion of the telemetry intercepted by the Turkish and Iranian ground stations, the Iranian stations being better situated than the Turkish ones.

Political/security issues involve the agreements to which the United States must come in order to gain access to foreign territory. The existence of such bases can subject the United States to blackmail or extortion in order to be maintained. This blackmail could focus on additional aid funds or political and weapons support for a possibly authoritarian government. Second, there is the inevitable possibility of U.S. expulsion at a future date.

Another question arises concerning U.S. responsibilities to the populace. In many cases, U.S. installations can create a nuclear target. It might be argued that the United States bears no responsibility as long as it is honest with the host government, regardless of whether that government is elected or not. However, long-term U.S. interests do not necessarily agree with the short-term interests of the present power structure in a given country. Revelation of U.S. activity at a future date might produce a hostile reaction and feelings of U.S. duplicity. That the host government might have been a willing partner might only exacerbate the feeling. Possibly, by revealing the functions of an installation from the outset, the United States can avoid such a reaction and avoid expulsion. It should be noted that the functions of such installations will usually be known to the Soviet Union, which can leak the information to cause problems for the United States.

These policy and management issues have been with the U.S. intelligence community since its inception. They are not likely to be resolved anytime soon.

NOTES TO CHAPTER 16

1. Joseph Fromm, "Inside Story of Battle to Control Spying," *U.S. News and World Report*, August 8, 1977, p. 27.
2. Victor Marchetti and John Marks, *The CIA and the Cult of Intelligence* (New York: Knopf, 1974), p. 78.
3. James Schlesinger, *A Review of the Intelligence Community* (Washington, D.C.: Office of Management and Budget, 1971), pp. 5-6.
4. Letter from The President's Board of Consultants on Foreign Intelligence Activities to the President, December 20, 1956, *Declassified Documents Reference System* 1978-204C.
5. John Eisenhower, Memorandum of Conference with the President December 16, 1958, December 22, 1958, *Declassified Documents Reference System* 1981-621B.

6. A. J. Goodpaster, Memorandum of Conference With the President Febru-
    ary 2, 1960, February 5, 1960, *Declassified Documents Reference System*
    1981–622B.
7. James R. Killian, Jr., *Sputniks, Scientists, and Eisenhower: An Memoir of
    the First Special Assistant to the President for Science and Technology*
    (Cambridge, Mass.: MIT Press, 1982), p. 222.
8. U.S. Congress, Senate Select Committee to Study Governmental Opera-
    tions with Respect to Intelligence Activities, *Supplementary Detailed Staff
    Reports on Foreign and Military Intelligence, Book IV* (Washington, D.C.:
    U.S. Government Printing Office, 1976), pp. 62–63.
9. Ibid., p. 73.
10. Ibid.
11. U.S. Congress, House Select Committee on Intelligence, *U.S. Intelligence
    Agencies and Activities, Part 1*, (Washington, D.C.: U.S. Government Print-
    ing Office, 1976), p. 114.
12. Marchetti and Marks, *The CIA and the Cult of Intelligence*, p. 90.
13. Central Intelligence Agency, *CIA Fact Book* (Washington, D.C.: CIA,
    1978), unpaginated.
14. Author's interview.
15. Tom Wicker, "A Policy of Hypocrisy," *New York Times*, October 21,
    1983, p. A35.
16. Sensitive Compartmented Information Nondisclosure Agreement DD
    Form 1897–1, January 1983.

INDEX

"Active measures." *See* Covert action
Advanced Imagery Requirements and Exploitation System, 38
Advanced Range Instrumentation Aircraft (ARIA), 124
Advanced Range Instrumentation Ships (ARIS), 128
Aerial sampling operations, 159
Aerospace Corporation, 15, 145
Aerospace Defense Center, 79
Aerospace Defense Command, 78–79
Aerospace Defense Intelligence Center, 79
Agee, Philip, 181, 186
Agents: clandestine, 177–81; double, 220, 221, 223; turned, 178; walk-in, 178
Aircraft reconnaissance systems, 115–17
Air Force Electronic Security Command, 19–20, 49
Air Force Intelligence Service (AFIS), 49–50, 184, 307; Directorate of Attaché Affairs, 50; Directorate of Evasion and Escape/Prisoner of War Matters, 52; Directorate of Intelligence Data Management, 50; Directorate of Intelligence Reserve Forces, 50; Directorate of Operational Intelligence, 50; Directorate of Security and Communications Management, 50; Directorate of Soviet Affairs, 50, 52; Directorate of Targets, 50; Special Activities Center, 50, 52
Air Force Office of Special Investigations (AFOSI), 225, 285

Air Force Office of the Assistant Chief of Staff, Intelligence (OACSI), 49–50; Directorate of Estimates, 50; Directorate of Intelligence Plans and Systems, 50
Air Force Regulations, 273–74
Air Force Space Command, 78–79
Air Force Special Plans Office, 45
Air Force Special Projects Office, 14, 287
Air Force Special Reconnaissance Activities Program, 287–88
Air Force Systems Command, Foreign Technology Division (FTD), 37, 49–50, 52–53, 56, 126, 188–89, 205, 254–55, 274, 313; Directorate of Administration and Support, 56; Directorate of Data Services, 56; Directorate of Plans and Operations, 56; Directorate of Sensor Data, 56; Directorate of Systems, 56; Directorate of Technology and Threat, 56
Air Force Technical Applications Center (AFTAC), 50, 56, 58, 160, 274, 305
Alaska Long Period Array (ALPA), 160
Aldridge, Edward C., 14
Alfa, 139
Allende, Salvador, 24, 204, 232–33
Allied Intelligence Bureau, 197
ALTAIR–4 radar, 154
AMAN, 205–6
Anderson, Richard, 175–76
Andropov, Yuri, 174, 177
AN/FPS radar, 154
Angleton, James Jesus, 23, 207, 223

Anglo-Iranian Oil Company, 233
AN/GPS search radar, 154
Anti-satellite targeting, 150
Arbenz, Jacobo, 229
ARGUS satellite, 298
Armed Forces Medical Intelligence Center
    (AFMIC), 35, 43-44, 272-73
Armed Forces Security Agency (AFSA),
    302
Army counterintelligence operations, 67
Army Intelligence Survey (AIS), 67-68
Army Material Development and Readiness
    Command (DARCOM), 287
Army Office of the Assistant Chief of Staff
    for Intelligence (OACSI): Counter-
    intelligence Directorate, 66; Foreign
    Intelligence Directorate, 66; Foreign
    Liaison Directorate, 66; Intelligence
    Systems Directorate, 66
Army Regulations, 274
Army Space Program Office, 287
Army Special Operations Office, 45
Artamonov, Nikolai, 221-22
Artemko, Lt. Col., 173
Atlantic Command (LANTCOM), 80, 82,
    84, 259
Atlantic Undersea Test and Evaluation
    Center (AUTEC), 148
Atomic Energy Commission (AEC), 156
Australian-New Zealand Military Intelli-
    gence Service (ANZMIS), 200
Australian Secret Intelligence Service
    (ASIS), 203-5
Auxiliary General Environmental Research
    (AGER) ships, 128
Auxiliary General Technical Research
    (AGTR) ships, 127-28
Aviation Week and Space Technology,
    13-15, 111
Azores Fixed Acoustic Range (AFAR)
    system, 148

Baker, James, 278
Baker-Nunn cameras, 150, 152
Ballistic Missile Early Warning System
    (BMEWS), 154
Barrier project, 148
Bay of Pigs, 25, 229-30, 241
BBC Monitoring Service, 177, 201-2
Begin, Menachem, 205
Bennett, Donald V., 307
Berlin crisis, 245
Bethe, Hans, 175
Bhangmeters, 157-58
Bissell, Richard, 179
Blake, George, 271
Blunt, Anthony, 224
Board of National Estimates, 229, 329-31

Boland, Edward, 1
Boyce, Christopher, 120-21
Brezhnev, Leonid, 174
British Radio Security Service, 315
Bronco project, 148
Brownell Committee Report, 15
Brown, Harold, 299, 338
BRUSA Agreement, 196, 315
Brzezinski, Zbigniew, 5
Bureau of Intelligence and Research (INR),
    11, 95-98, 241, 253-54, 280, 284, 313,
    330, 332
Bush, George, 206
BYEMAN, 41, 316, 318-19

Caesar arrays, 147. See also Hydrophone
    arrays
Campbell, Duncan, 211
CANUS, 79
Carter administration, 5, 14, 68, 156, 187,
    206, 220, 236, 242-45, 264-65, 275-76,
    279-80, 287, 289, 299, 331, 338,
    342-43
Casey, William, 25, 206, 243, 245, 343
Castro, Fidel, 229-31
Central Asian Research Center, 176
Central Command for Southwest Asia,
    80-81
Central Intelligence Agency (CIA), 11-14,
    16, 20-30, 38, 40-41, 44-45, 71-72,
    75, 82, 96, 100, 102-3, 111-12, 116,
    120-21, 123, 145, 148, 172, 180-81,
    183-88, 190, 195, 201-11, 221-36,
    241-42, 246-48, 254, 264, 266-68,
    270, 279-80, 284, 286-87, 298-301,
    307-8, 323, 328-32, 338-41; Center
    for Insurgency, Instability and Terrorism,
    28; Central Cover Staff, 23-24; Counter-
    intelligence Staff, 23-24; Covert Action
    Staff, 23-24; Directorate of Administra-
    tion, 21-23; Directorate of Intelligence,
    21, 25, 28-29, 186, 247-48, 313, 329,
    331; Directorate of Operations, 21-25,
    29, 186, 207, 227-29, 308, 318;
    Directorate of Science and Technology,
    14, 21, 29-30, 186, 207-8; Domestic
    Collection Division, 25; Evaluation, Plans
    and Design Staff, 23-24; Foreign Intelli-
    gence Staff, 23-24; Foreign Resources
    Division, 25; Office of Central Reference,
    25, 28; Office of Communications, 21;
    Office of Current Operations, 25, 29;
    Office of Data Processing, 21; Office of
    Development and Engineering, 14, 29;
    Office of Economic Research, 28; Office
    of Finance, 21, 23; Office of Global
    Issues, 25, 28; Office of Imagery Analysis,
    25, 28; Office of Logistics, 21, 23; Office

of Medical Services, 21, 23; Office of Personnel, 21, 23; Office of Political Analysis, 28; Office of Research and Development, 29; Office of Scientific and Weapons Research, 25, 28; Office of Security, 21, 23; Office of SIGINT Operations, 14, 29-30, 208; Office of Soviet Analysis, 25; Office of Strategic Research, 28; Office of Technical Service, 29; Office of Training and Education, 21, 23; Office of Weapons Intelligence, 29; Publication Review Board, 14; Staff D, 23-24; ZR/RIFLE, 24

Central Intelligence Board (CIB), 301

Central Security Service (CSS), 19-20, 52, 67, 272

Chalet satellites, 120-22, 301, 318

Charged couple devices (CCDs), 153

Charyk, Joseph, 12-14

Chayes, Antonia, 14

Chernenko, Constantin, 8

Church Committee, 289

CIA and the Cult of Intelligence, The, 13, 104, 121, 181, 184, 186, 338

CIA-subsidized publications, 235

Circularly Disposed Antenna Array (CDAA), 126-27, 146, 200-201, 211

Classic Bullseye, 64, 146

Classic Outboard, 64, 146

Classic Wizard, 64, 140-41, 143, 200

Cline, Ray, 202

Clipper Bow radar satellite (RORSAT), 64, 143-45

COBRA DANE radar, 125-26, 155, 189

COBRA JUDY radar, 126, 189

COBRA TALON radar, 126, 154

Cockburn, Andrew, 174

Coherent light signals, 119

Colby, William, 14, 29, 228, 242, 289, 298-99, 330, 341

Colossus, 147-48

COMBAT CATCH, 159

Committee on Foreign Intelligence (CFI), 276

Committee on Imagery Requirements and Exploitations (COMIREX), 269, 283-84, 299-301, 338, 342

Communications Security (COMSEC), 16-17, 19-20, 64, 66, 213, 344

Communications Security Establishment (CSE), 197

COMSAT, 17

Consolidated Cryptologic Program (CCP), 19, 68, 287, 303

CONSTANT DOME, 159

CONSTANT FISH, 159

CONSTANT GLOBE, 159

CORONA project, 111-12

COSMOS 954, 143

Counter-covert action, 344

Counterintelligence, 2-4, 11, 72, 182, 219-27; defensive, 219; definition of, 3, 219-20; offensive, 23, 219; studies, 41

Counterterrorist Joint Task Force, 319

Covert action, 2-3, 11, 21, 23-25, 40, 71, 219, 227-36, 265, 275-76, 278, 339, 342-44; in Afghanistan, 227-28, 236; in Angola, 234; in Chile, 232-33; in Cuba, 229-31; in France, 227, 229; in Greece, 227; in Guatemala, 229, in Iran, 233, 236; in Italy, 227-28; in Lithuania, 229; in Nicaragua, 71, 236; in Poland, 229; in the Ukraine, 229; in Zaire, 234

Covert ground sites, 56

Critical Intelligence Problems Committee (CIPC), 282-83, 302-3

Cuban missile crisis, 147, 245-46, 304, 318, 329

Cuban Revolutionary Council (CRC), 231

Cubela, Roland, 230

Curtin, Richard B., 13

Deaver, Michael, 278

"Defector in Place," 220, 222

Defectors, 183-84, 306-7

Defense Advanced Research Projects Agency (DARPA), 151

Defense Communications Agency, 285

Defense Counterintelligence Board (DCIB), 285

Defense Foreign Counterintelligence Program, 68, 287

Defense Intelligence Agency (DIA), 11, 35-41, 44, 58, 62, 64, 75, 80, 104, 158, 185, 188, 205, 209, 222, 241, 246-53, 271-74, 282, 284-86, 289, 300, 302, 307, 313, 326, 330; Directorate for Attachés and Training, 40; Directorate for Estimates, 41; Directorate for Foreign Intelligence, 40; Directorate for Intelligence and External Affairs, 38; Directorate for JCS Support, 39; Directorate for Management and Operations, 39; Directorate for Plans and Policy, 40; Directorate for Resources and Systems, 39; Directorate for Scientific and Technical Intelligence, 41; Directorate of Human Resources, 39; Directorate of Research, 41; General Defense Intelligence Program, 38, 68, 287; Office of Security, 41

Defense Intelligence Commentaries, 249

Defense Intelligence Estimates, 249

Defense Intelligence Notices, 39, 250

Defense Intelligence Officers (DIOs), 40

Defense Intelligence Staff, 39, 49

Defense Investigative Service, 285
Defense Logistics Agency, 285
Defense Mapping Agency (DMA), 35,
42-43, 50, 272
Defense Meteorological Satellite Program
(DMSP), 78, 159
Defense Reconnaissance Support Program
(DRSP), 286
Defense Satellite Communications System
(DSCS), 16, 19, 126, 148
Defense Signals Directorate (DSD), 197-98,
200
Defense Special Missile and Astronautics
Center, 272
Defense Special Plans Office (DSPO), 35,
45, 272
Defense Support Program, 58, 78, 158-59,
346
Defense Support Project Office, 286
De la Torre, Vitalio, 231
Deno, Francisco Caamano, 71-72
De Silva, Peer, 23
DESKTOP program, 149
DGI, 225
Digital Network-Defense Special Security
Communications System (DIN/DSSCS),
19
Digital Terrain Evaluation Data, 42
Director of Central Intelligence (DCI): role
of, 339-41
Director of Central Intelligence Directives
(DCIDs), 269-72, 283-84, 307, 319,
323, 326-29
Discoverer satellite, 112
Disinformation, 3, 8n, 9n
Dollar stability, 1
Domestic Contact Service (DCS), 184
Dominion Radio Astrophysical Observatory,
141
Dozier, James, 71
Drones. See Remotely Piloted Vehicles
Drug Enforcement Administration, 101-3
Dulles, Allen, 123, 233, 339-41
Dulles, John Foster, 339

Eden, Anthony, 202
Eisenhower administration, 5, 13, 35, 111,
129, 234, 287, 304, 320, 340
Eisenhower Surprise Attack Panel, 116
Electronic Countermeasures (ECMs), 17,
116
Electronic Security Command (ESC),
52-53, 55, 213; intelligence directorates,
53; operations directorates, 53
Ellsberg, Daniel, 224
El Mercurio, 233
Emigrés, 183-84
Emitter Programs Listings (EPLs), 18

Encryption, 120-21
European Command (EUCOM), 80, 84
European Defense Analysis Center
(EUDAC), 90, 260
European Defense Community, 229
Executive Orders, 263-65, 276, 279, 317,
319-20, 326, 344
Export Administration Act, 98
Extremely Sensitive Information (ESI), 319

Federal Bureau of Investigation (FBI), 16,
103-4, 187, 205, 207, 222-24, 264, 277,
279-80, 301
Federal Communications Commission
(FCC), 30, 196, 285
Federal Emergency Management Agency
(FEMA), 285
Federal Research Division (FRD), 104
Ferret satellites, 122
Filatov, Anatoli, 180
Fleet Intelligence Centers, 87-88, 260
Fleet Ocean Surveillance Information
Centers (FOSICs), 82, 87-88, 140, 199
Fleet Satellite Communications
(FLTSATCOM), 148-49
Ford administration, 234, 264, 276, 289,
299, 320, 343
Foreign Agriculture Service (FAS), 101
Foreign Broadcast Information Service
(FBIS), 29-30, 177, 201-2
Foreign Instrumentation Signals Intelligence
(FISINT), 119
Foreign Intelligence and Security Services
(FISS), 225
Foreign intelligence services, 224-27
Foreign Material Exploitation Program
(FMEP), 63, 190-91
Foreign Science and Technology Center
(FSTC), 66, 69, 71, 205, 254; Army
Foreign Material Program Office, 69, 71;
Intelligence Production Directorate, 69;
Technical Services Directorate, 69, 71
40 Committee, 234, 276, 306
Forum World Features, 24
Forward-looking infrared (FLIR) sensors,
146
FPS radar, 154-55
Free Cuba Radio, 235
Freedman, Lawrence, 112
Freedom of Information Act, 66, 199
Frei, Eduardo, 232
Friedman, William, 197
Fulbright, William, 314-15

Garthoff, Raymond, 175-76
Gates, Jr., Secretary of Defense, 13
General Agreement on Tariffs and Trade
(GATT), 101, 289

General Electric, 145
General Services Administration (GSA), 285
General Defense Intelligence Program (GDIP). *See* Defense Intelligence Agency
Geodesy, 42
Glomar Challenger, 162
Glomar Explorer, 148, 189-90
Golitsin, Anatoli, 222-23
Gore, Albert, 314-15
Government Communications Headquarters (GCHQ) (Britain), 197, 202, 212
Government Communications Security Bureau (GCSB) (New Zealand), 197-98
GPS satellites, 159
Grechko, Defense Minister, 174
Greenland-Iceland-U.K. (GIUK) gap, 146, 149
Greer, Brigadier General, 12
Gritz, James Bo, 71
Gromyko, Andrei, 174
Ground Based Electro-Optical Deep Surveillance System (GEODSS), 152-53
GRU, 221, 223
Guevara, Che, 72
Gulf of Tonkin Resolution, 314

Helms, Richard, 223, 232, 279, 307, 341
High-resolution photography, 298-99
Hillenhoeter, Roscoe, 173
Hinckle, Warren, 230-31
Holystone submarine reconnaissance program, 129-30, 304, 318
Honorable Schoolboy, The, 219
Hoover, J. Edgar, 103
Hope Report, 204-5
House Permanent Select Committee on Intelligence, 1, 175-76, 236
Hughes Aircraft, 15, 140, 145
Hughes, Howard, 190, 229
Huizenga, John, 330
Human Resources Committee, 269, 282, 307-8
Human source collection, 171-72, 177-85; management of, 306-8
Hunt, E. Howard, 186
Hydrophone arrays, 147-49

Imagery, 28, 38, 41, 50, 63, 66, 68-69, 79-80, 90, 107-17, 172, 206, 274, 282, 288, 297, 299-301; enhancement, 109; exploitation, 67; photographic, 108-9; radar, 108-9, 272
Imaging. *See* Imagery
Infrared photography, 108
Inman, Bobby, 102, 182
Institute of World Economy and International Affairs (IMEMO), 183

Integrated Tactical Surveillance System (ITSS), 145, 288
Integrated Undersea Surveillance System, 149
Intelligence: acoustic (ACOUSTINT), 147; analysis of, 2-4, 11, 21, 30, 62, 66, 241-60, 313-14, 327-32; bases abroad, 343-46; classifications, 314-27, 344-45; collection, 2-4, 11, 21, 23-24, 30, 52, 60, 71, 103, 172-77, 265-67, 297-308; communications (COMINT), 16-17, 19, 24, 28, 118, 124-25, 146, 198-99, 272, 282, 301-3, 323; cooperation, 196-213; cost of activities, 11, 14-15, 19-21, 25; definition of, 2; economic, 8, 253-54, 268, 271, 282, 327-28; electronics (ELINT), 16-17, 19, 39, 80, 84, 90, 118-19, 123-25, 146, 203, 256, 260, 271, 282, 301; human (HUMINT), 11, 40, 50, 66, 68, 80-81, 171-85, 195, 203-5, 287, 297, 306, 308, 342; managing access to, 313-27; medical, 43-44; military, 7, 327-28, 338; narcotics, 24, 28, 95, 98, 101-3, 302-3, 330; national, 241-46; open, 6; political, 6, 327-28; radar (RADINT), 118-19; scientific and technical, 254-55, 282-83, 327-28; secret, 6-7; signals (SIGINT), 11-12, 15-17, 19-20, 29-30, 39-40, 50, 53, 64, 66-68, 72, 80-81, 84-85, 113, 118-30, 140, 182, 187, 195-203, 207-8, 213, 259, 267-68, 270-72, 282, 287-88, 297-305, 338, 340, 342, 345; tactical, 298, 300, 338; telemetry (TELINT), 119; utility of, 5-6
Intelligence Advisory Committee, 280, 282, 329, 339-40
Intelligence and Security Command (INSCOM), 19, 66-68, 126-27, 182, 213, 222, 274, 285
Intelligence and Threat Analysis Center (ITAC), 67-68
Intelligence Community Staff (ICS), 279-80
Intelligence Identities Protection Act, 344
Intelligence Information Handling Committee, 282-83
Intelligence Oversight Board (IOB), 287
Intelligence Producers Council (IPC), 284
Intelligence Resources Advisory Committee (IRAC), 341
Intelligence Support Activity (ISA), 66, 71
INTELSAT, 17, 120
Interagency Defector Committee (IDC), 183
Interagency Intelligence Memorandums (IIMs), 242, 246, 280, 327

International Telecommunications Union, 141
ITT, 181

Jaruzelski, Wojciech, 180
Johnson administration, 264
Johnson, Louis, 15
Joint Atomic Energy Intelligence Committee, 282-83
Joint Chiefs of Staff (JCS), 15, 35-36, 39, 41, 44, 64, 67, 76, 250-1, 256, 258-59, 276-79, 284-86, 301, 305-6
Joint Intelligence Organization, 39, 49
Joint Reconnaissance Center (JRC), 40, 80, 82, 286, 305
Joint Reconnaissance Committee, 306
Joint Reconnaissance Schedule (JRS), 306
Joint Strategic Connectivity Staff, 76
Joint Strategic Planning System, 44
Joint Strategic Target Planning Staff (JSTPS), 76

Kasavubu, Joseph, 234
Katz, Amrom, 172
Kennedy, John (administration), 12, 35-36, 230-31, 264, 287, 340-41
Kerr, Governor-General, 242
Keyhole (photographic reconnaissance satellites), 12, 14, 21, 40, 42, 85, 112-15, 122, 140-41, 151, 206, 288, 299-300, 317-18, 338, 346
Key Intelligence Questions (KIQs), 289
KGB, 171, 177, 180, 222-25
Khadafi, Moamar, 178, 236
Khomeini, Ayatollah, 236
Killian, James, 340
Kimmel, Husband, 315
Kissinger, Henry, 6, 103, 182, 330
Kistiakowsky, George B., 13
Klass, Philip, 112
Komaraov, Vladimir M., 17
Kosygin, Alexei, 17
Kovshuk, V. M., 223

La Nacion, 231
Lansdale, Edwin, 230
Large Aperture Seismic Array (LASA), 160
Laser Radar Intelligence Acquisition Technology (LARIAT), 154
Launch sites, satellite, 141
Lausche, Frank, 314
Lay, James B., 15
Le Carre, John, 219
Lee, Andrew Daulton, 120
Lessiovski, Victor, 224
Letelier, Orlando, 103
Limited Test Ban Treaty, 56
Lindsey, Robert, 120

Lockheed, 15, 111-13, 116, 145
Low-altitude satellites, 203
Low resolution area surveillance systems, 299
Luce, Claire Booth, 228
Lumumba, Patrice, 234

Magnetic anomaly detector (MAD), 146
Maheu, Robert, 229
Mail interception, 172
Mail opening, 185-87
Malvern, Linda, 211
Management issues, 337-42
Manhattan Project, 319
Mann, David E., 143-44
Marchetti, Victor, 13, 104, 121, 181, 184, 186, 338
Mark, Hans, 14
Marks, John, 13, 104, 121, 181, 184, 186, 338
Marine Corps Intelligence, 72
Marshall, George, 315
Martin, Graham, 228
Martin Marietta Corp., 111, 143, 145
Material acquisition, 187-91
Material exploitation, 172-73, 187-91
Maui Optical Tracking and Identification Facility (MOTIF), 155
McCone, John, 298, 331, 340-41
McDonnel Douglas, 145
McMahon, John, 331
McNamara, Robert, 36, 314-16
Medvedev, Zhores, 175
Meese, Edwin, 278
Meyer, Cord, 242
M1 Group, 68
Military Intelligence Board, 286
Minitrack antennas, 150
Missile Intelligence Agency, 66, 69
Moles. See Agents
Monarch Eagle, 45
Moorer, Thomas, 182
Morrison, William L., 249
Mosely, Leonard, 233
Mossad, 205-7, 225
Mossadegh, Prime Minister, 233
Muller, Joseph P., 128
Murphy Commission, 14
Mutual and Balanced Force Reduction (MBFR), 7, 39, 41

Narcotics, 24, 28; intelligence, 95, 98, 101-3, 302-3, 330
National Aeronautics and Space Administration (NASA), 151, 298, 344
National Command Authorities, 306
National Communications Security Committee (NCSC), 285

National Communications System, 285
National Emergency Airborne Combat Post (NEACP), 39
National Executive Committee for Special Navy Activities, 305
National Exploitation of Tactical Capabilities (NETCAP), 339
National Foreign Assessment Center (NFAC), 331
National Foreign Intelligence Board (NFIB), 68, 267, 269, 279-80, 282, 284, 297, 299, 302-3, 307, 319, 321, 326, 328, 331-32, 342
National Foreign Intelligence Council (NFIC), 279-80, 284
National Foreign Intelligence Program (NFIP), 39, 98, 276-78, 287, 308, 341
National Intelligence Analytical Memorandums, 242, 246
National Intelligence Council, 279-80, 330-31
National Intelligence Digest (NID), 241-42
National Intelligence Estimates (NIEs), 37, 41, 96, 175, 242-45, 249, 270, 280, 327, 330, 332
National Intelligence Officers (NIOs), 40, 330-32
National Intelligence Program Evaluation (NIPE), 341
National Intelligence Resources Board, 341
National Intelligence Situation Report (NISR), 242-43
National Intelligence Tasking Center, 280, 342
National Intelligence Topics (NITs), 289
National Photographic Interpretation Center (NPIC), 28-29, 41, 268, 300, 313
National Reconnaissance Executive Committee (NREC), 12, 284, 297-99, 338
National Reconnaissance Office (NRO), 11-15, 35, 64, 79, 102, 115, 279-80, 287-88, 298, 338-39, 341, 344-45
National Security Act of 1947, 20-21, 227, 279
National Security Agency (NSA), 11, 14-20, 24, 35, 39-40, 52, 100, 102, 119, 123, 128-29, 195, 197-99, 205, 211-12, 264, 267-68, 271-72, 277, 279-80, 282, 284-87, 301-4, 313, 317, 338-39, 342; Office of Communications Security, 18-19; Office of Plans and Policy, 19; Office of Programs and Resources, 19; Office of Research and Engineering, 18-19; Office of Security, M5, 19; Office of Signals Intelligence Operations, 18-19; Office of Telecommunications and Computer Services, 19; W Group, 14

National Security Council (NSC), 1, 15, 20-1, 99, 227, 245, 264, 272-73, 275-78, 299, 302, 304, 321, 329
National Security Council Intelligence Committee (NSCIC), 276, 341
National Security Council Intelligence Directives (NSCIDs), 15-16, 29, 265-69, 272, 301, 307, 319, 322, 326, 328
National Security Decision Directives (NSDDs), 263, 265, 272, 319, 321, 326, 344
National Security Planning Group, 278
National SIGINT Requirements List (NSRL), 303
National Strategic Target List, 37, 76
Naval Administrative Services Command, 182
Naval Electronics Systems Command (NAVALEX), 14, 64, 143
Naval Intelligence Command (NIC), 58, 60, 62, 64, 82
Naval Intelligence Processing System Support Activity (NIPSSA), 62, 257
Naval Intelligence Support Center (NISC), 62-63, 222, 254-55
Naval Investigative Service, 285
Naval Reconnaissance Center, 286
Naval Research Laboratory (NRL), 140-1, 143, 158
Naval Security Group (NSG), 210-11, 213
Naval Security Group Command (NSGC), 20, 58, 64, 128, 141, 143, 146
Naval Space Surveillance (NAVSPASUR) System, 153
Naval Special Warfare Group, 45
NAVSTAR Global Positioning System, 158
Navy Operational Intelligence Center (NOIC), 62-64, 88, 140
Navy Space Project (NSP), 12, 14, 64, 102, 143
Navy Special Reconnaissance Activities Program, 287-88
Nixon administration, 181-82, 232, 264-65, 275-76, 330, 341
Nonimaging infrared sensors, 119
Non-Proliferation Treaty, 56
North American Aerospace Defense Command (NORAD), 79, 126, 155, 255
Norwegian Security Service, 212
Norwegian Seismic Array (NORSAR), 160, 212
Nosenko, Yuri, 223-24
NSAM 156 Committee, 12
Nuclear detonation monitoring, 78, 156-62
Nuclear Detonation (NUDET) Detection System (NDS), 158-59, 346
Nuclear Regulatory Commission, 314

"Nuclear Weapons Employment Policy," 156
Nutmeg detection system, 148

Oak Tree installation, 160
Ocean surveillance, 139–50, 197, 199–201, 203, 211
Ocean Surveillance Information System (OSIS), 62–63, 87, 140, 200–1
Ocean Surveillance Requirements study, 140
Office of Export Enforcement (OEE), 99–100
Office of Management and Budget (OMB), 266, 276
Office of National Estimates (ONE), 329
Office of Naval Intelligence (ONI), 44, 58, 221, 302
Office of Space Systems, 14
Office of Strategic Information, 99
Office of Strategic Services (OSS), 20, 95, 174, 207, 212, 318
Official Secrets Act, 199
Ogordnik, Aleksandr D., 180
OPEC, 181
Open source collection, 172–77
Operation Gray Plan, 40
Operation Neptune, 319
Operations Advisory Group (OAG), 276
Optical radar, 153, 155, 158
Optical surveillance, 154–55
Organization of American States (OAS), 231
Overseas bases, U.S., 210–13

Pacific Command (PACOM), 80–81, 90, 258
Pacific Radar Barrier (PACBAR), 154
PACOM Intelligence Board (PIB), 80
Palestine Liberation Organization (PLO), 8, 207
Paramilitary operations, 24
Parapsychology, 185
Partial Test Ban Treaty, 156
Partia Y Libertad, 103
Passive interferometry, 140
Pave Paws radar, 154
Peaceful Nuclear Explosion (PNE) treaty, 56, 156
Penetration, 23, 178, 220–23, 225; agent, 185; technical, 185–87
Penkovsky, Oleg, 179, 221
Perimeter Acquisition Radar Characterization System (PARCS), 155
Periodic Intelligence Summary, 250–51
Phased array radar, 125–26, 140, 154–55
Philby, Kim, 178, 221, 224, 233
Photographic reconnaissance satellites, 107–15. See also Keyhole

Pied Piper project, 111
Pierce Morgan Associates, 182
Pike Committee, 37
PILOT FISH program, 150
Pipes, Richard, 175–76
Plessey Corp., 212
Policy issues, 337, 342–46
Policy Review Committee (PRC), 275
PONY EXPRESS, 159
Popov, Peter, 179, 221, 223
Poseidon submarines, 146
Pot, Pol, 236
Powers, Francis Gary, 117, 304
Praeger, Frederick, 235
PRAIRIE SCHOONER program, 150
Precise Bathymetric Navigational Zone Charts, 149
Precise Bathymetric Naval Zone Charts, 42
President's Board of Consultants in Foreign Intelligence Activities (PBCFIA), 339–40
President's Daily Brief (PDB), 241–42
President's Foreign Intelligence Advisory Board (PFIAB), 287, 307
Priority National Intelligence Objectives (PNIOs), 267, 269
Propaganda: activities, 235; black, 3, 45, 344; covert, 24; grey, 3, 45; white, 45
Psychological operations, 44–45
PYRAMIDER agent communications satellites, 21, 318–19

Radar ocean surveillance satellites (RORSATs), 143
Radio broadcast monitoring, 30
Radio Free Asia, 235
Radio Free Europe, 235
Radio Liberty, 235
Rapid Deployment Force, 81
Rapidly Deployable Surveillance Systems (RDSS), 66, 149
RCA, 111
Readiness Command (REDCOM), 80, 84
Reagan administration, 14, 21, 40, 45, 156, 232, 236, 243, 245, 264–67, 278, 284, 287, 289, 298, 306, 321, 331, 342–45
Reconnaissance missions, 303–306
Reconnaissance, overhead, 202–203
Reconnaissance satellites, 11–15
Reference Mission Satellites, 115
Regional Seismic Test Network (RSTN), 161
Remotely Piloted Vehicles, 111, 117
REWSON Project, 64, 66, 128
Rhombic antenna array, 127
Rhyolite satellites, 12, 14, 21, 120–21, 210, 298, 301, 318, 338, 346
Rockefeller Commission, 4
Roosevelt, Franklin D., 315
Roosevelt, Kermit, 233

Rositzke, Harry, 180
Rosselli, Johnny, 229
Rubel, John H., 13

Saguy, Yehoshua, 206
SALT, 2, 17, 39, 174, 182
Sandinista government, 25, 236, 250, 343
SAMOS (Satellite and Missile Observation
  System), 12-13, 112
Satellite Control Facility (SCF), 203
Satellite Data System (SDS), 16, 114, 122,
  159
Satellite imagery targeting, 300
Satellite radar, 145-46
Satellites, real-time, 299
Satellite Reconnaissance Advance Notice
  (SATRAN) system, 79, 151
Satellite reconnaissance, management of,
  297-301
Satellite reconnaissance programs, 12-15
Savimbi, Jonas, 234
Schlesinger, James, 25, 299, 341
Schneider, Rene, 232-33
Science Magazine, 141
Scientific and Technical Intelligence
  Committee, 282-83
Sea Nymph satellite system, 143
Sea Spider array, 148
Secrecy, 344-45
Secret Intelligence Service (SIS), 203, 221,
  233
"Secret political action." See Covert action
Security Committee (SECOM), 326-27
SEEK SAIL radar, 154
Seismic arrays, 160
Seismic Data Analysis Center (SDAC), 212
Seismometers, 160-62
Senior Interagency Group-Intelligence
  (SIG-I), 276-77, 306
Sensitive Compartmented Information
  (SCI), 62, 66, 273, 315-16, 319, 321,
  323, 326-27, 344-45
Sensor systems, 146, 151-62
Service Cryptological Authorities (SCAs),
  19-20
Shin Bet, 205, 225
Ship-based sensors, 127-30
Shuttle mission, 7, 151
Signals intelligence aircraft, 123-25
Signals intelligence satellites, 120-23
Sinclair, John, 233
Single Integrated Operational Plan (SIOP),
  5, 27, 42, 76, 319
Smiley's People, 219
Smith, Walter Bedell, 15, 339
Sonars, 147
Sonobuoys, 146, 149
Sound Surveillance System (SOSUS), 66,
  87, 147-49, 189, 212, 288

Southern Command (SOUTHCOM), 80, 82,
  259
Soviet military publications, 173-74
Space-based surveillance systems, 151
Space Infrared Experiments (SIRE), 151
Space Infrared Surveillance Program, 151
Space surveillance, 78-79, 139-46,
  150-55, 162
Space Surveillance Technology Program,
  151
Space Tracking and Detection System
  (SPADATS), 151, 153, 155
SPACETRACK system, 151, 154
Space Transportation System (STS), 12
Special Access Programs, 319, 321
Special Coordination Committee (SCC),
  275-76
Special Defense Intelligence Estimates, 249
Special Defense Intelligence Notices
  (SDINs), 250
Special Intelligence Service (SIS), 103
Special National Intelligence Estimates
  (SNIEs), 37, 96, 242-43, 245-46, 249,
  280, 327, 330
Special Operations Division (J3), 35, 44-45
Special Program Office for Exploitation
  Modernization (SPOEM), 42
Spectrum analyzers, 147
Sputnik, 111, 150
Spy Who Came in from the Cold, The, 219
START, 2, 8, 39
Stealth aircraft, 151, 319
Stillwell, Richard, 45
Stockholm International Peace Research
  Institute (SIPRI), 147, 160
Strategic Air Command (SAC), 75-78, 122,
  124, 151, 155, 255-56, 298
Strategic reconnaissance aircraft, 21, 29, 76,
  78, 90, 111, 115-17, 123-25, 159,
  202-3, 206, 211, 213, 286, 304-6, 318,
  338
Strategic Reconnaissance Center, 78
Submarine signature identification, 18
Sullivan, William, 308
Summa Corporation, 190, 229
Sun Tzu, 6
Surface Towed Array System (SURTASS),
  66, 149, 288
Sylvester, Arthur, 12

Tactical Cryptologic Program (TCP), 303
Tactical Exploitation of National Capabili-
  ties (TENCAP), 90, 287-88, 339
Tactical Intelligence and Related Activities
  (TIARA), 287-88
Talent-Keyhole (TK), 41, 316-17
Tange, Sir Arthur, 249
Target Data Inventory (TDI), 37
Technical surveillance, 185-86

Technological Capabilities Panel, 5-6
Technology transfer, 98-100, 220
Technology Transfer Assessment Center, 25
Technology Transfer Intelligence Committee, 282
Telemetry collection, 298-99
Telephone interception, 17, 24, 104, 172, 185-86, 211
Television broadcast monitoring, 30
Teller, Edward, 175
Terrain Countour Matching (TERCOM), 42
Terrorism, 28, 41, 67
Theater command intelligence units, 255-60
Thermal infrared scanners, 108-9, 112
Thieu, Nguyen Van, 186
Threshold Test Ban Treaty, 56, 156
Tinker, Tailor, Soldier, Spy, 219, 318
Toroella, Louis, 229
Treaty compliance, 56, 119, 139, 175
Trevor-Roper, Hugh, 6
Trident submarine, 146
Truman administration, 15, 20, 228
TRW Corporation, 15, 114, 120, 143, 157, 318
Turner, Stansfield, 25, 120, 206, 245, 299, 338, 341-42
Turner, William, 230-1

UKUSA Agreement, 195-99, 202-5, 207
ULTRA, 196, 315-16
UMBRA, 316-17
Unconventional warfare, 44, 88
Underseas surveillance, 11, 146-50
Undersea Surveillance Project, 64, 66
Underwater sensors, 88
United Fruit Company, 229
United Nations Food and Agricultural Organization, 231
United Nations Registry of Space Objects, 345
USA and Canada Institute, 175, 183
U.S. Air Force Europe (USAFE), 84-85, 90, 257
U.S. Army Intelligence Operations Detachment, 66-67
U.S. Army Special Forces (Green Berets), 43, 66, 71-72
U.S. Atomic Energy Detection System (AEDS), 56
U.S. Department of Agriculture, 5, 100-101

U.S. Department of Commerce, 1, 95, 98-100
U.S. Department of Defense (DOD), 1, 3, 12-16, 35-37, 39-41, 43-45, 52, 60, 64, 67, 75, 99, 115, 145, 187, 249, 267, 271-73, 279, 284-85, 287, 289, 297-98, 300, 314, 319, 326, 328, 339, 342
U.S. Department of Energy (DOE), 1, 95, 100-101, 161, 280, 314, 318-19
U.S. Department of Justice, 95
U.S. Department of State, 1, 3, 11, 20, 30, 95-98, 100, 286, 313, 332
U.S. Department of the Treasury, 280
U.S. Government Organization Manual, 16
U.S. Information Agency (USIA), 45
U.S. Intelligence Board (USIB), 15, 36, 267, 270, 280, 282-83, 299, 307, 321, 329, 340
U.S. Secret Service, 24
U.S. Signal Intelligence System (USSS), 301
U.S.S. Liberty, 128, 304
U.S.S. Pueblo, 128, 304-5
Ustinov, Dmitry, 28

VELA satellites, 58, 157-59, 168n, 274
Viktor III, 139
VOLANT CHUCK, 159
VOLANT CURRY, 159
VOLANT DOME, 159
VOLANT SPECK, 159
VOLANT TRACK, 159
Vought Aero Products, 189

Washington Post, 13
Weapons and Space Systems Intelligence Committee, 282-83
Weather reconnaissance, 78
Weekly Intelligence Summary (WIS), 39, 249-50
Weekly Watch Report (WWR), 242-43
Weinberger, Caspar, 205
Weissmann, Stephen R., 234
Westinghouse Electric, 140, 145-46
White Cloud ocean surveillance satellites, 12, 14, 64, 140-43, 162n
Whitlam, Gough, 242-43, 248-49
Wigner, Eugene, 175
Wiretapping. *See* Technical surveillance

X-Rays, 158

Yamomoto, Admiral, 315

ABOUT THE AUTHOR

Dr. Jeffrey Richelson is Assistant Professor of Government in the School of Government and Public Administration of The American University, Washington, D.C. Previously he was a Senior Fellow at the Center for International and Strategic Affairs, UCLA. Dr. Richelson has published in the areas of intelligence, nuclear strategy, and social choice theory. His publications have appeared in the *Journal of Strategic Studies, Journal of Conflict Resolution, American Journal of Political Science*, and *Review of Economic Studies*. He is the coauthor (with Desmond Ball) of *The Ties That Bind: The UKUSA Intelligence Network*, and author of the forthcoming *Sword and Shield: Soviet Intelligence and Security Service Operations* (Ballinger, 1985).